YOUNG WANDERLUST

Young Wanderlust

Names and identifying details have been changed to protect the privacy of individuals.

ISBN-13: 978-1492214465
ISBN-10: 1492214469

Cover and graphic design by Elizabeth Feder
www.elizabethfeder.com

Book design by Maureen Cutajar
www.gopublished.com

YOUNG WANDERLUST

A TRAVELER'S NOVEL

BY

EVAN KENWARD

INTRODUCTION

It wasn't looking good. Gill called me with weeks to spare, urging that we consider a plan B. "We could bike up to Nova Scotia and back." He said it in that tone that mothers use when trying to appease their child because their theme park vacation was cancelled. "We could go out back and you can play on the jungle gym!"

Fuck that.

The only part of Canada I planned to see on this trip was BC. "Beautiful British Columbia" was what it said on their license plates—or so I've heard. I've never been to British Columbia, nor anywhere else in the Pacific Northwest, nor just about anywhere else on my well-planned trip across the great North American continent. This was a trip I had been planning for months, years, eons—hell, it was planned out for me long before I was born. And after all this planning, all the stress and excitement and anticipation, with two weeks before we were to leave, Wallace's car—the car he promised would take us three thousand miles away from home and back—decided to break down. Gill said it needed a new transmission—I was wondering why Wallace hadn't been answering my calls.

Just like I always did, I brushed it off. Gill was right, it was time to come up with plan B. But car or not, the West was my destination. I would take a cop-out-bitchy flight across the country if I had to, so long as I got away from the East Coast. I was not sticking around the place where I was born, the place where I grew up, went to school, University of Massachusetts, fall foliage, sliding around a mountain covered with ice on skis, maple syrup—no. I was not spending the money and time I had saved, to bike to Nova-fucking-Scotia. Besides, I didn't own a fucking bike. *Fuck.*

Not that I did not love biking, or New England. Nor had I ever been to Nova-fucking-Scotia. But I had to get out west and it was going to be hard to convince me otherwise. I could settle for biking up the Pacific Coast. Something like, San Francisco to Vancouver—*wait I can't buy a bike.* On to Plan C. Maybe fly to Vancouver, rent a car, and drive around British Columbia. There was a national park that I saw on the map which looked like the size of Florida. It ran from north to south, splitting the peaceful borders of BC and Alberta called, Jasper National Park, set conveniently in the middle of the Canadian Rockies. As I stared at the map of the US and Canada—the one I pinned to the wall in my room—I could see ice fields, mountaintops, and hot springs that spotted the park's geographical landscape. I also noticed a highway that ran directly down the center of it. The two-dimensional map of colors and words entered my head, opening into a wild excitement of imagination: driving along a desolate highway, surrounded on both sides by lush green pines, with snow-capped rocky mountain tops, and sky-blue glaciers running down the ravines.

I ran across the room to my computer. Google Images gave me similar snippets, tantalizing my senses with hints of what was to come...or at least what could be. It could all be a simple fantasy, a traveler's dream that fell on the (apparently weak) shoulders of this son-of-a-bitch transmission. "If it gets fixed," said Gill, "we'll know by Monday."

I considered myself an optimistic person. I did not take a potential tragedy for a tragedy, until it became reality. So I put this ridiculous car idea in the back of my mind and got up from staring at the fantasyland pictures. I walked back over to my map on the wall. In front of the map were a chair and a table. The chair was there for me to sit in while drooling over the map. The table was my road-trip-planning headquarters. Scattered across it were various tools: a stack of state maps that I got from AAA (free with a membership), a small tin of thumbtacks, and a notebook with a tacky purple yin yang on it that my mom had given me in preparation for my trip. I had graciously accepted the ugly thing while biting my tongue. *Thanks Mom, but style just ain't your strong suit.* I reached over to my planning headquarters, grabbed a thumbtack and stuck it in the middle of the Florida-sized park in the Canadian Rockies. Then I sat down and studied the rest of the map where I placed similar tacks:

Start in Amherst, Massachusetts. Head south three hours, making a detour to Port Chester, New York. Why? For Pat's Hubba Hubba. This would be one of the two places on the trip that I've already been to—many, many times. It was a tradition to make Pat's your first and last stop on any road trip heading out of the Northeast. Take a left on the main street at the fork, park in the back alley, find the undisclosed white door, and head in to a long, narrow room, covered from wall to ceiling with dollar bills. Sit down on a bar stool and order a wedge, hot dog, fries—anything your grease-craved heart desired—with chili. Don't forget a side of Hubba Water (tap water with a splash of fruit punch), the perfect complementary beverage to wash down the authentic Hubba's chili. Why does this need to be the first and last stop out of the Northeast region of the United States? There is no real explanation, although in some legends of folklore, it is said to be the "gateway to the Northeast." If you've ever been to the Northeast, you'll notice there is a giant wall that encapsulates it from all sides. Pat's Hubba Hubba is the threshold that sends you off into the vast, cruel world with a delightful chili meal in your stomach. Or it will welcome a weary traveler back into the Northeast, giving you the reminded reassurance that no matter how spicy, greasy, or mal-nutritious the Northeast is, it is still so good to come back to, again, and again, and again.

From Pat's we head out with horrible stomach cramps to stay with my friend Jenny, in northern Michigan. She was a sweet Midwestern gal whom I had met when I studied abroad in Italy, two years prior. It was a big detour but she promised it was worth our while.

Next stop is the long haul to South Dakota and the Badlands. Everyone I had met who crossed paths with this place, told me it was not to be missed.

The Black Hills, Mt. Rushmore, then in Wyoming comes the real West: Yellowstone National Park and the Grand Tetons. My grandparents spent thirty summers in the Tetons and this was my chance to carry on their legacy.

Spend a few days there, then head south to Utah and hike around Bryce and Zion National Parks, the second of two places I had been to before. I hiked Bryce and Zion as a bright, young, innocent lad, and I was dying to go back as an old, pot-smoking, binge-drinking adult.

West from there, through the deserts of Nevada to the mountainous Sierra Nevada's: First Yosemite National Park, then north to Lake Tahoe.

From there we make the final push west to San Francisco. This will be the middle of our trip, where we'll all split up—because of how sick of each other we'll be—and spend a few days with our respective family members (which each of us had in that area).

After a few days, regroup and head north up the coast, through the redwoods, up to Portland. Jut back out to the Oregon/Washington coast—I heard there are seals—and jut back in to Seattle. Head west to the Olympic peninsula and check out Olympic National Park. Google Images makes that place look like a mountainous rain forest!

Then up to Vancouver, spend a few days there and see if its "green" reputation upholds itself. Head west to Vancouver Island and island-hop back to Vancouver. Then head up to Whistler, home of the number one ski area in the North American continent, which arguably makes it the best in the world.

Explore the mighty BC, make our way to Jasper, and head down that tantalizingly drool-worthy highway. Then straight south to Montana where we'll run into Glacier National Park—google image that shit, you won't be disappointed. By the way, if by now you're thinking that it sounds like I google image national parks like a high school freshman looks at porn, you're on the right track.

By this point, our projected month trip should be almost finished. High-tail it back across—don't forget Pat's—then roll on in to Amherst and shit out the chili just in time to get ready for the long awaited/long avoided post graduate "real world."

There it was, the great American road trip, laid out simply on a piece of paper pinned to my wall. The three of us had done our share of traveling around the world, but we had yet to fulfill our civic duty as citizens of the United States of America: to travel by car from the green hills of the Northeast, to the rich farmland of the Midwest, through the western

ROUTE

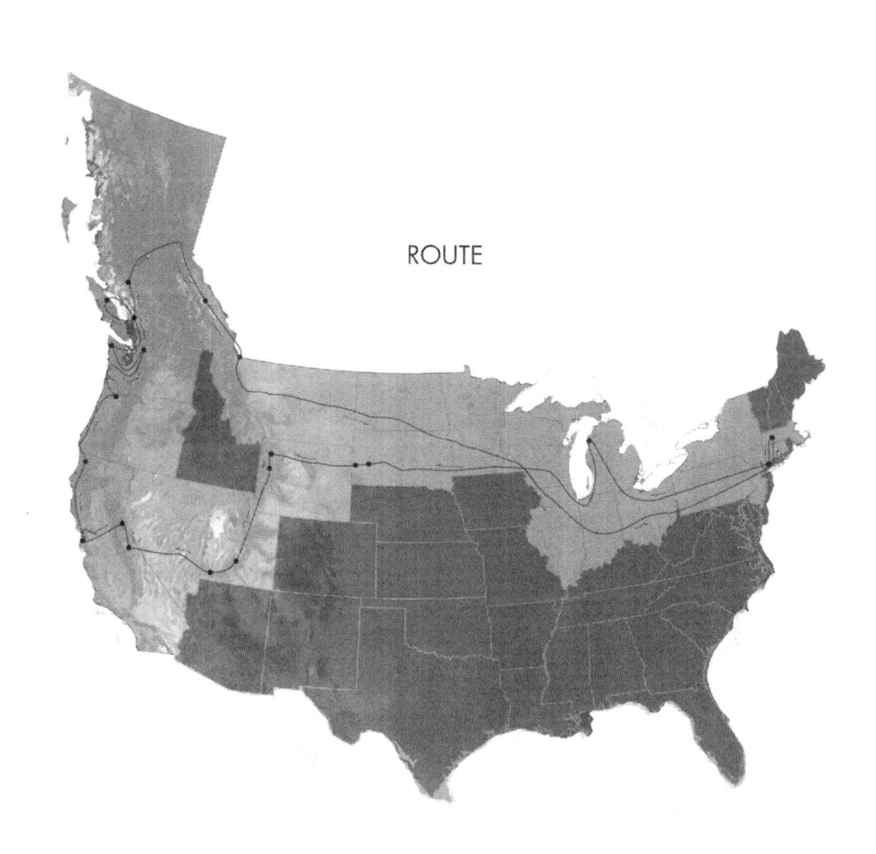

prairies and mountains to the rocky California coast, white with foam, from sea to shining sea. God bless America, my home sweet home—plus a little bit of Canada. God Save the Queen.

The next week was torture. After multitudes of unanswered phone calls, Wallace got in touch with me. He was calling from a town a three hour's drive north called, Burlington, Vermont, where the car broke down and was currently getting worked on. He had gone to the University of Vermont to visit his girlfriend Kath for the last precious time before heading off on the big adventure. Wallace informed me that once they replaced the transmission, he had to take it to *his* mechanic back home in Massachusetts. He insisted that it needed to get checked again, to see if the poor thing would make it across the country and back. I was beginning to loathe this car...

Meanwhile, I had a few things on my mind. The following Saturday would be my college graduation. It was not the event of the year that I was most looking forward to. I ultimately made the decision to go, because there was going to be a graduation party at my house afterward and I *had* to go to that. So instead of sitting around, anxiously waiting for the keg of Opa Opa (one of my favorite Massachusetts microbrews) to arrive at my house, I figured I might as well occupy my time during the day.

Along with graduating on my mind, there was preparation not only for this trip, but to entirely move out of the Amherst area, out of my house, and out of my college home which treated me so well for four years. I will always say, if college taught me anything, it taught me how to party. God bless the liberal arts.

Along with that, I was stressing about this girl I had met at the very end of the semester, whom I was hoping to squeeze into my bed before I packed up everything and headed out. We had met in a gardening class, as part of one of my "senior slack" electives. *Oh, to be surrounded again by sunshine, dirt, and beautiful girls. I'm beginning to miss college already.*

All these issues swirled around my mind, but for the majority of the time, I had nothing to do besides sit and wait. I would find myself lying on my couch, staring out the window to the mountain that rose up behind our backyard. Most of the yellowish, budding spring leaves on the trees were matured and it was almost full summer green. I had enjoyed climbing this mountain many times, but as I looked at it then, I developed a distaste for it. It looked tired and small like a hunched-over old man. *It's not a mountain, it's a hill.* I wanted to see young, sprightly, snow-capped peaks that could tower over this petty lump and crush it with their pinky toe. My roommate Niko would walk by and say, "You look like you're waiting for something." I would respond, "You're right. I'm waiting to get the fuck out of here." As good as these past four years had been, my restless spirit was pushing me to move on.

There was one last imperative issue which stressed me out the most. Wallace's car was a stick shift. Up until that point in my life, I could not consider myself a member of the "Stick Shift Society." But I hoped that I would have enough time to get practice on his car before the trip. This was why I kept trying to get a hold of Wallace, and why it stressed me out even more that he wasn't returning my calls.

Wallace was the kind of person that rarely picked up his phone. If I was lucky I could leave a message. Usually I got an automated female robot voice, telling me that I couldn't leave a message because, "This person's mailbox is full, goodbye." I was the kind of neurotic person who constantly checked my cell phone—especially in cases like this. There was a big problem if we ended up doing the trip and I had no practice on stick. I would not be able to drive at all, which would not be fair for the other two. And it didn't make it any better once he got a hold of me, telling me he would not be back in the area until the Monday after graduation. My projected time of departure was the following Wednesday.

Shortly after that, Gill called me from a state a twenty-four hour's drive south called, Florida. He was there with *his* girlfriend, exchanging *his* precious last face time, telling me he would not be back until Tuesday, maybe Wednesday. It was becoming apparent that leaving Wednesday was out of the question—if we were to leave at all.

This did not make a happy Evan. I was ready to leave at any moment. I would have been ready to go in an hour if they told me. I kept staring out the window, as if miraculously Wallace's car would come flying over the mountain to swoop in and snatch me up, leaving a glittery rainbow air-trail in its path. I rearranged my position on the couch to get more comfortable. *We're never leaving on this trip. And if we do, I can't even drive. I still have to pack up my room. I hate packing. And I need a nice atmosphere if I can get this girl in there. But dammit, she won't answer my calls either!*

"Hey Evan," I looked up in panic to see Niko laughing above me. "Did I startle you? You look like you've been in a trance."

"No, I'm just tired," I replied, unsure if he was right or not.

"I've been staring at my computer for too long," he said. "I need to get outside. You want to come hike up the mountain with me?"

I shifted in my seat. "No thanks."

"You sure? It's a damn nice day out there."

"No, I'm waiting for a call from Wallace."

Niko shrugged. "Suit yourself."

He walked out the back door and I drearily watched him walk into the field. *Have fun on your boring hike up a boring hill, Niko.* I was saving my energy to scale rocky cliffs and waterfalls. I watched him disappear behind a grove of trees. *Maybe I should've gone... Whatever.*

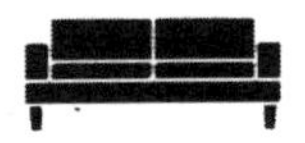

Graduation was an uplifting, yet arduous event (as expected). I sat baking in my polyester robe under the hot late-May sun, with thousands of my classmates. We sat in the middle of the football stadium, surrounded by packed seats, bringing the number up to roughly twenty thousand overheated individuals. I didn't consider the graduation ceremony to be anything remarkable. It seemed out of place, separate from the rest of the college experience. I knew that I was *supposed* to feel differently. This was the culmination of my educational career. Now it was time to go out into the real world, and get a job, and make something of myself. Well I still hadn't had a clue of what to "make of myself" and I was sure I was not alone in that cultish, cardboard-capped crowd. *Whatever, I have the rest of my life to think about that. It can wait one more month.*

The nicest part of the ceremony was being able to sit next to my old college chum Casey. Casey and I had been friends since a few weeks into the start of my college career. We initially bonded over music, then an insatiable love for the outdoors, and eventually we grew connected by our similar views on how to generally pass through life in an enjoyable way. In the following years, we attended many concerts, hiked and camped around New England, and took some amazing road trips. Most of these trips headed south during spring breaks. Many college kids preferred a cop-out-bitchy flight to warm climates during their spring break, especially in the north, where winter was making its final stab in the middle of March. But there was nothing like getting in a car and driving out of the cold to a warm climate. Casey whole-heartedly agreed.

I tried to convince Casey to come on our road trip. In the prior months when I was planning, he was working on getting a job somewhere out west, preferably in or around a national park (being the avid outdoorsman he was). So I figured if the timing was right, we could drive him out west and drop him off at his job. He was open to the idea, but the consensus was to play it by ear. "If it works, it works," said Casey with a shrug. That was the kind of laid-back attitude that made up Casey. I learned a lot from him. One of the most important lessons he taught me was that there was no room in life for complaining. He never said this directly, but I realized that every time I would get worked up and begin to bitch about something while instinctively expecting him to agree (a popular trend among ungrateful adolescents), he would shrug and say something like, "I don't know. It doesn't seem to be that bad." Those level-headed words would send me back into reality, forcing me to take a breath and say, "Yeah, I guess you're right."

It is this kind of mentality that is necessary on a road trip. When traveling, especially to new places, the senses—all of them—are constantly bombarded by newness. New sites, new sounds, new smells, everything. It is human nature to want to experience new things. That is why traveling is such an amazing, natural human desire. The opposite is monotony. Monotony creates depression. Once something has been seen and experienced enough times, the appreciation for it is lost. The mind stops thinking about it, and focuses on other things: "I got to pay my bills." "My girlfriend's being annoying." "I got to be home by eight o'clock, or else I won't find out what happened after Danny cheated on Sally with her best friend, on my favorite TV show, which takes me away from my monotonous life and I can marvel at the wonderful, perfect lives of the rich and famous." But when things are seen for the first time, it all has to be taken in and enjoyed for what it is. The mind, the life, and the well-being are a little more expanded because of what is being experienced. And with all that, there should not—there *cannot* be any room for complaining. People still find ways to complain. But on a road trip, cooped up in a car, maintaining a short distance between you and your fellow road trippers for such an extensive period of time, there is no room for complaining. There is no room for *any* drama. This isn't a sorority house reality show. This is life. No matter what happens, the atmosphere needs to stay positive, stay chill. It did not take much for Casey and me to maintain this "Code of Chillness" on our road trips. It came naturally and that was a big reason why I was trying to convince him to come with us.

Casey had learned a lot of his outdoor appreciation from his parents. For his whole life, his "family vacations," which included his parents, his brother James, and Penny, his golden retriever, were almost always a multi-day hiking trip somewhere mountainous. I envied this. I never walked farther than a mile with either of my parents. Not that I held it against them. Even if they wanted to do a multi-day hiking and camping trip with me, the thought of spending that much time with them may force me to kindly decline the offer. I mean, my parents like, seriously drive me crazy! Oh my God, like last week they—wait sorry, I forgot this was a book and not my diary.

During graduation, as the two of us sat restlessly in our seats—Casey couldn't wait for the keg of Opa Opa either—we inevitably began discussing the trip. He filled me in on the latest development from his side. It turned out that he had a plan of his own. He was also going to leave that following Wednesday and drive across the country with his brother James. Then in Reno, Nevada, they would pick up their parents at the airport and drive down to Yosemite, for a week-long hiking trip. Then after another installment of the "Casey Family Vacation," he would drive up to the northeastern part of Oregon, where he had finally landed a job, working for a wilderness conservation organization. While he was looking for a job, I promised him that we would be able to stop through on our trip, wherever he ended up, since I assumed anywhere out west would be "on the way." When we got back to my house and he showed me on the map where he would be living, I incredulously shook my head. As it turned out, he could not have picked a more awkward spot to go. Our planned route essentially took us in a huge horseshoe around him, where we would be no farther than ten hours but no closer than five hours away. "Oh well," Casey shrugged, "if it works it works. You guys are always welcome."

Casey was all set to drive across the country the same day I planned to leave, and he had figured it all out no more than a week before his departure. Then there was us, the three stooges: months into planning and it was all about to crumble to pieces because of this goshdarn cottonpickin' motherfucker car. But I wasn't thinking about that when I headed straight for the grilled chicken and keg cups at our graduation party. As I relaxed on my back deck and enjoyed the last official day of my college career, my phone rang.

"Hello?"

"Hey buddy." It was that unmistakably intense bass of a voice, as if you were listening to a narrator of an action movie trailer.

"Wallace! What's up! I just graduated and I'm drunk!"

"Aww, sweet, congrats that sounds awesome."

"You should come over, have some beer and food."

"Thanks, I can't though, I'm still in Vermont. I just got the car out of the shop and I have to deal with some stuff."

I shot up in my chair like a puppeteer had yanked my strings with all his strength. "Really??"

"Yeah," he said. "The tranny's fixed."

I looked over and stared at the mountain that had mocked me for so long. "Does that mean all systems are...go?"

"Yep," said Wallace, "all systems are go."

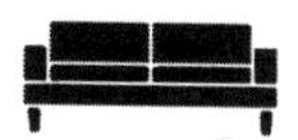

The next few days were filled with anxiety, preparation, and unprepared anxiety. I kept pulling for an earlier departure, while Wallace and Gill kept pushing for more time. Saturday was looking like the projected day of departure, and that was "cutting it close," said Wallace. He was insisting (among other poor excuses) to still get a thorough check of the car from his mechanic.

It's going to take a miracle to get us on the road. Like I said, I did not accept a tragedy until it became a reality. The same applied to a victory. Until we were physically in a packed car leaving my driveway, I would have my doubts.

On a more positive note, Wallace finally gave me a chance to practice stick on our road trip car to-be, his 2003 hatchback Suburu Outback. He boasted it had the most unforgiving clutch of any car. "If you can drive this," Wallace proclaimed, "you can drive anything." Intimidating, but I was up for the challenge. Realistically, I had no choice.

As frustrated as I was with Wallace and his lack of communication, it was good to see him back from the north country. John Wallace was a direct descendent of William Wallace, the Scottish war monger from the thirteenth century (refer to Mel Gibson's film, Braveheart). He was a burly fellow with a perpetually scraggly beard, and the most vibrant, brightest blue eyes you have ever seen (on a hairy Scotsman)—the ladies loved it. He was a cheery fellow, who more likely than not, laughed at your jokes, no matter how funny or not funny they were. He was a good man and a good friend. Let it be mentioned on the record as well that he loved his weed and would not shut up about California. "Cali bud, dude, Cali bud."

Planning and preparing and a whole lot more waiting (on my part) ensued. A definite advantage to the delay of departure was the extended opportunity for me to lure this lass into my room for the night, which I finally did. A small victory. *Maybe if the trip gets cancelled, I can hang out with her more and find that I found my true love. We'll get married and for our honeymoon take our own road trip across the country, maybe the world. We'll make beautiful children and—oh, what's the use.*

Gill also had a car with a stick shift, which I managed to successfully drive from my house to his. He calmly coaxed me through my shifting, his soothing, collected voice guiding me through it. "Easy there, buddy, now slowly ease off the clutch, there ya go, well done."

Jacob Gillman, aka Gill, Gilligan, Gilly Bob Thornton, was a thin, soft-spoken fellow. He maintained an aura of calm and polite composure about him at all times—always cool. Gill was home from college, staying at his parents' house in the rural woodland town of New Salem, Massachusetts. Getting there entailed a picturesque twenty-mile drive from Amherst, on windy roads through dense forests and undulating hills. My reward for successfully driving stick, was the pleasure of spending time at the Gillman residence, which I referred to as my dream home. It was an old, white colonial, two-story house with a beautiful open barn attached to it, and situated on a small quiet street, lined with similar houses built in the early days of New England (when it was still *new*). I held fond memories of this place, which dated back to high school when Gill would throw parties when his parents were out of town. This was how I knew Gill and Wallace—not the partying part, the high school part—correction, both.

Even though my fellow travelers were my high school brethren, we were entering into a foreign territory of our relationship by doing this road trip together. I had never traveled with them on an extended trip. But I trusted their credentials. Both had vast resumes of travel.

At one point in the week, all three of us were able to get together at my house and sit down to study the map on my wall. We discussed certain logistics and made a few changes. One change, which I expected would happen, was to nix Utah. That was the most out of the way location and none of us were dying to make it there. The next big change was our direction. We decided, instead of heading southwest from the Tetons to Yosemite, we would head north to Glacier National Park, then do the rest of the route backward, heading up to Jasper, around to Vancouver, and down the coast. We also added a few stops on the way, like St. Paul, Minnesota, where I found out that Sam, my good friend from childhood, was living in his place a few more days before he moved out. He had recently graduated as well—from Macalister College—and was moving back to Massachusetts. If we got there in time, we could make it a good resting point between Michigan and South Dakota. Then came a devastating change. Wallace's girlfriend lived in Rochester, New York, located off Route 90, on the way to Michigan. She was leaving in a few days to spend the summer in Guatemala, to learn Spanish. So the choice needed to be made: either my love for Pat's Hubba Hubba or Wallace's love. We couldn't have both. I held in my lustful desires for the world's best chili sandwiches, and agreed to entertain his lust for a pretty girl—the same one he *already* said goodbye to in Vermont—*what the fuck!... It's okay Evan, be cool, just be cool... Okay, okay, I'm cool.*

"Fine," I said. "That's the plan. I'll call Jenny and let her know when we'll be arriving. Is there anything else we need to discuss?"

I looked at Gill who was smiling. "I'm ready!"

I looked at Wallace who was looking down nervously at his hands.

"Wallace?"

"There's one more thing," he said.

Uh-oh. "What's up?" I asked reluctantly.

"I took the car to my mechanic and he looked it over."

"He said it was fine, didn't he?"

Wallace nodded. "Yeah. But he wasn't too convincing." Wallace looked over at Gill. "What's up with your car, Gill?"

Gill's eyes lit up in shock, unprepared for such a big question. "Mine? No. Well, it's not really my car in the first place, it's my parents'. Plus, that thing is an old lady, she wouldn't make it halfway across the country."

Wallace looked at me for a second, but knew I had no solution. "The mechanic," he said, "he told me it was fine, but he said I would need to be *really* careful." Wallace paused and looked back down at his hands. I could understand his dilemma. Clearly his car was in a fragile state, especially after the transmission scare. But he knew that the fate of the trip was in his hands. "I don't know, I guess I'm just being paranoid."

"Don't worry, the car will be fine," I said reassuringly. "We're going to take care of your baby."

Wallace cracked a smile. "She's a big fucking baby, that's for sure." We all laughed.

The stage was set. We would leave Saturday night and make it to northern Michigan the following day. I gave Jenny a call and told her when we would be arriving. "It's a sixteen-hour drive so I'd say we should get there around late afternoon."

"No problem! Can't wait!" was her reaction. And then she added, "Are you guys really going to drive through the night?"

Another road trip tradition has been to leave at night and get a good chunk of driving in without worrying about traffic. The excitement of starting the trip helps keep you awake through the night. It also helps put the body's internal clock out of whack. This may seem counterproductive, but it helps. On a grand adventure like this, you don't sleep when it's time for bed. You "rest" at an advantageous time so as not to miss a thing. Lastly, there is nothing worth seeing within ten hours outside of the Northeast anyway.

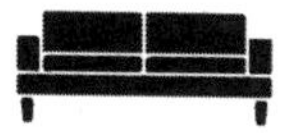

Saturday finally came. As I was packing up the rest of my room along with last minute packing for the trip, some strange news came to me. Gill called to tell me that Wallace's parents had taken the car an hour and a half drive west to a town called; Albany, New York.

"Why the hell did they do that??" I asked, as irritated as I was confused.

"I don't know," said Gill seemingly unaffected.

"Are they coming back?"

"I think so."

That didn't sound convincing. I hung up, then looked up Jenny's number and stared at it. *Do I call her to let her know our plans have changed?... No. Not yet. Just hold out Evan.*

As the day wore on, Gill gave me updates. "Wallace is saying he might not be able to leave today."

"No!" I put my proverbial foot down, as my real feet paced around my empty room. "That's not an option. He can sleep in the fucking car if he wants."

"...Okay, I'll tell him that."

Wallace was most likely only communicating with Gill because he knew I would react this way and it was the last thing he wanted to deal with. We hadn't begun the trip and I was already breaking my Code of Chillness, but something had to be done.

By dinnertime I got the call. "We're good to go. Wallace will get his stuff together, come and pick me up, and then we'll come to you and leave from there."

Of course I'm the last to be picked up. Nothing was easy, all the way to the bitter end. It was as if they knew how unbearably anxious I was and had no problem with taking advantage of it. "What time do you think that will be?" I asked.

"Tonight," Gill said. For such an ambiguous answer, Gill's voice was reassuring. As anxious as I was, he maintained his cool. I didn't like his answer, but I trusted him.

With a few hours to kill, it was time for my last supper in Amherst. I called up some last remaining college friends still lingering in town and we went to Wings. Amherst was blessed with a plethora of quality delivery places, but Wings reigned king. They cooked beefy, boneless, chicken wings, dipped in different kinds of delectable sauces. Aside from delivery, they had a restaurant to eat at called, the Hanger, where neither the waitresses, nor the spicy style of wings, showed mercy. Their ribs and nachos were worth getting as well. For my last supper, we got it all. The only problem was with it not being the healthiest meal. You were reminded of that, no more than an hour after it had been digested (even faster than Pat's). I felt apologetic toward what I was about to put my fellow road trippers to-be through, and I felt more apologetic toward what I was about to put my gastro-intestinal system through, but I could not leave Amherst without saying goodbye to Wings. They can take my Pat's, but they will never take...my Wings! Didn't Wallace's Uncle William say that?

At ten o'clock in the evening, as I lay on my "waiting couch," staring out the window into darkness, my front door opened and the only two people I wanted to see in the whole universe walked through. "Hey buddy, you ready to go?"

"No," I said dryly, "I think I'll sit on this couch for another three weeks."

We packed the car with my stuff, then I went to my room one last time. I took down the map, and as I was about to leave, I noticed the purple yin yang notebook lying on the floor where the table had been. I hesitated. *I don't want that ugly thing around... Get over yourself. It's an ugly purple cover, but a notebook is a notebook. You never know when it comes in handy... Fine.* I grabbed it and walked out.

We got in the car around ten-thirty. I sat in the back seat and had trouble taking in the reality. *Are we actually doing it? Yes. We are.* The long haul west had begun. For the next month, we would experience beauty from all kinds of areas, climates, culture, and everything else under the desert, mountain, cornfield, grassy sun. For months I planned, stressed, anticipated, dreamt. It was a good feeling making a dream a reality. Many people try and fail. Many more don't even try. I was doing it. At least at the moment I was. If there was one thing I knew for sure about a road trip, it was this: It can be planned and prepared for ahead of time as much as humanly possible. But once that car hits the open road, you might as well throw all the plans out the window, because anything can—and will—happen.

PART I
THREE SEMI-DECENT CAMPERS

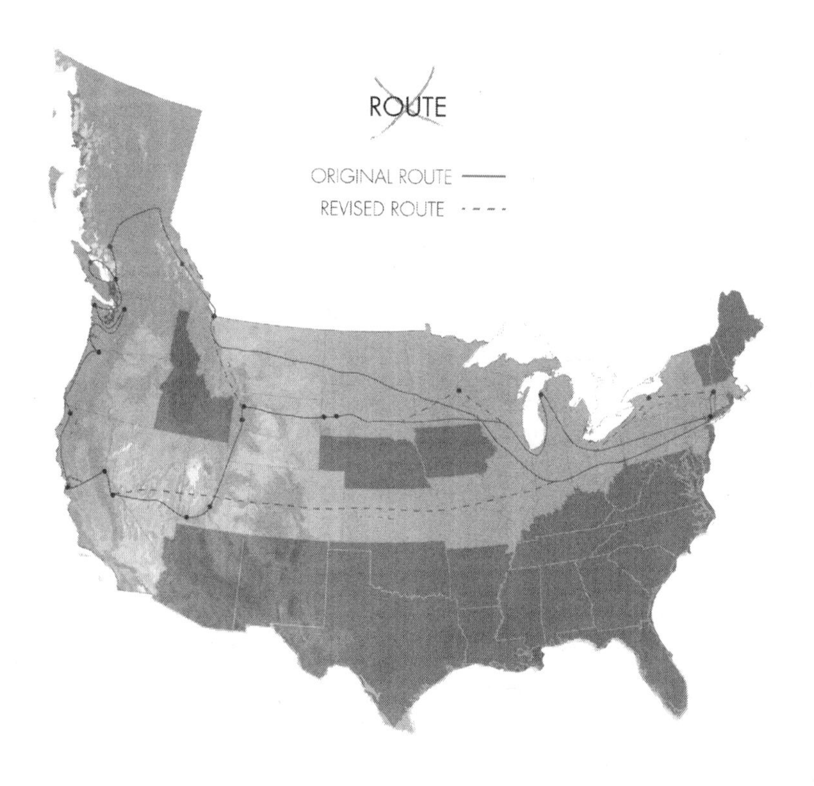

DAY 1

It was ten-thirty on a Saturday night. The warm early summer air still lingered from the hot daytime with a touch of humidity adding a little thickness. The full summer humidity would not set in until late June, early July, around the time we would be in this exact spot, but instead of us backing out of my driveway, we would be pulling in, most likely cheering and kissing the ground. We would forget for a second about all the woes of our long trip, like the arm that Wallace lost, or that old man in South Dakota we had killed and thrown in the river. But none of this had happened...not yet. The adventure had just begun.

From Amherst we headed to Northampton to get on Route 91 south toward Connecticut. This was the road I had taken so many times to start my spring break road trips. 91 south connects to Route 95 south which goes all the way to Miami (Pat's as well). But this time we were on it for a mere twenty minutes to connect to Route 90 west. 90 would take us through Rochester, all the way to southern Michigan. We could take it clean across the country to Seattle if we wanted, but if all went as planned, we would be approaching that Northwest village a different way.

Wallace had a hectic day. He had driven his parents to the Albany airport and back (a three-hour round trip), packed all of his stuff, and rushed out to please my obstinacy. I figured after all that, he would have slept in the back. It turned out that he snorted an exorbitant amount of adderall and decided he would drive all the way out to Michigan. *Suit yourself bud.*

None of the reality had entirely set in that we were embarking on a month-long vacation across the North American continent. Maybe it was due to the fact that we were heading out on a dark highway, with an eighteen-hour drive ahead of us. Jenny texted me from the comforts of her Michigan home, asking how we were.

"Have a good night's sleep," I wrote back. "We'll see you tomorrow afternoon."

Spirits were high. We blasted P-Funk on Wallace's sound system as we sped along the dark roads, flying by the occasional car.

A brief word on Wallace's sound system, which he had spent a pretty penny on installing in his Suburu: When the choice came to keep the one foot by three foot subwoofer in the trunk, or take it out to free up packing room, we were mutually pleased with our decision as we bobbed our heads to George Clinton's scratchy, funkified voice bumping from the front to the back.

Adrenaline pumped through all of us (some more naturally than others) all the way to Rochester. Hours went by like minutes, yelling about our plans over the music.

We pulled up to Kath's quiet suburban house around four a.m. She sleepily gave Wallace a loving embrace and then offered us breakfast and cooked eggs in a basket. A generous gesture and I ate it, but it was too early. I slumped into her living room couch and enjoyed her gentle Rottweiler, Ophelia. The Band's song Ophelia entered my head. I turned to Kath and asked her if the dog was named after the song.

"What?" she replied.

I replied, "Never mind," and slumped back into the couch. I didn't feel like explaining the intricate drum/vocal work of Levon Helm at this hour of the day.

We hung out for an hour, talking about God-knows what—the usual conversations had at four a.m. and sober—and were briefly interrupted by Kath's father, who was a reverend. But he shyly stood by the doorway, hidden behind a wall from my view so I only heard his reverend voice without seeing his reverend face.

Somewhere on Route 90 between Syracuse and Rochester, Wallace briefed us on his relationship with her father. He said he was terrified of him, because they had prior interactions that Reverend Dad did not exactly approve of. Some of these included seeing Wallace walk out of the shower in nothing but a towel and walk into his innocent daughter's room, flashing the bold Mowery tattoo on his arm which he drunkenly acquired, somewhere on the North Island. Or when Wallace helped Reverend Dad move Kath's bed when she was moving out and the bed fell apart, with Wallace sporting a guilty look and a shrug. Gill and I applauded him for that. In the world of lovemaking, you should receive a medal for breaking a bed. Silver for your own bed, gold for hers. It should be called, the Honorary Fucking Medal. Because when the bed breaks, that's not making love, that's fucking.

At around five-thirty a.m., we walked out to the car to head on our way. The sun was coming up and the birds were singing their wake-up song.

"Do you want to switch up driving, Wallace?" asked Gill.

"No way man, I'm ready to go! Let's do this!" was the amphetamine-induced answer.

Suit yourself bud.

I laid out in the backseat and attempted to sleep, as Wallace steered the car westward toward Ohio. Sleeping in a car isn't easy. That comfortable position cannot be found to rest the body. It almost happens, but the mind gets stuck in a grey area, not quite awake with the eyes closed, but not asleep either. Don't ever think about dreaming, it never happens. Reality is always lingering in the background. It can be heard, but attention is not given to it. However, a slight awareness is maintained, so if something sounds interesting like when someone in the car says, "Holy shit!" or "Wooow!" the head perks up immediately for a couple seconds. *Are we passing something outside that's worth getting up to see?* The mind groggily interprets the situation before the head lies back and the eyes close again.

When I opened my eyes again, the sun was up. It was a bright morning and I nudged myself upright in time to see us driving by Cleveland. We passed over a river reflecting the blue sky. The city skyline was close enough to reach out and touch, with the great lake as a backdrop. This beautifully clear Ohio day made Cleveland actually look like a nice city. To think it was always at the butt of my jokes. Like when Hurricane Katrina hit New Orleans, I thought, *why did such a terrible hurricane have to hit such an amazing city? Why couldn't it hit some place like, I don't know, Cleveland?* Well I am here to say I apologize, Cleveland. From the highway you look like a beautiful city, not worthy of getting destroyed by a catastrophic natural disaster.

I "woke up" after my roughly four-hour pseudo sleep, as we turned off 90, heading north into the giant mitten. The way I planned it out meant we would drive through the majority of New York and Ohio in darkness. I had zero desire to see what those states had to offer aesthetically. Then I could see Michigan in all of its glory. Traveling through Michigan would mark the beginning of my curious adventure into the uncharted territory of Evan's mere twenty-one-year existence.

I took out a map to see the ground we covered. I didn't realize until then that we had briefly crossed through Pennsylvania. When looking closely at a map, a tiny part of the state can be seen, that juts up in between New York and Ohio like a little chimney. Judging by the geography, this was a purposeful Pennsylvanian power play to weasel its way onto a fifty-mile stretch of coast on Lake Erie. They insisted on ruining their perfectly shaped rectangular state so they could get onto the lakeshore. Prime real estate without a doubt. Amazing what people did to get a little piece of the pie.

It was noon and we were about halfway up the mitten when Wallace called it quits on driving. We pulled into a gas station with a big banner on the front of the convenience store advertising fresh jerky. I loved jerky. I considered myself an extraordinaire and I can be a harsh, unforgiving critic.

When we walked into the convenience store, I could see that when it came to jerky, Michigan did not mess around. They had a counter space set aside, which was shelved and encased with all kinds of fresh-made hunks of dehydrated meat. Imagine a showcase normally occupied by donuts and substitute with jerky. Lots and lots of jerky. They had beef, turkey, elk, venison, and all of them in various flavors. Gill and I bought one pound of a large variety. It was like being in a candy store of savory delights. Well done, Michigan.

Wallace turned to me holding out the car keys. He had deep, dark, puffy patches under his bloodshot eyes. His hair was sticking up in different directions, and held together in clumps by grease. His beard looked extra scraggily. In the deepest voice I have ever heard from this already baritone individual he said, "Adderall's worn off. Your turn to drive." He dropped the keys in my hand and hobbled to the backseat.

My moment of truth had come. Would I be able to contribute my share of the driving? I stepped into the driver's seat and went over what I was taught. *Clutch in, put it in neutral, start the car. Okay, switch to first—*

"E-brake!"

Oh yeah, shit. "Thanks Wallace. Sorry."

"It's fine, just take your time."

E-brake down, put it in first, ease out the clut—nope it stalled.

Gill giggled, entertained by this pathetic pledge to the Stick Shift Society. After a few tough stalls, I managed to get the bastard back on the highway. I knew once I got to fifth gear, it was smooth sailing. I took a victory bite out of my venison teriyaki jerky. *Mmmm.* The dry yet juicy meat let out succulent, savory flavors as I chewed. This state knew jerky.

Our destination was Petoskey, Michigan. To say it like a true Michigander, treat the "o" like a bunch of "a's." It's situated on Lake Michigan, in the northwest region of the state. To locate it without a map, put your right hand up with your palm facing you and your fingers extended and together. Petaaaaskey is situated around the crack between your ring finger and middle finger.

It was a couple more hours before we veered off the highway onto local roads with traffic lights. This gave me a chance to work on my practical stick shifting, which was both fun and nerve-racking. One little fuck-up on the clutch and I could be the reason for the car to break down and the trip to end. The same thought must have crossed Wallace's mind and after a few traffic lights, he made me pull over and took the wheel. I had a good run. But not worrying about destroying our already delicate car let me sit back and enjoy the quaint, northern Michigan scenery.

We had reached rolling hills and farmland, with the road rising up and down like calm waves. Out in the fields, the hay was freshly cut. Perfectly put together hay bales sat in various lonely spots. They sat alone but proud, like they were on pedestals, showing themselves off at the county fair, competing for the perfect spiral.

Back when we had gotten off the highway and I had still been driving, I called Jenny and gave the phone to Gill to get directions. When traveling with people in such tight quarters, certain attributes can be found about your partners that you would have never expected. I had known Gill for the better part of a decade, but it was at that moment that I learned something new. As he was on the phone, I listened to the soft muffle of Jenny's voice. She seemed to be giving Gill many details. He replied every so often in his typical suave, everything-is-under-control voice, simply replying, "Uh huh. Okay. Yeah, sounds good. Yep. Yeah, I got it. Okay, Jenny, see you soon." When he hung up, I asked if he remembered all of the directions, to which he replied, "No. But don't worry, I'll get you there."

Jenny told us that we were about ten minutes away. A half hour later when we were still roaming around back country roads, Gill stayed adamant that we did not need to call her back, despite our pleas and utter confusion. We had been in the car for eighteen-plus hours, we were within a couple miles of our destination, but Gill (being the typical man that he is—God I hate men) continually refused to let us call. He promised over and over that he would get us there. "She said we would pass a line of mailboxes. I know we're close, I can feel it."

"Feel it? What the hell do you feel, Gill? You know what I feel? Tired."

"Don't worry guys, just trust me. It's right up ahead."

At this point we had been up for so long that the whole situation was comical. I didn't think any of us knew what was going on, which explained why neither Wallace nor I took the initiative to call Jenny back. *Where are we? Michigan? How the hell did we end up here?* I chewed on another piece of jerky to settle my senses.

After ten more agonizingly confusing minutes and Wallace's escalating threats of violence, Gill gave in and called back, and five minutes later we were pulling into Jenny's driveway. A line of large, healthy oaks passed us as we drove in. There was a big green front lawn, very well manicured, which led up to a big white house, as if we pulled up to the front cover of a homes and gardens magazine. We got out and each had a victory stretch. The warm Midwest air hit us with a combined cool mist from the great lake, which had yet to be seen, but was oh-so close. Jenny came out to greet us. This was a smiling, familiar face I hadn't seen in two years' time, on another continent. I gave her a big hug. It was great to see her after so long, it was even better to be out of the car.

It was five-fifteen on a Sunday afternoon in Petoskey, Michigan. The sun was still shining strong and the sky was pitch blue. We had one thing on our minds, something that Jenny had promised me a long time ago, as we sat in Torino, Italy, slurping pasta and wine. "If you ever visit me," she said with that inherent hospitable charm, "I'm taking you out on the boat so I can show you what Michigan is all about." No more than five minutes after we arrived, we had our bathing suits on and were strolling down a small dirt path from her house. The path led us one hundred yards down to a private neighborhood marina. I was expecting her to live on one of the great lakes, but it turned out we were on a smaller lake called, Lake Walloon, which was a stone's throw away from the big one.

The five of us—Gill, Wallace, Jenny, me, and Murphy, their Black Lab—headed out on the lake in the motorboat. The water had a light, greenish-blue color that made it look like we were in the tropics. Not what I expected from northern Michigan. This was a change from New England lakes, which, nice as they were, often sported a dark, muddy color. Gill and I took turns testing our skills on water skis, as Wallace groggily watched from the boat.

"Wallace, this is awesome!" I said as I flopped onto the boat sopping wet. "You want to try?"

"Tomorrow," Wallace mumbled. "I can't keep my eyes open right now."

A few runs around the lake had built up our appetite and we docked the boat and headed up to the house. Murphy led the way.

Jenny was a hospitality management major at the University of Michigan, Grand Rapids. I found this out in Italy when she would never fail to find the opportunity to speak the world about Michigan, making it sound like the Garden of Eden. "...and the lake is beautiful in the summer, and then in October we have an apple festival and..." She would tell us this over a gourmet-cooked meal she had whipped up with ease. Her best friend Melony and I would sit at the table with our mouths full, nodding, "Uh huh, uh huh." I felt compelled on this trip to take this northern detour, so I could finally give Jenny a chance to live up to these hospitable promises. Lo and behold she managed to far exceed my expectations.

When we arrived back at the house, we followed her into the large, modern kitchen. "I hope you guys like pork chops," she said as she pulled out a big bag of thick, marinated hunks of meat. She went and threw them on the grill. Then she presented us with another dish. "These are some gourmet mushrooms I handpicked from the woods behind our house. They're in bloom this time of year. You guys are real lucky because they cost forty dollars a pop at the five-star restaurant I work at in town."

There wasn't much to say as we stood there in awe. We had to focus more on sucking back our watering mouths. She cooked up all this, as well as an elaborate salad (all fresh vegetables from the garden) as a precursor to our feast.

For as long as I had known her, Jenny had always been a motherly figure. She cooked for, and generally took care of everyone around her. This was especially true with her best friend, Melony. In Italy on our abroad program, they were inseparable. In fact I could not see Melony ever functioning without Jenny. Especially because Melony was an epileptic and her life had been saved by Jenny, multiple times. Melony's parents understood Jenny's importance in their daughter's life so much, that they refused to let Melony go to Italy without Jenny.

None of this had changed two years later, sitting in Jenny's house. Gill, Wallace, and me (and Murphy), watched Jenny do all of the work, scurrying around the kitchen, concocting the perfect meal and atmosphere. Although she did miss a step to perfection and accidentally "burned" the pork chops. We all insisted they were fine, but she refused and made a call to her mother, who did not hesitate to swing by the supermarket on her way home and buy a full set of fresh pork chops.

Jenny's mother, Silvi came home and chatted us up as soon as she walked in the door. It did not take long to see where Jenny got her hospitable attributes from. Silvi was a beautiful, slim, and fit woman in her forties with a big, bright smile which Jenny also inherited. Jenny's father never came home. We learned that Mr. Breadwinner was away on some business trip.

We proceeded to feast while sipping on a deliciously balanced and light microbrew local to Michigan called, Bell's, while they excitedly asked us about our trip, and we excitedly answered. We also got to share some stories of Italy, and our enchanting hikes together in the Alps. Talking about the Alps sparked more memories.

"Jenny!" I blurted. "Do you remember that classic conversation that Melony had with her mom on the phone?"

Jenny furrowed her brow and shook her head. "What conversation?"

"What conversation?? Oh, you'll remember." I began the story as the table listened in. "After the hiking trip that Jenny, Melony, and I went on, Melony was on the phone with her mom, telling her all about it. 'I had so much fun this weekend, Mom! I got to go hiking in the Alps!' Confused, her mom asked her where that was. 'You know Mom,' Melony confidently responded, 'the Alps? Like the *Alp*alacians?'"

The table erupted in laughter. "Oh my gosh!" said Jenny. "I totally forgot about that!"

I hadn't thought about these great stories in two years and they were better than I remembered. As the old saying goes, "Like a fine wine, it gets better with age." Especially when it's Italian wine.

After dinner, Wallace had reached his limit. The adderall had finished draining his life –not a detail we shared with our hosts—and he bid good-night to all. I went upstairs to take a shower. In the shower I thought about the next day and our plans. *Chill on the lake some more, maybe play tennis on Jenny's private court, and leave for Sam's place in St. Paul, Minnesota by mid-afternoon...damn. I am going to be in St. Paul, Minnesota tomorrow!* And that was when it hit me. All of the excitement and anticipation from months and months of waiting. I was doing it. We were already in Petaaaskey, Michigan and tomorrow we would be in St. Paul, Minnesota. The words sounded better than being told I was receiving a million dollars. For my whole life I had only heard about such places like St. Paul. Now they were becoming part of my reality. And there was so much more ahead of that. So many mountains, and cities, and people, and states, and microbrews!

It was ten p.m., almost twenty-four hours since we left my driveway. The sun was still out and we headed back to the boat for a sunset ride. Michigan was gifted enough to be the western-most state on Eastern Standard Time. It would never be light at ten o'clock in Massachusetts, not even on the longest day of the year. There were still five in our sunset party because Silvi substituted for Wallace. She also drove the boat so Gill, Murphy, and I could watch Jenny show off her slalom ski prowess in perfect form. She gracefully skimmed over the then purple-orange water reflecting from the sunset. Gill and I relaxed, sipping on Michigan beer fed from the boat's cooler, as the warm evening lake wind swept through our hair. I raised a glass and Gill met me with a cheers as we laughed and shook our heads. "Can you believe we did it?!" said Gill.

"Gilligan, my man," I paused and took a long swig, "this is just the beginning."

When we got back to the house, fatigue hit Gill and me and we traded going out to a local Michigan bar, for a morning tennis match. We reluctantly decided on seven a.m. as a wake-up time. "You can sleep when you're dead." This became the motto on our little adventure.

"Okay," said Jenny, "breakfast should be ready by seven-thirty."

DAY 2

I woke up in my sleeping bag on a soft, clean carpet in a pitch-black basement. The ceiling above me creaked from human activity. This was a good sign because we were directly under the kitchen.

I walked up and opened the door. Blindingly bright light blasted into my squinting eyes. I couldn't see anything but I could hear people laughing at me. My disheveled hair must have complimented my actions as I stumbled around the house. When my sight returned, I was confronted with a glorious spread on the dining room table. Cups of freshly squeezed juice were laid out at each well-placed table setting. In the middle of the table was a king-sized silver platter decorated with eggs, sausages, chocolate chip and blueberry pancakes, and whatdayaknow, the burnt pork chops. We had begged Jenny the night before to save them. "If it comes down to putting them in the garbage or my stomach," stated Wallace, "you know where to put them." Gill and I had nodded in agreement.

As Jenny stood over the stove cooking poached eggs, she turned to me with a her five-star smile. "Would you like some Italian coffee? I saved it from our trip and only bring it out for special occasions."

"No thank you, Jenny," I've never been a coffee drinker, although in hindsight I should have made an exception to get a small taste of Italian nostalgia. "But you know who would love some? Gill. He loves—oooh, speak of the devil."

Gill made an entrance mimicking mine, first stumbling blindly, then staring wide-eyed at the breakfast feast. We sat down ready to devour.

"Should you wake up your friend John?" asked Jenny.

"Who? Oh you mean Wallace?" Gill and I looked at each other and shook our heads. "No. Judging by how loud he was snoring down there, he's going to need a lot more time."

Silvi joined the three of us for a post-breakfast tennis match. Murphy was our spectator, panting peacefully in the shade. Jenny's private court was right above the docks, which made for a picturesque Michigan lake backdrop as we played. It could have been considered a distraction, but Team Massachusetts was unfazed. Gill and I were focused on beating Team Michigan on their home court.

Something that our two states have in common is that they are the only ones that can be shown on a body part. I already mentioned Michigan (on the palm of your hand). As for Massachusetts, curl up your left arm like you're flexing your bicep, and voila, Cape Cod! To find Amherst, point between your pectorals (or breasts), which is appropriate, since it's set in a valley.

By the time we finished two sets, the sun had warmed up and the all-encompassing thought came back to everyone. We headed back to the house to wake up sleeping beauty.

"Wallace! Get up, we're going back on the boat."

"Mmmmrrrr," came a low growl as if we were waking a bear from hibernation. "I'm still exhausted. Go on without me."

"Come on, Wallace. Look I got a pork chop!" I waved the piece of meat in his face.

He took a sniff and opened his eyes. "Mmm, that smells good."

We were back on the lake in no time.

Yesterday's main event was water skiing. Today was wake boarding and tubing, including relaxing breaks in between with beer in hand. The weather seemed more beautiful than yesterday, if that was possible. From my optimized reclined position, I reached out my beer. "Jenny! Cheers!"

Jenny laughed and extended her glass. "Cheers, I'm so glad you guys made it up here!"

"So are we."

"You guys brought the good weather too. I think yesterday was our first real summer day."

"Really?" I asked, surprised. For some reason, I couldn't imagine this place as anything but blue skies and beautiful all year.

"Yeah," answered Jenny. "I would say the nicest day of the year so far—or maybe today is the nicest and yesterday comes second."

"That's great to hear. Cheers to that!"

Jenny laughed again. I was always good at making her laugh.

"Are you almost finished with your major?" I asked.

Jenny nodded. "One more semester."

"Cool. Then what?"

"Then I move back here."

"Like, until you find a job?"

"Yeah, but probably for good."

"Really?"

"I have some great connections with hotels up here. I'm going to get into hotel management."

"You don't want to go somewhere else?" I asked as if it was some obvious choice.

Jenny shook her head without much thought. "Not really, maybe a couple towns up shore. I love it here. I love the lakes, I love the seasons, my whole family's here. It's comfortable. I know it as well as I know myself. Plus I love showing it to people like you!"

I smiled and nodded, but I couldn't relate. The thought of staying in one's hometown never sat well with me.

"What about you?" she asked.

I shrugged. "I don't know. But I don't think I would go back to my hometown."

By two o'clock, the time had come to tear ourselves away from this idyllic lake resort and head back on the road. Although Jenny and Silvi didn't let us leave until they filled our gullets again with juicy burgers and homemade pasta salad.

After I ate I went to call Sam to tell him we were heading his way.

"Sounds great, Evan. Looking forward to seeing you guys," said Sam.

"I know man, I can't wait. It's been so long."

"Hey, I almost forgot," he said excitedly. "You have some good timing."

"Why's that?" I asked.

"If you stay over, we can go see Obama, who just so happens to be in St. Paul tomorrow to make his victory speech." Illinois senator, Barack Obama had just won the presidential candidacy (over Hillary Clinton) for the Democratic Party.

"Are you serious!?" I wasn't a big political buff but how could an opportunity like this be passed up when it was put right in my lap? "That's amazing!"

Another incredible aspect of road tripping can be summed up in the simple phrase: "Shit just happens." Do not ask why or how, but on the open road, luck likes to lean itself in favor of the road tripper. We had no idea Barack Obama would be coming to St. Paul at that exact time. But the road trip gods decided to treat us well. All they required was for us to put in that little bit of effort and courage to make the choice of getting in the car and going. They would take care of the rest.

When I got off the phone, I told everyone the good news. Jenny and Silvi nodded politely in that awkward way which hinted that they did not care for Obama, nor the Democratic Party. I forgot about Jenny's political stance. *Toto, I don't think we're in liberal Massachusetts anymore.*

It goes to show that those types of issues do not need to be discussed. One of my teachers in high school told me that there are three controversial subjects in this world that should rarely be discussed out of the privacy of one's own home: religion, sex, and politics (he said it with half irony because he was a religion teacher). Back in Italy I made sure never to bring up the subject of politics with Jenny because it had the potential to negatively affect our relationship. One time we began to get into a pro-life/pro-choice argument, but I "aborted" the conversation before it got too messy.

We took this cue to leave before anything could be stirred up. After thanking everyone profusely while hugging and taking pictures, we were back on our way. It was hard to break away from such an amazing place. Jenny and Co. treated us like kings and it would probably be the best treatment we would get for the entire trip. Although that was an assumption...

Since we were so far north in Michigan, it didn't make sense to go back down and around past Chicago. Jenny suggested we head north and then west across the Upper Peninsula. The UP as it is commonly called, is a strange part of the country. It borders Wisconsin in the west and is connected to Michigan in the southeast by the Mackinac Bridge, which goes over a narrow channel of the great lakes. It is also connected to Canada in the east, but a lot of it is sandwiched between Lake Superior and Lake Michigan. Jenny and Silvi acted strange when it was mentioned. "It's...different up there. We call them the 'U-py's.'" On my fold-out map of Michigan, one side of the map showed the mitten and was labeled, "Michigan." The other side showed the UP and was labeled, "Michigan's Upper Peninsula." Why was this place referred to as something else? Why was it not just part of Michigan?

As we drove north closer to the bridge, we left our beloved Petoskey blue skies which were substituted by clouds and mist. This made it hard to see Lake Michigan, which we were now driving in close proximity to. It rained as we crossed the Mackinac Bridge. To the left of us was Lake Michigan. To the right was Lake Huron. The two giant bodies of water were dark and ominous. I missed the tropical waters of Lake Walloon, which already felt like a distant memory.

Grey skies lay before us. On the other side of the bridge, a sign read, "Michigan's Upper Peninsula." I found it so strange that they labeled a part of their state like that. It was part of Michigan, yet it was referred to as Michigan's subsidiary.

As we veered west, we drove over endlessly straight roads, with little to see but trees and telephone poles. The scarce signs of civilization were overwhelmed by forests, topped by grey skies. If horror movies haven't been made about this place, producers please come flocking. It should have been its own country: a random, desolate nation wedged between the US and Canada. It did not belong anywhere, like purgatory. I was able to lift the strange mood we all had when I thought up the phrase, "UP, we watch." Get it?

We soldiered on to Wisconsin. When we crossed the border, the environment immediately changed for the better. We were hungry driving through the UP, but we unanimously decided not to stop *anywhere* until we crossed the border.

It was getting late and few places were still open but we managed to find a crappy pizza place. My goals in Wisconsin were to eat cheese and drink microbrews, which both had impressive reputations. But alas it was too late in the day. The cheese stores were closed and we didn't have time to stop and drink some beers. Our only opportunity was wasted on the crappy pizza place, which had both cheese and beer options: processed mozzarella and Budweiser.

I drove for my second installment across Wisconsin. It sucked. There were no major highways close by, so it was only small routes to kiddy corner down to Minnesota. I had to stop frequently, make numerous turns, and drive slow through one small town after another. On top of all that, it was raining and every road decided to have construction. Shit just happens...

I nervously clutched the steering and gear shift, while Wallace and Gill were knocked out from the cheesy, doughy pizza we had reluctantly consumed. The worst part had to be in God-knows-where Wisconsin, where I pulled over to get gas and on my way out, I could not get the damn car to stop stalling. Wallace groggily repeated, "Try again. Try again." I had no idea if he was awake or asleep.

It was unfortunate that I couldn't get to see my surroundings. Take away a stick shift, rain, construction, and darkness, and I was sure this would have been a pleasant drive. I was curious to get an idea of the *real* Midwest, and going along these small roads through so many towns would have presented a great opportunity. I fantasized about being part of a Ray Bradbury novel, driving down quaint streets with friendly faces sitting in rocking chairs and waving from their porches. Or kids with tucked-in shirts and parted hair racing around on tin bicycles. Instead I was in the other part of Bradbury's novels, driving through dark, evil streets, not knowing what will pop out around every corner. I could barely make out some rolling hills and farmland with barns and wooden houses with big front porches, but only so much detail could be illuminated from the dark roads and scarcity of street lamps.

We were approaching St. Paul around three a.m., which was not the best time to arrive at someone's house (save for significant others). I called Sam.

"He-Hello?" It was obvious I woke him up.

"Hey Sam."

"Hey. Um. Are you here?"

"No, we're about twenty miles out. Did I wake you up? I'm sorry."

"Um, kind of," he sounded in no state to be tending to company.

"Sam, what time is Obama's speech?"

"Um, it's at four or five o'clock."

"P.m.?" *That was a stupid question, why the hell would he be making a speech in an hour?* "Never mind, don't answer that."

I thought about our situation. *Was it worth staying for Obama's speech? It's a once in a lifetime opportunity to celebrate this momentous victory. But that's a long time from now.*

"If we go," said Gill, "we probably would need to skip the Badlands and go straight to Yellowstone."

"I agree. What do you guys think? Badlands or Obama?"

I looked behind me and Wallace was snoring.

I looked at Gill who shrugged. "I don't care."

Executive decisions had to be made. "Sam," I said, "go back to sleep."

"Okay," he said obediantly. He hung up, and we marched on.

Before making the even longer haul out to western South Dakota, I wanted to take this opportunity to make a small detour and drive through downtown Minneapolis. When driving past a metropolis during the wee hours, it's a fun road trip activity to take a quick drive through one of the main downtown streets, where you can catch a rare glimpse of an empty major city. We got out and stood in the street under the immense, empty buildings. No traffic, just an occasional car. It was surreal, like we had survived the apocalypse and were the only people alive.

We enjoyed our post-apocalyptic prelude before continuing toward our next destination, the Badlands of South Dakota. Gill took over driving and I passed out. *Good night, Minnesota.*

I managed to get a few hours of car sleep, or so I thought. It felt like we had been driving for a long time but I'd occasionally pop my head up and ask where we were to which Gill replied, "Still in Minnesota." My car sleep had warped time and maybe I was sitting up every five minutes, but it felt like hours.

I woke up for good around nine a.m. to find us parked at a gas station off the highway. Wallace was in the driver's seat. "Welcome to South Dakota," he said. His tired, unenthusiastic tone didn't hinder my curiousity and I got out to inspect my new surroundings. The gas station was raised slightly in elevation, enough to give me a 360-degree view of far stretched plains. This was prairie land. Never in my life had I been able to see so far and so wide in so many directions. All there was, was prairie and power lines, with the occasional cluster of grazing cows. I looked at where the highway went and where we came from. It extended straight as an arrow off into the distance in both directions, shrinking into the horizon. We were back on Route 90 which we had last left back in Ohio to take our little detour. I noted how overcast, grey, and cold it was before my attention was drawn to a big truck pulling into the gas station hauling a large metal grate with small holes. Shrieks and squeals from what sounded like hundreds of unseen hogs came from inside. *Welcome to South Dakota indeed.*

South Dakota is one of the square states. It has no cities. The map shows big empty areas with no roads, no names of towns, just nothingness. When the map shows a road, it is perfectly straight and turns at right angles due to zero natural obstructions. Massachusetts on the other hand, is so hilly that it's tough to find a straight road on any map. The far west side of South Dakota is where interesting stuff starts popping up, like the Badlands and the Black Hills. We were still hours away from all that, stuck in the nothingness blob of prairie land. But I welcomed it all with my virgin eyes. I focused on the newness of the nothingness.

We went into a trucker-stop diner: nothing special. We got an order of nothing special eggs with a side of nothing special hashbrowns and bacon, served by a nothing special waitress. I bought some postcards of the Black Hills and we continued west.

The prairie is the start of the big country—the wide open west, where the gap between the sky and the earth seems to have widened exponentially. As we drove, I noticed the sun occasionally breaking through the clouds. Great misty beams of light shone down from the heavens to the flat fields. There was one rare moment when the clouds broke apart and the sun changed the dark shade of the prairie, bringing out bright, vibrant colors. New shades of green and orange came out of the grass which weren't visible from the overcast skies. There were giant spots of shadow casted down onto the prairie where the clumps of clouds still covered the sun. They were maybe miles in diameter, which I was able to see in its entirety from my vantage point. This will not happen in the east, where a cloud casts a shadow on the world because there is always a hill too close by to see far off. The prairies, on the other hand, leave nothing to hide.

By the middle of the state we approached hilly terrain. Nothing substantial—maybe shallow ravines were a better description. We began passing billboards for the Badlands and its respective tourist traps. I looked on the map and noticed we had recently crossed into Mountain Time. I was happy to make the announcement. "Hey guys, just a quick update, we are now in the Mountain Time Zone." I reached for my watch to set the time back which I realized had to be turned back *two* hours because I had not changed it for central time. That made sense because we had crossed it last night and last night was a blur of rainy dark highways and pseudo sleep.

"Wait," said Gill, "we should keep our clocks on Eastern Time."

Wallace and I exchanged a look like this wasn't the Gill we had known for all these years. And after that shenanigan he pulled getting into Petoskey, who knew what else was going on in that skinny man's brain.

"My friend told me to do this on our trip. He's gone on a lot of cross-country trips so I trust his advice."

"And what will that accomplish? Will we travel back in time eventually or something?"

"I know it sounds pointless, I was skeptical too when he told me. But he swears by it. This way we can get up really early, but it will feel a lot later because we'll be tricking our minds into thinking we're on Eastern Time."

Wallace and I looked at each other and nodded. It was so crazy it just might work.

"Consider it a fun experiment."

"Okay, let's do it. All clocks shall hereby remain on Eastern Time until otherwise noted."

"Agreed."

Around the same time of the historic Eastern Time Continuum Agreement, I noticed some interesting terrain appearing on the horizon. Instead of nothingness, there were jagged lines popping up. They looked like distant mountaintops, but they were too low to the ground to be. Not long after this strange sighting, we made it to the Badlands exit. A right turn took us to a tourist trap advertised on the billboards called, Wall Drug. We all made a "yuck" sound like we just ate a piece of licorice flavored liver, and turned left instead toward the Badlands. We were three bold travelers unfazed by petty tourist traps and the strong temptations from the billboards were no match. No, I don't want any fireworks. No, I don't care about dinosaur mini golf. No, I don't give a shit about the giant wigwam tent. Not that these places were designed to lure in a pack of young men like us anyway. Their tasteless target market zeroed in on kids and tacky old people.

We drove what seemed like miles through more prairie. *Where are these confounded Badlands?* Confusion set in but faith was not lost. It was a couple miles till we made it to the national park gate. We had decided during our trip-planning phase that the three of us would pitch in for a national park pass. This would be a one-time purchase to use in every national park around the country for one year. We knew we were planning to visit a good amount of national parks, at least enough to make it worth the eighty-dollar price tag for the pass. This would be the first of hopefully many national parks on our trip. Giddy with anticipation, we purchased the pass and received a load of maps and information from the nice ranger. He looked like an overgrown boy scout in his little hat, outfit, and handkerchief tied around his collar. "Here you go guys!" he said with a winning smile. "Enjoy the Badlands, as well as the rest of the parks. There's a whole heck of a lot to explore!" If I had a badge to give, he would've gotten it.

Up ahead was a dirt road and still more prairie. But about one hundred yards ahead, the land stopped and there was only sky, like we were heading toward a cliff. We pulled up and found where the prairie ended and these long awaited Badlands began. It was an immediate and drastic change of landscape. Behind us was flat green grass. In front of us were multi-colored jagged formations of earth, rising no higher than the ground we stood on, but dropping hundreds of feet down to ravines. It was like the earth opened up and swallowed the prairie in giant mud-slides and after thousands of years, formed into these colorful valleys. The succession of erosion could be seen, because the ravines had lines that were parallel to the ground, and could be followed straight across. These lines were a few feet thick and either purple, pink, or yellow. Most of the formations were grayish, but these multicolored lines gave an appropriate contrast.

Looking down on all this was like looking down on a massive jagged mountain range from high up in the sky. But they weren't mountains. Like I said, they didn't rise higher than the prairie. Nor did it look like there was any rock involved. It all seemed to be comprised of some kind of soil. On the other side of the Badlands, the prairie continued but not at the same level as where we stood. The other prairie started at the bottom of the Badlands. This made for an even more spectacular sight, with the Badlands in the foreground and hundreds of miles of prairie behind.

We drove on a road that took us along the ridge of the park, then curved downward so we were driving in between the ravines. There were parts where we could pull over and step out onto a narrow plateau so we could be surrounded on either side by a steep ravine. There was nothing I could compare this to. I had never seen earthy structures and formations on such a large scale. The Badlands had to be one of a kind.

We drove about ten more miles admiring our unique surroundings. The big grey overcast cloud had finally broken up some, and the sun was able to creep through, along with patches of blue sky. Great masses of cloud shadows were once again casted over the lower prairies beyond the Badlands. From our high-up vantage point, I could see the vivid outlines of the shadows. If I looked hard enough, I could watch them move across the prairie like floating ships.

At the other end of the park, we got to the visitors center. We stopped in to get information on camping, or to steer us in the direction of campgrounds close by. The rangers gave us the rules of camping, which left me in utter astonishment.

Rule #1: You can camp anywhere you want in the Badlands, except:

Rule #2: You must be camped at least half-a-mile or more from any road and:

Rule #3: Your campsite cannot be visible from the road.

That's it?? I couldn't believe it. Most national and state parks I've camped in have had strict rules pertaining to camping and specific places to camp, as well as a load of other useless rules. The Badlands, on the other hand, was a big camper's playground. I had the initial impression that they would not want us to even touch the fragile-looking soil. But it was the opposite. We could touch it, walk on it, roll in it, sleep on it, pee on it, and explore every nook and cranny our hearts desired. This was no strip club. We could look *and* touch.

What we needed before camping was food and booze. We drove out of the park a couple miles to the closest town called, Interior. "Interior, South Dakota, population 200," was what it said on the sign, as we entered into a tiny town comprised of trailer homes and shacks. A small shack on the side of the road, which looked like an outhouse, had a painted sign on the side that said, "Town Jail." At first I thought this was a joke, but the more I looked around, the less funny it became.

We walked into the general store. This depressing room with a couple rows of supplies should have had a sign that read "Supermarket." We bought some vegetables, tortillas, canned beans, a bottle of hot sauce, and a six-pack of some generic beer—no South Dakotan microbrew here—and headed back toward the park.

On the road back, we passed by a man walking on the road who looked Native American. His dirty, weathered face watched the three young white boys drive by. Wrinkled lines on his brow and cheeks stuck out like black ink on white parchment. I could tell by the way he looked at us that he knew exactly who we were. The word "privilege" stuck out in my mind in sparkling Dirk Diggler-esque letters. After thinking about it, I figured that Interior must be a small, Native American town. But "town" seemed inappropriate. "Ghetto" was a better fit. The people running the supermarket also looked Native American. I could only speculate, but they could have all been part of some tribe that was given a small amount of resources by the US to build a town, being promised revenue by the tourists that came through to the Badlands. Not a good situation I gathered. People like us were the revenue, offering a measly fifteen dollars for a few groceries, which was just enough money coming in to keep them in poverty.

I couldn't imagine that these people wanted to "stay in their hometown" like Jenny. But it was not a matter of choice. Choice came with privilege. I chose to leave my beautiful home in Amherst, a place far more livable than Interior, South Dakota. *Amherst should not be taken for granted, Evan. Remember that.* I was sure anyone in this town would have killed to live in a place like Amherst if they had the choice.

Our next task was to drive through the park and find the absolute most perfect spot to camp, since we had the freedom to do so.

"So guys," I said, "what should our criteria be for our perfect camping spot?"

"I think it should have a semi-high elevation to give us the most ideal view in the most directions," said Gill.

"Yeah, and it would be freakin' sweet if we could see the sunset, or sunrise," said Wallace.

"Or both," I said.

"Agreed."

We drove through a lower elevation area, which was tempting because it had a unique geography from the rest of the park. Instead of the tall grey jagged structures, it was a succession of low-rounded mounds, colored purple, green, and yellow. We appropriately named this place, "Teletubbyland." Teletubbyland was taken note of as a prospect and we drove on.

We were backtracking to where we had originally entered the park and it became apparent that we were heading toward a dark, menacing cloud which looked like it was moving in. Fast. We turned around and tried to make a quicker decision. An area was decided on, which surrounded us in Badlandness for about a mile in every direction. It also had a higher elevation and we were a visible distance from Telletubbyland.

Thus began our first camping escapade. Of the three of us, there was no real hardcore camper. We were all on a similar level of having a handful of experience, but all of our prior experiences had been with people with much more experience than us, so we didn't have much to worry or think about. We figured that the three of us combined, probably made one whole somewhat confident camper. We promised ourselves though, that by the end of our trip, we would be master campers. This time was considered the "trial camping run," where we wouldn't be far from the car if any sort of camping emergency were to arise.

As soon as we parked the car, the dark cloud had moved faster than we had expected and the rain fell. We sat looking at each other like, "Who's going to make the first move to start gearing up?"

Evan: "Fuck."

Wallace: "Shit."

Gill: "Fuck it!" And he ran out.

Wallace and I looked at each other and reluctantly followed suit. We got our ponchos on, ripped our backpacking packs out of the car and started throwing shit in. No one knew who was bringing what. There was no communication. We were trying to get it all done with, so we could shut the car without getting too much stuff wet inside.

Shortly after we geared up, locked the car and headed out, the cloud thankfully passed and the sun was out again. As we headed out onto the Badlands, we learned exactly what this strange area was made of. It was some kind of semisoft, earthy clay, and thanks to the brief rain shower, it was given a muddy, sticky texture. It took just a few steps for our boots to accumulate giant Badland mud globs underneath, making the boots ten times as heavy. But once we ascended the ravines, we left the mud and reached hard, dry, stable clay.

We explored the area, hiking up and down mounds and peeking into crevices. The bareness of this area should be emphasized. Trees did not exist. We had the freedom to walk everywhere and see everything around us at all times. Maybe that was why the park was so lenient on camping. There was no real concern with starting a fire, which was the biggest concern in most national parks.

Wallace scampered on ahead while Gill and I played with a video camera we brought, trading off corny narrations. We were trying to be witty, but nothing came out besides cliché phrases like, "Well here we are in the Badlands of South Dakota and it is just beautiful. I've never seen anything like it... Um, I don't know what else to say. Evan? Do you have anything to add?"

"No, Gill. Turn the camera off."

Meanwhile, Wallace called to us from across a ravine where he had staked out a flat grassy spot on the side of a mound. We headed over and checked it out. It had a clear view of the eastern side of the park, which meant a prime sunrise vantage point. It was fairly low and we couldn't see much else, but there was a big round mound next to us. We put down our stuff in our designated base camp and hiked up the mound. Just as we expected, we got an amazing 360-degree view of the area. Our camping spot was a success. We had staked out a covered area for sleeping, and a lookout spot for intruders. Our forefathers would have been proud (especially Uncle William Wallace).

We confidently strolled back down to set up base camp. Tent? Check. We set it up with all tent pieces present and accounted for. Three chairs? Check. Unfolded them. Six-pack? Check. Cracked open three cold ones. So far so good.

Time to eat. Gill pulled out a small camping stove while Wallace and I pulled out food. Refried bean fajitas was the menu that evening. I grabbed an onion and a Swiss Army Knife and went to cut—"Wait a minute, did anybody bring a cutting board?" We sat there giving each other idiotic looks like three Neanderthals. Wallace grabbed a frisbee and handed it to me. I took it, looked at him, looked back at the frisbee, shrugged, turned it over and cut the onion on the back. I looked over at Gill's camping stove and frowned. From the second I laid eyes on it, I knew it was trouble. I have seen many camping stoves before and this did not classify as one. It had all these weird tubes and wires, and some kind of metallic object resembling a fan, which Gill awkwardly placed around the "stove." It looked like it was meant to land on Mars, rather than cook our food. Needless to say, we couldn't get it to work. It was a good thing this was our "trial camping" run. I had brought an extra stove which was in the car, a mere half-mile away. The owner of the "Mars Lander" was the obvious choice to make the trip back to retrieve my stove.

"Is there anything else we're missing before I head back?" Gill asked.

We looked around scratching our dumb caveman heads. "Um, I don't think so."

"Okay," said Gill, "I'm leaving. But I'm only making one trip."

The backup stove was big and awkward. It was questionable to realistically take on our future, more serious camping escapades, but it did the trick for the night. The fajitas were no burnt pork chops, but they were delicious.

There was one more small problem which was out of our control. The "Interior Supermarket" sold us a hot sauce bottle with a broken cap, which spilled everywhere after the wrapping was taken off. It was a good thing we were not in the middle of some mountainous wilderness where big hungry animals were snooping around with spicy palates. Although who knew what the nighttime would attract to the Badlands... We cleaned up as much as we could, used some of the sauce for our dinner, threw away the rest of the bottle, and hoped for the best.

After dinner we walked up to the lookout point at the top of the mound and Wallace pulled out a victory joint to smoke. The sun was reaching close to the Badlands' jagged backdrop and the colors began to change. It was a victory not only for our first successful camping escapade, but for a more solid feeling of being on the road. Michigan was spectacular but it felt like the real adventure began here. This sparked some excitedly stoned, inebriated discussions about what was ahead of us.

"I feel like I could spend a whole week exploring this place!" said Gill.

"Gill, my friend, like I said, this is merely the tip of the iceberg of awesomeness of what is to come!" I spoke as if I knew what I was talking about.

"This mound is a great dancing platform," said Wallace.

As we talked and danced around, cars would stop every so often on the side of the road which was visible about a mile away. We could distantly see their excitement as they took out their wildlife binoculars, curious to identify what peculiar animals they spotted on that big mound. We considered performing a choreographed dance, maybe to Michael Jackson's, Thriller (which commonly played in one's head when one got stoned). I was sure most people were disappointed to see three ridiculous kids dancing to Thriller in their view-finders. Hopefully it worked out for at least one party who spotted us and just so happened to be listening to Thriller in their car. We giddily laughed like school girls at this preposterous scenario. One could only dream of such perfect circumstances.

But this *was* a dream we were living, surrounded by such extraordinary beauty as the sun set over the silhouetted mountains. The sky had stolen the colors from the Badlands and tossed them up in every direction, casting out vibrant purplish-red streaks. The best part about it, was that this light show was being put on just for us. There's an amazing feeling you get when given the chance to experience such natural beauty with no one else around. Rich people buy their own secluded islands to get what we were getting on our private mound.

We headed back to base camp before it got too dark. Gill and Wallace had headlamps but I foolishly forgot mine in the car, making it a challenge if I was to maneuver down in total darkness.

It was a clear night and I tried to stay awake to see the stars, but the two days combined into one had finally caught up with me and I was fighting to keep my eyes open. Gill and I crawled into the tent to go to sleep. Wallace decided to sleep outside under the stars. He was a good distance from the tent but I could still hear him snore. *At least he'll keep away the animals... I hope.*

DAY 3

I woke up several times in the night for various reasons. One was from the sound of snarling and sniffing. I lay perfectly still, listening to whatever was snooping around our campsite. I hadn't a clue as to what kind of animal it was or how big or small. It sounded like it was inches from me, with nothing but a thin layer of tent fabric between us. You never feel entirely safe in a tent. The rustling that's heard could be a friendly squirrel, or a deadly wombat. I imagined whatever it was, ripping open the tent and dragging me away by my head. Imaginations were dangerous tools.

The second time I woke was to the tent opening and a dark figure stepping in. *Speak! Are you friend or foe?*

"Shit!"

Oh it's Wallace.

I could hear light rain pattering the roof of the tent. Wallace collapsed like a fallen tree and there was silence again except for the rain. The next camping test was to see if our rain tarp was going to work...

...Nope. I woke up in the morning in a puddle of water. *Fucking rain tarps never work!* I also figured out we were camping on a small incline which I was conveniently at the bottom of, getting all the water to sleep in. I woke the others and we got up in a hurry, packing all of our shit up even faster than when we were at the car.

I looked at my watch. It was eight o'clock. *Eight o'clock?? How did we sleep that late? Wait a minute, that's Eastern Time! That's right, it's only six o'clock!* Gill's crazy idea may have been working. It was a mental thing but being mentally prepared was all that really mattered in life.

Neither Eastern Time nor sleeping in a puddle helped us to get up early enough to catch the sunrise. But we may have missed it regardless, due to the piece of shit rain cloud above us that happily flooded our tent. It felt as if this cloud was following us across the country.

Our boots accumulated more Badland mud as we trudged through the rain to the car, as if we were walking with concrete blocks on our feet. Our boots were so built up by the time we got to the car, that if we were thrown off a bridge, we would've dropped like stones and slept with the fishes. All the clay on them was too much to deal with at the moment so we threw them in a big trash bag. We threw the rest of our wet stuff in any place we could find and got the hell out of there. At one point not too long ago our car was nicely organized. So much for that.

Damp and rudely awakened, we marched on past the Badlands. The next plan of action was to drive through the Black Hills and give in to our rarely present tourist tendencies by visiting Mount Rushmore. The Black Hills were a mere couple hours from the Badlands, which at this point felt like an easy puddle jump compared to our previous twenty-hour treks.

We got off an exit with signs for Mount Rushmore. At this point we were in the foothills of the Black Hills, and we hit torrential rain. The sky was almost black with zero visibility, but we got through it as we ascended elevation on a windy pass. This brought us back to what seemed to be the norm: overcast and grey. We also reached trees and vegetation, something we had been missing in the great prairie state of South Dakota.

We drove through a tourist-catered town in the middle of the hills. Flashy signs pointed to hotels, mini golf, or restaurants that advertised, "Mount Rushmore's premier all-you-can-eat buffet!" No one was impressed. Nor were we excited to see Mount Rushmore. It was one of those, "We're driving through so we might as well check it out," scenarios. This was so we didn't have to listen to Mom and Dad say, "You're telling me you drove through South Dakota and didn't even stop to see Mount Rushmore!?! What were you doing this entire trip?! Smoking reefer?" ...Yes.

We were able to spot Mount Rushmore as we were driving up the road that led to it. There were old George, Tom, Ted and Abe, watching us joylessly drive up to say hi. We were like ungrateful children visiting their grandparents who they *should've* appreciated but couldn't.

When we reached the site, we approached a tollbooth guarding the parking lot. We stopped before we got there and pondered the dreaded "Ten Dollar Fee" sign.

"Do we really want to pay that?"

"I don't know, we're here, we might as well."

"Let's see what they have to say."

Wallace drove up to the booth and an old lady greeted us.

Wallace: "Hello."

Old Lady: "Hello boys!"

Wallace: "We're not sure if we want to pay the parking fee."

Old Lady: "Oh, it's definitely worth it."

Wallace: "Okay! Well you sold me! Gill, gimme ten bucks."

Really Wallace? You're that easily convinced? I wonder what else you've been convinced to do, and by old ladies for that matter.

We drove in, parked, and walked up to the mighty Mount Rushmore, which was not so mighty up close. Every monument turns out to be smaller when seen in person—which strangely applies to Hollywood actors as well. We spent ten minutes there and realized we were starving and did not want to eat at the overpriced Mount Rushmore food court. So we left. That ran the bill to approximately a dollar a minute. I cursed the people parked on the side of the road where we had initially seen Mount Rushmore for free. They could see it as clearly as we had seen it up close, and were ten dollars richer. They looked satisfied. I wondered what they were going to do with their ten dollars. The possibilities were endless.

"Definitely worth it, Wallace, definitely worth it."

"Shut up."

We drove back to the tourist town and ate breakfast in a German restaurant. The place was packed, which felt strange having this foreign establishment located next to one of our nation's most patriotic landmarks. The cooks spoke German and our waitress was a petite Japanese girl who couldn't speak English. But the biscuits and gravy were out of this world. God bless America.

After breakfast we took a scenic route across the Black Hills toward Wyoming. I didn't find the Black Hills to be impressive. They were mountainous but not extreme, comprised of a few lakes, some rocks and trees, but nothing noteworthy. We didn't stop anywhere to take pictures and rolled on through to the Wyoming border. The grey cloud wasn't helping our lackluster moods either, but I couldn't wait to get to Wyoming. South Dakota was the grey area—literally and figuratively—between the Midwest and the West. The Midwest was nice, but the West, like I said, was the real deal. Hopefully it would be sunnier too.

When we left the Black Hills and crossed the Wyoming border, the landscape made a drastic change. It flattened out again and we were back to driving in wide-open country, but we were no longer in prairie. Instead of green grass and grey earth, turquoise sagebrush and red soil was abound. Every so often we would pass a wooden structure on the side of the road. It was two beams standing vertical, with one beam connecting the two, horizontally on top. The unique colors and cuts of these beams reflected the time and care that was put in by their owners. A dirt road ran through them and traveled far out to a humble house, or over hills to an unseen oasis. These were the ranches of the "Wild West." I was getting a firsthand understanding of what this coveted term came from and where it was. Like I had predicted, Wyoming embodied it. I became a true believer when I saw a tumbleweed bounce across the road in front of us. This was distinctly beautiful country. The ranches complimented the landscape all too perfectly. I didn't know what it was about these simple three-beamed thresholds that I liked so much. They were so simple yet so aesthetically pleasing. Maybe it was a reminder of the simplicity of natural beauty out here, where there were no cities, just wide open country.

We stopped at a gas station off an exit and it was apparent who stood out in the crowd. Every single person had a cowboy hat, a tucked-in, button-down shirt, blue jeans, and cowboy boots. It was a good ol' fashioned-fashion standoff: the cowboys against the—actually I didn't know what we were. We had on T-shirts, cargo shorts, and sandals—the jobless college grads? I liked their style. Not that I would've personally worn it, but it suited them.

When we got toward the middle of the state, we saw signs for Yellowstone and Teton National Park. They were still a ways off on the western side, but we were directed off the main highway to the Bighorn Scenic Byway, which we would take through the Bighorn National Forest. I wasn't sure what the difference was between a national forest and a national park, besides the fact that the latter had overgrown boy scouts collecting money to let us in. I was sure there was a logical explanation but boohoo, we didn't have Wikipedia available in the car. *Where's my computer?? Man, this road trip sucks.*

We rose in elevation and drove up what seemed like a mountain pass. The incline was steep, steeper than anything we had experienced yet. The Suburu was slowing down and visibly struggling.

"Come on baby," said Wallace, "you can do it."

I sensed the tension in his voice. It made us all tense.

The sky darkened and it rained again in big heavy globs that splashed on the windshield. Our windows fogged up from the drastic change in temperature and pressure. I wiped down the window to see outside. The area was covered in—*What the hell? Is that snow?* Suddenly we were surrounded by a white landscape.

"What's going on?! It's June!"

"What in God's name is going on?"

"Gill! What's happening?!"

"I don't know!!"

We looked around yelling in delusional disbelief. I was so cold, and felt like death was upon me. I desperately dug through my bag and grabbed my sweatshirt.

"What is—what is that over there to the right?"

"Is it? I think it's a lake."

"OH MY GOD IT'S FROZEN!"

"AAAAAHHHHHHH!!!!"

Wallace locked the doors and put his foot on the gas.

"GO WALLACE! FASTER!"

"I'M TRYING GODDAMMIT!"

Our horror episode passed as we descended in elevation. We were back to the "real world" with no snow and were rewarded to our delight by a beautiful canyon. The walls on both sides were a mix of alpine trees and reddish rock patches. This lifted our spirits in anticipation of what was to come, but the rain still lingered to keep our spirits at bay. The sky was a dark grey and wet mist crawled through the canyon, forcing me to continue wearing my sweatshirt and keep my raincoat on standby.

Eventually we were back on flat land. We survived the canyon and the "Bighorn National Snow Field." The landscape changed again to lush green pastures growing over blood-red soil.

By early evening we made it to the foothills of Yellowstone National Park called, the Shoshone National Forest. We drove through a canyon, surrounded on all sides by steep rocky cliffs. Once we deemed ourselves sufficiently inside the national forest and close enough to the park, we pulled in to the next campground we came across. It was raining, of course. Not hard, but enough to make setting up our tent a horrible experience. We didn't want a repeat of the night before, so we took extra precaution and rigged a tarp over the tent, tying it to nearby trees. I could tell we were starting to see the light, on the path toward the ancient sacred ways of the camping master.

We also needed to put a canopy over an area to cook and eat. There was a picnic table five feet from us, but the rain had rendered it unusable. When it comes to camping, rain is the threshold, separating the experience between good and a nightmare. Bugs fall under that category too, but rain gets the number one spot.

Luckily we were able to pull our ingenuity together. We dragged half of the table under the tarp. One person had to hold up one end of the tarp, while we cooked on the stove. It wasn't pretty but we made it work. We stood huddled around trying to keep warm and dry as we scarfed down some canned soup and bread. We wanted to get it over with so we could go to sleep. It wasn't late (even for Eastern Time) but we crawled into the tent anyway, in preparation for our first day in a big national park. I knew the three of us were thinking the same thing as we fell asleep. *Maybe tomorrow the rain will stop.*

DAY 4

The East Coast Time Continuum worked like a charm. We were up at eight o'clock our time, six o'clock local time. The sky was mostly cloudy, but the sun was slightly visible and there was no water falling down on us. If it had rained last night, our tarp had done its job because I was bone dry. The crisp morning forced me to keep my sweatshirt on as I walked twenty feet down from our campsite toward the sound of running water. I came upon a wide, steadily flowing river. This was the good kind of water. It was contained and pleasing to the eye, unlike that crap from above. I unzipped my pants and added some of my own water to the river while observing my surroundings. On the opposite bank was a towering rock wall that spanned wide in both directions. I turned around to look across the valley and noticed a similar geological wall, which led me to wonder if this valley was cut straight through by some glacier, millions of years ago. Beyond the rock wall I could see a snow-capped peak, peaking up in the distance. This was a welcoming sight to see. It was about time that we got ourselves into the real mountain country. This was the Rockies, home to some of the most beautiful mountain scenery in the world, as well as a richly diverse wildlife, The String Cheese Incident, Coors, and Coors Light (Silver Bullet!).

We decided to reorganize our mobile home before we rolled into Yellowstone National Park. This was a long delayed chore since our rushed Badlands exodus. It's impossible to keep a car organized on a road trip. Everything starts neatly placed in its perfect, easily accessible spot. Then something is pulled out the back and carelessly thrown back after it's served its purpose. That throws off the equilibrium and in no time everything is getting dug through, with shit getting even more carelessly thrown about, because all I need is my goddamn headlamp and if I could just move the bulky folding chair, I can get to the bag with the right pocket, because I'm having trouble hooking the propane up to the camping stove, because all I care about at this very moment is to get a warm, half-cooked hot dog in my belly, and bullocks to keeping the car organized! It happens. So time must be taken every so often to pull every goddamn thing out of the car, and put it all back in again, in an organized fashion.

Once that chore was finished, we were on our way to Yellowstone. We made it to the gate in a half hour and eased right in with the help of our shiny all access park pass. The ranger gave us more guides and pamphlets about Yellowstone. All of the Badlands literature lay in a muddy mess on the floor of the passenger seat. These new papers would soon see the same fate. I noticed one bright yellow pamphlet and grabbed it. On it was a cartoon picture of a bison running with its head tilted down. A tourist-looking fellow, with binoculars hung around his neck, was in front of the bison, sideways in the air, arms and legs sprawled out. On the top of the paper it read, "Warning: Do not get close to the bison." Under that were some bulleted statements. "Bison are unpredictable animals. Bison weigh over three thousand pounds. Bison can run three times as fast as any human." And the last bullet point was, "They will outrun you." We scoffed at the warning, but secretly made note never to try to fuck with a bison.

On we drove through windy roads in woods and valleys of tall pines. We came to a point where all the trees were bare and black for hundreds of acres. These were poor victims of forest fires. It looked like the fire could have happened barely a month ago. But in reality it could have been years, even decades. Forest fires were becoming a more common occurrence, especially in the West. I was sure this would not be the only patch of dead forest we would pass on our travels. I hoped it would be, but I accepted the reality. It was a horribly depressing sight, but it complemented the ever-present gloomy weather all too well.

The shades of grey and black parted when we arrived at a pure sky-blue lake. Across the lake (miles away) we could see a vast snow-capped mountain range, which reflected like a mirror on the water. As we drove along the shore, we could see patches of smoke coming up at various spots. We pulled over and got out to investigate. We walked up to a group of holes in the ground, five feet in diameter. The smoke was coming up from bubbling water inside the holes, like a boiling pot—or a hot tub. The idea of jumping in was tempting but I valued having skin.

This is a unique part of the world where boiling hot water surfaces from the ground. Some of these "geysers" build up pressure and shoot water up hundreds of feet into the air. Old Faithful is the famous one. It's supposed to shoot water out at around the same time every hour like clockwork. All this geothermal activity under the park is so turbulent and volatile that it is supposedly liable to explode at any given time. If that happens, it will take a good portion of the country with it. And that's enough on geysers and Yellowstone facts. You want to learn more? Do your own goddamn research.

We looked at the map of the park and plotted our course for the next few days. Today we would drive through the park, down to the Tetons. We would spend two days there, then head north back through Yellowstone, spend one day doing a hike, maybe check out Old Faithful for as long as we can stomach the tourists, then head up to Montana. The thought of taking a break from going, going, going was especially nice. We could relax in the Tetons and get some time to get to know a place, as opposed to speeding through the country and only catching what was on the surface.

We headed on the road that led south out of Yellowstone, and into Grand Teton National Park. The Tetons would be my first major anticipated attraction on this trip, said to be the most beautiful and unique part of the Rocky Mountains. I had mentioned that my grandparents had spent thirty summers visiting this area, going hiking, camping, and fly-fishing. They have some magnificent framed pictures of the Tetons displayed around their house. I grew up gazing at these pictures, wondering when I would get my chance to pay a visit. In preparation for this trip, my grandmother had given me some suggestions for hiking, which I promised I would carry out. They were written down on a piece of paper that I kept in my backpack. I took this opportunity to reach back and take it out.

The Grand Teton National Park and Yellowstone National Park are interesting parks because they border each other. Exiting Yellowstone to the south, leads straight into the Tetons with no ranger station in between. These geographic landmarks have lived peacefully as neighbors for generations. However, lest we never forget the great Yellowstone-Teton war of 1855. So many young men stripped of their youth. I was but a young lad when my pappy went off to fight—but I digress.

It was a quick half-hour drive through short pines that were very Black Hills-esque—meaning nothing worth noting. Then it opened up and on our right was the start of a lake. On the other side of the lake, the ground drastically sloped up. That was the start of the Grand Teton mountain range. They were named by French fur trappers who likened them to the French word for breasts. But these beautiful breasts were nowhere to be seen. This piece of shit rain cloud had beaten us to our anticipated destination and planted itself over the mountains. All we could see were the foothills sloping up and disappearing into a giant mass of muffled grey. This dark grey cloud reflected off the water, which made the lake look like a giant puddle of mud. *It will clear up. It will get better.* I clutched my grandmother's hiking itinerary for dear life.

We traveled along a straight, flat road in a perfectly flat valley. It was numerous miles in length and width, but unlike South Dakota, massive chunks of earth and rock rose up thousands of feet in a perimeter around it. The Tetons remained to our right, with herds of Buffalo grazing in the fields of sagebrush. They didn't look like they wanted to kill us, but I heeded the warning of the pamphlet: "Bison are unpredictable animals." I tried not to make eye contact.

It took us an hour to span the length of the valley and make it to the southern tip of the park, where we reached the town of Jackson. We found a tourism center on the edge of town and stopped to check out information on campgrounds. They instructed us to go back out of the town and into the park. Following their directions, we drove along a road heading east, away from the Tetons and farther into the flats, where we found a nearly empty campground. The rest of the country seemed to have gotten the memo about the shitty weather and knew better than to go out camping in these parts. The joke was on us.

We pitched our tent at a site. It was cold. It was June. We were confused.

We weren't as discouraged as we drove back into Jackson to spend the evening, since we had a couple things to look forward to. The first game of the NBA championships was that night, between our home team, the Boston Celtics and the Los Angeles Lakers. This meant we could relax, watch the game, eat, drink, and forget our weather woes. We were excited to sit and drink. It was something we had not had time for since we reclined on Jenny's boat, which already seemed like ages ago. But it was early yet for such activities. First we had to take in the sights of Jackson.

Jackson, Wyoming is a town which on the surface is made for tourists, but different from the tacky tourist traps of the Black Hills or Wall Drug. Jackson focused on the "authenticity" of the "Wild West," while at the same time catered to the wealthy tourist crowds who came from around the world. Every storefront replicated the classic look, with flapping wooden doors, tin overhangs and wood planks for a porch. But inside, the store was an expensive art gallery, or souvenir shop, or a themed bar and grill.

A small ski mountain lay at the edge of town called, Snow King. There was a prominent trail going down the middle of the mountain which looked like it headed straight into town. We later learned that this trail was one of the steepest in the country. This peaked my interest, being an avid skier.

"Check it out guys! These people could walk out their back door and hit the slopes!"

"What? Oh. Cool, I guess."

Wallace and Gill were not avid skiers. I knew that, but I couldn't contain my excitement. After all, I was in the home of one of the world's premier ski resorts called, Jackson Hole. I had to see it with my own eyes before we left (even though it was devoid of snow—or maybe it still had snow and people were skiing since it was June and nothing in this country made any fucking sense).

We walked around the town square to where a crowd was gathered. Everyone was watching a group of men and women dressed in "Wild

West" garb, acting out a scene. They had wireless microphones and their animated Disney-like voices were projected out of a PA system. Two of the "cowboys" were having a "standoff." They stood ten paces apart and faced each other with hands dangling by their holsters, ready to release cap-gun carnage. Tension grew as they spat off cliché phrases like, "Looky-here partner, your kaand ain't welcome round these parts." And, "I reckon you ain't the man to decaaad." I hadn't seen a campy production like this since a trip to Six Flags sometime last decade. Our interests began to peak, in hopes of some death and blood capsules exploding into the crowd.

Right before the tension was to snap and the violence was to begin, a lady in a fancy western dress sprang out into the center wielding a shotgun and fired off a round into the air. "Now hold on just one cotton-pickin' minute!" Her voice was loud and clear through the PA system. Then it all happened so fast. She rattled off some kind of speech about forgiveness or something, and before we knew it, there were dozens of these people doing a line dance and singing about praising Jesus. That was about the time we walked away.

It was nearing dinnertime and we figured it would be a good idea to find a nice local, to steer us in the right direction of where to eat. I wasn't sure why, but something compelled us to walk into an expensive leather store. A dorky looking clerk in his late twenties with bleached, parted hair and bright blue eyes met us with the town's ever-present, Disney-like smile. We were greeted with a hokey, "Howdy y'all! What can I do for ya today?" He appeared to be the embodiment of a tourist town archetype with that plastic, animated smile and perfectly spoken Wyoming accent.

"Um, hey dude. We were hoping you could give us some suggestions on a place to eat."

"Sure, I can help with that! You got lots of options. What were y'all in the mood for?"

"We're looking to eat somewhere good and local. Maybe not a place where all the tourists go."

At this comment I saw something change in his face. The Disney smile went away and he gave us a more genuine look of relief. "Okay, I got a few places in mind."

He told us about a tiny burger joint to try, which he explained was started by an immigrant from New York City. Then he recommended a bar where apparently the highest percentage of girls went in town. "Unfortunately for us fellas, Jackson has a shortage of ladies," our new guide said with a sly smile. "'Round here, girls are like parking spots. They're either handicapped or taken!" That warranted a good laugh.

The conversation continued and we got into talking about the Tetons, which he respected us for inquiring about. "I tell ya, most people walk in here and ask me how to get to Old Faithful. It's not very often I get the pleasure of telling some good travelers like yourselves about our area. There's a heck of a lot to explore in the Tetons. You won't find anyplace like it."

We nodded in agreement. "That's what we're here to do. I don't even know if we'll make it to Old Faithful. Tourist spots aren't high on our list."

"Oh! Hold on one second." He reached under his checkout desk and pulled out a detailed hiking map of the Tetons. He could not be more enthusiastic about pointing out his favorite hiking spots. "...and here is a beautiful canyon you can get to. There's a heck of a nice waterfall at the end..."

After giving us some good suggestions, he also recommended we check out the disc golf course at the Jackson Hole ski resort. This peaked our interest since we all loved disc golf and planned on playing on our trip. It would work out as well since I wanted to check out Jackson Hole. This guy turned out to be a fantastic resource.

It feels good when traveling, to get recognition by a local when they understand that the visitor is there to genuinely explore and learn about their home. There's a big difference between asking a local about the popular tourist spots and asking what *they* like to do. That is where the true essence of an area and culture is found. On the surface, this town looked like a big tourist trap with dancing Jesus freaks. But there was so much more to explore if we took the time and were interested. And if people see that genuine interest, they are happy to show off the good things. They still like to keep their favorite spots secret from the masses, but that is what the big tourist sites are for. Let the masses have their Old Faithfuls and "Wild West" souvenir shops. That leaves the rest of the area open for our enjoyment and exploration.

We took the guy's advice and found the burger joint. It was a little hole in the wall connected to a bar, which we wouldn't have noticed if we walked in without prior knowledge. My spicy jalapeno cheddar burger hit the spot.

From there we headed downtown to the sports bar where he had recommended to watch the game. We ordered a round of draughts from Snake River Brewing Company (Jackson's local brewery) and secured a prime viewing table in time for tip off.

As we sat openly cheering for the Celtics, we caught the attention of an older gentleman sitting behind us. It turned out he went to Amherst College (the small, private college next to mine), "Back when it was a real college, men only!" he proudly proclaimed. Naturally he was rooting for the Celtics and was happy to tell us about their "glory days" which apparently preceded Larry Bird's time, when "Havlicek stole the ball!" I had no idea what he was talking about but he chanted this Havlicek phrase throughout the game, like it was the Celtics' chant. Amherst College an all boys school? Havlicek steals the ball? Yeah, this guy was old. But he announced with pleasure that he was on his honeymoon as he slung his arm around his partner. She bashfully smiled and nodded.

We turned around and gave him a big cheers. "Congratulations! Havlicek steals the ball!"

"That's the spirit boys!"

During halftime, Wallace and Gill stepped outside to smoke cigarettes. I came with, not to partake, but to enjoy a beautiful sunset over the Wyoming-Idaho mountains. The clouds had broken a bit and the sun cast golden shades over the western frontier. We looked out reminding ourselves of this awe-inspiring land that was still so new to us.

Gill and I took this all in as Wallace struck up conversation with a young, rugged dude smoking a cigar and sipping whiskey. He looked like he just came back from either climbing up a mountain or biking down one. Apparently they got into a conversation about weed, after Wallace had expressed interest in wanting to use the gentleman's cigar for something else. By the time Gill and I made our way over, the guy was on the phone with his friend, asking if he could take us out whitewater rafting the next day, for a discounted price, and all of the smoking and drinking we desired along the way. We all wanted to go whitewater rafting at some point on this trip, but we knew we couldn't afford the full price. This seemed like the perfect opportunity with some added perks. Once again the power of meeting locals and relating to them, which is transferred to extraordinarily unexpected opportunities. Or in this specific case, "weed networking." Wallace got his number and we agreed to hook up the next morning.

One downside of my night was losing in a rock-paper-scissors match, which landed me as designated driver. But I didn't care since I was content with my couple of Snake River beers. As long as I could get a taste of the local brew, I was happy.

Staying sober also gave me a good chance to drive in traffic. I stalled once at a traffic light as it turned green.

"Dammit Evan! Quick, let me take the wheel!"

"I got it Wallace, you're drunk."

"I'm not drunk!"

I got the car going again on my first try and it was smooth sailing back to the campsite. Wallace got out of the car and stumbled. "You're right," he said in a slur, "I'm drunk."

We prepared for an "early" wake-up. The cigar man told us to give him a call around seven and we could get on the water nice and early to beat the crowds.

"Is that too early?" he had asked.

"Not at all," we replied. Nine o'clock would be a great time.

DAY 5

My shivering body woke me up. I uncovered my head from my sleeping bag and tuned in to the dreadful sound of rain hitting the tent. *Fuck.* I felt under my sleeping bag for any wetness. Thankfully the tent held up under the rain this time (nor did I pee myself). I reluctantly managed to pick up my frigid carcass. Gill and Wallace were out cold. "Hey. Guys. Gill. Wallace. Wake up." A shift and a grunt was all I got.

I opened the tent and stuck my head out. Light yet frigid rain violated my face. *Double fuck.* Pathetically defeated, I dragged myself to the car and grabbed all the warm clothes I had brought, and put them on. This was the worst morning yet. I would have been surprised if the temperature exceeded forty degrees. I looked over past the campground. From our campsite I could see across the wide valley to the Tetons. They were completely, utterly, shittily shrouded. *What the fuck! It's fucking June! Why such shitty weather? And why oh why during my road trip? I don't know how much more of this I can take... Wait, no!* My determined side came back like a mighty phoenix. *We're going fucking hiking in the fucking Tetons and we're not going to let this fucking shitty weather ruin it.* I boldly turned my back to the absence of Tetons. It was time for breakfast.

I brought the cooking stove over to the picnic table. As I was chopping vegetables in the frisbee, Gill climbed out of the tent. He had the same grim look that I had before, but my new look was one of defiance.

"Good morning, friend!" I said with a jovial smile. "What would you like in your breakfast burrito? We have eggs, cheese, pepper, and onion. Sorry, no hot sauce."

That put an immediate smile on Gill's face and he played along, something he did best. "Oooooh buenos dias amigo. I will take it all!"

Gill was a positive person. I realized from these five days that he was great to travel with. He saw the shittiness of the situation like me, but was able to move past it with ease and stay in high spirits. I had never heard him complain once about this weather we had. Gill was in the know about the unspoken code of "chillness."

Wallace on the other hand, had completely sunk. We poked our heads in the tent to let him know breakfast was ready.

"No man, I can't get up. I think I'm getting sick, and I'm fucking freezing!"

"But Wallace, you have to get up. You're just hungover, you'll get over it. Come on, we have to call that guy to go rafting and then get a good hike in."

"No. I can't. You guys go without me. Come back and wake me up when you're done."

"Wallace, just get up, you'll be fine. I made a delicious breakfast burr—"

"*No*!" This was a startlingly angry tone. "I'm sick. I need more rest or else I'll get sicker."

Wallace probably had a bad hangover, but he certainly was not ill. Our effort was hopeless so we let it rest and geared up to go.

Gill and I drove toward the Tetons information center to get some maps and other trail info.

"Maybe by the time we get back from the information center he'll have come to his senses," I said.

"Hopefully," said Gill. He took a deep breath. "Unfortunately this is typical Wallace."

"Really?" I asked.

Gill looked at me. "Do you know how long I've known him?"

"A long time, right? Like middle school?"

"Elementary school actually. And I've come to accept the fact that he can often turn into a big baby. I've been in many situations similar to this, where we'll be ready to go out and do something, but he'll get lazy and rattle off some kind of excuse about something paining him. Or like this time, feeling sick."

I prefer not to hear things like this. I don't like having nasty conversations about other people. I think it is dull gossip, spoken by people with dull minds. I am also a nonjudgmental person as a general rule. But when I hear someone's negative opinion of someone else, I cannot help but be affected by their judgment and as much as I do not want to create a bias toward someone, I feel like I'm forced to. Especially in this situation, I did not want to form any negative opinions toward either of the two people I would be spending almost the entire waking and sleeping moments of a solid month with. I didn't let Wallace's backing out of the hike bother me too much. I just hoped this would not be turning into a trend, like Gill had warned.

When we got to the visitor's center, the rain had let up a bit but the clouds kept their intimidating demeanor. The building had some woods to the side of it and as we walked toward the entrance, we saw two moose grazing a few yards away in the trees. *Now this is a good omen.* They looked like they were searching through the low-lying branches for an omnivorous breakfast. I took out my camera (which I always kept in my front pocket) and cautiously snapped some photos of these big, beautiful creatures. They were ignoring the small group of us, which had accumulated to five or six passerbys. I remained cautious at this short distance. Even though we did not receive a warning pamphlet on moose, I was sure that they could do just as much damage as a bison if they felt like it.

We walked into the building and the first thing I noticed was a board on the wall, giving the multi-day forecast. I reluctantly walked over to meet my fate. Today: rain, temps in the mid-forties; Tomorrow: the same, maybe worse; The next day: probably worse. This bad dream was turning into a nightmare. We walked over to a forest ranger for some hopeful clarification. I wasn't sure what I was expecting. Something like: "Don't look at the weather forecast, because it will be sunny and warm today! I recommend the peppermint trail, where you can pick peppermint candy canes off the trees!"

He assured us that the weather was bad, and most of the trails were not even feasible to hike on yet, because there was still too much snow. I had to ask him a few times to convince me that we were really in the month of June and we did not fall into some wintery time warp, taking us back to February.

"Nope, this is June in the Tetons," he said matter-of-factly. "We had gotten a lot of snow this winter, which I have to admit made for an excellent ski season!" He was pouring salt in my wound and didn't even know it. "But it's typical to have this weather this time of year. Spring comes very late for us and there can be a lot of rain as the snow is melting. Our summer often starts at the end of the month. But this weather is unusually bad. I guess that's the trade-off for having such a great winter!"

Great dude. Thanks for letting me know that I missed an amazing ski season, and came just in time for the worst weather of the year. I was going to do to this guy what that bison did to the tourist, except I had arms to bash his face in after the trampling.

"If you guys want to hike, I would recommend a low elevation trail because it will have the least amount of snow cover. But your options are kind of slim."

As we walked back to the car, the rain started again and turned to a torrential downpour. Freezing droplets pelted my face, like an ice cube machine gun. The moose were gone, most likely seeking shelter. *Bad omen.* This was it. The tipping point, the final place to draw the line.

"Gill," I said, "it's time to look into other options."

We got in the car and drove toward Jackson.

"What are we going to do?" asked Gill.

"I don't know but we're getting the hell out of the Tetons. Fuck this place." I never thought I would hear those words come from my mouth. My grandparents would have slapped me.

We decided to find internet and look up the weather forecast. We had a lot of options of places to go from here, all we needed was the right information. It was still very early in the morning—for the West at least—and we drove around town to find that everything was closed. But we weren't going to wait for places to open. We had to figure out our plan fast, and get the hell out. There was no more time to waste in this wasteland.

We pulled up to a café, which I noticed had a "free wi-fi" sign. There were lights on but the door was locked with not a soul in sight. I knocked but there was no answer. This was futile. We got back into the car and sat there thinking as the windows fogged up around us.

I decided to use up a lifeline: call a friend. *Of all my friends, who will be doing nothing right now, sitting in front of a computer, and happy to help? Maybe Niko?* I dialed his number and put on the speakerphone. Gill and I held our breath as we stared at the phone, listening to the ringtone.

"Hello?"

"Yo Niko, what's up?"

"Oh hey, not too much man, just sitting looking at truck parts on my computer."

Fucking perfect. "Oh really? Well could you do us a big favor?"

"Yeah sure. How's the trip? Where are you guys?"

"Jackson, Wyoming."

"Oh, no way! That must be real nice!"

"Actually it fucking sucks. That's why I called. Could you look up some weather forecasts for us?"

"Yeah, no problem."

We told him to look up locations that were feasible options from Jackson. Northwest Montana (Glacier National Park): rain. Next. Eastern British Columbia (Jasper National Park): rain, cold. Next.

"Umm," I tried to think but I was running out of options. "Try Olympic National Park, Washington—"

"Hold on guys," Niko cut me off. "I'm looking at a map of North America, and there seems to be a giant rain cloud, which spans from Vancouver to Montreal, and covers the entire northern section of the US."

Gill and I looked at each other. "Oh my God." It all made perfect sense! We had entered this giant storm cloud in Michigan and had experienced the same weather all the way here. This weather wasn't coincidentally following us, it had enveloped us.

Then more bad news from Niko. "I'm looking at an extended forecast. It will stay like this for two more weeks before anything lets up."

You've got to be kidding me. We're stuck in a three-week rainstorm situated on every point of our planned route.

Gill shook his head. "That's not good."

"I know," I said, and we sat in silence for a moment, staring at the foggy windows.

A thought suddenly occurred to me. "Niko, check Lake Tahoe."

"Okay, hold on..." We waited, staring at the phone. It seemed like hours.

"...Oh," said a curious voice on the other line.

"What?"

"Interesting."

"What is it!?" I yelled.

"I pulled up the seven day forecast for Lake Tahoe," he said.

"Yeah?"

"Are you ready?"

"Of course I'm ready, you ass! Spit it out!"

Niko continued. "Forecast for Lake Tahoe: sun, sun, sun, sun, sixty degrees, seventy, seventy, seventy, seventy."

"And what about Yosemite?" I asked.

"Let me check... Same."

I turned to Gill, eyes wide with a fiery determination.

Gill shook his head. "No."

"Yes," I said, "we're going to Cali."

Gill looked in shock. "No we're not! That's impossible!"

"Yes, it's very possible. We're going to California!"

Gill knew it was inevitable but he couldn't accept it yet. "But that would be taking a complete one-hundred-and-eighty-degree turn from our plan!"

"I know!" I yelled. "Isn't it great?!"

Niko was laughing on the other line.

My lifeline worked! "Niko! I love you! You changed our lives!"

"Thank you, Niko!" said Gill with some apprehension still in his voice, but I knew he was on board.

"No problem guys, good luck!"

I started the car, cranked the heat to defog the windows and we hauled it back to the campsite to break the news to Wallace and pack up. There was no time to waste. We had to get out of this shitcloud and get to sunny California. It felt like my soul had been invigorated.

"Are we really going to California?" asked Gill.

I nodded, "I couldn't be more sure of anything in my life!"

This event was a perfect example of the single greatest aspect of a road trip: spontaneity. Like I said—and it bears repeating—no matter how long or how much a road trip is planned for, you must be ready at any moment to throw every plan out the window and start from scratch.

It is a concept that must be accepted as well as embraced. There were no restrictions. Our car was a vessel, which we had the freedom to use anywhere on this great playground, known as the North American Continent.

We weren't sure how Wallace was going to take it. I didn't want to be skeptical, but I couldn't help it after my talk with Gill earlier. Wallace was still asleep in the tent when we arrived.

I stuck my head in. "Wallace!"

"Mmmmmmrrrrr."

"Wallace! We're going to California!"

"Mmmrr-what?"

"I said we're getting the fuck out of here and we're going to California, where the sun shines and the women flow like delicious wine!"

Wallace opened his eyes and blinked a couple times. "Oh. Okay."

And that was it. We packed up the tent and car and were flying out of Jackson by ten a.m. As excited as I was to leave, a part of me was disappointed that I was going to miss the Tetons. So much for following in my grandparents' footsteps, but they wouldn't have wanted me to see it like this anyway. *Oh Tetons, your bountiful breasts may have eluded me this time. But I'll be back. Oh yes. One day, I will be back.*

Gill recounted our monumental phone call to Wallace as I looked at the map of our playground, to plan out the best route. We had to first head east over a mountain pass into Idaho. From there we would begin a succession of staircase drives—south, to west, to south, to west—through Nevada and down to mid-eastern Cali.

As we drove, it occurred to me what Casey had mentioned about his trip: "Drive across the country with my brother, pick up my parents, and head to Yosemite National Park."

I called Casey and left him a voicemail. "Hey Casey, it's Evan. We're heading out of Jackson, Wyoming at the moment. We had a change of plans and now we're heading to Lake Tahoe. After that we're going to Yosemite. I don't know where you're at but if you happen to be getting there soon, let me know." I was sure that such a lucky encounter wouldn't work out, but a simple phone call didn't hurt.

The mountain pass from Jackson to Idaho was the snowiest route we took so far, with snow coverage that could have been measured in feet. I was still shocked at the sight. Mother Nature's work in the Rocky Mountains was something I had truly underestimated.

Wallace's car struggled on the pass. He insisted on driving again even though he was "sick" and he nervously cursed, "These goddamn hills are too much. Too much for this car. We're not going to fucking make it back to Massachusetts, I swear." Wallace's moody negativity was stemming from his hangover—I hoped.

Once we declined in elevation, Idaho welcomed us with green pastures and I finally felt warm enough to take off my sweatshirt. We turned onto Interstate 15 south, which would run us down the southeastern edge of Idaho. Then it curved west along the bottom. We would take it till we dropped south again into Nevada to begin our "stairway to Heavenly" route.

We were heading south for an hour when the grand, long awaited moment unveiled itself in front of us: We had reached the edge of the storm. This alone was an amazing sight to see. The dark edge of this mega cloud, which stretched past the horizon both east and west, passed over us and we entered pristine blue skies. It was like walking out of a huge ominous awning, to the clear outside world. The bright blue beauty brought bubbly tears to my bleak, bloated eyes.

Idaho had an interesting landscape. Rolling hills made up our northern horizon and behind those loomed snow-capped peaks. To the south and west were vast fields of emerald green. We guessed the long flowing grass to be potato fields, since everyone knew Idaho loved their potatoes. It was a wonderful sight to gaze out at the pure green grass hills below the pure blue cloudless sky. All I could think about was the popular picture from the Windows 98 desktop (fish out an old computer, they all have it). Besides that, there wasn't much else to Idaho, although we knew that what little scenery it had should be cherished, before we got to the arid deserts of Nevada.

It took us about five hours to scale south, then west, then south again, toward Nevada. By the looks of it, Idaho was predominantly uninhabited. There were no sizable towns to speak of until we turned south off the interstate. Suddenly we were engulfed by strip malls and franchises galore. But what caught us off guard was crossing a bridge over a deep wide gorge that dropped straight down hundreds of feet, like someone had dug a giant trench. We stopped on the other side of the bridge and walked to the edge. It was a majestic, deep canyon which snaked out on either side as far as the eye could see. We couldn't see very far since the land on both sides was completely flat, but that made the drop into the canyon more dramatic. It was the deepest canyon I had ever seen. I later learned that this geographic wonder called, Hell's Canyon, snakes through most of Idaho, bordering half of Oregon and Washington. It is also the deepest canyon on the North American continent—deeper than the Grand Canyon. So it was probably the deepest canyon that *most* people had ever seen.

This was an amazing sight, but we had to continue on our journey—maybe we didn't *have* to, but we wanted to, because California was beckoning to our call. As I walked to the car, I noticed a family of four walking back to their car. There were two angsty looking teenagers sporting a punkish twang, followed by two neatly dressed parents. They looked like some classic American family but their license plate said, "Beautiful British Columbia." This was the first BC plate I had ever seen (and the rumors were right). I forgot we were getting in closer proximity to BC. In fact we were one state away (one big state). I found it interesting to see this Canadian family on their own American road trip, with every element similar to an American family, down to the teen angst. It was a nice indication of people's similarities to one another, regardless of national boundaries. One of the kids noticed me looking at them and I saw him look over the three of us. I knew what he was thinking, "Those lucky bastards. Out on the road on their own, free of their *stupid* parents. God, life sucks! No one understands me!" *Patience young one. Your time will come.*

Shortly after we continued on, we crossed into Nevada and so began our long desert journey. We looked at the map and confirmed our "stairway to Heavenly" route down to Lake Tahoe. Tahoe was another beautiful ski-centric community that I couldn't wait to check out. I thought back on the pictures I had seen of it on Google Images: A big blue lake surrounded by snowy mountains.

"Hey Wallace," I said, "didn't you say you've been to Tahoe before?"

"Yeah, I was there a couple years ago."

"I've been there too," said Gill. "A few times actually."

"Oh really?" I was sorry they wouldn't be able to share my excitement of exploration.

"I don't mean to throw another wrench in the plan," said Gill, "but what if we skipped Tahoe and went straight to Yosemite? Then we can spend more time there instead of rushing around."

"Yeah," said Wallace. "I've never been to Yosemite."

"What do you think, Evan?"

I nodded, "I can smell what you guys are stepping in. You would rather spend more time in a place that you haven't been to."

"Yeah," said Gill, "Tahoe is nice, but I'd like to see something new."

"Okay," I said, "it's settled. Yosemite it is. Agreed?"

"Agreed."

"Meeting adjourned."

I would have loved to see Tahoe, but I could understand where they were coming from. This was an experience of exploration for all of us. Plus, I was all for spending more time in one place. We had planned to do that anyway in Wyoming so Yosemite sounded like more than a fair substitution. Yosemite is farther south than Tahoe, but that didn't make a difference. It would be a two-day journey regardless.

The map through Nevada is what one would call "sparse," making South Dakota look like an overcrowded metropolis. There are long stretches of road, with few towns in between. Some are merely labeled, "Ghost Town." One of the roads we would be driving on is nicknamed "the loneliest road in America," where there is a one-hundred-mile-plus stretch of road with nothing in between. Mental note: *Remember to get gas before driving on said lonely road.*

On our stairway route, we planned on taking a detour over what looked on the map like a dirt road leading to a ghost town. Gill's friend who gave him the time strategy, also recommended this specific ghost town to check out called, Belmont. Seeing as how we were convinced this guy was a master of time, we took this advice for a detour without question. Visiting a Nevada ghost town sounded like a cool thing to check out anyway. But that wouldn't happen until tomorrow. It was getting to be late afternoon and our goal was to get close to Belmont by dark.

We continued along a main highway which curved west for a while. Then we spotted a cool-looking smaller road on the map a few miles ahead of us heading south. We took the exit. The opportunity to take small roads and get off the main highways is an exciting opportunity. There is always the high probability of seeing more. When I was planning the trip, I thought of only taking smaller roads across the country and avoiding the interstates. If you have read Blue Highways by William Least Heat Moon, you know what I'm talking about (if not then read it because it is a great book—but read mine first). However, small roads mean small distances traveled. William Least Heat Moon spent one year traveling around the country on these small roads called, "Blue Highways." We had one month. Strictly small roads were not a feasible option. But that made it more exciting for these opportunities when we could take advantage.

We stopped at a pit stop off the exit to get ready for a stretch of lonely Nevada road. We filled the gas tank, grabbed some munchies, and I snagged a sweet buck knife for five dollars. <Footnote: I still have that knife to this day and it is still sweet. Five dollars well spent.> The pit stop was half a convenience store and half a casino. A wide-open entrance from the store led to a dark room with neon lights emanating from slot machines. Welcome to Nevada.

The sun was low in the sky as we embarked into the desert. The cold chill of the Wyoming mountains was a long gone memory. We were all in shorts, T-shirts, and sandals, as it damn well should have been—it was fucking June goddammit! But alas we were in the desert now and I could already feel the temperature dropping. It was still warm but once the sun set, I was sure I would be grabbing for my sweatshirt and pants. At least this was something to be expected.

The road started out windy and narrow, snaking through rocky hills. There were vibrant colors of blue, orange, and red splayed about the rocks and vegetation. In the distance surrounding us were tall rocky mountains—not the actual Rockies, we were past those. It was all surprisingly beautiful. I expected Nevada to be a long stretch of wasteland, but there was more to the desert landscape than met the eye.

As we cruised along this picturesque, desolate road (speed limit seventy-five mph), I saw this as the perfect opportunity to bust out one of my favorite albums to blast as loud as possible, Daft Punk, Alive 2007. It was a requirement for that album to be played at full volume, so this was our opportunity to find out if Wallace's bulky subwoofer was worth taking on our trip. The power of this music can move you and it definitely moved our car. As the sound of hard electronic bass pulsated through our bodies, I looked over at our chauffeur. Wallace remained pensively fixated on the road. His wide-open bright blue eyes pierced what lay ahead, with both hands gripped tight to the wheel. I looked down at the speedometer slowly rising. Eighty, eighty-five, ninety...

The road had straightened like an arrow far past the horizon. Flat desert spanned out a mile on both sides, leading to towering mountains silhouetted by the setting sun. Ninety-five...

The music got louder, the bass pumping harder. The landscape flew by in a blurry mess, colors meshed together. Ninety-seven...

Red and orange crawled out of the tops of the mountains onto the darkening blue canvas of the sky, then mixed and swirled with the setting sun's radiant gold. Ninety-nine...

As we pushed one hundred mph, a pickup truck flew by us, speeding twenty mph faster. Wallace sported a mischievous grin. "Looks like we got a canary!" Then he dropped his foot on the gas and the blurry landscape became one whole mixture of light. The only solid vision was the road ahead and the truck that creeped closer and closer as we went faster and faster, the music louder and louder. Harder, better, faster, stronger.

Now the sky was blood red. Streaks of purple and orange exploded in spontaneous directions. The more vibrant the sky became, the darker the mountains became. But the darker the mountains became, the more defined their silhouettes became. My hair stuck out straight in the back of my neck. Unbelievable beauty was all around me, attacking all of my senses.

Everything finished at the same time. The album ended, the colors dissipated, the sky went black, we exited desolation, arrived at a town, and Wallace slowed down. My heart stopped palpitating and my surroundings became real again. I had been in some dream state, but didn't realize it until the music/sky/car/road stopped.

I took out the map and saw the town we entered was called, Eureka. It was a one-street town, lined with poorly maintained general stores, small dive bar/casinos, and empty, long-forgotten storefronts. Judging from the map, it was the most populated area for hundreds of miles.

The next challenge was to find a campsite. We stopped into a few promising places but they turned out to be sketchy looking trailer parks. We settled with a rest stop on the side of the road about a half-mile out of town, equally as dark and sketchy as the trailer parks. It seemed to be the lesser of two evils, but we were three able young men. Plus I had a shiny new buck knife.

We set up the tent and stove in a flash and threw on a few hot dogs. As we cooked, a cop pulled up to the rest stop and idled twenty yards away from us. We looked at each other unsure of what to do. He wasn't approaching us yet, so we acted normal and kept cooking. A few minutes later, another cop stopped next to the other. This car said "Sheriff" on the side. They idled there, talking to each other. We were worried, but more perplexed. Questions were raised.

"Are we allowed to camp here?"

"I don't see any signs that say we can't."

"Do we look suspicious?"

"I don't think so, but I don't know what defines suspicious in Eureka, Nevada. Maybe they think we're drug dealers."

Fuck, I knew Wallace shouldn't have brought weed on this trip. They're going to search us, bust us, and we'll be stuck in Eureka, Nevada, where they "Don't take kandlee to boas from Massa-too-shits."... No, they can't search us. They have no probable cause...

Whirlpools of random thoughts swirled in our heads but we kept our cool and quietly went about our business, trying hard not to look over in their direction.

Then one cop moved. It was the sherriff. He pulled around next to us and rolled down his window. An older looking gentleman in uniform stuck his head out, looked at us, then over at the stove. "I like mine medium rare! I'll be back in ten minutes!"

We all looked at each other speechless, and then laughed in secret relief. "Okay! We'll have it ready!"

He smiled and pulled away, along with the other car. So ended our interaction with the Eureka, Nevada law enforcement. This state was growing on us minute by minute.

We scarfed down our menial sustenance, and were off to bed. We had a big day ahead of us. By the time the sun set again, it would be under California skies. Correction: I *hoped* it would be under California skies. I also hoped to be in the Tetons, but instead I was sleeping in a tent in a rest stop in the middle of Nevada. *Dammit I love road tripping.*

DAY 6

I woke up to my alarm which had been set for eight o'clock Eastern Time, *five* o'clock local time because we were now in the Pacific Time Zone. Perfect. The three of us excitedly sat up, which was the opposite of the previous morning. Nobody was hungover, or "sick," or cold. We got up and out quickly and efficiently, ready for the day. No more clouds, or cold rain. The sky was blue and the warm breeze in the cool morning hinted at the hot day to come.

Once the tent was packed, we headed into town in search of a hearty breakfast. The main street was quiet with a couple scattered dusty pickups parked on the side. There wasn't a dramatic difference to the town from night to day besides a mere visible difference of some desolate hills that rose up behind the buildings. If this town wasn't marked "ghost town" on the map, I couldn't imagine what the *actual* ghost towns were like.

Out of the plethora of breakfast options, we managed to decide on a place called, the Owl's Club, which looked like a café and naturally had to have a small casino attached. There was one old man in the casino, slumped over a slot machine. It was five-thirty in the morning. He could have just gotten there, or been there all night, or been there for hundreds of years. His slouched posture and tired, lifeless face showed no hint of passage of time.

The dining area was a quaint, conventional short-order space, with a tired waitress hovering around—she must have been fresh off of playing the slot machines. She did not appear to be phased by our bright, smil-

ing, Massachusetts faces, but that was okay. We enjoyed our simple hearty meals and were so amused by her T-shirt that we each had to buy one. On the front it said "Owls Club, Eureka, NV," with a picture of a little owl. On the back it had an acronym for the word WRANGLERS, which could've only been the masterwork of a genius:
Western
Rangers
Against
No
Good
Leftist
Environmentalist
Radical
Shitheads

Knowing that these three guys from Massachusetts were thoroughly amused by their slogan had melted our waitress's cold, cold heart and she finally cracked a smile. Humor brings people together. I should have told her that we wished we had these shirts in St. Paul at the Obama victory speech...or maybe it was better that I didn't.

After breakfast we felt it was time to tear ourselves away from this bustling metropolis and we headed on our way. We continued onto Route 50, which was hailed the "loneliest road in America." There had to have been nothing, because as I write this, I cannot recall a single landmark or any notable feature. It was complete and utter desert as far as I remember. What I do remember is what happened at the end of this lonely road. It is something I will never forget for as long as I live.

We crossed up and over a scenic mountain pass that descended into the next closest town called, Austin. We needed to stop there to fill up before we plunged into the desert wilderness in search for this elusive ghost town. Austin was another small one-street town like Eureka but had more character since it was set on the side of a mountain. The road curved dramatically downward through the main street and into another vast open desert which could be seen in its entirety from our high-up vantage point. We stopped at a gas station and I filled up while Wallace walked in to ask about the ghost town and fill our water bottles. He came out with a sour look on his face which was noticeable enough for Gill and I to inquire. "What happened?"

"What a bunch of bitches!" sneered Wallace.

"What?"

"There were two crotchety old ladies in there who *refused* to tell me anything. They didn't let me fill the water bottles either. We're going to die in this desert because of those old hags!"

Water bottle refills were desperately needed for our desert journey. How could they refuse giving us water? Maybe Wallace's charm only worked on cigar-smoking stoners. Or maybe this town was happy to be away from any civilization because they hated people. That was *their* loss keeping themselves closed-in from the rest of the world.

We tried the competing gas station down the street and the three of us went in for back up. We didn't want another screw up here or we would be lost and without water. A smiling man in his fifties greeted us as we walked in. He stood behind the counter with a nametag that read Carl.

Carl was happy to let us fill our water bottles. "No problem boys, have as much as you want. The water's okay to drink."

"Thank you! We really appreciate it."

"Where are you boys heading?" Carl asked.

"Yosemite, but we wanted to stop by a ghost town we were told about on the way. It's called Belmont. Have you heard of it?"

"Yeah, I know how to get to Belmont. But,"

"But?"

"But it's okay," Carl said with a lackluster shrug. "Not worth coming all the way out here for. Do you know about the hot springs?"

Our eyes lit up. "What? No."

Carl reached over to the "Austin Tourism Information Center" (a brochure stand) and pulled out a brochure. He explained how to get there. "You go back up over the ridge, then take your first right and then your first left onto the dirt road. And then you take a left after you pass under the power lines. Got it?" Not really but we were sold. The ghost town could wait, we needed to find these hot springs.

We crossed back over the pass from where we came from, and descended back onto the wide open plain. Soon after we veered onto a smaller road. Soon after that we veered onto an even smaller dirt road. Carl was right so far. We traveled straight for a while and I felt myself sinking deeper and deeper into the arid dessert landscape. It made me nervous to be without any sign of life or natural resource. Where was Carl *really* leading us?

We made it past the giant power lines that stretched into the horizon on either side. Our supposed final turn should have been coming up soon. We spotted what maybe looked like a road but we passed it off. We were hoping to see some kind of legitimate road leading to some kind of legitimate area with legitimate hot springs, surrounded by palm trees and beautiful, scantily clad, exotic...MEN. Haha! You thought I was going to say women! –Actually that is what I meant to say. Naked Women. Lots and lots of naked women. But there was nothing. We scanned the area but all there was, was scantily clad, exotic desert. There were no more turns and the road began to veer right toward some impending hills. We decided to turn around and try that tiny road near the power lines.

At second glance the road looked even smaller, which could be classified as no more than a dirt path barely as wide as our car, with massive bumps and potholes. We reluctantly turned onto it. Fortunately this was nothing our Suburu couldn't handle. Inclines were not so good, but Suburus loved bumps and dirt. The road curved up a large mound and as we ascended, some figures came into view. There were a couple cars and a small microbus scattered in various spots around the mound. The road broke off into multiple paths and we took a path that led toward the closest parked car. Next to the car was a small circular pool the size of a hot tub, with steam rising from the surface. Neatly laid stones made up the perimeter and a small wooden platform was built just above. A man sat inside with his eyes closed. He opened one eye for a second and looked in our direction, then shut it again like a lazy lizard who couldn't be bothered. We drove further up to the next pool where the microbus was parked. A nude older dude was stepping out of the pool, and grabbed a towel from the wooden platform. We continued on in hopes of finding a vacant pool.

We drove to the top of the mound. No pool, but we got an aerial view of the desert valley in its entirety. It stretched out for miles in every direction with snow-capped mountains lining the horizon. We also had a bird's eye layout of all the pools. It was amazing how none of this was visible from the road. With no natural obstructions, you would think these could be seen from anywhere around this valley. The desert held more secrets than you would expect.

There were only a few pools and they all looked occupied, but we noticed that the Nude Dude was putting on clothes. We drove back. The Dude formerly known as Nude was getting into the bus when we arrived.

"Excuse me sir, are you leaving?" Gill asked in his polite tone.

He turned and smiled. "Yeah, it's all yours."

"How's the water?" I asked.

He stepped out of his bus and walked over to our car. "Well that's the tricky thing. You see that small upper pool?"

We looked over and noticed there was another pool slightly above the one he had been in, and a pipe with a valve ran out of it and into the lower pool. "Yeah."

"You have to let a little bit of the spring water into the pool to get it perfect. Just turn the valve. I tell ya, every time I come here, it seems like someone messed with the damn valve and I got to go and adjust the temperature again. Don't people understand..."

He rambled on for a bit and we weren't sure if he was talking to us, or himself. But eventually he left and there it was, this beautifully inviting hot spring just for us.

We walked up to the wooden platform. The water was calm, and looked like a royal mirror that a medieval king would use to gaze upon himself. Stones made up the entire inside, glowing from the warmth. We stood there for a minute unsure of who would make the first plunge. Just like in the Badlands, out fearless leader Gill took the reins, and in a most unexpected way. "Okay, fuck it." He tore his clothes off, all the way to his bare white ass. After Wallace and I had a shockingly amused laugh at this bold move, we looked at each other, shrugged, and followed suit. There we were, three young men, naked as the day we were shot out the womb, standing proudly on a hill in the middle of nowhere, Nevada. It was a sight to behold—thank God nobody was there to.

We stuck our feet in to find it hot, but bearable. Then it seemed we were back to where we started, looking at each other unsure, except now we were ass naked. I decided to take the leap of faith. The water was hot and soothing. It was a good thing Nude Dude was there before us to tamper with the temperature, because it was perfect. Wallace and Gill got in and we all relaxed like we have never relaxed before. A collective "aaaahhhhh" went around the pool. Stone seats were conveniently built, so we were able to comfortably sit, submerged up to our chests. It was the most perfectly unexpected situation we found ourselves in.

This was one of those places that man searched for his whole life to find: your own private paradise. We found one in the Badlands but this was even better. Places as amazing as these were not supposed to be like this. They were always crowded and built up as a tourist site with convenience stores, gift shops, and steep fees to boot. We not only had the magnificent pool to ourselves, but there wasn't a soul in sight, neither in our close proximity nor anywhere out across the vast desert, which we could see splayed below us for our viewing pleasure. I imagined what this same view would be like on a clear night, galaxies upon galaxies stretched across the sky.

Aside from the amazing beauty and soothing water, it occurred to us that this was our first opportunity to bathe since Michigan. It wasn't perfect and we didn't use any hygienic products, but simply soaking in there seemed to sufficiently cleanse our bodies (and souls).

After our long solid soak, we stepped out rejuvenated as if we were reborn (the nakedness helped with that). We dried, put on fresh clothing and headed on our way. I promised myself I would come back here. Who knew when, but a place like this must not be forgotten.

I pulled out the brochure that Carl gave me and it had some other notable spots marked on this same road. Apparently up ahead in the hills we had approached earlier, there were cave paintings. And after that was some sort of "punch bowl." Sounded good.

The road curved to the right and when we were fully into the hills, the landscape changed to small spiny trees and big thorny bushes. A rocky cliff stuck up to the left. The road remained dirt and bumps while the Suburu remained at ease. I think I was finally warming up to our little car which I started out having little faith in.

We spotted a sizable gash up in the cliffs which fit the description in the brochure so we pulled over. There was a short trail to hike up which was fun to climb because of how steep and rocky it was. Gill leaped ahead, bouncing around the rocks like an excited bonobo. I tried to keep up but couldn't contend with his energetic antics.

Wallace slowly climbed, huffing and puffing. "How long is this stupid trail?"

"Not much farther! It's right up here!" yelled Gill. "Oh my God!"

Wallace and I made it up to a flat dirt landing where Gill stood. In front of us was a cave. It was wide but not too deep, sinking in barely fifty feet with a twenty-foot high ceiling. Faded designs covered the walls. These Native Americans picked a great spot. It was comfortable, fully sheltered, with a flat floor for fires and sleeping. Not to mention a phenomenal view. Rolling hills surrounded the foreground with a wide desert backdrop that sunk into the horizon. Potential dinner could be easy targets to spot, creeping through the small trees and bushes below. Just needed a few friends to carry the carcass back up the rocks—which had to be a non-issue for a physically fit native—and cook a nice meal while watching the sunset. Then take some peyote and draw on the walls. Sounded like a perfect Indian evening.

These old paintings were in amazingly good condition, only a bit faded. But they were tough to see because a great steel fence blocked the entire entrance from top to bottom. There was a big ugly sign hanging that said no trespassing, "By Ordinance of the State of Nevada Preservation Council." I guessed it was better this way. A place like this could not be open to the general savage public, armed with spray paint and greasy, inconsiderate fingers. But a certain member of our party had the strong desire to see it up close.

"Gill, what are you doing?"

He had a look in his eye that shouted determined mischief. He inspected the fence and fixated his gaze on a narrow gap between the side of the cave and the fence. "I can get through that."

"Are you crazy? That gap is inches apart!"

"I know," he said with professional confidence, and he grabbed the fence.

I underestimated his skinny physique. Wallace and I watched in wonder as Gill shimmied up the wall like a clever chimp and slowly slid his body parts through the gap. He made it through without a scratch and received a respectful golf clap from his audience as he pranced around the cave. He was probably committing a felony. Good for him.

Wallace and I watched him walk around inspecting the paintings. "Here," I said, and I passed my camera through the gate.

As he browsed around taking pictures, his mood visibly changed. His prancing, celebratory gestures slowed and his face grew serious. I sensed some fear. "Gill?" No answer. His head and eyes slowly swiveled around like he was in a trance. "Gill, what's up?"

"This is...crazy." He walked calmly to the gate and slipped back over. "I got such a strange feeling in there."

"What do you mean?" I asked.

"I don't know, it was a crazy feeling. I can't explain it."

We all looked back into the cave. The sun bounced off the walls, illuminating the paintings in different shades and shadows. I looked at the pictures he took. They weren't figures of anything tangible, mostly different symbols and shapes. They sat there idly but their mysterious history was palpable. Gill had felt it.

We drove on in silence, each of us deep in our own thoughts about the paintings. The brochure had a brief description about them, saying it was a religious gathering spot for a certain tribe. These symbols were not tangible to our eyes, but clearly meant something to some group of people. It was insignificant to us, just like the Christian cross must have been insignificant to these people when they saw it. These paintings could have been there long before the Western World came over and took charge. This is a perfect example of evidence of a different religion, which is just as legitimate as all the others. It proves how inferior and unrelated every religion is to any other. A religion like Christianity merely gained more legitimacy with power. And it is bullshit for a particular religion to say that theirs is the only true religion in the universe. Christianity was as irrelevant as dust in North America, before Christopher Columbus touched its shores. It was refreshing to know religious symbols like this existed, to help denounce intolerance. My apologies for my stringent, unrelenting religious views.

The next site in our brochure was a noteworthy mound called, Mary's Punch Bowl (it appeared Christianity *did* eventually make it to these parts). We kept our eyes peeled for some noteworthy mound but not much stuck out between the spiny trees. Eventually we made it out of the hills and back to flat desert. The road came to a T, and with no direction known, we threw a shot in the dark and took a right. We drove on, only the sun watching from above, knowing if we were going the right way or not (along with any other unseen eyes).

After a few miles we spotted a large mound protruding from the ground. The top was bleached white. It stuck out of the flat earth like a big fat pimple ready to pop. We had to veer off our dirt road again to another smaller one and stopped at a detachable wooden gate that guarded the mound. It was eerily easy to open, just a metal wire to unclasp. We were falling straight into someone's trap. *Carl! I knew it was you!* I got out and opened the gate to let the car pass through. The mound was steep but looked somehow drivable and we had gained so much confidence in our little Suburu that we decided to chance it and we continued up and around like peeling an orange. It was a hell of a smart idea to chance something like this in the middle of nowhere. I imagined our car broken down on the top of this mound, no tow truck service in sight, let alone cell service to call for one, let alone any soul passing by to send for one. We were on a dirt road, off of a dirt road, off of a dirt road, off of the loneliest fucking road in America. Who knew how often people traveled through these parts. Days? Weeks? But that was mere common sense talking and who listened to that crap? The drive of exploration was what pushed us forward.

When we reached the top, Wallace stopped short. "Whoa, shit!" Had we driven any farther, the car would have dropped nose first into a one-hundred-foot pit, straight into a pool of bubbling water. Steam rose, so hot that we could feel its heat this high above. We cautiously got out and surveyed. This mound turned out to be what looked like a miniature volcano, with the top portion cut off and a hollow interior. The water at the bottom had a blindingly bright amber tinge. Who knew how far down it went. Only the ones who had the misfortune of falling in and lay in their graves at the bottom, knew. I imagined that the same Native American tribe used this mound to tie people up and execute them by pushing them in, like pirates of the desert. My apologies for my violent, twisted imagination.

Mary's Punch Bowl was the last site in our brochure. I looked at my watch and saw that it wasn't even eleven o'clock! We were having an amazing time catching some rare, unbelievable sites, and it was barely time for lunch. This meant we could still check out the ghost town and make it to Cali before dark. I looked at the road map. I could only guess where we were. I could see Austin and I could see small roads that branched off. After all, this was not a local map, it was a map of the entire state. These roads were probably too insignificant for a state map. Then again this was Nevada. Tiny dirt roads probably held more significance than what someone would have thought, coming from an overpopulated, overdeveloped place like the Northeast.

We traveled no more than ten minutes from the Punch Bowl before we ran into yet another site worthy of stopping for. Off the side of the road was what looked like the site of a dried-up lake, that had left a flat, multi-colored, mile-long piece of land. There was nothing growing, only changing shades of color in the ground from pink, to yellow, to purple in the middle of desert grey. We parked and semi-cautiously walked onto it. The ground was crusty, but solid. This time Wallace had a fit of possessed determination and he broke out in a sprint (Wallace never sprints) out toward the middle for a few hundred yards, then immediately turned around as if he ran into something terrifying and sprinted back.

He returned panting. "I don't know why I did that. It seemed fun, but when I got too far out, I got scared being there alone and it was fucking weird with all the colors. I thought something was going to pop out of the ground and eat me."

I wouldn't have been surprised if weird stuff went on in this area. This was the middle of nowhere, Nevada. Just like the paintings and the Punch Bowl, we could only guess what this actually was, with such little information to go by. There were no tourist centers or plaques with descriptions to tell us what was what and why. Area 51 was in Nevada, nuclear bomb testing was in Nevada, who knew what the hell we were standing on.

We walked back to the car and found a middle-aged couple who had parked their giant SUV close to us. This was the first sign of life since the hot springs. The man was a boisterous-looking fellow, pouting out his barrel chest and sporting numerous rings on his fingers, which could have passed him as a mob boss. The small woman hung onto him for dear life as she laughed and made inebriated swaying motions.

"Hey boys! How's the water!" asked the Mob Boss.

We laughed. "A little dry!"

"You could say that! Fuckin' wasteland isn't it!"

That's a bit harsh. "Yeah, not much going on but it's beautiful," was our diplomatic reply.

The man looked around as if he were trying to figure out what beauty we were referring to. "I guess so. The real beauty is on the inside. Right baby?" She giggled and rubbed his belly. "Where are you boys heading?"

"We're trying to find a ghost town called, Belmont."

"Belmont? Hmm. Don't know if I've heard of that one. But there are tons of ghost towns. Keep driving and you'll run into one. Hell, every town is a ghost town around here. But if you run into my mine, tell the boys Big Jim said hi and get the fuck back to work!" Him and his lady let out a bellow of a laugh.

"You run a mine out here?" Gill asked.

He nodded casually, "Yeah I got a few." He pointed, "Just on the other side of those hills. Me and the old lady came up from Reno to check on everything, make sure those dumb amigos aren't sitting around drinking tequila and are actually working on my clock. The boss has to roll in every so often to keep them on their toes, know what I mean?"

We nodded. Funny running into a mining tycoon in a place like this. I guess we weren't as far out in the middle of nowhere as it seemed.

"How are you boys doing on water?" Big Jim asked.

"We got a few water bottles," answered Wallace.

He walked to the back of his SUV. "Well you can never have too much out here. Take these." He pulled out two big gallon jugs of water and handed them to us.

"Wow! Thank you! That's so gracious!"

"No problem boys. Good luck finding that ghost town. Just do me one favor," Big Jim said with a sly grin.

"What's that?"

"Invest in mining. You'll help me out, and I guarantee one day you'll be able to afford as many jugs of water as your hearts desire."

We drove away confused. It felt like we were accepting "dirty water," from the classic movie bad guy who had all the money from stripping away the world's natural resources. I didn't care how much money this guy had. I couldn't imagine ever living a lifestyle of making tons of money by stripping away natural resources anywhere, let alone revolving my life around the middle of the desert. Hot springs, cave paintings, ghost towns, and mining tycoons. What other secrets would this great state reveal?

We drove through more nothingness before we came upon some broken down rubble. A sizable smoke stack still stood on its own. We guessed that we had made it to Belmont but there were no signs to make it official. We got out and walked around. There wasn't much besides rubble and a smoke stack, and we continued on completely underwhelmed. This was an anticlimactic finish to our eventful morning. But it was better this way. Had we gone straight here, I would be writing volumes about how amazing it was to see a giant smoke stack surrounded by rubble.

Sure enough, a mile down the road we ended up making it to Belmont, with an official sign and everything. In fact it was a functioning town with some occupied houses and stores. But alas it was too little too late and we drove straight through. We were starving and sick of stopping and there was no way this town could have topped all the things we had already seen and done.

The closest legitimate town was a few miles away called, Manhattan. The mining tycoon had told us to go there for lunch and find some guy whose name none of us remembered, whom he knew would give us free drinks if we mentioned his name, which none of us remembered.

Manhattan was no bigger than the ghost town. We found what looked like the one bar and stopped. It was a small dive bar with three people inside. Two old men sat opposite from the bar, each at their own slot machine. Neither paid any attention to us as we walked in.

Then there was the bartender, an older man with a friendly face who met us with a welcoming gaze. "Are you guys with the group?" he asked.

We looked at each other as if one of us somehow knew what he was talking about. "Uh, what group?"

"The riders."

"Riders?"

"Yeah, the motorcycle group that's supposed to arrive now for lunch. You guys are right on time but I guess you're not them."

"No, we aren't with the motorcycle group but we were looking to get some lunch."

The Bartender nodded with a smile. "Oh, well you boys should help yourselves. We made a lot of food for these guys and we'd hate it to go to waste." He pointed past the bar to another room around the corner.

We walked into a pristine, untouched spread of salad, pulled pork, baked beans, and bread, all in immense serving bowls. It appeared we had found the desert oasis. Jaws dropped, we turned back at the Bartender with an "Are you sure?!?!" look.

"Go ahead!" he said. "Dig in!"

We each grabbed as much as we could fit on our plates and brought it back to the bar where we bought a round of beers and merrily dined and chatted with the Bartender.

"You boys came all the way from Massachusetts?" he asked sounding impressed.

We gave a proud nod. "Yeah and I don't have to tell you that our East Coast Manhattan is a little different than yours!"

The Bartender nodded. "You got that right. That's how we like it out here. I'm from LA originally." He shook his head and gave a sour look. "Too many people crammed into too little space. So I said to myself, I'd choose the life of a hermit any day of the week over living another second in a place like this. So I found myself in Manhattan and I wouldn't live anywhere else in the world. Unless maybe a Greek island all to myself, but until that day comes, I'm happy right here."

I thought that maybe this was the guy who the mining tycoon was talking about. "We ran into a man earlier who said he owned some mines around here. Do you know him?"

The Bartender's face turned grim. One of the men at the slot machines perked up. "Hell with him!" I forgot those guys were still sitting behind us.

"Yeah," said the Bartender. "We don't got many nice words to say about him. Those mines seem to be taking up more space every day. One of these days I'll wake up and they'll be mining my backyard."

The other slot machine spoke up. "They'll have to get past my shotgun if they want to mine in *my* backyard!"

"Hell with him!" repeated Slot Machine One.

I was glad we were fortunate enough to see the two sides of the coin in one day, and all of it had fallen into our laps. *Everything* had fallen into our laps.

After we filled up our gullets with good food, nice conversation, and cold beer, we asked about the damage. The Bartender looked at our beers. "Well those beers are about two-fifty each, so we'll just make it an even seven."

"Seven? That's it? What about the food?"

"No no, that's already paid for. We just don't want it to go to waste."

A delicious meal and three beers for a grand total of seven bucks—or roughly two dollars and thirty-three cents per person. We tipped him well and left with our wallets as full as our stomachs.

We couldn't contain ourselves as we walked to the car. "You scc?" I told my compadres. "Shit just happens!" I don't know how it happened, but we traveled to it, and *it* met us there. So far this whole day had been a prime example of my theory, and the day was only half over!

All of the action, combined with a big meal and a beer put me into a peaceful nap. We were mere hours from the California border so it was a good opportunity to get some rest before I focused my energy on getting to Yosemite. I suppressed my urge to keep my eyes open and watch the newness go by. I was content with what I saw in Nevada. This state had far exceeded my expectations.

I woke up to my phone ringing. I opened my eyes and looked around before answering. We were still driving through desert, but some taller, more majestic mountains loomed in the distance. Cali was close. I picked up my phone and it was the one person I hoped it would be. "Casey! Tell me something good!"

"Hey man! I'm currently in Reno, Nevada. My brother and I just picked up my mom and dad and we're on our way down to Yosemite. I got your message. Bummer to hear about Wyoming. The weather in the middle of this country was total shit, wasn't it?"

It was comforting to know we weren't the only ones suffering from it. "Tell me about it! I thought it would never end! Thankfully we got some weather info and I think we made the right choice."

"You definitely did. Where are you guys?" he asked.

"We're somewhere in Nevada." I picked up the playground map. "And if I'm reading this map correctly, we are just about as far from Yosemite as you guys are, except we're coming from the east instead of the north!" *What an interesting coincidence. Shit was happening...*

"Well then I guess I'll see you in Yosemite!" Casey laughed.

I laughed too. "I hope so! Where are you guys heading to?"

"We aren't exactly sure. We were thinking about staying outside of the park tonight, maybe around a place called, Mono Lake. Tomorrow night we have a campsite reserved inside the park. Then the following day we'll be heading into the back country for a week."

"That sounds awesome. Why don't you just find a campsite in the park tonight?" I asked.

Casey laughed mockingly like I had just asked the most ridiculous question. "Have *you* tried to find a campsite in the park?"

"Umm, no. We figured we would get one when we got there."

"Good luck, my friend. Do you know when my dad booked our campsite? February. And there weren't many sites left even at that point. Right Dad?"

I heard the upbeat voice of an older man in the background. "You betcha!"

"Are you serious?" I said. *Booking that far in advance for a measly campsite?? What is this place? Do the campsites come with bidets and dancing bears?*

"Believe it," said Casey. "Welcome to California."

"Okay," I said, "so that sounds like a lost cause. Where is this Mono Lake? Maybe we can meet you there." *Mono Lake. Sounds sickly.*

"It's not far outside of the eastern entrance to the park. You should be able to find it on a map. Unfortunately we still don't know where we're going to camp. I guess we'll have to be in touch."

"Sounds like a plan. See you guys tonight? Maybe?"

"Hope so! Safe travels!"

I hung up and updated Wallace and Gill. "What the hell?" said Wallace. "This place was booked up in February?"

"Apparently so," I said. "I've never heard of that happening. I've always been able to drive into any campground and find a spot."

"Doesn't surprise me," said Gill. Then he turned to me. "You're excited to make it to California, right Evan?"

"Obviously."

"Well you're not the only one."

I nodded. "I'm picking up what you're putting down, Gill, and I'm still excited," I said defiantly. "All we have to do is worry about tonight. Tomorrow Casey said he had a campsite reserved in the park. Let's cross our fingers that we can set up on their site."

"Cross your fingers that you'll be able to find him in the first place," continued Gill. "I heard Yosemite is the most crowded park in the country."

"One thing at a time guys," I said. "Let's see what Mono Lake is like. Worst comes to worst, we'll just park our car on the side of the road, hike into the park, and pitch a tent in the woods. We're going to be in a national park. How hard can it be?"

Everyone nodded, agreeing that that was a fair assumption.

"By the way," I said, "how far are we from California?"

"Just a few miles at this point," said Wallace.

I gasped. This was an exciting moment for me. California was a place I had wanted to go for my whole life and we were minutes away from the border. It was an amazing feeling to think back on how long I had wanted to do something like this, and how many times I had heard about it, and in a very short amount of time, this myth would be turning into a reality. One of the strangest things about physically being somewhere for the first time, is the feeling of familiarity, like you've been there many times before. As a result of all the exposure to a place on the media, in pictures, in books, internet, magazines, and in tv shows and films (this especially applies to California), it feels like you've been there hundreds of times. I feel the same way about far reaches of the world that I have never come close to.

I was far more excited than Wallace and Gill. They had both made it to Cali numerous times, and took amusement watching me sit there anxiously poised with my camera in my hand, ready to grab a picture of the welcome sign. I hoped that other states I had been to for the first time on this trip didn't take offense: Michigan, UP, Wisconsin, Minnesota, South Dakota, Wyoming, Idaho, Nevada, thanks for the memories. But come on, this was California!

I chatted excitedly with the guys, "...and isn't it crazy? 'Cause like, I haven't been to Cali before but I *feel* like I have, you know? Because of all the media and..."

Wallace was driving fast as usual and all of a sudden the "Welcome to California" sign popped up out of nowhere. "...it's like you've already been—Shit! There it is!" It was as small as any other road sign. I was expecting some great, ostentatious banner saying, "The Golden State of California Welcomes You, Evan!" or something appropriately comparable. But the sign came and went before I could get a picture. I thought of telling Wallace to turn around but it wasn't worth it. I sulkily held up my map that said California on it and took a picture with the desert in the background. Such is life. However, I grew solace in the thought that one day I will look back at that measly picture of my California map with the desert in back, and know what it meant, realizing it will have been exactly the same as if I took a picture of the actual sign.

The desert lasted a little longer before we began our ascent into the Sierra Nevada mountain region. We cruised up a windy road and the landscape changed to a forest of burgundy red cedar trees. They were enormous and I thought at first we were looking at the infamous redwoods, but Gill assured me that, "You will know when you finally see a redwood."

After a few miles we left the forest and entered another depressing forest of burnt trees. Talk about buzzkill. This state had the worst problem of any, in regards to this. I shed a tear and we moved on.

We came around a bend and below us in a valley was a large lake. More burnt trees surrounded it, making it look like a barren wasteland. Welcome to Mono Lake. It looked as sickly as its name. I would have withstood mono rather than taken a vacation around here. I tried to call Casey to deter his plans but he didn't answer. A few minutes later I received a text. It read, "Meet me tomorrow evening at the Grove of Giant Sequoias." *What??* I tried to call him again but it went straight to his voicemail. At that point I knew there was no chance of us meeting up. Once we got into the park, cell phone service would become obsolete and I would have to rely on this vague text to find him in a nondescript place at a nondescript time. It sucked to think we both traveled across the country, to be in a fifty-mile radius of each other, and were never going to meet up. *So it goes. We must move on.*

Bushwhacking in the park became our camping choice for the night, but this meant we needed to hurry. The sun was descending and darkness was not far off.

Once we passed Mono Lake, the real mountains began. The road curved more and the incline steepened. Giant snowy ridges rose from the road with flower patches of yellow, green, and purple sprouting out of the cliffs. We were ascending Tioga Pass, which would lead us to the eastern entrance of Yosemite National Park.

We stopped at a turnout in the road which looked out over a deep canyon that dropped down to God-knows where. We stepped out and absorbed everything. The air was crisp and I could feel my breath catching quicker from the altitude. There was an amazing aromatic smell that seemed to come and go with the light breeze. I looked around at the different flowers and bushes, then picked a few and sniffed. The culprit ended up being a lush green plant that looked similar to sage. It smelled like amazing perfume that was concocted in the Fertile Crescent by ancient nomads who obtained a recipe that was passed down from the gods. I have never come across such a pleasantly potent plant in my life. The smell complemented the gorgeous vista that surrounded us.

The canyon fell directly down from the edge of the road and shot back up immediately a hundred yards away, giving me the feeling that if I reached out I could touch the other side. This narrow canyon snaked through the mountains taking sharp curves on both ends to unforeseeable territory. We would have to keep driving to find out more. This majestic scenery made the flat deserts of Nevada long forgotten, despite the fact that we were there no more than a couple hours prior. I had never witnessed landscape make such a drastic change in such a short period of time and distance.

We couldn't stand around for too long, unless we wanted to bushwack in the dark. We kept ascending, up and up, twisting around hairpin turns, following the groove of the canyon. The Suburu had been through a lot today, but she was a champ and muscled on. "Not much farther. You're doing great," said Wallace soothingly as he pet the dashboard. "God, why can't this fucking incline end?" *Easy Wallace, forget about the car and appreciate your surroundings.*

Soon prevalence of snow was around us once again. But the temperature remained steady from the remaining heat of the near-setting sun. We made it to the park gate as the sun disappeared over the mountains, casting shadow around us. It was still light and the sky remained brilliantly blue, but we would not see the sun again until morning. I grabbed my sweatshirt.

Once inside the park we turned into a wilderness guide shack. We marched in with our fresh smiling, East Coast, naïve faces and walked up to the counter where two rangers stood, a guy and a girl, both young and attractive.

"Hi!" I said. "We were looking to get some stuff to help us hike in and camp today. Do you recommend any trails, or a bear-uh-canister or something?"

They looked at each other like I would imagine a couple Parisians would, in response to an idiot English tourist asking them how to get to the Eiffel Tower. The guy turned to us with a twisted, ugly smirk on his face and said, "You're not hiking out tonight."

We were taken aback at his curtness. The girl stood quietly but was clearly amused. The guy grabbed his fingers one by one while he rudely spat out his points. "It's too late in the day, you would need to hike at least four miles in to camp, and–" this one crawled under our skin and made our hair stand up "—you're unprepared."

Our three mouths flew open, but none of us could make a sound, we were in such shock.

"Here's what I suggest you do," he continued. "Go get a campsite outside of the park—because you're sure as *heck* not going to find one inside. Organize your stuff," then he had the gall to try to scam us, "and take one of these maps to help you out." He pulled out a map and put it on the counter. "This is the best map around, I highly recommend it."

"Um, okay thanks." I went to grab the map, but he pulled it away before I could touch it.

"That'll be ten dollars." A sly smile drew across his disgustingly clean-shaven face.

"What??" I pulled my hand away. "No thanks."

"It's super worth it, bro."

Don't call me bro. I'll bro my fist straight into you fucking bro face. You think you're impressing your little lady by demeaning us then assuming we're stupid enough to buy your overpriced map?! We turned around and walked out.

As right as he may have been, his blatant douchebaggery made us feel inclined to ignore everything he said and head straight into the woods, map or no map, solely to spite him. How the fuck would he know how prepared or unprepared we were? But we had to face the facts. There was no choice but to find a campground outside the park. We had spotted a small one before we reached the gate, so we backtracked in hopes for an empty site. We got there and by the grace of God, there were a couple free spaces left. This easy solution lifted our spirits again. We weren't going to let Prettyboy Ranger Dick ruin our epic day.

Once we secured our spot, we decided to head back down the pass to the nearest store and stock up on food for a feast. We were sick of little canned meals and hot dogs on the stove. Our campsite had a fire pit with a grill fastened on top, which was about to get utilized. Hell yes Yosemite, it was grillin' time!

When we reached the bottom of the pass, I checked my phone, which squeezed out a couple reception bars, so I called Casey. It went straight to his voicemail again, so I decided to leave my own vague message for the hell of it. "Hey it's Evan, we ended up getting a campsite in a campground right outside the park. Um, I'm not sure what entrance we're near, I think we went up some road called, Kiona? Tiona? Something like that. Anyway, that's where we'll be tonight. Later."

There was a small general store by the entrance to the pass. We picked up corn, squash, sausages, buns, and a bottle of whiskey, and were heading back up onto the pass in five minutes' time.

The campground was small, consisting of one short loop. There was no official front office. In fact there was no park staff around, period—just a little dropbox at the entrance for site fees. This place was probably used for our exact purpose: temporary overflow sites for "unprepared" people. Fine by me. It was beautiful, overlooking a small lake, surrounded by mountains. What was discouraging was the abundance of snow. Even the lake was still frozen. Seeing that made me realize how cold it had gotten since the sun went down and I went to grab all my layers. But like I have said: no rain, no bugs, equals no problem. At least it didn't bother me...or Gill.

"Fuck!" said Wallace. "I don't know about staying here guys. It's too fucking cold! If this keeps up, I'll tell you straight out, I'm not going to fucking do it."

Shut up Wallace, I don't want to hear your bitching... easy Evan, easy. I pretended to ignore it. "I'm going to go collect some wood. Gill, do you want to chop up that squash?"

Wood wasn't hard to come by and we started the fire with ease. By the time we threw on the corn and sausages, the sound of them sizzling was music to our ears. The warmth of the fire was also welcomed with open arms. Hopefully cooking over a fire like this was a sign of many more to come. As I stared into the dancing flames, I had a small daydream of camping out in the Canadian Rockies in Beautiful British Columbia. I imagined a scene just like this, a crystal clear lake mirroring the towering mountains in the background. Then my mind wandered to Olympic National Park in Washington, walking out of a rain forest onto a pristine, sandy beach. Then I was taking a leisurely walk through a forest of redwoods in Northern California, admiring their size and beauty. All of this and more was yet to come.

What a day it had been. And with all of the unexpected things to happen, I thought about the rest of the trip and what would *actually* end up happening, as opposed to what I envisioned and planned.

I was throwing chopped squash onto the grill when a car pulled up in front of our site. It was a familiar-looking, small, black sedan. I saw someone on the passenger side. He looked like Casey's brother, James—*holy shit it* is *James!* And there was Casey smiling in the driver's seat. I threw up my arms and screamed for the whole campground to hear. "Heeeeeey!!" I couldn't believe they found us. Of all the campsites, in all the national parks, in all the world, and they drive into ours.

Casey pulled the car over to the last remaining vacant site. *What a day, what a day.* Casey walked over followed by James and his parents,

David and Dolly. We traded greetings and introductions. No introductions were needed for me though. I knew Casey's whole family from various encounters over many years. I have stayed at their house multiple times in Andover, Massachusetts and even gone on a couple ski trips with the whole family, like an adopted son.

I slapped Casey on the back. "How the hell did you find us?"

"We started out around Mono Lake, which looked like what camping in hell would be like," began Casey.

I laughed. "Tell me about it!"

"Then I got your encrypted message and we decided to go for it."

"Yeah, well it was better than your text," I shot back.

Casey nodded. "You're probably right."

We shared our roaring fire with them to cook, and our feast turned into a banquet with the scrumptious addition of four cheese macaroni. We all sat around the picnic table, merrily noshing while trading off some general travel experiences. But the main topic was Yosemite.

"What do you all plan to do?" I asked.

"Well," said David, "tomorrow will be our 'taking it easy' day. We'll be driving around the park at a leisurely pace and at some point make it to our campsite down in the southern part of the park."

"Our campground is near the Mariposa Grove of Giant Sequoias," said Casey, "which explains my text...sort of."

I nodded in agreement. "Sort of."

David continued. "Then the next morning we hit the trails and we're out in the backcountry for four nights."

"That sounds awesome."

"Yeah, this place takes some work to prepare for," said David. "I did most of the planning and permitting over the winter."

"Permitting?" Gill asked.

David nodded. "You need to obtain backcountry permits."

"Wow, this place is on lockdown. I guess we couldn't come with you guys then!" I said.

Wallace shot me a look that told me, "Are you crazy?! Five days in the backcountry?!"

"Unfortunately not without a permit," said Dolly.

"I know," I laughed.

"But we can probably squeeze them into our campsite tomorrow night, right?" said Casey.

David gave a casual shrug (and I could immediately see where Casey got it from). "I don't see why not. And you guys can do some small hiking tomorrow if you want. I think your mother and I will be taking it easy though."

"Yeah," said Casey, "we'll figure out something short and sweet. We got a bunch of great maps."

Maps! Thank God! That reaffirmed our rejection of buying the overpriced map from Douchey-Mcdoucheington. This was another fortuitously splendid reason for our meeting, aside from hooking up with a good friend in a cool destination. We had been placed in the hands of a group of exceptionally prepared, expert hikers. We were no longer lost, innocent, naïve wanderers—well, still innocent and naïve, but not lost.

Casey's parents pitched their tent on the other site and went to bed shortly after dinner. Casey and James pitched their tent on our site and we had no intention of going to bed any time soon. We had a pile of wood and a bottle of whiskey to burn through. Casey and James took it upon themselves to venture out with their headlamps and doubled the size of our wood load. We sat around the fire, trading whiskey, joints, and travel stories. Casey and James had some interesting adventures themselves: tornadoes in South Dakota, buffalo stalking in Wyoming—

"Wait," I interrupted, "didn't you get that yellow pamphlet on the dangers of buffalo?"

Casey nodded. "Yeah, it had a funny picture, didn't it? But no, that didn't stop us. Those animals looked way too peculiar not to stalk. We must've followed them for, how long James?"

"Five miles at least," answered James.

It took *us* a while just to get through explaining everything that had happened in the past twenty-four hours. "And all we expected to happen today was drive through the desert, see a ghost town, and camp in the woods!"

"Wow, that's an action-packed day."

We gabbed and gawked around the fire until the flames were practically out and the coals glowed softly like they were peacefully breathing, almost asleep. It was two a.m. East Coast time when we called it a night.

It took a lot of work to run down all the adrenaline built up from the day, but the whiskey, joints, a warm fire, and good people to share it with did the trick. We were out cold like three newborn babies in a blanket (clothed this time).

DAY 7

"And on the seventh day, God said, 'Let them reach California.'
And it was all good baby bay-beh."
Evanicus 4:20

Day seven. Seven days on the road from Massachusetts to California. A week ago today we were setting out on a warm summers night, toward Rochester, New York. Today we woke up nine thousand feet above sea level, next to a frozen lake in the middle of the Sierra Nevadas. I considered this to be a huge success, especially with everything that had happened so unexpectedly—to be so expected from a road trip.

We got everything packed and prepared to follow Casey's family, wherever they chose to lead us. It was nice to be able to put ourselves on auto-pilot for the day and let them call the shots, a relief from seven days of "tough" decision-making.

We headed into the park and drove along a road lined with tall pines. Our destination was a place called, Glacier Point. It was approximately an hour drive to get there, counting random stops to check out vistas and slowing down for sharp, steep curves. At one point we were driving down in the Yosemite Valley, where towering bald rock faces shot up thousands of feet on either side. An occasional waterfall spurted down the rocks and fed into a crystal clean river that would run along the road, then disappear around a curve only to faithfully return later down the road, like a curious dog romping through the woods.

This geography had to be some of the most dramatic mountainous scenery I had ever witnessed—

"Evan's Book of Life World Records" Item #3266: Most dramatic mountain scenery.

At points it looked like a scene straight out of some fantasy book. It was like an artist had intended to portray the most ideal scene of valleys and towering rocks with waterfalls perfectly placed in between. It was no wonder that this place got more human traffic than any other national park. Every roadside vista was packed from end to end with cars, and people, and cameras, all trying to snap that perfect shot to go on their mantelpiece.

We climbed back up from the valley floor, rolled around a large ridge, and made it to the Glacier Point parking lot. The lot was packed—like everywhere else—and it felt like we were trying to find a spot in a busy suburban supermarket lot. These crowds were getting to be overwhelming.

It was a brief walk down a straight, flat, handicap-accessible path to Glacier Point. We walked out in the open and in front of us looked like the entire world. There was an amphitheatre viewing area at the edge of a cliff. I looked over the edge, which was like looking straight down from the top of a nine thousand foot tall skyscraper. The cliff dropped down what seemed like nine thousand feet, into the valley that we were just in. In actuality I was looking down thirty-two hundred feet. That was still a hell of a long way. Even though I've been up this high in elevation before, I had never been able to look straight down such a far and vast distance—

"Evan's Book of Life World Records" Item #3267: Highest point to stand and look straight down—You know it's a good day when you're breaking multiple life records.

The valley sloped up on the other side, showing some spectacular waterfalls, one feeding into the other, dropping for multiple thousand-foot levels, down to the valley. Next to these falls stood one of the most famous sites in Yosemite, the Half Dome. This towering rock (which is literally half of a dome shape) is a prevalent monument that can be seen from many lookout points around the park. There was an extension of the valley that led away from us which began at Half Dome. It was amazing to see exactly what some giant glacier had done thousands to millions of years ago. The glacier's visible path (the valley) managed to cut this dome-like rock straight in half.

This breathtaking view was but a fraction of what this park had to offer and the majority of visitors here will only experience this tiny portion. But to truly experience a park like this, is to hike into the backcountry. It is to walk through the narrow trails through dense forests surrounded by the region's horticultural species. It is to camp on the earth and sleep under clear skies unobstructed by light pollution from manmade objects. It is to listen to the diverse sounds, and smell what is distinctly unique to where you are at that very moment, isolated, alone, and at peace. This is the fundamental difference between a tourist and a traveler. Most of the people at Glacier Point were tourists. They came there on their coach buses or family SUVs, parked in the "Glacier Point Parking Lot, Restrooms are to the Left," and stepped out a few yards to snap some pictures of themselves holding a peace sign and a plastic smile, with Half Dome in the background. Some were clearly city or suburban folk, who dressed like they were going to leave Glacier Point and head straight into "da' club." Glacier Point is an Old Faithful. It is a trap, a big piece of bait for all of these people to come get lured in and stuck to. Meanwhile the travelers go to see the real attractions in the backcountry. Casey's family was a family of travelers. They went out and took time to experience what the area truly had to offer.

I would consider Gill, Wallace, and myself travelers, but I'll call a spade a spade and admit that we were more like tourists for this section of our journey. We planned to get a little bit of hiking in, but nothing that would cover a lot of ground or a need for overnight backpacking. Big endeavors like those were planned for later in the trip.

We relaxed at the amphitheatre area for a bit. Casey brought out his hiking stove, which looked far more like a legitimate compact stove and far less like it could land on Mars. He made some of his signature quesadillas for all of us, which were brilliantly simple and have fed us on many a camping trip.

Casey's Signature Quesadillas

Ingrediants: Flour tortillas, summer sausage, pepperjack cheese, hot sauce with workable cap.

Directions: Cut up some pieces of summer sausage, put them in the hot pan and wipe them around. This will achieve two things at once: It will cook the sausage as well as grease the pan. Fill a tortilla with cut up pepperjack cheese and the cooked sausage. Fold the tortilla in half and stick it on the greased pan (keep some sausage under the quesadilla for outer flavor). When the cheese is melted, take it off, open up the tortilla, sprinkle or douse in some hot sauce, and it's done.

*Those are all cheap, light, non-perishable items that will fit well inside of a pack.

Once we were sufficiently fed, it was time to figure out an appropriate hike for the situation. We wanted a hike close by, which would not take us too far, maybe a two to three hour endeavor. Casey's parents took their car and would meet us at the campsite later on.

As we looked over the map discussing our options, Wallace started limping around and giving us looks of pain as he rubbed his back. "Oh man, my back really hurts." This got me fuming. It was no coincidence that he was again trying to make up an excuse right before setting off on a hike. Bad thoughts raced through my head. I dreaded the thought of bigger hikes in the future and having to hear this same gimpy bullshit from this sad sap. We were all men here and he was not going to get any sympathies from us, especially me. He could either come with us, or sit in the car all afternoon cradling his balls in his hand.

Thankfully once we had figured out a hike and were putting on our hiking boots, Wallace seemed to get the picture of his alternatives and quietly sucked it up.

Our destination was a waterfall about a two-mile hike downwards from Glacier Point. When the five of us entered the trailhead to begin the hike, the number of people around dropped exponentially and after ten minutes it was practically just us. The occasional hikers would pass us going the other way, exchanging the friendly hiker's nod and hello. These people all looked and acted less like club-goers and more like travelers.

It was a solid hike, passing some extraordinary stuff like prehistoric looking pinecones the size of our heads—

"Evan's Book of Life World Records" Item #3268: Largest pinecone.

—and neon green moss hanging from tall red pine trees—

"Evan's Book of Life World Records" Item #3269: Most neon colored moss.

Half Dome was in view for most of the hike and we were given a plethora of different angles as the trail made downward switchbacks. A blue bird (twice the size of a Blue Jay) with a crowned feathered head, followed us for the last leg of the hike to the waterfall. It bounced from tree to tree and made cheerful chirping sounds as if it was excited for us to check out this cool waterfall. "You'll love it!" it was saying. "Follow me!"

We made it to a rushing river and soon realized we had reached the waterfall—we were above it. We walked over to a cluster of rocks a few feet from where the river ended and the water met its fate. We relaxed, hanging our feet over the edge as Casey passed around a bag of victory trail mix. Peanuts, raisins, almonds, and M&Ms: my favorite. The whole scene was therapeutic. The rushing water got propelled over the edge with such force that it had an angled trajectory extending far past the cliff like the water was being shot out of a fire hose. Down below, a cool mist rose from where the gallons of water fell hundreds of feet and crashed onto jagged rocks. The beaming, unobstructed sun hit the mist, which created a multicolored chemical reaction, otherwise known as a rainbow.

The rivers and waterfalls around the park were especially strong this time of year because of the winter snow runoff. It was the "start of spring" in Yosemite too. At this point we were used to this "extended season" crap.

Sufficiantly satiated by this special scenery, we headed back up the trail to Glacier Point, which was all incline. Wallace took up the back, huffing and puffing and swearing under his breath. At one point I thought I heard him whisper, "This is fucking bullshit." But I forced myself to believe that I was hearing things. He never outwardly said anything and the big baby managed to make it to the end. *Good job. Here's your prize: an amazing hike you finished. You better be fucking thankful.*

In the parking lot, a throng stood in the middle of the road, looking up and pointing in the same direction. They were staring up a hill to the top of a tall pine tree where a big brown bear clung to the trunk. I got out my camera and joined the group of tourists. Regardless of how far we were from the bear and how many people were around, I had a sense of nervousness. The bear was the animal I was most afraid of—no cartoon pamphlet needed to remind me. Those enormous hunks of muscle and teeth will outrun, outswim, outclimb, and outfight any human, no matter what belt you've earned in karate. Don't think about shooting them either, that will only make them angrier. We watched it shimmy down the tree and mosey off into the woods, paying no attention to its spectators. Even though I was deathly afraid of these massive creatures, I could not help but ignore my fear and let out an affectionate "Awwww!" with the rest of the crowd. These furry guys had the potential to be cute as hell. I just had to get past the fact that they also had the potential to rip my limbs off.

We headed south to our—I mean Casey's family's campground called, Wawona, which was another half hour south from Glacier Point. It was a similar drive as the last, meandering through tall pines, around ridges and vistas that took your breath and threw it away, over the cliff. Wawona campground was right off the main road and we found our—I mean Calab's family's campsite empty, except for their parent's tent already set up. We found a note attached to a tree telling us that they went to the Mariposa Grove. "They wanted a little time for themselves," said Casey. "Mariposa Grove was where they spent their honeymoon and this is the first time they've been back."

"That's adorable," said Gill.

"Let's go," I said. "We'll just make sure to keep our distance if we run into the two lovebirds."

It was early evening as we entered the Mariposa Grove of Giant Sequoias. This was the place and time where Casey had told us to meet in his text. I was still confident that would *not* have happened.

A very, very, very large tree stood at the entrance to the grove. "Hooooooly shit," I said as I stuck my head out of the car and looked up.

"See what I mean?" said Gill. "They're hard to miss."

"Evan's Book of Life World Records" Item #3270: Largest tree.

We drove down the road to a parking lot loop. In the middle of the loop was another gargantuan hunk of wood, even larger than the first—

"Evan's Book of Life World Records" Item #3271: Largest Tree.

These Giant Sequoias had to be at least fifteen feet in diameter and I could not begin to guess how tall. I was informed that these trees were larger in circumference then redwoods, but were not as tall. "You mean redwoods are even taller than these?" I asked Gill.

"I guess so," Gill shrugged. "What do I look like, Evan? A...uh, tree scientist?"

"They're called Dendrologists," said James.

"Yeah," said Gill, "what he said. What do I look like? I Dermatologist?"

"*Den*drologist," corrected James.

"Whatever, my hypothesis is that these trees are fucking huge."

"Agreed."

We found Casey's parent's car and parked by it. "They must still be out on their romantic walk," commented Casey.

"Well boys," I said clasping my hands together, "I guess it's time we take a romantic journey of our own!"

Right before we embarked on a trail, Wallace finally gave in. "Guys, uh, I think I'm going to go back to the campsite."

We turned around. "Why?" asked Gill (he knew the reason, but he asked anyway).

"Um," Wallace stammered, "I want to take a shower. I can come back later and pick you guys up."

It was apparent that Wallace simply didn't like to hike. I didn't want to accept this as the truth, since I knew this would cause future problems. He knew full well what was planned on this trip. But I forced myself not to be bothered at this point. We would address that issue when it was necessary. "Fine," I said curtly, and turned around toward the trail.

The four of us took a mile-long loop, which was an easy stroll around the grove. The forest wasn't very dense with each pine tree keeping a safe distance from each other and blanketing the exposed floor with pine needles. The Giant Sequois popped up in various spots, often standing alone, with none others in their general vicinity. We asked ourselves what a grove was. No one was sure. There was no dermatologist around to answer these questions. My educated guess was a concentrated area, with an above average number of the same plant species.

After a mile of walking through the grove, we came to a more populated area. Paths wound different ways, some passing through a cut-out section at the base of the sequoias. They were big archways that at least six people could all fit through at the same time. As I walked through the center of the tree, I had the fortunate pleasure of looking at all the shit that people selfishly engraved on the inside bark. For instance, couples pronouncing their marital status with initials in a poorly drawn heart, or self-righteous pricks boldly announcing what year they were there to deface the tree. People around us proudly took pictures of themselves in front of the openings. I took a few pictures of the people taking pictures. A framed picture of a random Pakistani couple is currently hanging on my mantelpiece. I often admire it as I sip my brandy and review the trade journals.

When we got back to the parking lot, Wallace was waiting there talking to Casey's parents. He looked clean and cheerful.

"We had a great walk," said Dolly. "It was the same hike we did on our honeymoon twenty-eight years ago."

"Sweet!" said Wallace with a grin and a chuckle. Correction: Wallace looked clean and cheerfully stoned.

"Happy anniversary guys!" I said as we walked up.

"Thank you!" said David and he put his arm around Dolly. "It's been twenty-eight wonderful years!" Dolly's face was glowing and Casey and James grew huge smiles. *What a great family*.

"Is everyone as starving as me?" announced Casey.

We all nodded aggressively. "Fuck yeah!—I mean, yes." said Wallace with a sheepish glance at the parents. You can take the foul-mouthed boy out of rural Massachusetts, but you cannot take the rural Massachusetts foul mouth out of the boy.

"I don't feel like cooking anything tonight," said Casey. "How about some real food before we get on the trail?"

Everyone nodded in agreement. "I think a Celtics-Lakers game is on tonight," said Gill. All the Massachusetts residents of the group nodded in enthusiastic agreement. All the non-Massachusetts residents in the group could fuck off. It was a good thing we had no non-Massachusetts residents in the group.

We followed Casey's car out of the south gate of the park with our bets on finding a restaurant close by, which would be moderately priced with cable TV, and preferably a bar. It was an unsure bet being in the middle of nowhere in the mountains outside of a national park, but we were also in AMERICA.

We drove down a winding road that was radically different than Tioga Pass, since it was lower in elevation, meaning no snow (Wallace was visibly relieved). Nor was it as dramatic. But there were no complaints cruising through winding corridors of a dense pine forest. *Everything* here was nothing short of beauteous.

Sure enough we spotted a restaurant no more than twenty minutes outside of the gate. It had all of our specifications, especially the bar. It wasn't an ideal sports bar like in Jackson, but it would do just fine. A small TV was mounted at the top corner of the bar. It wasn't playing the basketball game, but when the bartender wasn't around, Gill utilized his freshly acquired Indian-cave-painting-slithering-maneuver and slinked around the bar to change the channel.

After an active day, it felt good to relax with a beer and some unhealthy greasy food. We ordered cheeseburgers and fries with pints of New Belgium, Fat Tire to wash it all down. I immediately nominated Fat Tire as my favorite West Coast beer so far. It was brewed in Colorado (which unfortunately didn't make the cut for this trip...yet...) but I cursed the East Coast for not distributing this delicious brew every time its perfectly balanced amber taste touched my lips.

Our Massachusetts delegation boldly held down our "Boston pride" in this "Lakers territory," even though the restaurant was practically empty, not to mention we were the only people sitting at the bar, which meant we were the only people watching the game—go Celtics!

Afterwards we headed back to the campsite, set up our tent, and it was off to bed. Tomorrow would be a big day of more hiking as well as the eventual split up of our crew for the temporary hiatus in the San Francisco Bay Area. I drifted to sleep, listening to the calm sounds of the chirping, creaking, and burning-wood-crackling of the night. It was painfully easy to get used to this. As hard as it was to wrap my mind around at the moment, I thought about in a day's time listening to the less calm sounds of car horns, sirens, and wandering drunkards in the city streets of San Francisco. *Wow, Yosemite to San Francisco! I can't believe—... No!* I had to stop thinking such exciting thoughts and focus on going to sleep. The longer I was up, the better the chance of hearing Wallace snore in my face.

DAY 8

I woke up to a combination of the sun beaming in through the trees to our hot tent, and the busy sounds of Casey's family outside. I sat up and looked over. "Wallace."

"Rrrr, yeah I'm up."

"Gill."

"Owwwwww!" Gill winced.

"Gill? You okay?"

"Owwww! Not really."

"What's wrong?"

"Uugh, it hurts to breath."

Uh-oh.

Wallace perked up. "Where does it hurt? Like in your chest?"

"Yeah."

Wallace shook his head with confidence. "You may have liquid in your lungs. You're going to need to get medication for it. I've had it before."

Of course you have Wallace. So much for a morning hike. "Do you need to get to an emergency room now?" I asked.

"I don't think so," Gill answered feebly. "We don't need to rush out. Maybe have some breakfast first, and see how I feel." I trusted Gill's self-diagnosis. He was a trooper.

We got up and joined Casey's family at the picnic table for breakfast. We ate cereal with fresh berries, compliments of our hosts, and watched in admiration as they organized everything needed for their backcountry trip. All of the items were laid out either on the picnic table or on the ground in an organized fashion. They were rearranging things in different piles to ultimately fit in each members pack. I looked over all of the items. Each one looked light, compact, and equally as important. I felt like a total idiot looking at all of their gear. We had none of that stuff. I looked over at David who was messing with the settings of a pocket GPS system. *Sooooooo Jealous.*

After breakfast we packed up in a rushed fashion since Gill's chest was feeling worse. When the car was packed and ready, we walked over to say our goodbyes. "Good luck on your hike. I'm sure it will be an incredible experience!"

"Yeah," said Casey, "I can't wait to hike to the top of Half Dome."

"No!" I said shoving my palms in my ears. "Don't tell me anymore!"

"Thank you Dolly and David for sharing your campsite with us. That was very generous," said Gill. Even as he winced in pain he maintained his classic cordiality.

"Our pleasure," said David. "Good luck with the rest of your travels. Don't worry, you'll breath again."

"I hope you're right."

"Speaking of that," I said, "we should get going and bring this poor guy to a clinic."

"There'll be one in the valley," said David. "I know that for sure."

"Okay, thank you all again!" I said.

"Remember, the offer is still on the table," said Casey. "If you find yourselves in Eastern Oregon in a few weeks, you have a place to stay."

I laughed. "I'm not sure if it will happen, but thanks for the invitation."

"You didn't think you would be here now, right?" rebutted Casey.

I nodded. "You're right. I guess we'll see what happens won't we?"

We got in the car and headed back into the Yosemite Valley. It was another bright and clear day with the sky bringing new meaning to the color blue. The clinic was easy to find. Gill got out and hobbled toward the buildings with his hand on his chest.

"Good luck Gill! Don't die!"

Gill nodded. "I'll try."

Wallace and I waited out in the parking lot. Neither of us felt like changing our current environment for an indoor medical facility if we could help it. The clinic was situated in a shady nook of the valley with bald, rocky cliffs that could be seen looming over us past the shady pines. It was a bummer we couldn't get a good hike in today, but this area was so nice and peaceful that I didn't mind lying down in the shaded grass. The sun was hot and the shade balanced out the heat to a temperature almost too perfect. I embraced the fact that this was the first time during our trip that I could relax without rushing to the next thing. Wallace lay down nearby and dozed off.

I was woken from a quick nap by an RV rolling into the parking lot. A family of six stepped out, consisting of a mother, father, and four kids ranging from age three to eleven. Each member was blond and beautiful. The father said something to the kids in some language that I was only able to deduce as European. The kids nodded obediently and the man took his wife into the clinic while his children stayed outside and ran around the parking lot playing with a skateboard and a tennis ball.

Their unknown foreign identity peaked my curiosity and I walked over to them. They shot nervous glances at me but I didn't think they were at the age yet to understand the potential danger of a creepy looking stranger walking over to talk to them while unsupervised. I walked up to the two oldest boys who had to be twins. Their toddler brother sat on the skateboard and the twins took turns rolling him down the small hill of the parking lot. It seemed dangerous but if they hurt themselves, at least they didn't have to go far.

One of the twins looked at me. "Hello," I said with the most friendly, uncreepy smile I could muster.

"Hello," he said.

"Cool skateboard."

"Thanks." His English was clean with a distinct Nordic accent. Norway or Denmark were my guesses.

"Where are you from?" I asked.

"Holland."

Damn, I was close. "Do you like socce—uh, football?"

He shook his head with a smile. "No."

"No?!" *What?! A European that didn't like soccer?! Blasphemy!* I tried to drop some knowledge. "What about Van Nistelrooy? You have to like Van Nistelrooy."

He calmy shook his head, his coiffed blond locks whisping across his face. "No, I like tennis."

They were a wealthy family. He didn't say that outright, but he explained that they were on a yearlong expedition, traveling around the world. "We will spend time here, and then we drive to Florida. Then we get on a yacht and sail around the Caribbean. Then we sail to the Azores."

"Azores? Where's that?"

"Islands off of the coast of Portugal."

What?! Who are these people?! "Wow." I tried to sound impressed but not too impressed. "Then what?"

"We travel to Spain and back to Holland."

"What do you do for school?"

"Our mother teaches us." Clearly she was doing fine. They spoke better English and apparently knew more geography than me.

I had an initial feeling of jealousy. This family was not on a simple vacation. This was their *life*. I wanted traveling to be *my* life. This past week was amazing. Why not keep going? Don't turn around in British Columbia, go to Alaska, then across to Russia! Then down to Korea and Japan and—*Oh god you have to stop Evan, you're getting worked up*. My feeling of jealousy was followed by frustration. These kids weren't going to be able to fully appreciate such an amazing opportunity like *we* would have. Here was a family having their own adventure of discovery. Just like our trip, their travels would stay with them for the rest of their lives. Unfortunately it would not be the same. Traveling as a family is simply not as fun. Ask those angsty teens with the sullen faces at Hell's Canyon. A family cannot go wherever they want unless Dad says so. The local microbrews cannot be tasted, nor the sweet kisses from beautiful women. Music cannot be blasted out of a three-foot subwoofer in the trunk, because Dad's car doesn't have one. And even if he did, you wouldn't want to hear the Eagles "bumping from front to back." But more importantly these kids will not be able to appreciate what they experience as much as people our age can. This may sound like an arrogant presumption but it's true. I know because I've been there. Anybody who has traveled when they were young knows this. My appreciation for traveling matured along with my natural growth.

Here is an example. This was technically my second road trip out west. My first was with my dad and his girlfriend in an RV, driving from New York to Rocky Mountain National Park in Colorado, and back. I was ten (about the age of these twins). It was an amazing trip that I have many lasting, vivid memories from. I remember sitting by a campfire in a Rocky Mountain campground, and watching a herd of wild elk stampede past our site, their passing silhouettes reflecting off the light of the moon. I remember standing on a mountaintop, looking out across vast mountain ranges and deep valleys, while trying to keep myself standing with a fifty-mile-an-hour wind wipping up the valley and pushing my dad and me backward with a force I had never felt from nature before—

"Evan's Book of Life World Records" Item #542: Strongest wind hitting my body.

These, among many other great memories were once in a lifetime experiences that I will always remember.

I also remember being bored out of my mind, driving for hours on end on the highway, and sneaking to the back bedroom of the RV any chance I could. While we drove across the country passing by all of this new and exciting scenery, I watched movie after movie on a little TV. Thinking back on it now, I can't imagine all of the things I had missed. But at ten years old I didn't have the patience, nor appreciation to simply sit up front and watch this new world go by. This kind of appreciation didn't come to me until I was in college.

Certain factors contribute to this "appreciation" metamorphosis in the brain. The three most important are maturity, independence, and quite frankly, pot. A healthy level of maturity is reached at a college age, where a motivation has been developed to open the mind to new things like philosophies, or methods of living, or experiences. And as these new waves of thought hit, they become the most exciting parts of your life. Not only is this new world being introduced, but the old world is seen with different eyes. It is as if you've been blind since birth and someone just opened the curtain to let you see the truth. The second part is independence. You're finally out of someone else's grasps and for the first time the freedom is given to go out and experience everything that you're so motivated to see and learn. There's an overwhelming feeling of excitement by this newness, and that is where pot comes in. It helps to process all of this newness as well as expand it. And with that grows appreciation. All of a sudden, that three-hour drive up north through Vermont to go skiing—that I used to dread doing—is now something that I look forward to. Packed in a car with my friends, passing around a bowl, while watching the freshly fallen snow on covered elm trees pass by, I realize that winter scenery has a calm beauty that has always been there but I never *saw* it. Meanwhile my head is racing, connecting winter scenery with a million other thoughts, while simultaneously grooving to this unbelievable music group that I had never heard before called, A Tribe Called Quest.

Another thought on pot: Yes pot is an important piece to the process of discovery. But it is not essential. It is a drug like any other that should not be relied on. I have never said that I would only be able to enjoy something, e.g.: beautiful scenery, good music, etc, if I was high. Anybody who feels that way, has relied too heavily on the drug. Drugs should be used as a tool, not a crutch. I know too many people that use it the wrong way and it does a lot more bad than good. And that concludes my lecture on drugs in relation to self-discovery. Please read pages twenty-six through fifty-five in your textbooks for next week. Class dismissed.

I shied away from talking to the Dutch kids when I noticed their parents walking back. I didn't want to look like that creepy guy around people's kids. However, the act of noticing the parents and walking away, was probably what made me look more suspicious. The Dad gave me a strange look, before gathering up the inheritors of his estate and piling into the RV.

Gill walked out shortly after. He looked better.

"Diagnosis?" I asked.

"Apparently the layer of goo between my ribs and lungs are thin, so the ribs are poking my lungs a little."

"I was close," said Wallace.

"Treatment?"

"Advil," answered Gill.

"What?? You were in there for like two hours!"

"I know, that's all they gave me."

"Well do you feel better?"

Gill shrugged. "I'll be fine. It wasn't a heart attack or anything, I'm just too skinny."

That warranted a chuckle. "Ain't that the truth."

"Sweet," said Wallace, "let's get a move on to San Francisco. I just talked to my mom and she said that Bay Area rush hour traffic sucks, so we should get there before that happens."

I guess we could do that. It was still early in the day and I didn't feel the need to rush out of here just to avoid rush hour.

We got in the car and headed toward the western entrance of the park. We got a few miles from the clinic when I spotted signs for a waterfall that would be a short walk away. "Hey!" I said. "We should check out that waterfall!"

"No," said Wallace bluntly, "I don't want to get stuck in traffic."

And that was when it finally happened. The seed that Gill had planted in me in Jackson had incubated and I birthed an ugly beast. "So fucking what if we get caught in traffic!" I yelled.

Wallace yelled back. "Because I fucking hate traffic! That's why!"

"Well boo-fucking-hoo Wallace!" I screamed. "We're in a national park. This is a once in a lifetime opportunity. So excuse me if I don't want to simply rush out, just so I can avoid some bullshit traffic!"

Wallace got red in the face and didn't reply for a few seconds. Gill was holding his breath.

"Fine! Whatever!" yelled Wallace and he yanked the wheel and pulled over.

It was an easy couple minute walk down a flat path to get to the waterfall. I marched alone, with Wallace and Gill slowly trailing a few yards behind. I walked up all the way to the base of the waterfall. Wallace didn't follow me, probably in protest. Gill stayed back with him. I didn't care. I would do this all alone if I had to...

The waterfall was a couple hundred feet high and fell all the way to the bottom of the valley. Water spewed out the top like the other waterfalls in the park, surrounding me with ice-cold mist. Yesterday we stood proud on top of one of these forces of nature. Today I stood at the bottom, proud for other reasons.

We got back to the car and all was civil, our little tiff never spoken about again. I knew I had broken my Code of Chillness. I felt bad about it, yet on the other hand I felt justified. I could not sit idly by and accept a situation like that. To be in such a beautiful place and be worrying about something so trivial was unacceptable. I would trade an extra twenty minutes in Yosemite for an hour of city traffic any day. Although it seemed that our planned mid-trip hiatus away from each other was coming at a perfect time.

We left the park heading west and a little bit north, on the way to San Francisco. This would be the first city we would be visiting, aside from our nighttime stroll through Minneapolis. San Francisco would also be the end of our push westward and it was all points north from there, with Yosemite being the southern-most point on our trip. You may be asking yourself why I'm calling this a "great American road trip," when we're not touching the entire southern half of the country. Well to that I would congratulate you on your keen observation. Then I would call you a nozy little fuck and prefer you to stay out of our personal business.

As we descended in elevation, the tall evergreens became sparse. In fact all shades of green dissipated and the state of California convinced me that it lived up to its slogan as the "Golden State." Endless rolling hills of flowing fields of pure gold had surrounded us. If Idaho was a Windows 98 desktop, California was a Honey Bunches of Oats cereal box. We pulled over and I picked some gold from the ground. What I held in my hand was a tall, thin piece of golden straw. It stood erect, and at the top it curved downward where two or three bell shaped objects dangled. I'm no horticulturist, but these were some strange plant specimen. They looked like what I would have imagined hops to be. I had only vaguely seen what hops looked like but I wouldn't have minded if these delightful little objects were part of the ingredients of some delicious beer. So I called them hops. "They're not hops," said Wallace. *Thank you for your input Wallace, I don't care.*

At one point on the drive a sea of windmills inhabited these golden hop fields. They sprouted up from the ground in various spots all over the hills. I have seen windmills before, but maybe five at most in a small cluster. These had to number in the hundreds. Some people think that these creators of natural energy are an ugly eye soar. They must be referring to the (lack of) black clouds of pollution that protrude from them.

After the windmill fields, we came upon a town—or at least a part of a town. It was the part where you go to buy shit at big store chains and eat fast food. This was the first substantial form of civilization since we crossed Hell's Canyon in Idaho. *Oh how dearly we missed you Walmart, and Applebees, and Wendy's! You're all so conveniently together on a strip of road. You pop up on either side, tempting me with the best and latest in cheap shit. You're like a shopping mall, except you're spread out just far enough away that I have to drive to visit each one of you separately. Or I can be brave and walk with the traffic next to the guardrail. But I'd do it for you, Home Depot. And you, Chillies, and Burger King, and Barnes and Noble—Starbucks when I get fatigued from all the cheap deals. We're home guys, we're home!*

After filling up the gas tank, we stopped at an A&W drive thru. A poorly typed sign in the drive thru window read, "Tell us how we're doing? You could win a one thousand dollars!" A Mexican girl handed us our root beer floats and said "tank you!" *Grammatically incorrect signs in English written by immigrants? We're home guys, We're home!*

We laughed at the sign and "graciased" our server. Wallace put the car in gear and as he went to engage, a horrendous sound came from the inner depths of the vehicle, like something was grinding hard. "Fuck!" yelled Wallace. Our high spirits dropped like a thousand pound weight, straight onto our backs. Wallace's face twisted in frustration as he moved the shifter around. "Not a good sound. *Not* a good sound!" He kept repeating this and shaking his head. Once he shifted out of first into second, the grinding ceased. "It's got to be the clutch," he said.

The car continued to run but when we stopped at a light and started up again in first gear, the sound returned. At every light we held our breath in hopes that the sound would stop. It didn't. Every time it grinded we felt chills in our spines. Was this the beginning of the end of the Suburu? Of our trip? By this time on the trip, all worries and doubts about the car that had occurred prior to the trip, were a distant memory—

"I was waiting for this to happen. I knew it."

Correction: A distant memory for Gill and me.

The car had driven fine from Massachusetts to here. One of the backseat windows broke and could not roll down right, but that was a minor issue. This, on the other hand, was getting into serious territory. Certain things were necessary for this trip to continue. Gill needed to breath right, and the clutch needed to work. *If only the Suburu could get fixed with Advil too.*

"I'll be visiting my grandfather in Sacremento," said Wallace. "I'll take it into the shop there. Let's hope she can make it to the Bay first."

Neither Gill nor I said anything. I was starting to understand why Wallace may have been a bit more high strung than the rest of us on this trip. He knew his car wasn't ready to make a cross-country trip. *We're lucky though.* I had to be optimistic. We made it across the country to family. He would drop off Gill and me, and take it to his grandfather. *That's a good thing. Isn't it?*

The rest of the ride to the Bay was tense. Adding insult to injury, we hit some traffic outside San Jose. I might have taken this opportunity to make a snide comment like, "Man, that waterfall was worth it!" But it was better to keep my mouth shut. At this point I prayed for the traffic to break before Wallace did. It lasted no more than ten minutes and I was able to breath again. Gill let out a sigh of relief as well.

The beginning of our planned hiatus was to drop off Gill at his grandmother's house in San Jose. Gill informed us that she lived in a gated community called, the Villages. There are gated communities all over the country, often situated in warm climates and occupied by people who appreciate year round warm weather and closed-in, protected communities. This is where the hustle and bustle of the outside world is of no care. These types of people I'm describing, are people you may have heard of, or even seen before. They are commonly referred to as "old people." These are places where every single male enjoys golf and tennis, and every single female loves to play bridge and gossip. These are places where everyone has a two and a half door garage: two doors for cars and a little door for the golf cart. Places where the security guards are black and latino, and the residents are not. Also don't bother if you're Jewish (just kidding—actually I'm not, that's how it used to be). This was the place where Grandma Gill lived.

The Villages were on the outskirts of the city of San Jose. I won't bother describing San Jose—okay, I'll be brief: suburban sprawl.

We made it to the front gate in the late afternoon. Gill told the black guard who we were here to see and he nodded with a smile and let us through. It was like every other gated community: small streets that you could easily get lost on because they looked the same, similar houses with small, square yards, and every house was one story. Lord knows Grandma and Grandpa can't make it up any stairs these days after the surgery. It's interesting how these people are drawn to such homogenized areas. Maybe because they are the World War II generation and they all raised families in neighborhoods that looked the same. Or maybe when a certain age is reached, the mind goes numb to newness. We were on a trip to be bombarded with newness. These people haven't been bombarded since the war.

When we reached the cul-de-sac that Grandma Gill supposedly lived on, Gill looked around. "I've been here a bunch of times, but I can't remember which house is hers."

"I don't blame you," I said. I was already lost. If I was forced to navigate out of here, I would've required provisions because it could take me days without a map or compass.

"Oh! It's right here," blurted Gill. "I recognize her garden gnome."

We parked in the driveway and stepped out onto her front lawn. I could feel the fabrication of the grass as it stiffly crumpled under my feet. We knocked on the front door which was promptly opened, and a sprightly old lady stood there to greet us. "Hello Jacob! Hello boys!"

Who? Oh, you mean Gill. "Hi!" we collectively said with polite enthusiasm.

"Oh Jacob, it's so good to see you!"

"You too, Grandma!"

She gave Gill—I mean Jacob a big hug.

I extended my hand. "Hi, I'm Evan, I—"

"Hello!" she gave me a big hug. "Welcome to my home!" Wallace—I mean John—got the same treatment. "Make yourselves at home boys.

Feel free to use the bathroom or shower. Do you need to wash some clothes? Are you hungry?" She spat out suggestions like a true grandmother.

"Yes!" we answered to all of the above.

"Okay then," she continued, "the bathroom is down that hall, the washing machine is in the next room, and I hope you brought your appetites, because I got a big plate of lasagna baking and it's almost ready!"

"Thank you!" Grandmas rock!

It was a comfortable evening in the San Jose valley as the sun was making its final push for light and warmth before leaving North America. All bathed and clean clothed, we sat down on Grandma Gill's back patio and dug in to lasagna and salad as she chatted us up about the accomplishments of her children and grandchildren. "...And my son—Jacob's father—has built such a beautiful home in Massachusetts. I absolutely love visiting. I call it 'the Resort!'" I nodded. I knew exactly what she was talking about.

In turn she inquired and listened to our personal stories and life goals. She was a respectable grandma—or person rather. She would listen to you intently and nod, before delving deeper. "Oh yeah? That's a wonderful field to study. There's so much you can do with it. What do you plan on doing?" She was the kind of person who asked good questions that tried to delve below the surface. It was clear that she was genuinely interested in what we had to say.

It is easy to distinguish between someone who expresses genuine interest in you, and someone who doesn't care, and will only ask questions to be polite. For example, when I get back from this trip, one of my mother's disinterested but polite friends will inevitably ask me, "Oh really? How was it?" To which I will simply respond, "Good." Because I know that for them, an answer like that will suffice. A simple question gets a simple answer. The reality is, how can that person possibly expect you to sum up an entire experience you had in one sentence? This is what they are asking you to do because they don't care for you to go into any detail. And God-forbid you say, "It was bad." Then they would be forced to ask, "Oh really? Why is that?" But they dread to keep a conversation like that going because then they would have to express insincere sympathy over your woes.

On the other hand, a genuine person will ask details. And they won't give you that fake smile and dull eyes. They will give a thoughtful grin and nod when you say agreeable things, followed by asking questions specifically pertaining to what you said. Or they'll share stories of their own, from similar situations or places they have been to.

It's surprising how many people you meet, who do not care about others and have no motivation or interest to try to learn. Grandma Gill was not one of those people. A detail of our trip led to a similar story of her own, which led to us commenting on it, which led to a good conversation. This lasted all through dinner and into her living room.

"So Jacob, what good movies have you seen lately?" She asked him this as we all sat on her clean couches, sipping on Anchor Steam: a classic beer made in San Francisco that artfully combines an ale and lager taste. Grandma Gill was the most relaxed. She laid sideways in her armchair, legs draped over the arms.

"Evan and I watched Harold and Maude shortly before we left on the trip," answered Gill.

Her eyes lit up. "Oh yes! One of my favorites!"

Come to think of it, she had the same eccentricities as the character Maude from Harold and Maude. I found it hard to believe that an eccentric lady like this would live in a place like the Villages. I could see her more appropriately placed in a redwood tree house. I had to ask, "How do you like living here?"

She scrunched her face. I knew she could tell what I was getting at. "It's fine," she said with a sigh. "It's safe, people are nice. It can get dull, but it's safe."

I admired her honesty. I could feel the safety and comfort, especially after being out in the wilds of the country for eight days. For a short time we were protected from the evil temptations of mining tycoons and trail map salesmen. But as much as she tried to rationalize living in this place, I hoped that I would never meet this same fate, no matter how safe and comfortable it could be.

Grandma Gill offered all of us to spend the night (that probably came out wrong after the Maude reference). But even though it was getting late, we were too close to San Francisco, and Wallace and I had to reach our respected destinations. We thanked Grandma Gill and each of us gave her a big hug, followed by Gill. That little soldier was on his own now. I was confident he had learned enough in the last week for him to survive, as long as he didn't try to use his Mars Lander stove. "You guys be careful out there," he told us.

"You too buddy, take that Advil and keep breathing."

Grandma Gill struck a worried look. "Breathing? Jacob, what happened??"

"Nothing Grandma, I'm okay. *Thanks* Evan." He glared at me.

Woops, I let the cat out of the bag. "We gotta go! See you in a few days!"

And then there were two. Wallace and I set off north out of that city toward the *real* city, where he would be dropping me off at my cousin Becca's apartment. I gave her a call to let her know we were on our way. It was going to take us a mere hour to get to her apartment, which was like a minute in road trip time.

It's hard for me to explain how excited I was to get to San Francisco. This was the number one city I was most excited to explore in the entire world. The history and culture that San Francisco has created is unparallel to most other places. I spent my time in college reading Jack Kerouac and The Electric Kool Aid Acid Test. I've also extensively read about and listened to the Grateful Dead. Additionally I've been enraptured by documentary films like the Life and Times of Harvey Milk, or it's widely acclaimed successor, the Life and Times of Mrs. Doubtfire. All of this time I had dreamt about what it would be like to physically be in this place. I've carried an opinion of San Francisco for a long time, that if a band like the Grateful Dead and a band like Metallica could exist in the same place, then it must be a cool fucking place.

We drove through the industrially lit highways of Bay Area suburbia as Wallace chuckled at my giddy blabbering. "You see, you got the hippy movement, but what even predates that is the Beatniks, and believe me those guys were fly cats..."

Wallace watched the road and nodded. I was sure he didn't care nearly as much as me but he listened respectfully. His mind was no doubt on the potential fate of his car. But at least we were able to get past any hard feelings from earlier in the day. We may have shortly derailed, but the Code of Chillness brought us back on track.

"You would've liked the Beatniks Wallace," I proclaimed. "They took lots of Benzedrine—they called them Bennies, and talked twice as fast as I'm talking now."

Wallace smiled. "Sweet."

We rambled on until we came around a corner and my mouth stopped working. The San Francisco skyline revealed itself in its glorious entirety. The tall, eclectically shaped buildings had a luminescent glow, turning night into day. It was a skyline that I think could only be rivaled by New York. *I'm here, San Francisco. I made it. I know I don't have flowers in my hair, but I have a lustful heart that has yearned for you.*

Once we entered the city limits, I called Becca back to get directions. She lived in what she referred to as the "heart of the city." "I'm about a block away from Haight Street and Fillmore Street."

I had to fight hard to stay calm. These weren't mere street names. They were icons. Names like Haight Ashbury and the Fillmore West came to mind. These were names that held a strong presence back in my rural Massachusetts life for more years than I could count, and in a matter of hours I would be given the chance to explore their origins.

A few wrong and right turns and we pulled up to a three-story townhouse, painted pink. My cousin Becca walked out of her front door and smiled. This was a familiar face I hadn't seen since back in Massachusetts when she still lived there. She looked the same, a tall mid-twenty-year-old with dark hair and a warm smile. I expected her to have a flowery shirt and bell-bottoms, and her hair grown down to her knees. Not because that was the kind of person Becca was, but c'mon, this was San Francisco!

Becca made the big move out West a couple years back, driving across the country with a college friend. They were the only people they knew, moving to a place they had never been to before with no job prospects. She was an art major freshly graduated with nothing to lose, and she chose the path of the unknown. It was a huge risk and it turned out to be the best decision she ever made. At present time she found a good steady job, a solid group of friends, and a nice pink place to live, in a fantastic location. I would hear news back on the East Coast of how well she was doing and how happy she was, living where she was. I greatly admired this. It takes a lot to break away from your support system and move across the country, especially since we have no other family out

West. I respected her the most for embracing the challenge of the unknown. That's what traveling is all about. Or better yet, that's what living is all about.

We hugged and Wallace introduced himself, but got right back into the car and left. He was anxious to get to his destination, which was across the Bay Bridge in Berkeley, to stay with a college friend. The Suburu disappeared around the corner, which officially spread us out across the Bay Area, making our hiatus official. At this point I had forgotten what it was like to be immobile for an extended period of time, and I got to spend it in a city with endless possibilities at my fingertips.

Becca and I went inside and had a short chat, bringing each other up to speed on our current life happenings and excitement. She gave me some recommendations of what to do the following day since she would be at work. She handed me a map of the city.

"This is all I need," I said. "I'll figure out the rest."

We planned to meet for lunch in the downtown district near where she worked. That was a good enough plan for me: wander around the city and navigate my way to a specific location for lunch. I couldn't wait. I had seen some of America's greatest landscapes and mountains. Tomorrow I would find out what one of America's greatest cities had to offer America's greatest citizen.

DAY 9

I woke up late for a change. At this point there was no need for a morning rush—not to mention it was easier and more comfortable to sleep indoors and alone, as opposed to outdoors in a hot tent, next to two grown men. I was also naturally assimilating to the West Coast time change. The East Coast Time Continuum had served its purpose and could be left alone, so I changed my wristwatch back three hours to the local time.

I got up from the little side room, where Becca had set up a comfortable mattress on the ground for me, and I browsed through the empty house (Becca and her two roommates were already at work, doing real life things). I walked down a long hallway with bedroom entrances on one side and stairs on the other, leading down a few flights to the front door. Ahead the hallway opened up to a sizable living room, then a small kitchen at the end. Light poured in from big arching windows in the kitchen and spilled into the living room.

The most peculiar part of the apartment was the bathroom set up. There were two doors on either side of the hallway across from each other. One door led to a tiny room with nothing but a toilet. The other door led to a slightly larger room with a sink and shower next to it. This "split bathroom" model was apparently a popular design in San Francisco apartments. Maybe it was there to show who does and does not wash their hands after they use the toilet, so the unsanitary ones can get weeded out and ostracized. Thankfully they don't burn the unsanitary anymore. Who can forget the horrid San Francisco toilet trials of the late 1800's, which culminated in the great San Francisco fire in 1906. The city has really "cleaned up" since then.

I got dressed and headed out the door, equipped with a backpack and the trusty map of the city that Becca gave me. Inside my backpack I had nothing but a small water bottle, a pen, and the ugly purple yin yang notebook my Mom got me, figuring I might find a good spot to do some writing. Naturally there was the possibility of accumulating some items on the day's journey as well.

I had two hours before I had to meet Becca downtown for lunch, which meant two solid hours of wandering aimlessly. I was excited to have some time alone to explore. Traveling with others had its perks, but traveling alone had its advantages as well. I was the captain of my own vessel. I could make my own decisions and didn't have to answer to, or wait on anybody else. I could do things with speed and efficiency and didn't have to worry about anyone's well being except myself. I love to wander alone. I could be very inconspicuous, slipping through crowds unnoticed like a snake, in grass filled with snakes. And with the trusty map, I could navigate myself to areas that may have seemed less traveled by others. I was constantly in search of places where people rarely went. My goal was to find the beauty in the world that passed unnoticed by the untrained tourist.

Finding this untarnished beauty was something I did most of the time, except my current goal was the contrary. I was on a mission to get to the corner of Haight Street and Ashbury Street. This was the famous corner where a few doors down, the Grateful Dead lived and wrote their famed music in the mid-1960's and helped start a musical and cultural revolution. They would perform on the street to a packed crowd that spanned for numerous blocks. This was a crowd of people that no one had seen the likes of before. They had long, dirty hair, smoked grass, and tripped on LSD. Haight Ashbury was the center of the world for these "hippie freaks" and any hippie from that point on has known about this place.

This was no secret where I was headed. I knew that once I got there, there would be a bunch of people with their cameras in one hand and a tourist map in the other. I hated looking like a tourist. I hated standing out from the crowd because I was walking around aimlessly with a dumb look on my face. That was being a conspicuous tourist. A traveler was inconspicuous. But alas, sometimes you have to give in. I felt justified since I was visiting a place that held a deep importance to me.

When I stepped out of the apartment onto the street, the warm, unobstructed sun hit my face and I breathed in the fresh air. A light wind from the Pacific helped balance out the sun's warmth. I could tell that this wind was coming from the Pacific because for the first time on our trip, I smelled a faint salty hint in the air that was unmistakably the ocean. I thought back on our crossroads in Jackson and reminded myself of how good a decision it was for us to change our course. And from what I heard of normal weather in San Francisco, this sunny, cloudless sky was a blessing on its own.

I turned around and looked at Becca's house. It was pinker than it appeared last night. Becca lived up on the third floor. A Chihuahua stuck its tiny head out of the second floor window and casually stared at me with its batty ears perked up. I looked down the street at the other houses. They had a fairly similar "town house" style, but each one was distinctly different. Becca's house was the only pink one. The house next to it was the only blue one with white shudders. Next to that was the only red and yellow checkered house, and so on.

I walked around the corner and up a block to Haight Street. As soon as I got there, I caught a strong whiff of peculiarly pungent pot, which blessed me with a bright smile. I was in NorCal (Northern California) and it was already living up to its cannabis-centric reputation.

I looked at the map and made my first navigational decision to take a left. Then I stuck the map in my pack to make the tourist to traveler transformation. I figured out from certain signs that the area I was walking in was called, Lower Haight. Each storefront was either a cool-looking bar, ethnic restaurant, or neat little shop. Murals took up entire sides of buildings, which sent a clear message that the area welcomed the inspiring talent of street artists. A few blocks down on my left, there was the start of a park that sloped up dramatically. A road curled up the steep incline around the far end and distinctly beautiful houses lined the side facing the park. I stood for a while and admired these houses. Some had bay windows that curled around the corners. Others had beautiful balconies with accessible rooftops. Again I admired how different each house was from one another.

I continued farther down Haight for a few blocks and could soon tell that Ashbury wasn't far, because the pervasive prevalence of funkiness grew palpable as I perambulated onward. Thrift stores and garment shops took over every block.

When I reached Ashbury, my anticipated idea of a mob scene of tourists was merely a couple small groups of people standing by and taking pictures. The store on the corner was an overpriced Grateful Dead merch store—*surprise, surprise*. And yes, I bought something: an overpriced "Steal Your Face" sticker. I looked down Ashbury Street, trying to remember which number house the band had lived in. I couldn't remember and I was too proud to ask, so I moved on.

I decided to head back in the direction of the previous park I had passed. It was toward the direction of downtown, which I should have been heading to by now, since I would be meeting Becca in an hour. I veered off Haight Street on the way back to switch up the scenery. I walked up a block on Ashbury Street, then over, and was faced with a steep incline once I got close to the park. To my left the road curved down to Haight Street where I had passed before. I admired the same houses, seeing them from above. The view from the top made them look even cooler and more diverse, showing their beautiful roofs decked out with grills, lounge furniture, and well-trimmed shrubbery. *I could live there. And there. And there. And—damn I could live anywhere.* This place was the polar opposite of the Villages.

I headed into the park which was called, Buena Vista Park. I ascended a steep hill on a nicely kept path lined with a diverse species of plants. Then I came to a flattened area where the shrubs were cleared. I sat down on a bench and saw how this park got its name: I was given an unobstructed panoramic view of the San Francisco skyline. It looked far away, yet oh-so-close. Off to the left, I caught my first glimpse of the great big red structure, known as the Golden Gate Bridge, and behind that were the golden hills of California. Si senőr, a muy buena vista indeed! I loved seeing city skylines. A good skyline can be as beautiful to look at as a mountain range. I sat for a while as people walked by smiling, each walking a smiling dog. *Beautiful houses with beautiful scenery, occupied by beautiful people with beautiful dogs. This is turning out to be my kind of place.*

I walked to the other end of the park and down another steep hill. Once I left the park and was back on the street, I had to walk down an even steeper hill. It was lined with elegantly put together townhouses, each with a palm tree in front. This street was so goddamn steep. Parts of the sidewalk had steps going down to help out the passing "hiker." The cars were parked at right angles from the sidewalk and they looked like they could be tipped over by a simple poke of a finger and get tumbled down the hill.

At the bottom of the hill there was a stop for the MUNI, which is San Francisco's metro system. It's not as extensive as say, the New York Subway. Most of it is above ground, except for the main line which travels below, ending in the downtown district. This was what I needed to catch to go meet Becca.

As I waited for the MUNI, I looked down a street perpendicular to the one I was on. The street went down another hill and toward the bottom I could see a vertical sign sticking out which read, "Castro." Nearby an enormous rainbow flag waved proudly over all of the buildings. This was San Francisco's famous gay district. Back in the 1970's, a man named Harvey Milk was the first openly gay man to be elected for public office. He lived in the Castro and worked on the San Francisco Board of Supervisors, giving the gay community a powerful and admirable voice. He spent close to a year in office, before he was shot and killed by another member of the board. There are two well-done films about his life. One is the aforementioned documentary called, the Life and Times of Harvey Milk. Also Gus Van Sant made a bio-pic on him called, Milk. Okay, I'm done plugging for shit that I won't get credit for.

I took the MUNI to the downtown district. The San Francisco skyline is deceiving, because its downtown isn't as exceptionally large as it appears from afar. But the buildings were architectural wonders. The Transamerica building is the cities most distinguishable landmark in the skyline, built up like a slim pyramid.

I met up with Becca close by. She had on her business attire, *still* no bell-bottoms or flowers—*Unbelievable.* It was strange for me to see this art major, who decided to move to the center of hippie-dom, and now she was a business woman working at a stock investment firm. I had to admit to her how I felt. "Becca, I must say, I never expected that you'd get a job like this."

Becca chuckled. "I know what you mean. I never expected this either, but the job is much better than I thought it would be."

This got me thinking. Maybe today's San Francisco wasn't the same hippie-centric place it was in 1969. That's weird, how could a city possibly change after only *forty* years?? Apparently in that time, it became one of the financial (as well as tech) capitals of the world.

She took me up a building to an outdoor patio where we had lunch overlooking the downtown area.

"Where did you go this morning?" she asked.

"I walked to Haight Ashbury, then up to Buena Vista Park, and took the MUNI here."

She nodded. "Haight's a great street, isn't it?"

"I think I've been impressed by every single street so far," I said.

She laughed. "That doesn't surprise me."

We scooped chowder from sourdough bowls and munched on a farmer's market salad.

"You seem pretty settled in now," I said.

Becca nodded. "I am. It was tough at first, since I didn't have a job, nor any connections, but it's been about a year and a half and I'm settled and loving it." She looked around in admiration. "This place is hard to get sick of."

"Aesthetically I can see that that is totally true," I said. "I feel like everywhere I turn is something unique and beautiful."

Becca shook her head in agreement. "And it's more than that. There are tons of fun free or cheap events going on all the time."

The words "free" and "cheap" always perk me up like a dog hears the word "walk." "Oh yeah? Like what?"

"A lot of festivals: music, art, food, beer, wine, film—the list goes on."

I enjoyed all of those things immensely.

"And there's so much beautiful stuff to see outside of the city," she continued.

"True," I said, "it didn't take long to get here from Yosemite."

"Yeah, and there's a lot of great stuff even closer, like right over the Golden Gate Bridge. Ocean and mountains, we got it all."

"Wow. This place looks amazing and sounds even better!" I clapped my hands together. "You sold me!"

She laughed. "It's an easy sell!"

Our conversation was cut off by a call from Wallace.

I picked up. "Yo-yo! Mr. John Wallace! How goes it my friend?"

"Hey, I'm in Sacramento."

"Oh cool, how's that going?"

"I'm at the auto mechanic."

I paused. In all the excitement of the city, I had blocked the whole incident at the A&W drive thru out of my mind. "...Oh. Hold on," I excused myself from the table and walked over to the edge of the patio. I looked over the edge, down twenty stories to the street. I prepared to throw myself off, depending on what I would be told. "What's up?" I reluctantly asked.

"It's the clutch," he replied.

I grabbed the edge with my hand and dug my nails into the concrete. "Shit man, it was because of me, wasn't it. I'm such a novice at standard, I shouldn't have tried to drive, I—"

"No man, don't worry, this isn't at all your fault. You did well."

Aww, what I nice guy. I took a breath. At least I was personally off the hook, but my hands dug deeper into the concrete.

"But," he said and took a deep breath.

But? But what? But what?

He let out his breath. "They said it could take five hundred dollars to fix."

My mind worked quickly. *Okay, that's not bad. Five hundred is like one-seventy each, I can do that.* Not the best news, but I was able to breath a little.

Wallace continued. "But even if it's fixed, they said it might not make the rest of the trip."

I stopped breathing.

"We probably need to head straight home," he said.

My insides froze and I leaned over the edge. "Really?"

"Well, that's all speculation. They're still running diagnostics and will give me a full verdict eventually."

"Have you talked to Gill?" I asked.

"Not yet. He left for Santa Cruz with his cousin and I couldn't get a hold of him. I'll get back to you when they give me more info."

"Okay."

"Bye."

The phone went silent. I was dumbstruck. I decided not to immediately kill myself until I got more info. I walked back to the table with a visibly horrible look on my face.

"Everything alright?" asked Becca. I sat down and explained the news. She replied with a reassuring smile. "Well you're welcome to stay as long as you want." Her unconditional support got me thinking more positively and less about suicide. The idea of being stuck in San Francisco was not the worst situation. There were far worse places on this great earth to be stuck in. But the idea of ending the trip gave me a stabbing pain. I suppressed this horrible feeling since I knew that there was no official verdict yet. Everything was still in a stage of speculation. *Remember that, Evan. It's all speculation. You don't take a potential tragedy for a tragedy until it's reality, right?... Right.* I took out my city map and asked Becca where to explore next.

Becca pointed me in the direction of the famous bookstore, City Lights, which was not a far walk from where we were. I thanked her and told her I would see her later that night at the apartment. We parted ways, her's pointing toward the corporate world, mine pointing toward the wide-open one.

I was out of the downtown district after only walking a few blocks, and I entered Chinatown. It was easy to tell, as the percentage of English on signs narrowed, along with people's eyes. A few blocks more and I saw the noticeably traditional typeset letters that read, City Lights. This was another important "tourist" spot for me.

City Lights was to the Beatnik culture, what Haight Ashbury was to the Hippie culture. The Beatniks preceded the Hippies in the 1950's and were more of a group of select, talented individuals than an entire subculture, but they still made a huge dent in American history. They were comprised of mostly writers, poets, and intellectuals. The big writers were Jack Kerouac and William S. Burroughs. Kerouac wrote many acclaimed books but his seminal one was called, On the Road, which was the original document that sparked the American road trip tradition. His book embraces the spontaneity and rush of excitement of living, which is at the core of a road trip experience.

The most famous Beat poet was Alan Ginsburg who often hung out at this bookstore with people like Kerouac, and shining individuals like, Neal Cassidy. I will not get into explaining Neal Cassidy, because that could fill up this whole book. All I will say is that he was one of the most unique individuals ever to walk the earth. Alan Ginsburg's most famous piece of poetry is called, Howl, and it was in City Lights that he debuted it. Kerouac explains in his book, Dharma Bums, that he was in the packed audience passing out jugs of wine to everyone, while Ginsburg belted out his multi-page statement of passion. Imagine a 1970's punk rock show, and substitute poetry for music. That is probably hard to imagine, but if anyone could do it right, it was the Beatniks.

They were an incredibly influential group of people whom I discovered in college and immediately admired. They embraced life so passionately in a time where acting in such a manner was thought to be preposterous. These were people who drank all night while listening to bee bop, and yelled to each other about philosophy or any other outlandish concept that their hyper-intellectual stimuli could come up with. Then once morning broke, they got in a car and drove. Not to anywhere in particular, but simply driving for the sake of discovery, and exploration, and fuck it, because the jobs they had in that town were meaningless anyway.

My college friends and I tried to embrace this style of living, blasting our own music and trying to keep up with each other's ambitious, heady ideas. We wouldn't spontaneously get in a car at daybreak and drive off, but like I said, we took our share of road trips.

The road trips I took were amazing experiences, but they didn't satisfy my hunger to drive across the country. During these trips I couldn't stop myself from rambling on about getting my chance to fulfill my destiny of getting in a car and doing the journey from east to west. It was the Beatniks who instilled in me that riding across the country *was* my destiny.

The Suburu came back into my head. *If it can't keep going, what would I do? Give up? After all, I achieved my goal and made it across the country. But now I'm here, and all I can think about is moving forward. There's so much more to see! What would the Beatniks have done?*

City Lights was smaller on the inside. It had that pleasant, rickety bohemian feel that many old bookstores have, with little rooms branching off in different directions, left, right, up, and down. I ventured upstairs where there was an entire "Beat Literature" section. I picked out a "City Lights Edition" of Howl, which completed my tourist persona by purchasing the most common item sold in that particular tourist spot. I guess it was better then buying the, "I went to City Lights, San Francisco and all I got was this lousy T-shirt" T-shirt.

I did some more browsing and walked away with Howl and a few postcards. I stuffed them in my backpack before anyone saw me and I was back to my inconspicuous-passerby disguise before you could say, "Holy shit! Is that Jerry Garcia?"

The next neighborhood I walked through was called, North Beach. I figured out that this was the Italian section, as people's eyes got wider, along with the sausages hanging in the windows. It was interesting that the Chinese and Italians neighbored each other, since this is the same case in New York City. I bought a gelato and once again stuffed it into my bag before anyone could see—just kidding! I was making sure you were still paying attention.

I was heading in the direction of the coast at the north end of the city with a specific goal in mind. This was one of the main goals of the trip, as well as an important goal of my life, which was to reach the West Coast of America, and touch the Pacific Ocean. I was glad I was able to reach it for the first time by driving across the country to get to it, instead of taking a cop-out-bitchy, six-hour flight. I had traveled through rain and snow, across dessert and prairie—I even made it across the UP for God's sake! Just a few more blocks and I would be there. I was even able to ride in one of the open-air trolley cars for the last few victory blocks.

The trolley rolled over a steep hill, and out in front of me was the San Francisco Bay. I felt incredibly accomplished looking out at the Pacific. It had taken me twenty-one years to be at that very place in that very moment. Not that I necessarily worked my whole life to get to this point, but the idea would often enter my mind and I would patiently say, "That will be nice, I can't wait to do it."

I walked along and found a spot to sit with a little beach in front of me. Out in the bay there were numerous sailboats and kite-surfers gliding along the water. Each sail was a unique color and design, just like the houses in the city. To the left stood the great big red bridge that defined San Francisco. It towered over the bay, connecting the city to the hills of northern Cali. To the right a little island stood in the middle of the bay and a facility took up most of the land area. This was Alcatraz—"the Rock." It is the famous former maximum-security prison, now turned museum. I couldn't believe a maximum-security prison was put in the middle of the San Francisco Bay. I was sure it made people nervous seeing it there. Who knew when some inmate would have escaped and made it to land to terrorize the city.

I walked out onto the beach with my bare feet and touched the water. A numb-worthy chill was sent up my legs. It was way too cold to swim in, which immediately explained why a maximum-security prison was put in the middle of the San Francisco Bay.

The beach was crowded with people and dogs. It made me so happy to see all of these content canines frolicking freely. In my short time here, I could tell that this was the most dog friendly place I had ever been to. I watched one of the dogs with his owner walk off the beach and past me to a water fountain. The owner bent down and took a drink while the dog watched him, panting and wagging his furry tail like he was waiting for something. Then the owner pushed a button on the side of the fountain and water spilled out of the bottom into a bowl on the ground, which the dog excitedly lapped at. I didn't notice this bowl until now. It was identical to the fountain, but situated on dog level. *The water fountains have connecting doggy fountains??!!* I got this funny feeling in my chest. At first I couldn't figure out what was happening. I felt so emotional, but in a good way. I realized that this strange feeling was love. I was falling in love with San Francisco.

I sat down on a bench and took out Howl. I imagined what it was like for Ginsburg to read it in a packed, sweaty room inside City Lights, a place I could now clearly conceptualize since I had witnessed it with my own body and soul. Reading it compelled me to write a poem of my own. And now I am going to share it with you. So grab your jug of wine and enjoy:

I'm reading Howl overlooking the Golden Gate.
I thought it would be appropriate,
But it's all about New York.
But it was read in City Lights,
At the heart of San Fran,
As Jack helped the crowd inebriate,
Or so I've heard.

The connections between New York and San Fran
Are far and near.
The elaborate architecture, the alpine streets, the Union Square, the Chinatown/Little Italy matrimony, the friendliness, the clean water, the cold water, the breath of fresh air, the character.

I drove from the east to the west,
Three thousand miles.
I just touched the Pacific Ocean.
It's sandy like the east,
Cold like the east,
People are white like the east,
Cars, planes, highway signs like the east.
It's beautiful, like the east.

Did I really go far?
I guess so, people wear hats
But I've seen hats and hats.
I've seen Asians, and delis, and terriers, and homeless, and rich, and T, A, and everything in between.

Would a woman love me here like she would in the east?

I know a dog would love me.
Dogs don't care if we're on the East or West Coast.
I need a dog.
But do I need it more than a location or vocation?

The dog would probably say it needed me.
It would look at me with those expecting eyes filled with undying love and anticipation, saying, "Yes Evan, of course I need you! And I knew all along that you couldn't live without me."

No one ever said a woman was man's best friend.

-San Francisco, 2008

I closed my notebook with a content smile. I was no Alan Ginsburg, but it would do. My smile turned to a disappointed frown when I looked back down at the ugly purple yin yang. Suddenly an idea popped into my head. It was the best idea I had on my whole trip thus far. I took out the Grateful Dead sticker from my bag and popped it on top of the yin yang. It fit perfectly.

The sun was starting its downward decent and the sailors and kite-surfers were heading back to land. I walked off the beach and caught a bus going hopefully in the direction of Becca's house. As the bus pulled up, I noticed that it was connected to a wire grid that hung above the street. I realized that these wires hung over many of the streets, yet I had not noticed them until now. The bus made a light humming sound as it pulled up. *Electric powered buses??!!?* I was falling so much in love with this city that I had to conceal my raging erection as I stepped onto the bus.

I stood toward the back and watched the San Franciscan life go by. The style of houses near the water were different than the inland ones. The coastal ones had more pastel colors and were not the same town-house structure. They were flatter shaped and wider, but every house still maintained its own unique flavor. I had never been to a place where so many houses had so much variation and character. This had to have spoken a lot about the kind of people who lived here. These were people who had to have put thought into how they chose to live their lives, and were not going to settle for monotony. They each had to have a clear voice and individuality, along with being extremely creative. This would not be the case if every house looked the same. Life cannot be gone through, settling for less. And if care is not put into the place where you live, then there is probably not much care about many other important aspects of your life. Life is dull if you don't make it your own. Maybe when I'm Grandma Gill's age I'll think otherwise and settle for something "dull and safe." Until then I wanted to be like San Franciscans, who had a clear understanding for appreciating life.

I managed to get on the right bus. Every once in a while, a speaker verbally informed me about the bus I was on, and gave me some kind of safety message. Then it was repeated in Spanish (naturally). *Then* it was repeated in some kind of Chinese dialect. I perked my ears up. *Now that is interesting.* I had never heard Chinese spoken in a public setting like this in America. It is always English then Spanish. Was there really a big enough Chinese population here for them to consider it a necessity? I reminded myself that this was the West Coast. We were three thousand miles closer to Asia. Put that together with the influx of Chinese immigrants that worked on the railroad and this was all starting to make sense.

I signaled for a stop when I heard, "Ching chang, wing wang, ding dong, 'Haight Street.'" There was a door toward the back of the bus that I was closest to. When the bus stopped, I stood in front of the door, waiting for it to open...nothing happened. I looked over at the bus driver who was staring at me. Then he said something I couldn't understand. *What did he say? "Se-own?"* I looked at him confused, then looked back at the door. I gave it a little push but still nothing happened. People began to turn around and stare. I avoided their gazes but felt their thoughts: *What is he doing? Doesn't he know what to do? Great, another dumb tourist.* My inconspicuous disguise was wearing off and my true tourists colors were coming out.

The driver spoke again, louder and angrier but just as indecipherable. "Sit-down!"

What? Why would I sit down? I clearly need to get off! In a desperate, panic-stricken attempt, I reached out again and gave the doors a harder push. Everyone stared, appalled at my futile attempts.

"STEP DOWN!!"

I took a step down toward the door and it flung open and vomited me onto the street. The door slammed shut and the bus hummed on its way. I did the only thing I could do in that situation without making more of a fool of myself, which was to laugh. I smiled and shook my head at my most clueless tourist blunder of the trip so far. *Live and learn, Evan.* I could not be faulted for ignorance. I could only be faulted for making the same mistake after I've been shown the truth. From this moment forward, I vowed to step down for as long as I lived.

I walked a few blocks down Haight Street toward Becca's. As I neared the corner to turn, I once again caught a strong whiff of marijuana. This was the same general area where I had caught the stench of dankness earlier in the day. I followed my nose for a few doors down, and stopped in front of a storefront with no windows and a barred door. I couldn't see in, but the smell couldn't hide itself. A tough man, who stood like a bouncer would, was parked in front of the door. Wide-eyed, I walked over with an excited grin. The bouncer didn't look like he shared my excitement. Our conversation was brief:

"Is this—"

"Yes."

"Can I—"

"No."

"So how—"

"You have to be a California resident."

"So if I was—"

"You'd need a note from your doctor."

I nodded and walked away. This was my first encounter with a medical marijuana dispensary. I had only heard about them in passing stoner folklore. At the time, California was one of the only states to allow medical marijuana to be sold from a public retailer. But apparently they weren't open to "weed tourism." I couldn't buy a weed momento, and if I tried to take out my camera to get a picture in front with a peace sign, he probably would have peacefully snatched my camera and broke it. Even though it was legal in the state, the feds had the authority to shut these places down at any time.

I walked back to Becca's house and found her home from work. I told her about the rest of my day and we laughed again about the bus incident. "In my defense," I told her, "it was counter intuitive. How would I know to walk toward a closed door?"

Becca laughed and shook her head. "Step down!"

That night we got some burritos and then went to a bar close to her place on Haight Street called, Noc Noc. The peculiar décor made it look like Tim Burton had taken a lot of acid and took up interior design. The chairs by the bar had tall, skinny, oddly shaped backs and were painted different day-glo colors. In fact the entire bar was painted in all sorts of day-glo colors and shapes. A man sat at the bar with a little dog on his lap. There really were dogs everywhere in this city.

It was a relaxed night, sipping on a couple brews from Speakeasy Ales and Lagers (another San Francisco original), and talking more about living in San Francisco. After a day I was already completely in love and wanted to move here. "I have a question Becca," I began. "I had found it interesting that there was Chinese spoken on the bus, along with English and Spanish."

"Makes sense," she casually replied.

"I'd never heard Chinese spoken like that. There must be a big Chinese population here."

Becca nodded. "This is true. Our Chinatown is the largest outside of Asia, and the oldest I believe."

This all made a lot of sense. "Does that mean that there's good Chinese food?"

"There is *excellent* Chinese food," answered Becca. "There is excellent food in just about every category here, but Chinese food is at the top."

"Do you think we could get some at some point?" requested my inner fat boy.

Becca thought to herself then shook her head with conviction. "Yes. I know exactly what we can do."

I smiled and nodded. She sounded confident in whatever place she was thinking of, so I figured I would wait to find out at the appropriate time and be pleasantly surprised.

"By the way," she said, "did I mention that I got tomorrow off from work?"

"No, you did not."

"How about a bike ride around the city?"

"I would like nothing more," I said without a millisecond of hesitation.

"Great!"

After getting a day to wander aimlessly by myself, I was going to get a complimentary guided bike tour. "Wait," I said, "I don't have a bike."

"Obviously," said Becca. "That's not something you need to worry about."

I had very few worries at that time. It helped me when we arrived back at her place to fall right to sleep and dream like a San Franciscan.

DAY 10

Becca woke me up at nine. A tad on the early side, but when can I sleep? That's right, when I'm dead. We grabbed some quick cereal and wasted little time to get out of the house. The sun was beautifully beaming down again, surrounded by a bright blue sky. Even Becca could not believe this influx of good weather. "It was cold and foggy up until a few days ago. It seemed to clear up in preparation for your visit!"

"I know," I said, "you don't have to thank me."

We grabbed two road bikes from behind her house. One was hers, the other was her roommate's who was currently on a business trip to Dubai, or something. That explained the absence of one roommate. The other one I had only seen briefly when we got home from the bar. Busy city folk being busy with their own lives. It made a lot of sense. People had to make use of their time somehow when there weren't slot machines around to sit in front of all day.

"I didn't get a chance to ask him to use his bike but I know he won't mind," confessed Becca. Then with a half-serious look she said, "Just don't crash it."

"Sure thing!" I replied, and hoped for the best.

We began our journey heading north for a few blocks, then west on a main avenue. About a mile down we crossed into Golden Gate Park. This is San Francisco's largest and most popular park. The Grateful Dead used to hold free concerts here. As we entered the park, we rode passed groups of people lying around in the grass. Some were sleeping, some were sitting and staring at the ground. They looked like they may have attended these

Grateful Dead concerts and never left the park since. I heard a few of them mumble weed offerings as we biked by. Collectively they had an interesting demeanor, carrying a similar style with their clothing and accessories. They were dark and ragged from their clothes down to their skin, which wasn't ethnically dark, but incredibly tan to the point that it looked like leather. Some had mangy looking dogs on leashes—*Even the bums have dogs in this town.* The ones whom I heard talk, had raspy voices and rambled loudly about things I could not begin to comprehend. I had never seen such a similar group mind and style with bums. The bums on the East Coast are not nearly as organized. Over there it's "every bum for himself."

Once we passed the outer bum banks and reached the inner part, the beauty of the park was unleashed. There were lush gardens, and tall trees, and many open spaces where people were lounging, reading, playing music, tossing a frisbee, and generally doing something enjoyable.

The park is roughly four miles long. It's not nearly as wide, but wide enough to make me forget that I was still in the city. We biked through the entire park and when we reached the farthest end, we crossed an avenue and were immediately halted by the ocean. The majestic Pacific fanned out and met the blue sky at the horizon. We got off our bikes and marched out onto this beach, appropriately labeled, Ocean Beach. I wouldn't say it was the nicest beach I've been on, but I've never heard about San Francisco being well known for their beaches. SoCal (Southern California) apparently rules in that department. But so what. SoCal can have their pretty beaches. What it lacks in beaches, San Francisco makes up for in many other ways. But like they say, a beach is a beach, and we sat and relaxed, sipping some H2o and watching the waves.

At my most relaxed moment, legs crossed, head tilted, transfixed by the crashing waves, I felt my phone vibrate. It was Wallace. My heart halted as I stared at the phone ringing. Then I looked out at the ocean. One quick sprint and I could be engulfed by the frigid water and go to sleep peacefully among the fishes and the failed Alcatraz escapees, and not worry about this stupid car anymore. I gathered up the courage to face reality. *How much money is it going to cost? Is it dead? Maybe nothing's wrong. Yeah! He's going to tell me we're okay.*

I picked up and answered with a timid, lifeless voice, like I was answering to God on the other line. "Hello?"

"Hey," he said with enough morose to know that it was bad news. "She's pretty fucked."

"Like how fucked?"

"Like they totally need to replace the clutch."

Fuck. This really was my fault. I wore out the clutch, I knew it—

"But don't worry, it wasn't your fault."

Oh thank god.

"It was those damn Vermont mechanics. They fucked it up when they fixed my transmission. I *knew* that deal was too good to be true." Wallace sounded like he was making that comment to himself, as if he was going to go back to Vermont and do something violently vengeful to those mechanics.

"So what's going to happen?" I asked. "We're supposed to leave tomorrow."

"They haven't told me exactly what needs to be done yet. But they said that we might be able to finish off the trip, depending on what they can do. I'll let you know."

"Okay."

"Okay, later."

"Yeah, but—"

He hung up.

I thought for a second. It appeared that I was presented with three different scenarios. Two were awesome, one sucked. If the car died, I would be stranded in a beautiful city in Northern California: Awesome. If the car was fine, we would continue on our journey northwards: Awesome. If the car was "kind of" fixed, we would need to drive straight back to Massachusetts: Fuck no. All scenarios presented an unpredictable outcome to my trip. I was three throusand miles away from home and I was ready to accept any possibility. But then my optimism faded. There were so many specific things on my agenda that had yet to be done and they all required a car. I could feel the Northwest beginning to fade from my realm of reality. This did not make a happy Evan. Then determination set in. *No matter what, I will make it to the Northwest!... But How?* I lay back down. As stressful as the impending fate of the car was, I didn't find it hard to brush off and put in the back of my mind. It's hard to stay bothered when relaxing on a beach.

Becca spoke up. "Was that about the car?"

"Yeah."

"Is it okay?"

"I have no idea."

Becca got up. "Well that's not something we need to worry about now. Are you ready to go?"

I nodded and we got back on our bikes heading north. We worked our way up a hill that ran along the coast and when we came around a bend, the entire Bay was revealed. From our high up vantage point, the water glistened from the sun and lit up the Golden Gate Bridge. We continued on this windy hill and eventually entered a neighborhood set at the top. These houses had a view of not only the Bay, but also the city skyline on the other side. What gave away the worth of these houses besides their view, was their size: Every house was a mansion. "Robin Williams lives around here," said Becca. I turned my head enthusiastically as if I could guess which house would be the most Robin Williams-y. *C'mon Robin, give me a sign!... Nope. No sign.* We moved on.

We glided down the other side of the hill and made it to Big Red. The Golden Gate Bridge is magnificent. It has a deep red color that shines orange in the right light. I have seen many pictures of the bridge, but they didn't do it justice. It's a damn good lookin' bridge I tell ya. "Do you want to bike over the bridge?" asked Becca. What in this entire godforsaken world would have ever possessed me to reject such an offer?

There was a sidewalk on the bridge wide enough to bike on and for people to pass. A fence separated us on either side from both getting run over, and falling from a perilous height down to the water. I hoped Wallace didn't call me back at that moment. The jump was tempting enough without feeling suicidal. Seeing the bay and the opposing shorelines from this vantage point was a sight to behold. The edges of the shore we were approaching, shot up with cliffs extending from the bottom of the bridge, hundreds of feet up. Behind us the city of San Francisco sunned itself for us all to gaze upon like a bikini model.

We were leaving San Francisco but this would be a small tease. We would head this same way tomorrow and continue north—depending on the state of the car. Maybe these couple miles north of San Francisco would be the farthest northwest I would manage to go on my grand road trip. Or maybe I should do what Gill had proposed back in Massachusetts: bike it. Right now I could thank Becca and tell her to wish me luck and I will be on my way, peddling my sorry ass up the coast. *Shit, this isn't my bike... Who cares Evan, just take it!... But Becca's my cousin, I can't do that... Who cares? She'll forgive you. Don't you want to fulfill your* destiny?... *I don't know... Come oooon!... Fuck it, I'm not the stealing type anyway. Plus, she has my stuff at her place and the rest is packed in the Suburu... Pussy.* It was tempting but I think I made the right decision. It was in my best interest not to steal my cousin's roommate's bike, thereby not breaking my family's healthy dynamic, as well as not abandoning my friends. Road trips are all about important decisions. All you can do is pray that you're making the right one.

After the bridge we made it to a town called, Sausalito. The main street was littered with designer stores and boutiques. This was the ritzy town for the over-privileged who worked in San Francisco. I related it to heading out of New York City to a town like Great Neck in Long Island, with the exact same stores lining the main street. Needless to say, it wasn't my cup o' tea. But the area was glorious. Steep hills surrounded the town and were speckled with multi-story houses that fit into the hills like perfect puzzle pieces. I could only imagine the view from up there, of the Bay and the city behind it.

We decided that to get back over to the city, we wouldn't take the bridge, but instead take a ferry across the Bay. They ran often from Sausalito and we didn't have to wait long for the next departure. Once the boat had set off from the mainland, we got a great view of the Sausalito hills. This coastal town had beautiful scenery, with the hills rising up dramatically from the water. I was reminded of the Italian Riviera in the northwest corner of the country, where the lush green hills rise up from the Mediterranean. Sausalito didn't have the Italian Riviera beaten, but I admired their effort. Any dramatic hilly seaside town is easy on the eyes.

As we drifted away from the Sausalito hills, the Golden Gate Bridge revealed itself in the foggy distance. The Bay fog had thickened since we passed over the bridge, summoning the late afternoon. The bridge's deep red could still be seen, mixed with a grey fuzz to peer through.

Then came an island in our field of view. I didn't recognize it at first but soon realized we were seeing the Rock from the opposite side. "If you're looking for something to do, you should take a tour of Alcatraz," said Becca. "They have night tours which are supposed to be really fun."

"I don't know if I have time on this visit," I said. "Then again maybe I will if I stay."

The ferry landed at the northern edge of the city in the downtown district near where I had met Becca the day before. "This is the Port of San Francisco," informed Becca. "It's the popular spot where Critical Mass starts."

I turned to her. "Critical what?"

"You haven't heard of Critical Mass?" she asked.

"No, do tell."

"It's a biking event that takes place on the last Friday of every month around rush hour. Hundreds, sometimes thousands of bikers participate. They all meet at the Port, and bike together through the city and block traffic."

"Is it purposely done during rush hour?" I asked.

"Yep. It's a way of spreading awareness about biking and driving less."

"Sounds like an obtrusive way of spreading awareness."

"Yeah, but the city has gotten used to it. Even the police have helped out recently and they block off the streets for us."

"Wow," I was impressed. "Who organizes the event?"

"That's the best part. It's totally unofficial. People hear about it by word of mouth, so the city is caught off guard by where the bikers go. They choose a different route each time."

"Seems like a big deal. I'm surprised I've never heard of it."

"It started here in SF, but has spread to different cities around the country. However, I think it's more popular on the West Coast."

It nodded, convinced. "I'll be sure to add it to my 'If I'm stuck in San Francisco' list."

We walked through the ferry building and out to the square in front. Ahead was the start of Market Street, the main avenue in the downtown district. The financial monoliths rose above us and I was pleasantly reminded that it wasn't too long ago that I was looking up at cliffs this size.

Becca turned to me. "Are you hungry?"

"Starving."

"How about getting the best Chinese in the city?"

I grew a great smile. I knew she was cooking up a plan last night. Chinatown was only a couple blocks from us. "I have a general idea of where the place is," said Becca. "Chinatown's a little confusing but we'll find it and if we're desperate we can go with the millions of other options."

We mounted our greasy steeds and set off. It took us a few blocks to find the place, but the House of Nanking revealed itself by the crowd of people waiting out front. I was hungry but willing to wait. A line for a restaurant is always a good sign.

The House of Nanking was a small space, packed in tight with tables and people and bustling Chinese waiters that maneuvered around the narrow spaces with ease, like a bunch of Gills slipping through fences. Most of the customers looked Chinese which was also a good sign because the immigrant locals always knew best. *They* may have been in America but *we* were in *their* territory. We were packed in tight to a small, two-person table, inches from the next group of patrons, making me feel like I was in some hip bistro in downtown Manhattan.

When we sat down I picked up a menu, but Becca held her hand out to stop me. "Don't worry about ordering, leave it up to me." For the millionth time today, I was in no position to stop or question any of my cousin's actions. She may have been from Massachusetts, but she was a San Francisco local now.

A busy, bustling, short, old, enthusiastically smiling Chinese woman glided up to us. "Yes-yes, what would you like?" She even talked in that rushed downtown Manhattan tone that meant, "You better know what you want this instant or else I'm gone. No time to dillydally, time is money."

Becca asked with a bit of uncertainty, "Can we get the um, I think it's called the chef special?"

The busy, bustling, short, old, enthusiastically smiling, no-time-for-bullshit Chinese lady's eyes widened and she said, "Ooooh, chef special! Okay." She scribbled something down and then said, "Do you like seafood?"

Becca and I looked at each other. "Yes."

"Do you like beef and pork?"

"Yes."

"Vegetable?"

"Yes."

"How hungry are you? Very hungry?"

"Yes."

"Okay, thank you," and she bustled away.

Becca and I looked at each other with content anticipation. It was a rare treat to get ordered for and I loved the mystery of trying new food.

It wasn't a long wait before the waitress proceeded to bring out various dishes of pork, rice, beef, and calamari. These were all types of food that I never had prepared for in such a way. All of it was unique and delicious, especially the calamari which was marinated in some kind of spicy vinegar sauce. The squid melted in my mouth, slid down my throat, and was welcomed into my stomach with open arms. "Becca," I said with a mouth full of deliciousness, "this is exactly what I wanted."

After our exquisite, authentic meal, we biked off our digestion in the direction of Becca's place. She called some friends to come over and we decided to have a mellow night at her place with some wine. I was happy to chill-out for my last night in San Francisco and drink wine with some San Franciscans. *But is this going to be my last night?* No word from Wallace yet.

We got back to Becca's, showered and changed, and soon after, her friends came over. There were three of them, all attractive females in their mid-twenties. We sipped on some Merlot from Napa Valley and chatted about my trip and where I planned to go, as well as my unfortunate situation with the car. One of the girls, named Adalaide, looked at me with caring blue eyes and frowned with sympathy as I spoke about my car woes. She spoke up when I finished. "I'm sorry to hear that. You're more than welcome to stay in our wonderful city and we will be happy to show you around if you want!" She spoke with such a soft and natural, yet confident voice. She was a beautiful blond and her smile seemed to brighten the whole room. I was in love. But I soon found out that she was taken. This became apparent when the girl that sat next to her put her hand in Adalaide's, and gave her a loving nuzzle followed by a peck on her cheek that only a *girlfriend* would do. Adalaide's girlfriend seemed to be a nice, genuine individual, which made it difficult to feel scorn.

As the night wore on and the wine diminished, I gravitated to the corner of the room and nestled into a comfy loveseat. The wine mixed with the heavy amount of chatting estrogen made me drowsy and I was reduced to a fly on the wall, observing the habits of San Franciscan females. I especially lost interest in the topics of conversation when it shifted to "office talk." All four ladies worked in offices and had an equal number of boring stories to share about the goings on of each workplace. They could all relate to each other's anecdotes. I, on the other hand, could not relate at all, since my life up until now comprised of school, and more recently driving in a car. These people had entered the real world while I was still in fantasyland.

At one point Becca raised a topic that concerned her and her friends, as well as me, but not for the same reasons. "I have this coworker," she explained. "She's in her early thirties. Really cool, but has a 'serious boyfriend,'" she quoted with her hands. The girls nodded in understanding, meaning a wedding proposal was right around the corner. "And I've noticed that their relationship has taken a toll on her social life. Whenever I invite her to do something, like go to a concert, or hang out in the park, or even simply get a drink after work, she always has to check with her boyfriend to see if it's okay." The other girls listened with interest. "And that scares me!" exclaimed Becca. "I sincerely hope that when I reach the age of getting seriously involved with someone, I would still have the freedom to do what I wanted, without the consent of my partner."

Everyone agreed. Adalaide looked lovingly at her girlfriend. "We don't do that, right babe?"

Her girlfriend shook her head. "Of course not!"

I saw Adalaide caress her leg under the table. It should have been *my* leg.

I sat there in the corner feeling as scared as these ladies. But the reason I was scared was because I looked at all of these people, who were just a few years older than me, and all they talked about were their boring jobs.

Granted if they had cool jobs, it would be interesting to hear stories. But they worked in offices! That is some boring-ass shit! So while they sat there in fear of the next stage of their lives when they would be socially shackled by their significant others, I was in fear that the next stage of my life would be like theirs! I made a vow that whatever job I chose to do in the future, I would not let it take over my life, just like these girls had secretly vowed never to let serious relationships take over theirs. All we needed was some middle-aged dude in the room with a crappy job, bitchy wife, four kids, and a mortgage, to tell us that we were all ungrateful children.

Just then my phone rang. *Wallace! Oh shit, here comes the final verdict.*

"Hello?"

"Yo man." He already sounded dismal.

"What's up?"

"They finished checking out the car."

<Gulp> "Yeah?"

"The clutch is fucked up."

I looked over at the empty wine bottle on the table. *How easy would it be to break and drive through my heart?* While dying I could tell Adalaide that I always loved her and will meet her in heaven. "Okay."

"But they said it should last the rest of the trip."

I shot up. "What? Really?"

"Yeah, but I'm the only one who can drive from here on out."

"Okay, no problem!" I said without hesitation. That was the easiest condition that could be made!

"I'm heading to Oakland tonight. Gill will meet me there tomorrow morning and we'll pick you up between nine and ten. Later."

I sat there in paralyzed wonder, before noticing that Becca and her friends had stopped talking and were looking at me.

"I can't tell if you look relieved or dismayed," said Becca.

I looked at them and smiled. "It's relief."

I drained my glass of wine in a final, glorious gulp. Maybe tomorrow I would be drinking more in Napa Valley.

DAY 11

I decided not to set my alarm. Instead I turned my phone from vibrate to ring so I would be woken up by Wallace's call. I had made sure to pack everything up last night so I could get up and go. He said they would come between nine and ten.

Another reason I did not set my alarm was because I have a very accurate internal alarm clock. I can tell myself the night before to wake up at a certain time and I will usually do it within a close proximity to that time. This talent has been a big help in my life, although it has also worked to my disadvantage. I will sometimes wake up too early and then find it hard to go back to sleep, constantly checking my watch to make sure I didn't miss the time. That was what happened this morning. Although every time I woke up, I stopped myself from opening my eyes and looking at the time. I forced myself to keep sleeping, reassuring my brain, *Wait for the call. Just wait for the call.*

After a few repeated wake-ups, I got restless and opened my eyes. My first sight was out the window above my head to a bright sun surrounded by blue. This same weather was on repeat. No complaints there. I reluctantly lifted my arm and looked at my watch: ten-thirty. *Fuck!–Wait, I'm on East Coast time—Wait, no, I changed it two days ago—Fuck!* The same feeling grew in me that I had in Massachusetts: waiting on these fools, once again. I sat in bed for a while staring at the dull ceiling. This ceiling was not a unique, San Francisco ceiling. It was white and flat and like every other ceiling in any room. I hated being in this situation where what I was waiting for could happen at any second, but the time keeps dragging on and on. Seconds go by like hours. I looked over at my lifeless phone. *Ring, damnit. Just fucking ring!*

After ten minutes I couldn't take it anymore and called Wallace. Ring...Ring...Ring... Ring... "I'm sorry, you cannot leave a message because this person's mailbox is full. Goodbye." I scowled as that horrible robot voice hung up on me. *What now? Is he dead? Is he asleep? Did he drive off the Golden Gate Bridge?*

I called Gill. Ring...Ring... "Hello?" came a familiar voice.

Thank you Gill for always being reliable, unlike some people. I was getting annoyed with Wallace and we hadn't even started our trip again.

"Hey, it's Evan."

"Oh hey," said Gill, "did you talk to Wallace?"

"No, did you?"

"No. I haven't heard from him," he said.

"Where are you?" I asked.

"In Oakland having breakfast with my cousin. I'm waiting to hear from him so we can meet and then get you."

"I just called and he didn't pick up," I said.

"Hmm," pondered Gill. "I'll call and see if I get through."

"Okay, let me know." *God damn this kid. He must take joy in leaving us in suspense.*

I forced myself out of bed and got dressed. I set my bags by the stairs that led to the front door, then walked to the living room and sat down on the loveseat where I sat last night. Maybe the same energy from last night would be rechanneled, causing Wallace to call. I sat and stared out the kitchen windows to a palm tree. Its stiff, tropical leaves blew in the soft wind. East Coast or West Coast, it seemed that sitting in a chair and staring out a window was my greatest attribute.

Eleven o'clock...Eleven-thirty...

Becca walked into the room and startled me. "Hey."

"Oh! Hey! You got today off too?" I asked.

Becca gave me a blank stare. "Evan, it's Saturday."

"Oh, right." Days of the week were insignificant on this trip so I had lost track. I also forgot about work schedules. I had to remind myself that Saturday is on something called the "weekend."

"Where are your friends?" she asked.

"Good question. They could be dead so we may have to go back to plan B where I stay here forever."

Becca chuckled. "Okay, that's fine."

I smiled. I was going to miss this laid-back San Francisco attitude of going with the flow. This was a trait I hadn't been practicing this morning. I should say, "It's fine. They'll come when they come." But this was impossible for me to do.

By noon my head was about to explode. Finally, two hours, nine minutes, and fifty-two seconds after I was supposed to be picked up, my phone rang. It was Gill.

"Yeah?" I said, clearly sounding annoyed.

"Hey, you ready?"

"Yeah."

"Okay, we're parked outside."

"Really? Okay. What the hell took so long?"

"Just get out here, we'll explain." Gill said this with a tone of agitation and distress that I had never heard come from this normally placid individual.

"Okay, I'll be right down." *What the hell was wrong?* I expected the worst, like Wallace had traded the car for a horse and buggy or something.

I hugged Becca and thanked her. I was sure deep down she was relieved that she didn't have to entertain me for another few weeks. But it was comforting to know that she would have, if the situation arose. I was across the country, yet family was still close.

I grabbed my bags and headed out the door. There was the tired old Suburu parked on the street, trying to pretend it was all in one piece. My two companions each had sunglasses on and blank, emotionless looks from inside the car. Wallace was perched in the driver's seat, his new permanent position. I got in back and fought the urge to ask the angry housewife, "Where the hell have you been?" question.

"So—" I began but Wallace cut me off.

"The car got robbed."

"Huh? What? When?"

"Last night."

"Are you serious?" I looked around. The windows were all in one piece. And by the looks of it, all of our stuff was still packed in the trunk.

"I came out this morning and all of the doors were wide open. I guess I must have left the car unlocked last night," admitted Wallace.

"Really." My voice turned gruff.

"I know, I'm a fucking idiot," said Wallace sounding apologetic for the first time. "But here's the strange part," he continued. "As far as I can tell, all they stole was my cell phone and the loose change from the dash."

"Huh..."

We all sat there in silence, trying to wrap our minds around this situation.

"Where were you?" I asked.

"Oakland."

"You could've at least called me to let me know what the situation was," I said.

"And how could I have done that?? They took my cell phone, remember?"

I nodded. "You're right, sorry." He was right.

We sat in silence again. How could that have happened? Our car was packed full of stuff and all they took was a cell phone and change?

"I think we can agree on one thing," chimed in Gill. "Oakland crooks must be some dumb motherfuckers!"

That diffused the tense moment and we all laughed. "Okay, let's get out of here."

Unfortunately when shit just happens, it isn't always good shit. Sometimes there's free lunch in Navada, and sometimes change gets stolen in Oakland. Either way it's something to remember.

We were on the road again. Any stress from the morning flew out our open windows with the cool air. However, for an additional hour we drove around the city because Gill was navigating and once again had no idea where we were going.

"Don't worry, I got it," Gill assured us.

"Damnit Gill, use the map!"

"Don't worry about it, I already checked the map."

"Okay I'm calling Becca."

"Don't worry—"

"Shut up Gill!"

Becca helped us and we were sailing over the Golden Gate Bridge in no time. As we drifted over the Bay, I looked back at the city. The buildings and houses rose up and down like waves over the hills. *San Francisco is a good place. A damn good place.* I promised to make it back. Maybe when I went back it would be for good. But I wasn't ready for commitment yet. It was time to keep exploring north.

"So where to?" I asked. "I figure we should at least make a small detour through Napa Valley, maybe stop at a winery, and then we can head to the coast?"

"Did I mention that I had family I needed to see in Santa Rosa?" asked Gill.

"No, where's that?"

"It's on the way to Napa, just forty-five minutes north of here. We can stop in for like an hour or something and then be on our way."

I looked at my watch: It was one-thirty. Our late start wasn't helping the situation. But we couldn't deny a man seeing his family. And when there was family, there was always something free: food, supplies, etc. "Okay, but only an hour," I said, "it's already getting late."

The forty-five-minute drive was too short, feeling like we hadn't left San Francisco before we were getting off the highway. When we entered Santa Rosa, I was getting similar vibes as San Jose, which was the anxiety of being surrounded by plasticy, suburban sprawl. Everything looked fabricated and it got worse when we rolled through Gill's family's neighborhood. Every house was too neatly put together, with a perfect lawn and perfectly planted shrubs and trees. Giant SUVs were parked in front of each three-door garage.

We pulled into a driveway of a house that looked no different than the rest: same shrubs, same lawn. But there were even more cars parked in the driveway then could fit in their massive garage. Every car was clean and neat, not a scratch or speck of dirt. Our cruddy Suburu stuck out like a sore thumb.

Gill's Aunt and Uncle came out to greet us, followed by a boy looking around eighteen and a girl looking a few years younger. *Please do not tell me that there is a car in the driveway for each of these individuals.* There were four cars and nobody else came out of the house. *What a world.*

All members of the family were perfectly groomed, clean cut, with perfect smiles. A perfectly groomed cocker spaniel came out to greet us. My stomach started turning and I bit my tongue.

"Jacob! It's so good to see you!" said Aunt Gill. "Oh, and these must be your friends!"

We put on our happy faces and shook hands.

"Come in guys," said Uncle Gill. "Did you bring bathing suits? We have a nice pool in the back if you want to cool down from this heat."

Of course you have a pool.

They took us to the backyard where there was a belowground, stone-bordered pool equipped with waterfall and slide. Next to that was a trampoline (surrounded by safety barriers), and a lengthy yard to the side. When the unrealistically lush grass ended, some desert-like plants sprung up, and the ground was coarser. It was apparent that the desert was the native environment, while everything else was alien.

It's hard for me to see an area of complete fabrication. It attempts to give the environment "beauty" that it is thought to be lacking. This is an aspect of California that I had always heard about which I was now seeing first hand. Whether it be planting fake shrubs on a lawn, or putting a fake nose or breasts on your body, California has this obsession with altering reality to create "perfection." This idea frankly disgusts me. I do not believe that the goal to life is perfection. Life is about balance. If all of life was perfect all of the time, you wouldn't be able to fully appreciate the goodness that it brings. Bad times build character which ultimately makes you a better, well-rounded individual.

Take the seasons in the Northeast for example. Spring and summer are a beautiful time. It's warm, and plants and flowers are in bloom. Then in the fall and winter, everything dies. It is a common occurrence for people to get down, or even depressed during the cold, dead months. But having this time of death makes the spring and summer infinitely better. You can appreciate the world coming back to life and understand the cycle. Many people hate the winter and choose to move to places where it stays warm, year round. These people want perfection. They think that if they stay warm all of the time, they will be happy all of the time. But this is false. If things never change, they become stale. Monotony sets in, leading to boredom and ultimately depression. I have already talked about the innate human desire for constant change and why a road trip lends itself well to that notion. Life bares the same necessity. However, I'm also not so quick to judge. This family may have had four cars and a fake backyard, but that didn't make them bad, lifeless humans...yet.

We put our bathing suits on and took a refreshing dip. As we were swimming, Gill's youngest cousin came home. She was a tiny, spry child around eight, with cute dimples and the same perfect smile as the rest of her family. She couldn't have been more excited to see Gill and would not stop jumping around and screaming, "Jacob! Jacob! Jacob! Jacob!" Then she raced inside and returned in a bathing suit and jumped in.

Gill tossed Baby Gill around and she screamed in delight, up until she screamed in pain and ran out of the pool after Gill accidentally elbowed her in the face. Wallace and I looked at each other in mutual relief that it was their own family member that had to abuse our hosts' daughter and not one of the two grungy looking strangers.

We got out of the pool and stood there awkwardly as the family showered Baby Gill with attention, trying to softly convince her that she was okay. "Don't worry sweety, Jacob didn't do it on purpose." Wallace scoffed in disgust and walked away to a fake grassy patch in the yard to call his girlfriend.

Gill and I had the idea to challenge the three cousins to a soccer game. Baby Gill came back to the group looking unscathed but pouty. We stepped onto the fake grass and commenced our match. Gill and I were not only older, but superior soccer players. It gave our egos a much needed boost, being able to beat two teenagers and an eight-year-old.

After a quick goal I gave Gill a high-five. "Nice pass Gill."

Boy Gill stopped and looked at me with a screwed up face. "What did you call him? Gill?"

I nodded. "Yeah. Gill."

Clearly confused, Boy Gill looked at Gill. "Jacob, why does he call you that?"

"It's the nickname that all of my high school friends call me," he answered casually.

"Why?" he asked.

"Because it's short for my last name."

Boy Gill contorted his face more like it was the craziest thing he had ever heard. "What?! That's ridiculous!"

Sorry kid, your dull, untainted mind wouldn't understand.

We continued playing but soon the game had to take a five-minute timeout when Gill kicked Baby Gill and she started wailing again in the middle of the grass. Boy Gill and Girl Gill came rushing to her aid, again showering her with attention and sympathy. The whole scene made me sick. *Just let her cry it out! She doesn't need all that attention.*

Gill shared my sentiment and spoke up. "Come on guys, let's keep playing!"

Girl Gill looked at him in shock. "But Jacob, she's hurt!"

These whiny brats were making my blood boil. *No character I tell ya, none at all.*

I looked at my watch. We were getting into late afternoon. I turned to Gill. "We should really get going."

Gill gave me a helpless look that said, "I don't think we can pry ourselves away that easy."

Then Aunt Gill came out back. "We're about to start cooking dinner. You guys are staying the night, right?" Gill and I looked at each other and gave a defeated shrug. At this point it was inevitable, but free food and shelter never hurt.

This was not an impressive driving day. This was not an impressive day overall. In fact this day was quite bothersome. I had sat and waited in frustration, Wallace had gotten his change stolen, we had driven a shorter distance then we could have walked, and the afternoon had been spent with a bunch of whiney, sissy brats. *I can't believe they each have a fucking car.*

"But where's mu-mu-my car? Whaaaaaaa!"

Don't cry Baby Gill, you'll get yours soon enough.

I couldn't complain about the meal: fresh salad packed with delicious California avocados, corn on the cob, and grilled chicken. No microbrews to compliment, but they popped open a bottle of delightfully dry pinot grigio. The dinner conversation on the other hand, was painful. It consisted of the father talking about the different things he was going to buy his kids, while the kids prodded and pleaded.

"But Daaaad, you promised you'd get me that new computer."

"Yeah, and I need a new cell phone, mine's old."

Blah blah blah blah. Because your own car, trampoline, and pool isn't enough.

After dinner the family dispersed and plopped themselves in front of TVs and computers. I sat at the table and wrote postcards. I sent one from the Badlands to Jenny in Michigan, and one from Yosemite went to my Mom. These places already seemed like distant memories. We were in Michigan and the Badlands a week ago, but we did enough in that week to last a year.

When on an extended vacation like this, time starts to slow down and you're given time to sit back and contemplate. When vacations are crammed into a week or less, they go by in a blur and before your mind can catch up with everything, it's tragically over. It's like jumping off of a tall ledge as opposed to a short one, into water. When it's short, you jump and before you know what happened, you're in the water. But when you drop from a high enough point, your body reaches terminal velocity and begins to float. Your mind gets a grip on your body's action and there's time to contemplate your surroundings. Right now on our trip we had reached this free fall. It felt good to float.

Wallace, Gill, and I discussed what our next plan of action would be. The pinot grigio had reminded me of our close proximity to Napa Valley. Uncle Gill gave us a good recommendation of a vineyard to check out, where we could get a wine tasting and a tour. It was in the Sonoma Valley, which I had never heard of, but it was adjacent to Napa. Uncle Gill promised it to be no different and I wasn't ready to question him—at least on this subject. I ignored my opinion of their lack of character and accepted the fact that, due to their location and financial status, they probably knew a thing or two about California wine country.

Our morning was planned out and a rough goal of reaching Highway 1 (the coastal highway) was to follow, which would take us northward. The extended Gill family bid us goodnight and we laid our sleeping bags out on the cushy, vacuumed livingroom carpet. I disregarded all of the things that had bothered me today and mentally prepared myself for what was to come. One thought always led to another: wine country > coastal highway > redwoods > Pacific Northwest > British Columbia > mountains > awesomeness > more awesomeness...sleep.

DAY 12

We had a leisurely wake up, partly because we had fully aclimated to the Pacific Time Zone, and because a wine tasting and tour was not a seven a.m. activity. After a nice breakfast of assorted fruit and french toast, we headed out to the driveway where the extended Gill family saw us off. We put on our happy faces again and thanked them for all their hospitality. Baby Gill ran up and gave Gill a tight hug. "I'll miss you Jacob." Her tiny mind must have realized that after getting elbowed in the face and kicked in the shin, she was still in one piece, and love conquers all.

As lame and spoiled as I thought this family was, and for all of my complaining, I still could not deny their hospitality and generosity. I may have disagreed with their way of life, but it did not change the fact that they put forth a genuine effort to help us. I was sure as we rolled off in our clunky northeastern Suburu that they had lots of things to say and criticize about our unkempt selves.

"And did you hear them calling Jacob 'Gill'??"

"Yes how strange, and did you see that bigger one actually had a tattoo??"

We cannot all coexist on the same metaphysical level, but what we can ask for is to help and be helped by our fellow man and treat one another with respect (and no I'm not Christian, I'm merely human). That was what they did for us and so be it if they criticized us once we were gone, because that was exactly what we did. "Gill, your cousins are some spoiled fucking brats!"

"Yeah, I know."

Sonoma was a mere twenty-minute drive from Santa Rosa. Once we reached it, we got onto a two-lane road running through the middle of a valley. Rolling hills eased up on both sides and soon the vineyards took over. We would pass large, slightly modern, slightly Victorian complexes set a visible distance off the road, and surrounded by acres of grape vines, neatly stacked in rows. Each of these complexes belonged to a different winery, identified by an elegantly constructed welcome sign by the road. After passing a few, we turned into Uncle Gill's recommendation, the Kunde Estate Winery. We drove down a long, narrow path, passing row after row of grape vines before reaching the visitor's parking lot. This led up to a large, modern, wooden complex. The entrance was a two-story tall barn door that remained open.

Three scrappy travelers we, strolled into the building and straight up to the bar.

An older gentleman with a gentle face greeted us, holding a bottle of vino in one hand and glasses in the other. "Good afternoon gentlemen, welcome to the Kunde Estate. Would you like to taste some wine?"

"A good afternoon to you, sir. Why certainly, we would love to taste some wine from your beautiful establishment—and might I emphasize what a beautiful establishment you have!"

"Thank you gentlemen for those kind words. Shall we get started with the tasting?"

"Yes sir, I do believe we shall."

"Okay then, that will be ten dollars each please, so thirty all together."

"Oh...well, hmm." We looked at each other. "Should we do it?"

The man gave a reassuring smile. "Oh, it's definitely worth it."

"Okay! We're sold!"

I'm no wino, but the wine passed my test. The nice man gave us a handful of varieties, giving overly descriptive explanations to each kind about their flavor profile. Everything was over our heads, but I enjoyed it regardless. It felt like we actually got our money's worth. Some things were worth getting easily convinced of. Some things were not: My apologies to you, Mount Rushmore. To you, Yosemite ranger dude, well you can still go fuck yourself.

After the tasting we got a tour of the grounds, as well as inside the underground cellar where they stored their wine barrels for fermentation. I was glad that poor travelers like ourselves could enjoy a winery like this without draining our wallets. Wine culture had the potential to be financially intimidating.

At this point it was time to head west for our final drive in that navigational direction. Once we reached the ocean, north and east would be all that was left. Wallace took the reins while I took out the map of our NorCal playground to figure out the best (and most interesting) way to get to the coast. I figured a back road or two wouldn't hurt.

We backtracked a little ways out of the valley, through Santa Rosa, and then turned off on a side road. It was a narrow one-lane road which got windy and rural once we left town. The surrounding hills turned more golden and defined. Tall eucalyptus trees lined the roads, their arching branches hanging over, trying their hardest to touch our hood. We passed an occasional rustic house, situated in the middle of a golden field. "I could live there," I said to myself. I continued to say this after every passing house. This area was so picturesque with the rolling hills and trees. It became apparent to me that this was the most beautiful road we had driven on, on our trip thus far. It also occurred to me that of all the roads and scenery we had seen, this hilly landscape with winding roads reminded me most of the roads around our home, in and around Amherst. This meant that I was likening the most beautiful road on our trip to our origin. It gave me a newfound appreciation for my home as I realized that I lived in one of the most beautiful parts of the country—or world? This feeling of appreciation was followed by guilt. Maybe I didn't have enough appreciation for my home and I was too anxious to get away from what I realized I was taking for granted. Why did I need to go on this trip to search for beauty when I had enough of it in my backyard? This feeling of guilt was followed by realization that to truly understand and appreciate the beauty of my home, it was necessary to venture out and see other parts of this world.

We stopped at a crossroads with nothing around but a deli on the corner. It was a gourmet deli of course, with a parking lot filled with Audi's, BMW's, and luxury convertibles. Even though it looked like we were in the middle of nowhere, we were still very much in the heart of Californian country. Outside, a cool breeze lightly brushed through my hair, smelling like a mixture of wheat and salt. The Ocean wasn't far.

We loaded up on gourmet sandwiches with extra fresh California avocados and artisan bags of chips. Our goal then was to find the most pristine spot to sit and eat before reaching the coast. We continued on the route and it took us higher in elevation, out of the trees so we were engulfed by the golden hills of hops. When we reached the top of the hill with an excellent vantage point, we turned off the road. We drove through an entrance to a drive that led down the hill to a group of buildings looking like a compound. A sign by the road said something about a yoga retreat. We hoped that if we kept to ourselves and didn't disturb any meditation, the Yogi's wouldn't disturb us.

We ate our delicious sandwiches not far from the road, atop a rock sticking out of the hops. The fields in front of us sloped down to the compound and past it were more hills—hills, and hills, and hills, of gold. In the distance looking westward, rose a dense cloud of fog. There hadn't been much discussion since we left Sonoma, because we were all in awe of our surroundings.

As we ate, Wallace broke the silence. "So guys, I figure this is an opportune time to show you my latest purchase from Oakland."

"I thought the only purchase in Oakland was what a thief had made from *you*," I said.

"Not exactly." Wallace reached into his pocket and pulled out a bag of some delectable looking cannabis.

Gill and I turned into kids in a candy store, reaching out our grubby hands. "Oooh ooh! Lemme see, lemme see!"

"I want to smell it!"

"Me first!"

"Okay kids," said Wallace, "just be careful."

The goody bag was passed around and we sniffed and inspected. "Wow, Cali bud! Where did you get it?"

"My friend has a medical card," answered Wallace.

"Really??" I said. "So you got to go in a dispensary?"

Wallace shook his head. "No, those places are like Fort Knox. But I gave my friend a grocery list and she went for me. I got that bag, some hash, and an edible."

"That makes sense," I said as I passed Wallace back the bag. "I tried to go into one in the city and was turned away."

Wallace nodded and pulled out some rolling papers from his pocket. "That sounds accurate."

After Wallace finished rolling a big fat joint, we looked around. This was an opportune spot to eat lunch but not so much to smoke drugs because it was too close to the road and wide open.

"What's that?" said Gill. He pointed toward a lightly trodden path through the hops that led two hundred yards out to a rocky mound with a good amount of tree cover.

"To the mound!"

We gave two more head turns to see if anyone was in sight and then slipped into the hops. These golden plants stayed motionless, until a light wind would blow through the hill making a sweeping sound of whispers. I kept my eyes on the ground in hopes that the hops would be still enough for me to hear a snake slither through. This looked like a perfect home for such a creature.

The path led straight to the mound. We climbed up and walked around to the other side, settling on a comfy spot where Wallace and Gill nestled into some grooves in the rock. I climbed a tree and rested on a branch. This little tree conveniently shielded us from the sun and wind. Wallace sparked the joint and we passed it around, sucking in the delicious California smoke. It was heavy bud, at least from what us Easterners were used to. And with heavy bud, these words cannot be uttered lightly: We got really fucking stoned. The THC filled our minds with fantastic thoughts and it didn't take long for us to start bouncing over the mound and trees like monkeys at play, uttering half-articulate phrases about the universe and the Pacific Ocean. Ideas passed between us like we were all connected to the same circuit—which in a lot of ways was true.

We discussed our mutual excitement for the Pacific Northwest and all of its potential. "I want to hike in the redwoods."

"Yeah! I heard about this awesome trail that's set back from the road where most tourists don't go."

"Let's do it!"

"I heard there are seals on the Oregon coast."

"Cool, seals!"

"I heard Olympic National Park is like a rain forest!"

"Maybe we'll get stuck in Seattle because we'll all meet beautiful girls who love the rain because they like to stay inside and shag all day, and we'll move in with them..."

And so on and so forth. I wasn't sure what it was about our fantastic luck with mounds on this trip, but every time we crossed them, they gave us the times of our lives.

The drive of adventure was back in full gear, but one thing was on my mind. We had to make our final push west to the Pacific Ocean, so I was inclined to halt our stoned monkey banter to continue the task. We walked back through the grass and I picked one of the stalks. The little bell-shaped hops dangled from the golden stick, mesmerizing me to the point of hypnosis. I took a picture of it, with the field of gold in the background. <Footnote: This picture ended up framed and hangs in my house. Come over any time, I'll show you!>

When we reached the car, I stuck the stalk in the seat pocket behind the passenger seat so they hung out, the bells dangling with every bump. This added to our nature sample collection, which included some emerald moss from Yosemite that was wedged in the corner of the dash and windshield, and a dried glob of grey Badlands clay that was stuck to the middle of the dash. If all went to plan, by the end of our trip the Suburu would to be transformed into a mobile terrarium.

The road sloped around toward the west and we began our descent in the direction of the fog. I put on My Morning Jacket, Z on the stereo, and let that raw, emotionally-infused rock enter my ears and spread through my soul as we coasted downward. We swept around tight turns with nothing obstructing our view in front of us except the fog, which appeared to be dissipating as we got closer, revealing rippling ocean in the distance. The road took us down a hill and it dipped into a ravine so our view ahead was covered by a steep hill. The road soon sloped back up and when we reached the top, we reached the end.

There was an abrupt explosion of clarity as the view opened up to the vast Pacific Ocean. There was simultaneously an explosion of the sound of waves crashing onto rocks, a hundred feet below. The road had ended at a T. A sign that pointed north and south said, "California 1, Pacific Coast." We drove across the street and parked, and I got out and walked onto a jutting cliff. A bed of yellow and red wild flowers lined the edge, before it dropped down to jagged rock and crashing, frothing water. I looked north and south at the jutting line of the coastal cliffs, with the ocean violently splashing onto its rocky wall. I looked west to nothing but calm water glistening in the sun. I felt triumph. Triumph like I had rarely felt in my life. Even though I had reached this ocean in San Francisco, this unspeakably magnificent scene of the rocky coast had made my journey to the Pacific complete.

I took in a long breath of Pacific air and let it out in the loudest sound I could muster from my body and soul. Wallace and Gill watched behind me, smiling. When I finished they walked up to join me. The three of us stood, arms on each other's shoulders, and screamed out at the ocean. They had both been to the Pacific before, but they knew how I felt. Besides, no matter whether some of us had been here before or not, we had made the drive together and completed our goal. We had fulfilled our destiny and reached the light at the end of the three-thousand-mile tunnel. It was a cultural goal, one strived for by any American who wanted to travel across their homeland to see all of its diversity and beautiful potential. In fact it was a goal for any eager, curious traveler, anywhere in the world. We made it and I was proud. I was proud of myself, proud of my friends, proud of being part of a timeless American tradition. The only thing left to do now, was to keep going.

Back in the car, we reset our compasses. North was the new west as we headed up the famous Highway 1. This is a road strictly for pleasure driving. When planning on getting somewhere fast, this is the wrong road to take, because going faster than twenty mph will most likely end with the car smashed at the bottom of a cliff (there is no guardrail to stop this from happening). The road wound in and out of the incredibly uneven coast, so our car could not go more than fifty feet without hitting another hairpin turn. Wallace, still high as a kite (like the rest of us), took full advantage of this winding mess, pushing his Suburu to its limit. That was probably a bad idea due to the delicate condition of our little vessel, but get Wallace on an exciting windy road and all common sense flies out the window. With a perpetual grin plastered on his face, he screeched around the corners while Gill and I held on for the ride.

Back in high school, Wallace used to pick me up at school in his previous Suburu. We would smoke a bowl, crank up something like, Rage Against the Machine (in the same stereo system), and Wallace would go tearing through the back roads of rural Massachusetts. In that area, the roads are either gravel or poorly paved and all in the middle of the wilderness. Wallace would tear around corners, maintaining the same grin. Meanwhile I would be clutching the passenger seat, terrifyingly stoned. It took me a while to get used to this. My clearest memories of that time were thinking quite extensively about death. It was something that felt very close at the time, ready to meet us around the next hairpin turn. But to his credit, Wallace was a hell of a good driver, stoned or not (maybe even better in the former). I learned to trust him, reasoning that he had superhuman powers that gave him the ability to see around the blind turns and use the appropriate reflexes in case of unforeseen obstacles.

Now on Highway 1, in the exact same situation, ripping around corners, clutching the seat, stoned, I was not thinking as much about death. This allowed me to enjoy the amazing scenery as we weaved in and out of the cliffs. Looking down and around the rocky coast, I was reminded of travels I had made to other coastal regions like the high, serene cliffs of Cinque Terre in the Italian Riviera, or the grassy landscape and rocky shores of eastern Ireland, between Dublin and Belfast. The California coast was a hybrid of these places, adding a smooth golden finish. My breath was taken away, but it was questionable whether that was caused by the view, or of Wallace's driving.

As we drove my phone rang. *Who could be calling at such a time? Don't they know I'm busy working on exploration?* It was Sam. I had forgotten about my poor friend, whom we had barely missed in St. Paul. At this point he must have moved out and gone back east to Massachusetts.

"Hello?"

"Hey man, it's Sam. How's the trip?"

"Fantastic!" I exclaimed. "I'm currently driving up Highway 1 in Northern Cali. We're driving along the coastline. It's amazing. I couldn't be any better, in fact. How are you fine sir on this wonderful day?" *Shut up Evan, you're stoned and rambling.*

"Awesome!" said Sam. "I'm actually in Southern Oregon near the border, driving south to San Francisco."

I sat up. "Wait, what??"

"Yeah, kind of random, but after graduation, my girlfriend and I decided to fly to Vancouver, rent a car, and drive down the coast. I think your trip motivated me a little."

"Really. Tell me more..."

My mind was scheming as Sam continued. "After we reach San Francisco we're heading back up to Portland to meet Lena's sister, then we go back to Vancouver."

"Who's Lena?"

"That's my girlfriend."

"Oh, cool," I said. "So wait, let me get this straight. You're about to cross into California heading south, and we're in NorCal heading north."

"Um, I don't know what NorCal is, but yeah, that sounds about right."

Wallace and Gill were shooting me curious glances.

"Well then shit!" I yelled. "We're meeting up!"

"Yeah!"

"Yeah! Fuck yeah! Hold on, let me look at a map." I took out the NorCal map and looked for a good middle place to meet. I saw a town called, Mendocino a few hours north of us on Highway 1 and a few hours south of the state line. And with an enchanting name like Mendocino, how could we go wrong? "Hey Sam, do you think you could make it to Mendocino on Highway 1 by tonight?"

"Um, I think so, I'm not really sure. We're inland on Route 5 right now, but I'm looking at a map and I think we can cross over."

"Awesome! I'll give you a call when we're close to Mendocino."

"Okay, cool. I guess I'll see you later then!"

"Looking forward to it!"

Wow. How did this happen? "Hey guys!" I yelled. Wallace and Gill turned to the back. "Damnit Wallace, keep your eyes on the road!"

"Sorry."

"What's up?" asked Gill.

"I have a destination for us tonight. It's a town called, Mendocino where we're going to meet up with Sam."

"Cool," said Gill.

"Sounds good," said Wallace. "How do we get there?"

"Just keep going," I said. "And step on it!"

Wallace grew a grin.

"Wait!" I said. "Don't step on it! You're driving just fine."

"Aww, you got my hopes up."

This fortuitous occasion of happening shit, reminded me of Yosemite, and our lucky run-in with Casey's family. I imagined that by now their trek through the backcountry was finishing and Casey would be heading north to his new job in Oregon. I recalled back in Massachusetts when we ruled out the idea of visiting him. Then low and behold one week later, we found ourselves in Yosemite, a better place to meet up then most places on this great earth. And now fancy this. Another second chance given with a good friend whom we missed a week ago and now we were about to cross paths on the West Coast! I'm no religious man, but I was starting to believe that my wise-ass comment about the "road trip gods" was not unfounded.

The road continued to wind and it seemed like time had slowed down as much as our car. We endlessly weaved in and out, while sometimes passing small towns with a few houses planted on the cliffs, along with a general store. The sun was arching downward, and its final destination would be past the end of the earth, extinguished by the cold Pacific.

It was late afternoon when we were closing in on Mendocino and I grabbed my phone. I noticed that my cell service was only picking up a few bars. *Uh-oh, better make this call fast.* I dialed. Ring...Ring...Ring... "Hello?"

"Hey Sam."

"Hello?"

"Sam!"

"Oh hey."

"We're almost in Mendocino. Where are you?"

"You're in Mendocino?"

"No!" I yelled. "Almost in Mendocino! Where are you?"

"We're um, almost turn—...oute five—...ouple hours—"

"What? Sam? Shit." I lost him. We were still on the windy cliff roads. Natural beauty and cell service never mixed well. I figured we had to wait until we were in town before I could get some cell bars again.

The sun was low in the still-blue sky as we entered Mendocino. It was similar to the other quaint towns set up on the cliffs that we had passed, but a tad bigger. We were hungry and it was almost time for tip-off of another Celtics-Lakers clash. We drove up a hill that looked like one of the main streets and found a good 'ol Irish pub. The street went from east to west and the bar was at the top of the hill to the east. The hill sloped down to the west and eventually off a cliff and down, down, down, crash. From outside of the bar I looked at the sun still reflecting heavily on the water, shooting off millions of glints in every direction. A far off glint would briefly meet my eye but it was never strong enough to make me squint, only close enough to make me grin.

The bar was packed with small groups of eager adults standing around, happily clasping their pints. It was either the town's tourist bar, or the only bar in town. We managed to squeeze ourselves into a small table under the TV. Our successful day called for a pitcher of their local microbrew, appropriately named, Mendocino Brewing Company. This unassumingly delicious elixir helped wash down our succulent burgers and greasy fries. We rooted on our boys, who sadly lost (to the approval of most of the patrons).

I looked at my phone: no missed call from Sam and still no cell service. I walked out of the bar and managed to get a bar, so I called.

Ring...Ring...Ring... "Hey, this is Sam, leave me a—"

Shit, voicemail. How on earth am I going to explain this? Beeeep: "Uh, hey Sam, we're in Mendocino at this bar. It's an Irish place on the main street. I'm trying to look for the name of the street, I can't seem to find it...I guess I'm not sure how much longer we'll be staying here either." Then it hit me. *Wait, where* are *we staying tonight?* "So, um, I'll call you back when I get more details of where we're staying. Call me when you get to Mendocino." I hung up and stood there wondering. All the questions fell on the table at once. How were we going to meet up with Sam? Where were we going to sleep? And when we found a place, how would we get in touch with Sam?

These pressing issues were immediately halted when I turned around and looked west. The sun was creeping down over the horizon, radiating shades of orange, red, and purple over the water. All thoughts and body mechanisms left me and I was a drooling statue, staring out at this inspiring act of nature. I couldn't believe these people got a view like this every day. *Would you ever get sick of amazing sunsets? No, probably not.*

I stood there until the yellow orb sunk into the sea and waited a few minutes more for my bodily functions to return, finding relief in the fact that I had not soiled myself. I walked back to the bar. Wallace was out front smoking a cigarette, laughing with two guys. They looked like nice, clean cut gents in their mid-twenties.

"Hey Wallace," I said, "we have to talk. We haven't figured out—"

Wallace turned to me. "Hey! Evan!" Then he turned to the two guys. "This is one of my road trip buddies, Evan."

They said hello, we shook hands, and I turned back to Wallace. "So we need to figure out—"

Wallace ignored me. "You guys are from San Diego, right?"

They nodded. "Yeah, we're up here for the week going fishing."

"Sweet! Fishing! Oh uh, do you guys fish in that, you know," Wallace gave them a nudge and a wink, "secret spot?" Then he let out one of his famous bellowing, mischievous laughs.

They laughed too. I liked where this was going. They shook their heads. "Noooo, that's just where we go to um, you know." And then all three laughed in unison.

Then Wallace turned to me, and spoke almost in a whisper. "They were telling me about this sweet spot by the water where we can smoke. They said they got some really good weed from SoCal."

"Okay Wallace, that's great but—"

Wallace lifted his hand. "Oh, and they said they're staying at this campground that's all booked up but they could sneak us in."

"Oh." I said. "Really?"

Then all four of us laughed in unison. Gill walked out of the bar and soon there were five laughing in unison.

Wallace's skill for "weed networking" was getting down to a science. I just hoped this wasn't going to fall through like our potential rafting trip in Jackson. At least we didn't have to worry about the weather.

As the sun's remaining light left the sky, the San Diego Dudes were ready to go and we got in our car to follow. Then I remembered Sam. I took out my phone: nothing. I sighed and put it back in my pocket. We followed behind them and headed back the way we came on Highway 1.

After a couple miles we turned off onto another road, then another, and my bearings were off and I would not have been able to give Sam directions if my life depended on it. I took out my phone again: no reception.

Another ten minutes down a dark road and we pulled over. We got out and walked to their car. There was no sign of life around. They gave us a confidently sneaky look and said, "This way." We followed them down the road for two-dozen paces. Our way was slightly illuminated by a clear, bright moon. There was no sound around us, save for a not too distant drone of crashing waves and swishing water. It didn't seem to be coming from far below like usual, but closer to our level.

The Dudes turned an immediate right through an inconspicuous break in the trees where a small dirt path led us downward. We walked in single file down a steep decline with a few fallen logs that gave steady ground every few yards. It wasn't a long path and before we knew it, we were standing on a beach with the ocean less then twenty feet away. This little beach was set in a cove with rock walls jutting out on either side of us, with no more than fifty yards in between. Some lone rocks rose out of the water in front of us, their jagged outlines silhouetted by the light of the moon. It was one of those perfectly picturesque, secluded lagoons, which is supposed to only be imagined in one's hopes and dreams. "We come here every night," said the San Diego Dudes.

We sat ourselves on some logs and each party pulled out their goods. One San Diego Dude pulled out a cigar and he packed it with our smorgasbord of Cali bud under the light of the moon. We passed around the blunt that peacefully merged SoCal to NorCal as we fixated on the picturesque Pacific. The stars came out and lit up the sky, as well as casting tiny reflections on the rippling water.

This interesting encounter demonstrated the power of this crystal-green substance. Without it, we wouldn't have been in this magical place. If we weren't smoking, there would be no reason for these guys to take us there. A place like that would only be frequented by romantic encounters, or people wanting to dispose of something illegal in the sea. It would not have made sense for these guys to say, "Hey, you guys seem nice, want to check out a cool secluded spot by the ocean?"

We would have either said, "Sorry, we don't participate in gay orgies," or, "Listen buddy, if you got something to say to me, you can say it right here!" Weed can often be that brilliant social bridge which allows you to comfortably get taken to a strange place by strangers (who in this case happened to be very nice, straight, non-violent individuals).

After the blunt was finished and most of the kooky stoned talk dissolved, we hiked back up and followed them toward the hopeful campground. I got a bit nervous, realizing that all details were left out of the plan of sneaking us into a campground. Didn't campgrounds know how to avoid scofflaws like us?

A few more turns and we arrived. Sure enough it was late and the check-in station had been closed for the night. We followed the San Diego Dudes to their spot where there was ample room for us to set up camp. Easy as—getting high and eating—pie.

I took out my phone for one last effort. No missed call, one bar. I called: straight to voicemail. I left him a message similar to the one I had left Casey in Tioga Pass. I said we were at a campsite, I thought it was called this, and I thought we had taken this and that road. I even went back to the check-in station and posted up a note that said "SAM" in big letters and notified him of which campsite we were at. If Casey could find us in the middle of the Sierras, Sam could find us here. I was sure of it.

We pitched the tent, and I took one last glance at the starry sky before heading in. I could hear that our campsite was close to the ocean. On top of my exhaustion, weed, alcohol, and any other sleep inducing causes, what helped most in lulling me to sleep, was the unmistakably unmatched sound of the crashing waves.

DAY 13

I woke up to a chill, which could be categorized as brisk. This is in a milder catagory than say, deadly, which was the kind of chill I woke up to in Jackson. I stuck my head out of the tent and a cold, wet breeze hit my face. It was mid-morning and at first glance the area looked overcast. But I noticed that I could see chilly water particles floating through the air, which meant we were in the middle of a cloud of fog. This fog was thick but not thick enough to obstruct my immediate surroundings. I noticed that we made a significant decline in elevation last night. Cliffs shrouded in pines rose up on all sides except west. The campground was set in between these cliffs on a flat area that extended out one hundred yards to the sleep-inducing seashore. There was a tall bridge suspended directly above the shore that ran along the tops of the cliffs. I assumed we came from somewhere up there last night, although I did not remember crossing a bridge.

I put on pants and a sweatshirt and walked down to the shore. The beach was made up of dark-colored rocks, which met the grey, frothy water when it lapped lightly onto them in a rhythmically oceanic motion.

A man walked by with his Labrador, giving a smile and a nod. He wore a waterproof windbreaker and dirty blue jeans. I imagined this must have been the normal morning look around these parts throughout the year.

It was a serene morning in Northern California. I could have stood around watching this cove for hours, but I felt like I was missing something. Like something was misplaced or forgotten. Like—*Shit! Sam!* I walked back over to the check-in station. The note I had put up last night was still there, untouched. *Damn. Missed him in St. Paul, and just barely in Mendocino. I hope he didn't have to drive all the way off his course just to miss me... At least he has the chance to continue on Highway 1 down the coast.* I grabbed the note, crushed it in my hands, and walked back to the tent.

Wallace and Gill were groggily stepping out of the tent. I watched their reactions to the chilly fog. Gill gave a curious look around and nodded, intrigued. Wallace hugged himself, rubbed his arms, said, "Fuck!" and ran to the car to get warm clothes.

Gill looked at me with a smile. "Breakfast?"

"Oh ya."

"I'll grab the stove."

"I got the food."

"I'll get the bowls!" yelled Wallace as he hiked up his pants and reached into the car.

Before you could say, "Holy shit! Is that a Sasquatch?" we were enjoying huevos rancheros and toast on our wooden picnic table. A man in the campsite next to ours was sitting in a lawn chair outside his rickety RV, watching us.

I looked over and nodded. "Good morning."

"Good morning!" he said. "Hey! You fellas are some campin' professionals! I'm impressed!"

We gave each other a surprised look and laughed. "Thanks!"

Then I stopped and looked around. *Wait a minute, he's right!* I recalled how all this was handled back on our first expedition in the Badlands. This time we set up the stove and cooked with ease, everyone knowing their task and getting it done with precise efficiency. In the beginning of the trip I called us three semi-clueless campers combined to make one decent camper. But I felt safe to say that we had risen to the level of three decent campers, combined into one kick-ass camping machine. I was looking forward to later in the trip when we could show off our talents in the real wilderness.

After breakfast we packed up and sat on the picnic table with a map of our NorCal playground. "So," I started, "we all agree that we don't want to go crazy with driving up the coast. Right?"

"Correct," agreed my compadres.

"This isn't South Dakota, this is the Pacific Northwest. We need to enjoy it."

"No objections."

Mendocino was a decent ways up Highway 1 and in an hour or two, we would reach the end and hit Route 101. Route 101 would pick up where Highway 1 left off and take us up the coast all the way to Canada (if we wanted). "101 won't be the fastest route, but that's what we want to take all the way, right?"

"Yes. Minus some detours."

"Of course."

"We still plan to hit Portland and Seattle, right?"

"Indubitably."

"That reminds me," said Wallace. "I need to call a buddy of mine in Seattle. He said he can hook us up with a place to stay and he would take us around Olympic National Park for a few days."

"Awesome!" I said. "But we're getting ahead of ourselves. Let's figure out a destination tonight. It looks like we're five hours from the Oregon state line and the redwoods are around here." I pointed just below the California-Oregon border.

"Oh! That also reminds me," said Gill. "My friend—you guys know who I'm talking about."

"The space-time inventor?"

"Yeah, that guy."

"Of course, praise be him."

"He told me about this crazy looking canyon in the redwoods that's made out of ferns and I think he mentioned camping."

"Bam! Let's do it."

Destination: Fern Canyon, Redwood National Park.

We would have thanked the San Diego Dudes but they were already packed up and gone, no doubt on some early morning fishing expedition. After exiting the campground, we drove up a steep wooded hill. At the top was the bridge over the campground, but we headed the opposite way which took us north. After a few easy turns we were back on Highway 1. It seemed so simple and navigable in the daytime. I imagined Sam searching for us last night and driving over that bridge, then turning to his girlfriend and saying, "I give up. This is pointless." I hoped that he would have called eventually and told me what happened, but there was still no message on my phone. *Oh well.*

It was late morning and the fog was getting burned off by the rising sun. Soon we were on repeat of yesterday: winding coastal road under blue skies. This lasted for a brief time before the road veered inland. The landscape here was much different. We had entered the coast from golden hops. Now we exited into thick green forests:

Welcome to the Pacific Northwest.

The road was equally windy, making one-hundred-and-eighty-degree turns up smooth roads through dense forest. The strong sun shone through the trees, enhancing the green colors. It was a pure green forest, probably kept fresh and moist by the constant fog. *Mmmm, oxygen.*

Wallace was right at home, bending the car around the tight corners with so much force that at points I thought I could hear the car groan with pain. It was a gradual ascent toward the top of a hill and when the top was reached, we were out of the woods and had made it to a T. We were in the same situation with two signs in front of us pointing north and south, except these signs read "101." Something else on the side of the road caught our eye. It was a big touristy sign that pointed down a small road, advertising some big tree. "The Drive Through Tree!" it said. "Experience a tree so large you can drive through it!" We looked at each other with similar unenthusiastic frowns. "Does anyone here want to waste our time doing this?" A unanimous "No" resounded through the car. I was sure we would get our fill of big trees in the redwoods. We turned onto 101 North.

Route 101 was straighter and wider than Highway 1. It wasn't as exciting, but also wasn't close to the size of an interstate. Route 5 is the main north/south interstate on the West Coast. On that road you could speed down as fast as your heart desired from Canada to Mexico. But judging by the map, it looked dull. It took an hour's drive inland to get to it and there isn't much going on over there. Those windmills in the middle of the state were cool, but that was about it. Although that big dumb interstate should not have been our concern if we stuck to the plan.

101 was beautiful in its own way, with evergreens lining the road and dense, hilly forests in the background. I squinted my eyes into the hills,

looking out for any patchy areas that might be marijuana farms. After all, we were now in Humboldt County, the weed growing capitol of the US. Every so often I poked my head out of the window and sniffed the air. I shook my head at the other two. "Nope, can't smell anything."

Then I had an idea. "Hey, maybe we should go on a little expedition to find a farm!"

"Are you crazy?" Wallace said. "Do you want to get shot?"

"Yeah," agreed Gill, "I heard growers have all kinds of booby traps, like razor blade wires that will slice your eyeballs in the woods if you get too close."

"Nevermind then," I said defeated. That would be my last attempt at any kind of dispensary/weed farm tourism for Evan, on this trip.

We came upon an exit for another tourist attraction called, the Avenue of the Giants. "My friend told me about this too," said Gill. "It's supposed to be a beautiful drive through big trees." That was enough to sway our opinions so we turned off. By the looks of the map, it appeared to be a side road that ran parallel to Route 101 for a ways, and met back up with it eventually. It looked windy, similar to Highway 1. This was a concern because it would add time to our day, which we arguably did not have. After we turned off the exit, we stopped to have lunch and decide what to do.

We were pulled off the road in a gravel alcove, surrounded by green forest that gave us a cool shade with no breeze. We set up shop on the hood, with an assorted buffet of bread, mustard, new hot sauce, summer sausage, and a big block of cheddar. We took out the playground map and had a business lunch, eating as we discussed.

"It's just past noon," I said. "This road looks like it will take us about an extra hour to drive on, that is if we don't make too many stops."

"No," said Gill, "I think it's going to take longer. Look at <burp> excuse me, look at this distance on Route 101 and look at how windy the Avenue is."

"I would say if it's windy, it's probably sweet," chimed in Wallace.

"I don't doubt that," said Gill. "But if we take it, we won't have much light to set up camp. We're still at least four hours from Fern Canyon."

"Yeah, the way I see it, we can either spend time on the Avenue of the Giants and barely make it to the fern place by dark, or we can get back on 101 and make it to the fern place with time to chill in the ferns," I said.

Gill and I turned to Wallace. "What do you think?"

Wallace stared at the map and chewed pensively. Then he swallowed and took in a breath. "Well, this place looks sweet, but the fern place sounds *really* sweet, and on the map it looks like it's near the beach. So overall it sounds sweeter than the sweetness of the Giants."

We nodded in full agreement. "Ferns and beach sound fantastic. Let's do it."

The fellowship had completed its delegation. We finished our sandwiches, I got in the front passenger seat with the map, and we backtracked—dare I say it?—*south*, for only a couple miles and got back on 101 *north. Phew, that wasn't too painful.* A nice cruise for a few hours through Humboldt and we would be relaxing on the ferny beach in no time.

I studied the map as we drove. I noticed that we would be driving through a town called, Eureka. "Hey guys!" I announced. "Cali has a Eureka too!"

"Cool, I wonder if they have WRANGLERS there." We all chuckled. I was sure that everyone spent a minute with their own reminiscent moment of the enchanting deserts of Nevada.

I knew we needed some good tunes to help us with our NorCal cruise, so I grabbed my CD book and leafed through it. I figured something reggae-oriented might be appropriate to go along with the Humboldt theme. *Keep it classic with Bob Marley? Maybe, or I could go with Burning—*

"Oh Shit!" Wallace startled me. I shot my head up in time to see the car ahead of us make a sudden swerve, almost hitting the guardrail. Wallace braked and made a quick swerving meneuver to the other lane to keep a safe distance. Then the car swerved back into its lane. "Wow," said Wallace, "that was almost bad. Damn Humboldt stoners, can't even drive high. What a bunch of amateurs!" We all chuckled and I looked back down at the CD's.

The next thing that happened made me look up and drop the CD's on the floor because of what I both felt and heard. There was a loud "POP" and the car canted over toward the passenger side. "FUCK!" yelled Wallace louder than ever before and he gripped the steering wheel, trying to keep the car steady. It remained hunched over on the passenger side and Wallace tried his best to slow down while veering toward the shoulder. The next words I heard Wallace say burned my eardrums and were eternally branded into my brain. "That's it. That's the end of the trip."

My body sat tense and still as the car wobbled to a stop on the side of the road. There was a moment of silent shock before Gill spoke. "What the fuck was that?"

"I don't fucking know," said Wallace, "but it's not good. Not fucking good."

I still couldn't speak. Too many emotions were running through me. Denial: *It was a pop, probably just a flat. We're fine*—Anger: *Wallace, you fucking bastard. How can you just jump to such a negative conclusion? How are you so sure that the trip is over? I'm sick of your bullshit pessimism*—Acceptance: *He probably knows his car well enough to make such a brash conclusion. I guess we've seen enough on this trip, sucks it had to end like this but it was fun while it lasted*—Confusion: *Wait, what the fuck just happened?*

We got out and inspected the car, walking around and checking the tires. All the tires appeared to be in tact. The entire car seemed to be in tact (from the outside). That raised my fear ten-fold. A simple popped tire would be an easy fix. We'd be back on the road in a couple hours. All of our faces mirrored each other's as we stood around the crippled car scratching our heads.

"Well someone's got to call Triple-A."

"Where the hell are we?" We looked around. There were no signs anywhere. We were on a road with nothing around except trees, hills, and weed farms. I thought for a second about walking into the woods and climbing the tallest tree I could find, then jumping off making sure to hit every branch on the way down.

Gill picked up his phone and made the call. "Yes, hello, our car broke down. We're on Route 101...um, hold on." Gill looked at us. "Where are we?"

"I don't fucking know!" yelled Wallace as he stared at the crippled carcass of a car.

Gill talked back into the phone. "Um, I think we're about five miles north of the Avenue of the Giants exit...Okay, thank you, we'll be here."

I watched Wallace solemnly pace back and forth, looking at the ground and kicking gravel. *Is he right? Is this the end of our trip?* I thought back on what we had accomplished. We had successfully driven across the country and reached the Pacific Ocean. That couldn't be taken away from us. *But damnit! There's still so much more to see! We're only halfway through our expedition.* I needed to stop thinking about that. I was sure whatever was wrong with the car was fixable. But at what cost, was the next question. A tennis match continued in my head for a good while, before the tow truck came.

The piece-of-shit-asshole Suburu got hitched onto the bed of the tow truck and we all crammed into the front cab with the driver. It had one of those long, flat seats and we sat in a straight, cozy line. The driver was a soft-spoken young man with tired eyes, maybe a little older than us. He told us that he grew up in Humboldt County. He gave us truthful, unenthusiastic answers to our questions with no add-ons.

"Do you like Humboldt County?"

"Yeah, it's a pretty good place to live."

"I imagine the weather's pretty nice."

"Yeah, it's okay most of the time."

"Where are we going?"

"Eureka. That's the closest Suburu shop."

"Oh yeah? What's Eureka like?"

"It's alright I guess. I go to this bar downtown every so often."

"We're from Massachusetts."

"Oh, never been out that way."

"Yeah, it's pretty nice."

"Okay, I'll have to check it out one of these days..."

Jeez, what a tough crowd.

We drove through more forest and the road was straight, angling downward. The lower we went in elevation, the darker and cloudier the sky grew. I bid farewell to sunshine and good times.

We reached the Eureka city limits and were thrown back into "anytown USA," with traffic lights and franchises spread as far as we could see. We pulled into a Suburu dealership. The driver unhitched the car, then left us for dead. The sky was grey and it was colder here. I pulled out my goddamn sweatshirt.

A couple mechanics came out and Wallace went over to speak with them. Gill and I stood there shaking our heads. Gill turned to me. "What are you thinking, man?"

"Me?" I asked. "Shit. I don't know."

"Do you think this is it?"

I sighed. "I hope not." I turned to him. "Do you?"

Gill shrugged. "It's not looking good. Where the hell are we?"

We looked around. To our right was a strip mall and after that was an Applebees. That was about it.

"Fuck, I'm cold."

"Me too."

We walked into the dealership and sat in the reception area waiting for Wallace.

He joined us eventually and sat down. "They're going to check it out quickly to see if they can give an estimate on the damage. They're closing soon so they can't do anything today.

There goes the fern canyon.

"They said they can probably work on it early tomorrow morning, so we need to find a hotel or something. Apparently there are a few in walking distance from here."

Great, they must be wedged between the Applebees and the Dollar Store.

We solemnly sat for another ten minutes before the mechanic walked in. We were the worried parents and he was the doctor coming to give us our sick child's prognosis. *Is she gonna' live Doc? Tell me she's gonna' live!* The mechanics facial expression as he walked in looked more optimistic than the classic, "I'm sorry but there was nothing we could do" face. This made me less nervous. We got up and clutched each other, bracing ourselves for his verdict.

"Well guys," said the oil-stained Doc, "it doesn't look too bad. You seem to have busted a joint in the wheel axle. We can replace it tomorrow morning, probably a two hundred dollar fix and we can have you guys back on the road by early afternoon." A resounding "phew!" went through the room. *I could live with two hundred dollars, no problem.*

We took some stuff from the car and headed down the lonesome road. But things didn't look as bad now. We passed the Applebees, and after were some dingy-looking motels. They sat there with their nasty jowls gaping open, ready to prey on the desperation that came off of this foul strip of concrete. I ended up being wrong, we were wedged between Applebees and a *gas station. Oh, I remember gas stations. Those are places that people with the luxury of* working *cars get to use.*

We checked into the motel. It was called, "Lucky 7's," or some similar name of false promise. It was one of those long, two-story buildings where you walk down the outdoor hallway to get to your room. We brought our stuff to the room and immediately left to go fulfill the urge to eat and drink heavily. At least this time we didn't have to worry about a designated driver.

We went straight into—you guessed it—Applebees and ordered some food and drinks. It turned out to be happy hour—at least something was going in our favor. We proceeded to order pitchers of Blue Moon (the most exotic beer they had on tap) and Bud Light, and feasted on buffalo chicken bites and fiesta chipotle chicken sandwiches. It was a fucking fiesta for sure.

"So we're set back one day, that's not bad," I said.

"Don't jump to conclusions," interrupted Wallace.

I looked at him. "What do you mean?"

"I mean they don't know exactly what happened. They're not going to know until they get under there and really start to work on it."

"Wallace, buddy, it's going to be fine!" I slapped him on the back. "We'll be back on the road in no time!"

Wallace's face turned grim. "I don't know man, I don't know."

I could tell that he knew that whatever the mechanic said was not the whole truth. Wallace knew his car, it was an extension of himself. I couldn't ignore the fact that he had maintained this underlying melancholy throughout our trip, always being a little more on edge. He must have known something like this was bound to happen, ever since he had the problem in Vermont. It was just a matter of time until the shit and the fan met each other in messy matrimony.

"It was those sharp turns on Highway 1 that probably did it," continued Wallace. "I knew I was taking them too hard." He looked down and shook his head.

"Don't think that way, man," said Gill. "If it was bound to happen, it was bound to happen. It's not your fault."

Wallace kept shaking his head. "I'm just fucking sick of this car. I can't keep dealing with all the problems it throws at me."

Gill and I sat nodding our heads in silence. What could we say? "You're right Wallace, it's just too much to deal with. Let's go home." That was something I could never bring myself to say. Hell, I didn't care if the roof flew off. I was going to stay on the road for as long as I possibly could. But this wasn't something I could say. Unfortunately (yet fortunately) it was not my car, thus not my choice to make. I wasn't sure how Gill felt but we both kept silent.

"I'm sick of it. I'm just sick of it," Wallace took a big swig and finished his glass. "Well fuck it. Let's get drunk!"

Gill and I smiled. "That's the spirit!"

We left Crapplebees and went across the street to the gas station convenience store, where they conveniently sold thirty-racks of Pabst Blue Ribbon. We lugged it back to the room and proceeded to raucously consume thirty cans of PBR with some Cali bud thrown in.

Gill and I are Jewish, Wallace is Scottish, but that night, we were all Irish, mourning our car the proper way: by celebrating. We laughed and screamed, reminiscing on all the past events of the last two weeks.

"Remember that drive through Minnesota? I thought that farmland would never end!"

"Evan, you wouldn't remember that, you were passed out."

"Yeah, well you guys don't remember Wisconsin. That state was nothing but rain and traffic barriers. And I won't mention all the times I stalled."

"I don't remember that," said Wallace.

I laughed. "Really? I knew it! The whole time you were talking in your sleep, telling me to keep trying!"

"Are you serious? Does that mean I was 'backsleep driving?'"

"Yes! That's exactly what you were doing! Besides that, I think I drove pretty well."

"Yeah right! Remember in Michigan? It took you like twenty minutes to get the car started!"

"Whatever, that jerky was so good."

"Ooooooh! I forgot how good that was! It melted in my mouth!"

The festivities moved out of the room to the outside hallway. "Guys, I'm so glad they gave us a room on the second floor," I said. "Look at this glorious view we have of beautiful Eureka!"

We all gave an eggagerated gaze out at Eureka's magnificence. "Let's see, over there I can spot the bright Applebees sign. And over there I think I see—is that a Mobil? Or is it BP? I can't tell. Gill, fetch my binoculars!"

Our laughing slowly died and we grew less ironic and more solemn. "What the hell guys? How did we go from mountains and ocean to neon signs? I didn't travel across the country to check out the menu discrepancies between Applebees East and Applebees West."

"I know."

"I have to admit," said Wallace. We turned to him and listened intently. "I was pretty skeptical about this trip. I was worried about the car—for good reason—and I was worried about just being prepared. I didn't think we had enough planned, nor enough places lined up for us to crash. But I trusted you guys. And I realized that all we needed to do was to get on the road. Everything else followed naturally. And it convinced me that it was okay not to have a plan." Gill and I nodded as Wallace continued. "All that was important was communicating to each other, working together to put the tent up, and get the supplies. Or find that place on the map while someone else drove and the other made sandwiches." We all agreed and as I looked closely at the big bearded Scottish man, I swore I saw a tiny drunken tear well up in his bright blue eye. "And I have to say, if this car doesn't end up making it, I think I'm fine with that. Because this was a hell of a trip, and I'll never forget it."

"I couldn't agree more," I said, "and I'll take this sentimental moment to thank you guys for taking the chance with me on my big, ambitious idea. Remember when we all sat in my house back in March and I first brought it up?"

"Yeah," said Gill, "I didn't think it was going to happen."

"Me neither," said Wallace.

"Well when I say I want to do something, I fucking mean it," I said defiantly.

"I'm really glad we got to do this guys," said Gill. "I—" Gill paused and we knew what was coming.

"Say it."

"I—"

"Say it damnit!"

"Okay! I love you guys!"

"Ahhh! He said it!"

"Shut up! It's true!"

The rest of the night continued like this until there was no more alcohol to be consumed. After destroying the hotel room with beer cans, we passed out, sufficiently, sentimentally drunk.

DAY 14

I woke up to a phone ring and a headache. I didn't have to look at my watch to know it was early. I knew because my head was still spinning, meaning I had not slept long enough to make the full transformation from drunk to hungover. It was Gill's phone but I knew it was for Wallace. My eyes were shut but my ears were wide open. Gill answered and sure enough he turned and said, "Wallace, Wallace it's for you."

I heard a groggy Wallace answer. His deep voice was naturally deeper from waking up, and his added hangover made him sound like a constipated Alaskan brown bear. "Mmmmrrrr-h-hello? Oh hi....What? Really??...So it's another hundred to do the other wheel? Um, yeah sure I guess that's fine, go ahead."

I rolled over in pain. That meant three hundred dollars and *two* axles to fix. *Whatever, as long as we get back on the road by some decent hour.*

"Okay, thanks. Yeah, let me know."

Silence. I went back to sleep.

I was sure that I wasn't asleep for very long before I was woken again by the phone. My head was still pounding, harder now from stress.

Wallace knew to pick up. "Hello? Yeah. Uh huh. Uh huh...Really. No, no, no. Actually stop all the work. Yeah, just stop, I'll be there soon."

I picked up my heavy head and looked over. Gill and Wallace were sitting up.

Wallace looked bewildered, staring wide-eyed across the room past the mess of empty beer cans, into space. "Wow."

"What?"

"They said they've never seen anything like this."

"Like what?"

"The entire bottom of my car is rusted through."

"Seriously?"

Wallace pounded the wall beside him. "Where is my goddamn mechanic when I need him! This wouldn't even be a big deal if I was home!"

"What's wrong?"

"Apparently the joint that broke off is rusted into the axle. So they're afraid that if they try to pry it out, the entire rusty axle will split in half."

"And that would be bad?" I asked like a nagging, naïve girlfriend.

Wallace turned to me, his blue eyes piercing holes in my retinas. "Let's just say, *you* can't afford to fix that."

I nodded obediently. "Right."

We sat there groggily thinking.

"Fuck!" said Wallace. "Mechanics deal with rust all the time in New England! But apparently in perfect little *California*, it doesn't even exist!"

My headache started pounding like someone was playing a bass drum in my cerebral cortex.

Wallace got up. "I'm going to head over there and check it out. I suggest you two keep yourselves occupied for a while."

Gill and I moved our dumbstruck faces up and down. Wallace threw some clothes on while mumbling and swearing to himself and was out the door. I looked at Gill. "Breakfast?"

"Yep."

We left the hotel in search of some place halfway decent to eat. Although before we made it too far, I had to run back in to the hotel room to grab my sweatshirt, because I had forgotten we were still in the cold, cloudy void of hell they call, Eureka, California. We found a place along Route 101 not too far from the motel with a decent brunch setting. It had a crunchy, organic NorCal vibe. Not my favorite type of place, but at least it helped to remind me that I was in a specific part of the country and not American-Applebees-purgatory. We ordered some organic, free-range omelets with healthy things inside.

"So Gilly Bob," I said, "do you think we're stuck here?"

Gill looked at me with a nervous smile, then down at his free-trade coffee, stirring into the organic abyss. "I hope not." He remained staring and stirring and took a deep breath. "I kind of agree with Wallace though."

I furrowed my brow. "What do you mean?"

"I'd be okay with heading back. I'm pretty content with what we've done and to be honest, I miss my girlfriend."

"Yeah," I said, like I knew what he was saying, even though I could not believe what I was hearing.

"I also need to start getting ready," he continued.

"Ready for what?"

"I didn't tell you? I'm going to Guatemala for a few weeks for research."

"Really? That's awesome!" This was news that I actually was happy for.

"I'm flying down with my professor. We got a grant, which I just heard about when I was down in San Jose."

"Wow, that's great news! When are you going?"

"July."

"That's soon, isn't it?" I asked. "What day is it? We're still in June, right?"

"It's June twenty-first."

Cool, the first day of Summer! Wait, why do I have a sweatshirt on if it's the first day of Summer? Oh Right, because nothing in this country makes sense and especially not in this *hellhole.* "That's great to hear. I'm happy for you," I said.

"Thanks. What are you doing when you get back?" Gill asked. "You got any plans?"

I sat there frozen. *Plans? Plans? You mean besides where we plan to pitch a tent tonight?* Sure I had plans. I had plans to move to a nice place, plans to get a nice job I didn't hate, plans to make money for more road trips. But since graduation, all I've thought about was this trip. I stared into my fresh squeezed orange juice. *Should I be making plans? Is this trip over? Do I need to start moving on with my life?* Of course I had *plans*. Everyone has *plans*. But my plan was to make sure the car got fixed in a timely fashion because we should have been in the goddamn redwoods of Northern California by now! Instead we were hopelessly getting older in bumfuck Eureka living off organic omelets and fiesta chicken sandwiches, or whatever else could be scrounged up within a safe walking distance. Plans? My plan was to get the flying fuck out of this overcast hellhole as soon as humanly possible in some form of mechanical transportation and keep heading north! "Um, yeah," I said. "I guess I got some plans."

After breakfast we headed over to the dealership, where we found Wallace talking with the owner. He looked like a common car salesman type with a cheap suit and a greasy combover. Gill and I maintained a distance and I didn't listen to their conversation too intently, but it sounded like some form of negotiation was in progress.

I looked up at the clouds. Sometimes they cracked slightly, and desperate beams of sunlight crept through. I knew the sun was speaking to me, encouraging me. "Hey Evan, don't you like it when I shine on you? I'll tell you what: If you continue north, I'll give you a lot more than what your getting now. But I promise that as long as you stay in Eureka, you can kiss my sunshine ass goodbye!" The clouds filled the cracks and the light was gone.

The Suburu sat alone on the other side of the mechanics shop, like an abandoned, disabled child on the far end of the playground. Gill and I walked over to it and leaned on our broken home. "This place sucks," I proclaimed, finally breaking my Code of Chillness. Gill quietly shook his head.

Wallace walked over, his facial expression reflecting the sky. "She's pretty fucked. Not much they can do about it."

"What are you going to do?" asked Gill.

"I need to give my Dad a call. I think I'm going to sell this rusty pile-of-shit for parts and buy a new car. Gill, can I borrow your phone?"

"Yeah sure."

"Okay, um, then what?" I asked.

Wallace didn't hesitate to answer. "Then I'm driving my ass straight back to Mass. I'm sick of this shit. Anyone who wants to come with me is more than welcome."

That seemed to have made it official. The car was kaput and the trip was over—or was it? It was time for all of us to make a decision.

Wallace looked at me. "What do you think?"

Think? There was no thinking involved. I didn't hesitate to answer. "Hell no, I'm not going back."

"How are you going to continue?"

I shrugged. "I don't know, I'll figure something out."

We turned to Gill who looked back at us with concerned uncertainty.

"Come on, Gill," I said with a smile that had packed in all of the encouragement I could muster, "come explore the great unknown!"

Gill looked at Wallace, who simply shrugged. "I don't care, do what you want." Then he looked back at me. I still had my huge smile. Then back at Wallace, dejected.

Gill took a deep breath. "I don't know," he said nervously, "I think I'll probably head back with you, Wallace."

It hurt to lose my two companions, but I couldn't care either way. This trip was my baby. Wallace and Gill were along for the ride, yet merely a few extra joints in my rusty axle. Although unlike the piece of shit car, when I lost some joints, I had the ability to keep going. And that was exactly what I was going to do. Come hell or highwater, I was going to make it to British Columbia.

Traveling alone can be a daunting endeavor, but I had done it before in Europe and I was prepared at any point to do it again on this trip. In Europe I "studied" abroad, meaning I was enrolled in classes at my program, but that was a façade for my main objective, which was to travel. And travel I did. Whenever I decided where I wanted to go and when, I mentioned it to people on my program. If they wanted to come with me, fine. If not, it was fine just the same. Sometimes people agreed to come along, but more often than not, I was on my own to explore this wide world. I had learned a lot from traveling alone and it was time to continue that legacy. The question now, was how to do it.

My mind fled through possibilities. This was going to be a tougher process then backpacking through Europe. In Europe there is an elaborate train infrastructure, and the towns are small enough that the train station is always in walking distance. America is harder. Trains are practically non-existent and when they are, they are inefficient and expensive.

The bus system is reliable, but still not as accessible to find a station as it is in Europe. Eureka had to have had some sort of bus line running through it. I would have to look into that.

I could hitchhike, but "This isn't the sixties," as my hypocrite parents always said. "You can't hitchhike anymore. Too many psychos nowadays." Hitchhiking did have its danger factors. Although hitching a ride had to be way more exciting then the bus—

Wait a minute. Hitching a ride:.. Sam! Oh my God Sam! If my memory served me, he said he was driving down to San Francisco and heading *back* north. And I thought he said he was heading to, yes! Vancouver! *Oh my God, Sam!* I nearly ripped my pocket getting my cell phone out. This was going to be so easy! I was going to finish off my trip with another good friend of mine. It looked like I wasn't going to be alone after all.

Ring...Ring..."Hello?"

"Sam!"

"Hey man, sorry about Mendocino, we had to keep going and make it to San Francisco."

"No problem. Hey, are you still in San Francisco?"

"No, we left. We're heading back up north now."

"Is that so!" I was skipping around the dealership. "Oh my god, you wouldn't believe what happened to us!" <Proceed to tell Sam story of car.> "...and now I'm stuck in Eureka. Are you guys by any chance driving up Route 101?"

"Um, I think so," said Sam.

"And didn't you tell me you were driving up to Vancouver?"

"Yeah, that's our final destination."

"So, my friend, what do you say I hitch a ride with you guys up to Canada? *Eh*?" The "Eh" was in the best Canadian accent I could muster.

"Um, yeah," Sam stifled, "um I guess that could work. Ummmmmm can I call you back?"

"Of course."

"Okay, bye."

I proudly walked up to my *former* road trip companions. "Well boys, looks like I got myself a ride!"

"Already? How'd you manage that?"

"Remember my friend Sam?"

"Yeah, I think so. The guy who we never met in St. Paul and who never met us in Mendocino?"

"Precisely. So..." <Proceed to tell Wallace and Gill story of Sam.> "...and he said he could give me a ride!"

"Oh wow, you lucky duck."

I looked at Gill with my encouraging smile. "You know, I could ask them if you could come along. There's only two of them in the car."

Gill shook his head. "No thanks dude."

Fucking quitters.

My next task at hand was packing. I needed to go through everything I brought and condense it into my big red hiking pack. In certain ways I was still going to be on my own and it was necessary for all of my possessions to fit on my back.

Wait a minute, what's going to happen with the stuff I can't take? "Wallace," I said, "I have one last favor to ask you."

Wallace looked at me with an obvious expression. "You want me to transport your stuff back home."

"I promise I'll pick it up when I get back."

"I can do that, no problem."

Okay, case closed on that. It was time to sort. I sat next to the car and pulled out everything that was mine. Then I took out my pen and purple notebook with the Grateful Dead sticker on it, and wrote down all of the things that I thought I would need, and sorted them away from the big pile. First I had to think about survival: What were the things I absolutely needed? Then came hygiene. Then came clothes. Clothes take up a lot of room so I needed to choose wisely. Only one pair of something will often do, except for underwear—my boys had to stay cleanly. As the old saying goes, "Cleanliness is next to godliness and godliness is tucked in with your boxers." Besides, boxers were compact.

Then came a big decision about hats. I had a few hats that I brought on the trip and I knew I had to condense them to one. I had a couple baseball caps and a wicker cowboy hat. The wicker hat was the one I used only on special occasions, usually bringing it to music festivals or big, fun events. This road trip was obviously a special occasion and this moment was even *more* special, so the wicker hat won. Plus, I thought it best accentuated my "lone traveler" look.

After clothes, I packed up the big red pack. Then I made a pile of extras and put in anything that could fit. The final list came to this: Passport; sleeping bag; playground maps of Oregon, Washington, BC, and Alberta; purple notebook with Grateful Dead sticker; pens; phone charger; camera charger; nalgene; tooth brush; toothpaste; deodorant; floss; shampoo; shorts; shirts; socks; wool socks; sweatshirt; long sleeves; boxers; hat; sunglasses; harmonica; postcards; stamps; hackie sac; poncho; Emergen C; headlamp; buck knife. The last item on the list was Birks, short for Birkenstocks. I also had a pair of shoes, but as of today it was officially summer (at least outside of Eureka). In the summer I didn't go anywhere without my Birks.

"Here," Wallace said as he approached me with a handful of objects he had kept out of sight. "A little going away gift." He handed me a large nugget of weed and a wrapped cookie. "It's a taste of California you can take with you."

"Thanks!" I said. I held up the cookie. "What's this?"

"That's the edible from the dispensary," answered Wallace.

"Oooooooh," I said and slapped myself on my forehead. "A weed cookie! Thanks!"

Gill chimed in. "Good for bartering too!"

"Good luck out there," said Wallace with a look that was so beautifully endearing, I almost changed my mind.

I returned the look. "You too, guys."

Before this moment got too sappy, my phone rang. "Sam! Are you here yet?" I chuckled. "Just kidding. What's up?"

"Hey, um, so we need to talk." The nervousness in his voice was more than disconcerting.

"Ooookay, I'm all ears."

"I don't know if I can pick you up."

"What? What do you mean? Aren't you heading north now?"

"Yeah," his voice was tense and awkward.

"So then what's the problem?" I asked intently.

"Well it's just that I'm with my girlfriend and all, and..."

He paused, so I filled in the gap. "Okay, and I'm stranded."

"Yeah, um, hold on I'll call you right back."

No way was this happening. No fucking way. Was my best friend about to drive right past me—we are talking literally right past me because the dealership and motel were *on* Route 101—and not give me a ride? Maybe he didn't realize the severity of the situation. Maybe—*wait, how the hell could he not understand my situation?* He wasn't going to pick me up because he was with his girlfriend? His *fucking girlfriend?!* Maybe she wasn't giving him enough pleasure and the semen was backed up into his brain so he couldn't think straight. Maybe—

Ring...Ring... "Hello?"

"Hey, um, so I don't think we can drive you all the way to Vancouver."

"You don't *think* you can, Sam? Or you *can't*?" I was sick of this awkward pussyfooting.

"We, um, we can't. See, my girlfriend is picking up her sister in Portland, and she's driving with us up to Vancouver."

"Okay, so that means you can't pick me up? Couldn't you at least give me a ride to Portland?"

"Um, hold on." I could feel his cold hand blocking the receiver as he feebly groveled to his girlfriend on my behalf. "Yeah, I think that could work."

"You *think*?" I shot back.

"Yeah, yeah, we could give you a ride. To Portland. Just to Portland."

I couldn't believe what I was hearing. This chick had a vice grip on my friend's manhood. "How long are you staying in Portland?" I asked.

"I think a few days. Kara's sister booked a hotel room."

"Really? Do you think there's room for me to crash for like, a night?"

"Um, well I don't know about that."

"So what, you're just going to drop me off in the middle of Portland and say good luck?" Smoke started coming out of my ears.

"Well, no, not necessarily. Um, I'll talk to Kara about it, I'll call you back."

"Yeah, you do that." I hung up.

"I can't believe this shit!" I yelled in the middle of the dealership parking lot. "I've known this kid since fourth grade, one of my oldest and best friends, and he can't give me a straight fucking answer! This is ridiculous! I'm stranded three thousand miles from my home, he's driving by right *there*," I pointed to the road, "with the ways and means, yet he can't seem to release this Klingon death-grip that his girlfriend has on his balls!"

"Damn," said Wallace, "he sounds like a real dick."

"I know, right? This isn't like him."

I paced back and forth, my mind in multiple directions. I had to focus. What to do? Start with what I had: a ride to Portland. What I needed: a place to stay. What I really needed was a place where I could rest for a day or two and figure out my next plan of action. If I could convince Sam to let me stay just one night, then from there I could move on. I needed to get somewhere safe and I needed access to the internet. *Who do I know around Portland?... I don't know anyone! Near Portland... Nothing. Oregon, is there anybody in the goddamn state of—wait a minute, Casey!*

Ring...Ring... "Hey Evan, what's up?"

"Casey! You wouldn't believe what's happened!"

"I probably could, but try me."

<Proceed to tell Casey story of car and Sam.>

"Wow," said Casey, "this guy is your friend? Sounds like a real dick."

"I know! So where are you? Did you make it to Oregon?" I asked.

"Yeah, I actually just arrived. And like I said before, you're welcome to come. It's a small room, but we can make it work."

"Yeah, I really just need a place to crash for a few days so I can figure everything out. Do you have internet by the way?"

"I don't in my room, but the office where I work does, and we can use it as much as we want after office hours."

I started to skip again. "Oh my God, this is great. I think this is going to work. So where exactly are you?"

"I'm in a town called, La Grande in eastern Oregon, not far from the Idaho border."

"Do you know how far you are from Portland?"

"It's about five hours, but it's pretty easy, there's a bus that goes direct from there to here."

"Wow, I don't know how to thank you, you're really saving my shit right now."

Casey let out an amused chuckle. "Not a problem man, it's a little boring out here just to warn you. I'm already looking forward to company after a few days. It pretty much defines a 'one-horse town,' but lots of amazing mountains around. *A lot* of exploring potential."

"Sounds good—sounds great. I'll let you know when I'm coming, I still have some bullshit to figure out."

"Cool, just let me know, I'm not going anywhere."

Alas there was light at the end of the tunnel—well, maybe not at the end, but somewhere.

Ring...Ring... "Hey Sam."

"Hey, so I'm still not sure if you can stay with us at the hotel. Her sister booked the room and I don't know, I just feel kind of awkward asking."

"Fine, I guess I'll have to figure something else out. But you can still drive me to Portland, right?"

"Um, hold on..." (hand covered over phone, feeble groveling) "Yeah, we can do that."

"Okay." I hesitated, inclined to use this time to say "thank you," but I couldn't bring myself to. I stayed strictly business. "How close are you?"

"I think three or four hours away."

"Alright, call me when you're close."

"Okay, bye."

"Bye."

The awkward tension was unbearable. I gave a disgusted look to Gill. Wallace had walked away to deal with the car.

"So is he going to give you a ride?" asked Gill.

"I think so. Now the issue is whether or not I can stay in the hotel room for a night with his girlfriend and her sister. He says he feels too," I quoted with my fingers, "'awkward' asking—or at least that's the poor excuse that he's making up. I don't think he's telling me the whole story."

"Yeah," agreed Gill, "that sounds off to me. It doesn't seem that hard to ask for something like that."

The two of us stood in silent thought, then Gill spoke. "Maybe it's because he wants to be alone with his girlfriend."

I shook my head. "No, he mentioned the sister booking one room, so that must mean the three of them are sharing. But I guess that explains why he was apprehensive about letting me come along up to Vancouver. I guess he intended for this trip to be a romantic getaway or something."

"That makes sense. Why would you want to be the third wheel with that?"

"Yeah," I solemnly admitted, "I guess you're right...Wait! No! That's not right!" I yelled and flailed up my arms. Gill backed up to avoid getting smacked. "They're meeting her sister in Portland, and then she's riding with them up to Vancouver! What the fuck!" I shook my head in disappointment. This really was hurtful. "They're letting her sister drive with them, and Sam is like a brother to me, but I guess that's not good enough."

"Damn," said Gill. Then he gave me a reassuring shoulder rub. "If it makes you feel better man, I'd pick you up no problem. I wouldn't care if I was with my girlfriend, or the Pope."

I smiled. "Thanks man. It's times like these when you can tell who your friends really are."

"So when is he coming?" Gill asked.

"A few hours."

"So you're getting out of this one-horse town."

"Yeah, and heading to a smaller one. I'm going to Casey's place in eastern Oregon for a few days."

"Eastern Oregon, what's that going to be like?"

I shrugged. "I have no idea, but that makes it more exciting I think."

"Wow," Gill shook his head, "I can't believe the trip is over."

"For you," I said.

Gill looked at me and smiled in that pleasantly cordial way that he always did. "Yeah, I'm okay with that." That was why Gill was such a good guy. He always talked the truth, telling it like it was while remaining calm and collected, and you couldn't help but stay calm in his infectious presence.

We sat by the car, taking in the cool California air. I thought about what lay ahead. I had not the faintest idea. That was the way I liked it.

I had a few hours to kill (notice I said *I* and not *we*—something to get used to) before Sam would arrive. Wallace was busy with the car, and Gill and I didn't feel like waiting around a dealership parking lot anymore. We asked around and found out that there actually was more to Eureka then a strip of franchises. We were told about some piers to check out around the downtown district. It was in walking distance so we set off in that direction, with our expectations as low as they could get.

It was a mile walk before we reached buildings that weren't part of a strip mall and had no big-business affiliations. The buildings were standard, nothing flashy—Eureka wasn't trying to impress anybody. A block past the buildings were some piers, with a short boardwalk running along the water. The piers looked out to a bay which was dirty, but not too dirty, and scenic, but not too scenic. Bland was a good description. Maybe this town wasn't trying to be flashy. They had nothing to prove to us. We were some dumb tourists that didn't want to be there just as much as they didn't care for us to be there. We had a mutual distaste.

I realized this may have been the first place we had traveled to, where there was nothing noteworthy, nothing exceptional, nothing visually striking to please our senses. It was so damn appropriate to be stuck in such a place. I had mentioned back in San Francisco that if I ended up being stuck there, I would not have minded one bit. But fate will never pluck its strings to that nice a tune.

Gill and I headed away from the piers and into the "downtown district." We walked into a local brewpub to spend money on what we did best. It was the classis local brewpub with tacky shit on the walls, wooden tables, and a bar with that gross, shiny, plasticy finish.

We decided to try the sampler which is always a fun thing to get at breweries. They give out small glasses with a few sips worth of each beer they brew. They came in a wooden plank with holes so the bartender could give us all the beers lined up in a row, going from lightest to darkest. With it came a laminated sheet explaining each beer in as much flavorful detail as their (not so) creative beer minds could fabricate. It's fun to get these samplers but more likely then not, they all taste pretty much the same: heavy and hoppy with not much distinct flavor. The bartender proudly explained to us, "This here is our Belgian Blond, a very light wheat beer:" heavy and hoppy. "This here is our summer ale, light, with mild hops for flavor, and a hint of elderberry:" heavy and hoppy. "This here is our porter, a bit heavier, very full body:" too heavy. "And this is our IPA, for you hop lovers:" disgustingly hoppy. But beer is beer and especially in a local brewpub, the standards have to be set low with hopes to be surprised. And since we were in Eureka, our standards were extremely low.

The good news was that the final game of the Lakers-Celtics series was starting. It was imperative for us to get drunk so we could more easily laugh in all the faces of these Californians when their team lost.

Wallace joined us a little while later looking emotionally drained. "Give me a fucking beer."

"Would you like hoppy and heavy? Or extra hoppy and heavy?"

"I don't care, I'm finished making decisions for the day."

We slid over a brew and Wallace lapped it down like he had run a ten-mile race and finished dead last but tried just as hard.

"Did you sell it?" Gill asked.

"Yeah, finally. That dealer was a fucking dick. He tried to screw us left and right. But my dad and I talked him down and we were able to settle on something. I'll finalize the deal tomorrow morning and we'll get straight on the road. How does that sound Gill?"

"Sounds fine."

Wallace turned to me. "How about you Kenward, what's your plan?"

"My ride will be here in a couple hours."

"So that dude's balls finally dropped and he agreed to pick you up?"

I scoffed, "Yeah, he *agreed* to take me as far as Portland."

"Then what?"

"Find a bus that will take me to La Grande, Oregon. That's where Casey is. I'll hang out there for a few days, get my bearings, and figure out how to survive in British Columbia."

Wallace looked impressed. "Damn dude, you got it all figured out."

"Yeah I do," I said confidently, even though it was a lie. "And there's room for two more people in the plan."

They both laughed. "No thanks."

I couldn't understand why they refused to come. Wallace was going to get a fresh new car that surely wouldn't cause us problems. I knew he had to deal with a lot of shit up till now, but the hard part was behind us. I took a long sip of my beer and sighed to myself. *So it goes.* I wasn't going to press the issue any further.

We merrily enjoyed our last supper as the "three semi-decent campers," and celebrated a fine performance from the Boston Celtics who not only beat, but decimated the Lakers with a forty-point deficit. Afterwards we stumbled back to the motel for the last time as the "three semi-decent drunkards."

The sun was starting to set when I got the call. "Hey Sam."

"Hey, we're heading into Eureka now. There's a Suburu dealership on our left."

"Okay, you're almost here."

I gathered my bag together and checked my list, making sure I had everything stowed tight. When I was good to go, I plopped the wicker cowboy hat on my head and slung my big red pack over my shoulder. The lone-traveler transformation was complete. There was no turning back.

"Well boys, it's been fun," I said.

Wallace got up and barreled toward me. "Oh come here you bastard!" and he gave me a big bear hug. We may have had our tiffs along the way, but I missed the Scottish son-of-a-bitch already.

Gill gave me a skinny hug and a firm handshake. "We'll miss you, bud."

Sam's car pulled up and he got out. I fought to repress my inner frustrations and cheerily yelled, "Well hello, stranger!"

"Hello!" he said with a wave. For a second all woes were forgotten and we embraced. It was still good to see him, since it had been many moons in a far off land when we last crossed paths. I couldn't get over the surreal feeling of being so far from home and seeing someone so familiar.

His girlfriend got out and walked over: Dark hair just like Sam, dressed slightly hip yet slightly unkempt, just like Sam.

"This is my girlfriend, Kara."

We shook hands. "Hello, nice to meet you," she said politely.

My boyfriends walked out, dressed messy and disheveled, just like me. "This is Wallace and G—I mean, John and Jacob." They shook hands.

"Okay," said Sam before any further conversation could be breached, "we should get going."

Ugh, I hate rushing. "Alright." I said and turned around and looked at Gill and Wallace.

They looked back blankly. "We already said our goodbyes. Get out of here."

"I guess you're right. I'll see you all back east!"

"Indeed."

I turned my back to Wallace and Gill, my friends, my travel companions, my ticket home, and walked to Sam's car.

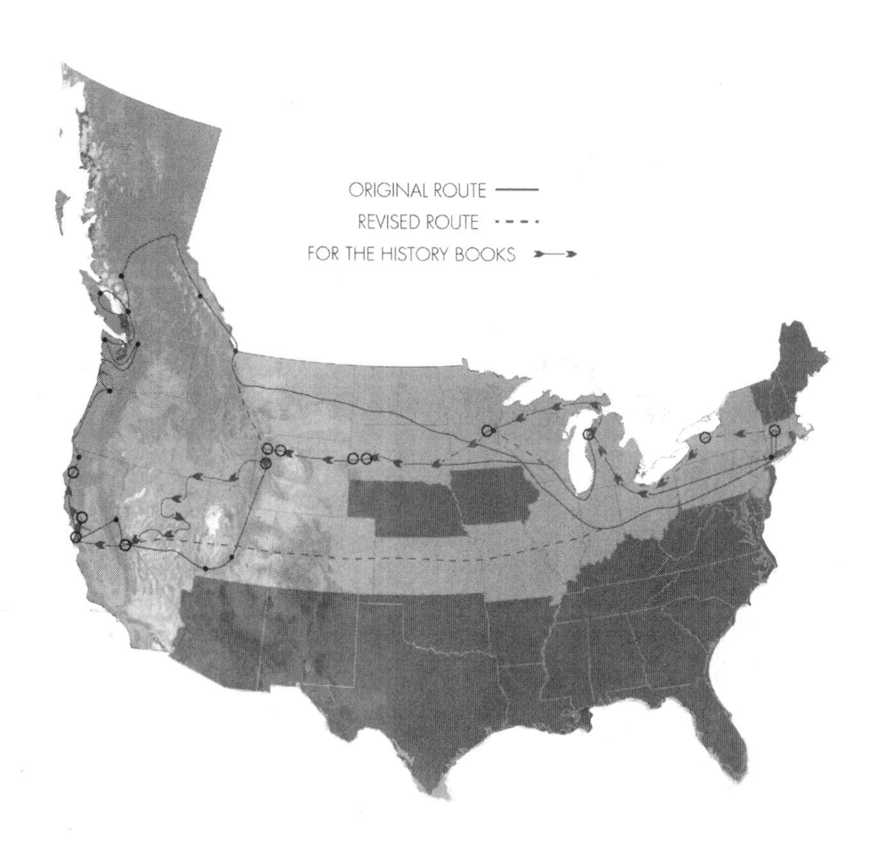
ORIGINAL ROUTE
REVISED ROUTE
FOR THE HISTORY BOOKS

PART II

ONE LONE TRAVELER

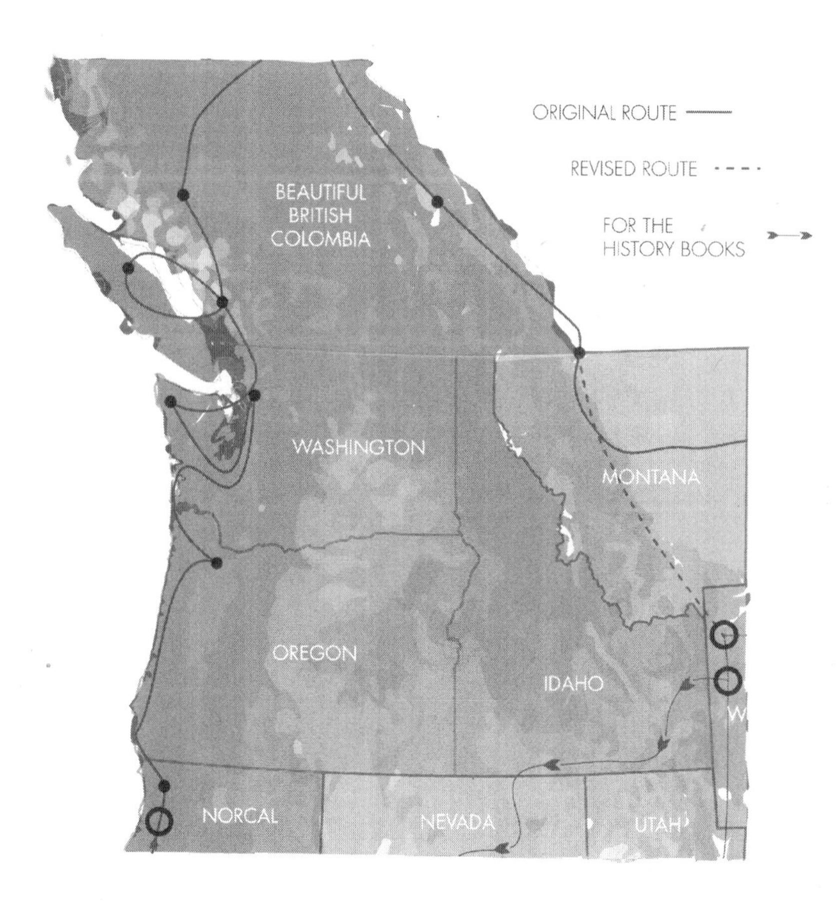

DAY 14 (CONT.)

The car smelled rental fresh. It was a stark difference from the funk that permeated throughout the Suburu. I put down the rear window which slid down like slicing through butter, unlike the Suburu's broken window. *This car is too new. It don't like it... At least it works, Evan. Just be thankful you have a ride.*

Sam and Kara occupied the front seats and they didn't spare a moment before we were backing out of the hotel lot and onto Route 101 north.

"Thanks for picking me up," I said.

"Yeah, sure," Sam said without turning his head away from the road.

This brief conversation was followed by uncomfortable silence. Sam spoke in a low tone to Kara, discussing directions.

I was too drunk to sit quiet, so I didn't. "So how was San Francisco?"

"Okay," said Sam, "we were only there for a few hours. But we got to see the Transamerica Building which was nice."

"A few hours? What do you mean?" I asked.

"We didn't have much time. We had to head back up."

"You mean you drove all the way down from Vancouver just to spend a few hours in San Francisco and head back?"

"Um, yeah, pretty much."

What the hell is wrong with these people? "So, uh, how was the Transamerica Building?"

"I have a cousin who works there," said Kara, "so we got to take a special tour and go up to the very top where the point is."

"It was pretty cool," said Sam. "Like a cramped little room."

"Oh, uh," *try to sound interested Evan,* "that's cool."

We continued on Route 101 and the daylight vanished. I thought to mention the fern canyon to stay for the night, but I figured I'd feel out the situation before recommending anything. After all, I was their guest. This scenario was no longer democratic. It was their way or the highway. Even though I was out on my own now, my freedom was strangely lost.

"What's the plan?" I asked. "Where we headed?"

"We have to get as close to Portland as possible tonight," said Sam. "We'll have to find somewhere eventually to sleep for a few hours, then get back on the road."

Kara chimed in. "My sister's flight is coming in to Portland early tomorrow morning and I have to be there to pick her up."

This was making more sense. They had been in such a rush the past few days because they needed to be back in Portland by a certain time. But I still could not believe they chose to drive all the way down to San Francisco if they knew they had such a tight deadline. That was some damn poor planning. Road trips are about spontaneity, but the brain still needs to be used when making decisions. When the brain is left out of the process, it's called being impulsive. Being impulsive is a bad trait and could land you in awful situations. Being spontaneous, on the other hand, is going by impulse and following up with intellect. Let's break down this scenario:

"Hey! Let's spend a couple days driving from Vancouver to San Francisco and back!"

Example of an impulsive response: "Okay!"

Nope. Not realistic. Why? Because they didn't factor in their deadline. They *had* to be in Portland by a certain time on a certain day. When working with a deadline, the trip must start with that, and then get planned around it.

Example of a response while using the brain: "Hmm, San Francisco seems kind of far for that amount of time. What if we spend a couple days at Crater Lake instead? That's not far from Portland. Then we can have an easier time to get back to pick up your sister."

"Oh, okay. That makes a lot more sense. Thanks Evan, I'm so glad you're here to make the sound decisions. You're way smarter than Sam. And might I add how attractive a trait that is. Let's have sex."

"Okay!" –Nope. Not realistic.

As a general rule on a road trip, deadlines should be avoided if possible. One side effect is it cuts down on flexibility. If we had a deadline at a specific destination, it wouldn't have been easy for us to make the decision to take the one-hundred-and-eighty-degree turn in Jackson. Another big issue is that everything needs to be rushed. Sam and Kara had to speed up and down the West Coast and all they got was a few minutes at the top of the Transamerica Building. *Wow, sounds like a fantastic trip guys!*

This rushing also meant that our goal of getting close to Portland tonight, entailed skipping through the redwoods. I looked out the window at the shadows of trees zooming by the peripherals of our headlights. My dream of frolicking through those enchanted forests would have to wait for another trip.

"Hey," Kara pointed as she gripped the steering wheel, "there's a sign for a connecting road to Route 5. That'll be much faster. Make sure I don't miss that turn, Sam."

"Okay," said Sam obediently.

And there goes the entire coast of Oregon from my trip. Fuck my life.

We drove on in silence, maybe because I had run out of questions to ask about the Transamerica Building. Or maybe I didn't feel like talking, after knowing that Sam and Kara just pressed the eject button on my plans of seeing the entire coastal Pacific Northwest.

Sam was glancing at the roadmap and Kara looked over at him. "Sam, put on some music."

"Okay," said Sam again in the same docile tone. He picked up the ipod sitting in the center console. Some angsty song came on by some hipster band I had never heard of. I didn't like it.

It wasn't taking me long to figure out that it was a blessing in disguise not to be riding with this crew all the way to Vancouver. Sam was a good friend, but an old friend. Throughout the many years that we'd known eachother, we had grown apart in different ways. At this point if we had gone to the same college, we would have had completely different groups of friends. Not that there was anything wrong with that. We still got along on a deeper level—at least I used to think so.

Kara turned slightly in my direction while watching the road. "So Evan, what are your plans?"

I shrugged. "I don't really know. From Portland I'm going to head to my friend's place in eastern Oregon and then keep heading north, by bus most likely, up to Washington and British Columbia."

"Where are you going to stay?" she asked.

I doubled my shrug. "I'm not sure. I probably have to get online and find some hostels around. Hopefully they'll be cheap because I'm on a tight budget."

Sam turned to me. "You don't know anybody north of Oregon?"

"I know you guys." I chuckled awkwardly but it rendered no response.

"What about Couchsurfing?" Kara chimed in.

I turned to her. "What? You mean like sleeping on people's couches?"

"Yeah, it's a website," she said.

"Oh? I've never heard of it." It sounded strange but I was intrigued. "So like, people let you stay on their couches?"

Kara nodded. "You search for where you want to stay and look at people's profiles and see if you can crash on their couch for a few days."

"But what if they're like, an axe murderer or something?" I asked.

Kara laughed. "No I think it's fine. I actually haven't done it, but my friend does it all the time and swears by it. She says it's the only way she travels."

"Cool, I'll have to check it out." Then I changed the subject. "Speaking of plans, where are we sleeping tonight?"

Sam shrugged. "I don't know, I guess we'll have to find a hotel eventually."

Ugh, nooo. Evan, it's time to speak up. "You guys don't have a tent do you?" I asked.

Sam nodded. "Yeah, we do."

"What size?"

"I don't know, pretty big I think."

"Like a four-person?"

"Yeah, that sounds right."

"Then why don't we just use that? If you want to quickly sleep somewhere and get up and go, I don't think it's worth paying for a night at a hotel."

"Um, I guess," said Sam. "But I don't know how we can find a campground—"

"We don't need a campground," I cut him off. The master camper was out in full effect. "Just pull to the side of the road somewhere."

Kara and Sam looked at each other in confused apprehension. They were silently saying, "I don't know, do you want to?" "I don't know, do *you* want to?" Sam gave a "why not?" shrug. "Um, I guess we can do that. But isn't it illegal?"

"Great!" I said taking the reins. "Let's get off at the next exit."

We pulled off the dark highway and found ourselves on an even darker road. We were still in wilderness with not much sign of life: perfect for guerilla camping. I could only assume we had made it to Oregon at this point. If there had been a sign, I had missed it in the darkness.

We came to an intersection and Kara looked at us. "Left or right?" To the right there was a sign pointing toward a town. To the left, the road sloped up a hill and around a dark corner.

"That one," I said, pointing to the left. We turned left and I scoured the area for possibilities. It appeared to be the right choice because the houses grew scarce, and when we came upon one, it was set far back into the woods with a long driveway. These were the kinds of homes that were meant for seclusion, set on a scarcely traveled road.

Every half-mile, wide patches of shoulder would extend off the road, wide enough for a car and a tent. "This looks good," I said.

"What?" said Sam.

"Right here," I pointed.

"Hmm, I don't know," said Kara as she drove by it.

Next one: "How about this?" I asked.

"No, too close to the road," said Kara.

Next one: "How about this?"

Sam finally backed me up, "Yeah, that looks good."

We pulled over, got out, and surveyed the area. It was a narrow dirt patch set away from the road, although there was an immediate slope up. This meant there was no room to venture farther into the woods, but it was fine by me.

"I—I don't think this is going to work," said Kara.

"Why not?" asked Sam.

"We're too close to the road. I don't know, I just don't think—"

"Are you sure?" he asked. "This really isn't that bad."

I kept my mouth shut and let the two of them duke it out.

"No," insisted Kara, "I don't feel comfortable with this. This whole area creeps me out. I think we should head back."

"Head back where?"

"I don't know, just back toward the highway."

"Okay," said Sam.

Oh my god. If we keep up this indecisiveness, we'll be driving around till dawn.

We got back in the car and turned around. A few miles down, a big dirt patch popped up ahead. "Here! Go here!" Sam and I said. Kara pulled over. This was a wider patch, plus the slope was even. I took out my headlamp from my bag and searched around. Sam and Kara put their poorly illuminating cell phones away and followed close behind me. I spotted an area a few yards into the woods with no trees and very little brush. "There," I said with assertiveness. "That's where we're pitching the tent." I think at this point everyone was too tired to argue so there was no opposition.

I led them through the steps of setting up the tent. "First we have to clear the brush, then put the tarp down, then lay out the tent pieces."

"Uh huh, uh huh, uh huh." It was obvious neither of them had touched this tent before.

I felt like the true camping machine that I had been training for. I had unknowingly moved up to sensei, where I could teach others the ancient ways, based on my extensive experience, refined technique, and polished intellect.

Thankfully, they were right about the size of the tent. I was afraid I was going to end up being the slice of deli-special honey ham in the Sam and Kara spooning sandwich, but there was more than enough room to spread out. I took my sleeping bag out of my easily accessible bag, got in, and curled up, using my bundled up sweatshirt as a pillow.

Sam and Kara were still futzing around. "Owe! Sam!"

"What?"

"There's a stick under the tent digging into my back."

"Oh, sorry, I thought we cleared it all out."

"Well you did a great job."

"Sorry."

Some romantic getaway this was.

I tuned out Tweedle Dee and Tweedle Dumb, closed my eyes, and tried to relax. I was back on the road again. Bunching up in my sleeping bag with sticks poking into me gave me a feeling of comfort. It was the feeling of being back on track. I wondered what Portland would be like. I had always heard good things. The "other" Portland. I was used to hearing about the small coastal city of Portland, Maine. I had been there once, coincidentally with Sam back in middle school. We went on a class trip to go biking, hiking, and rafting in Maine and spent a couple nights in Portland. We stayed in a hostel and Sam and I shared a room. I remember we stayed up most of the night bouncing around, relating to each other about twelve-year-old life and growing woes.

I remember looking outside in the middle of the night and seeing a group of scantily clad women walk down the street alone. "Look Sam! Prostitutes!" I announced.

"Really??" Sam ran over. "Let me see! Whoa!"

We giggled. "Hey!" Sam yelled. "Catch anything good tonight?!"

They looked up at us and we ran away from the window laughing hysterically.

"Why did you do that?!" I yelled. "You're going to get us killed!"

We then proceeded to scare ourselves with scenarios of pimps with guns knocking on our door.

Then I was reminded of the hiking and camping that we did. *Wait, Sam has done all of this camping before. Why couldn't he even set up a tent tonight?* I guess people change in more ways than one. Tomorrow we would see how different Portland, Oregon was, then Portland, Maine.

DAY 15

I was rudely woken by an obnoxiously faint beeping sound coming from the other side of the tent. I had not woken up to any alarm since Nevada, and that was set for the purpose of exploration. As much as I was still motivated to get up early and go, I knew that this alarm was set with a different intention. There was no exploration involved, only getting to some stupid airport on time.

"Sam! Sam! Get up! We have to go." Kara hadn't been awake for thirty seconds and she was already bossy.

Sam grumbled and picked his head up. "Okay."

I was still the new guy so she didn't yell at me. *Maybe I should lie here and see how long it takes for her to yell at the new guy... Bad idea, I'm already the unpopular one.* I got up.

I slithered out of my sleeping bag and stepped out of the tent. The sun shone through the multitude of greenery surrounding us, and through the cracks of the trees I saw blue sky. The sun had kept its promise, reaffirming my decision to continue on. This rejuvenated my soul and I was fully awake. I looked across the road where a steep incline shot far up. I turned around and saw that if we had walked a little farther into the woods, we would have fallen down another steep incline that dropped into a basin. I couldn't see the bottom but I could hear the faint sound of running water. This environment wasn't much different then where we had driven at the end of Highway 1. It was a green mix of deciduous and evergreens—although a much higher ratio of evergreens at this point. It gave off that perfect temperature from breaking the beams of the strong sun. These evergreens were the signature of the Pacific Northwest—at least it appeared that way. Why else would the Oregon license plate have a big ol' pine tree on it?

By the way, we are in Oregon right? "Hey," I turned around, "where are we, anybody know?"

Sam shrugged. "I have no idea."

"The middle of nowhere," said Kara.

"But do you know if we're in Oregon or California?" I asked.

"Oh, we're definitely in Oregon, that's for sure."

Okay then. Hello Oregon, sorry we weren't properly introduced. We got in so late last night, you were already in bed. You have a beautiful home.

"Nice to meet you Evan, I'm glad you found a place to put your tent. There's free-trade coffee and locally grown organic wheat muffins on the kitchen table, help yourself."

Thank you!

"Oh, and I almost forgot. Don't worry about pumping your gas, we'll do it for you."

We got the tent packed away and were back in the car, assuming our prior positions: Kara in the driver's seat, Sam passenger, and the bastard banished to the back. We retraced our steps on the road. The daylight had transformed this dark, spooky forest into an enchanting explosion of lush virescence.

We made it back to the highway, which wasn't Route 5 yet, but a route heading—dare I say it—*east* from Route 101. The wilderness didn't last for much longer before the world opened up. The trees fell away and grassy, hilly patches stood in their place. Along with this came Man. Man was everywhere. Franchises, cars, buildings, billboards, noise. The blue interstate signs loomed ahead.

Soon the transformation was complete and we were heading north on Route 5. The eighteen-wheeled giants barreled past us and bright billboards gave us superficial reassurance that everything would be okay. This overwhelming feeling I had, made me realize that driving along the California coast had spoiled me. There wasn't much scenery to speak of. We were inland and it was exactly like I thought it would be. Not a single pine forest was in view, and the high hills shrunk to small hills with dead grass on top. I knew the forest was out there somewhere, the Oregon license plates assured me. To think I could have been making friends with seals right now—*Don't think about it.*

We pulled over eventually to get gas and breakfast. Sure enough a man came out, greeted us, and pumped our gas. Oregon and New Jersey, what fine examples you lead.

"I'm starving," said Sam.

I nodded as I felt my stomach curdling. *Where could we find a nice, authentic Oregon breakfast?*

Kara pointed across the street from the gas station. "Let's get that McDonald's drive thru. We have to get back on the road, I think we're running late as it is."

Fucking great. I had to remind myself that what I was doing wasn't a road trip anymore. I was hitching a ride in a car with people who were going from point A to point B as efficiently as possible. I imagined this was what business trips were like: "We got to go! We're going to be late for the paper clip convention! Quick, what's the fastest route to the Chevron Convention Center? Interstate 5? Great. I hate back roads anyway. They make me carsick and trees are boring. Anybody hungry? Great, we got a choice of McDonald's or Wendy's. But we have to decide on one because we don't have time to hit both. I'd personally prefer McDonald's. They have better coffee. But be careful with the coffee. You don't want to be the guy walking into the convention with a stain on your tie."

I had to stop thinking horrible thoughts. Who knew if before long *I* would be worrying about that stain on my tie, or what color paper clip sold best this quarter. I sure had a lot to look forward to. Whatever I wanted to call the trip I was on, whether it be road trip or something else, I had to relish it.

I scarfed down a breakfast sandwich and sucked on my Minute Maid "orange juice" box. "Minute Maid orange flavored sugar water box," would have been a more appropriate name. Sam and Kara sat up rigidly, eyes locked to the road, one hand clamped to their coffee cups. Their movements were fast and rigid like robots: Coffee-to-mouth, sip-coffee-down. Mouth-sip-down. Mouth-sip-down. Eyes-on-road, hand-on-wheel, left-signal-engage, turn, change-lane. Lane-change-complete. Mouth-sip-down.

A couple more hours of nothing and the landscape turned busier and more developed, meaning we were nearing the metropolis. I had to remind myself that Portland was one of my original destinations on this trip and I was looking forward to it. The road took a curve to the east and as we came around the bend, the city—or at least what I thought was the city—was revealed. I had to second-guess myself if I was really seeing Portland because what lay in front of me was tiny. It was still a city with skyscrapers, but not what I was expecting. I didn't know what to expect, but this was surprising.

A wide river ran next to the skyline and it looked like a vast amount of low-level developments on the opposite side. We drove over to the low-level side and got off the highway.

"Maybe I should drop you guys off somewhere and I'll go pick up my sister..." Kara hesitated. "Unless you guys want to come with me to the airport."

That was a rhetorical question but Sam and I played along. "No, no! You can drop us off, that's perfectly fine!"

"Apparently this area is cool with a lot of shops and stuff. Would this be okay?" Kara asked.

"Yeah, it's great."

Kara pulled over on the side of what looked like a main street. We got out and Kara pecked Sam on the cheek, then looked at him with disciplinary eyes. "Don't get yourself in trouble."

Sam looked back, shoulders shrunk with a sheepish expression. "I won't."

I pretended not to watch and got some survival devices from my bag to stuff in my pocket.

Sam and I stood on the sidewalk and Kara got back in the car. She looked over at us, "I'll be in touch after I pick her up. We'll probably get a bite to eat and we can meet after."

"That's fine, we'll find something."

Kara drove off, and the boys were set free.

As Kara's life force drifted away from ours, I felt a distinct weight lifting off my back. Sam was visibly lighter as well.

I looked around us. All the buildings were low rises with funky looking shops and hip restaurants. The day was absolutely gorgeous, not a cloud to be seen and a shade of blue that seemed to have the California sky beaten, if that was possible. This squelched my second assumption of Portland because I heard it was a cloudy, rainy city.

"What do you want to do?" I asked.

"I don't know," answered Sam, "sure is a nice day."

"That's hard to argue with. It would be nice to find a park or something."

"Yeah," Sam looked at me.

I looked back with a mischievous grin. "Want to smoke?"

Sam gave an awkward laugh and looked down with a bashful smile. "Yeah."

"Say no more, let's find a park!"

We walked up Division Street in the opposite direction of downtown. More neat shops and cafés adorned the sidewalk. This area had the bustling culture of a city, yet kept a comfortable residential feel tucked inside. Houses lined every adjacent cross street, looking quaint with lots of vegetation around, as well as various accessories of lawn ornaments or nicely decorated front porches. It wasn't as flashy as San Francisco, but I could tell that people put time and effort into their homes.

A posted city map pointed us toward a park at the end of the street. We walked in silence, slightly awkward, but we were also occupied by taking everything in.

Sam spoke first. "I could live here. I like small cities."

"St. Paul is pretty small, isn't it?" I asked.

"Yeah, maybe a little smaller than Portland."

"You liked St. Paul, right?"

"I loved it. I could move back there. You wouldn't know it but they have a surprisingly diverse food scene."

"Really? I didn't know. I don't really know anything about St. Paul, or Minnesota for that matter. This trip didn't exactly help with that."

"Yeah, sucks you guys missed Obama, that was cool."

"Are you still trying to pursue cooking?" I asked.

Sam shook his head. "No, I gave that up a while ago. But I could confidently say that I've become a Korean food aficionado."

"Oh yeah! I forgot you studied in Seoul! Fuck. I never talked to you about that." I shook my head. "It sure has been a while, hasn't it?"

Sam looked at me. "Yeah man, it's been a while."

We got to the park and hiked up a steep hill. Flowery bushes adorned the sides of the path.

"Did you know," continued Sam, "that at restaurants in Korea, the waitress gives you an after dinner drink that's specifically concocted to enhance your sexual performance?"

"I did not know that. They give it to everyone?"

"Actually it's only given to the men."

"Oh, what do women get?"

"The bill. Ha! No, but seriously."

I broke out in a billowing laugh. This was the Sam I knew and loved. "That's so interesting!" I said. Then I added, "To me that shows a clear difference in culture."

"Why do you say that?" asked Sam.

"Because an American restaurant would *never* serve you an after dinner drink that enhanced your sexual performance. Can you imagine some chick at Applebees? 'I hope everyone had a good meal. Would you like to see our desert menu? Or perhaps our "after dinner fuck-drink" menu for you strapping young lads!'"

Sam laughed. "Your right. Our society suppresses sex."

"Ain't that the truth."

"But," added Sam, "it's also an example of the male dominated culture over there. There's a reason that there isn't a female alternative drink."

"Good point."

At the top of the hill it opened up to a grassy knoll with a bench appropriately placed in the middle. We sat down and got a nice view through the trees of the neighborhood we walked through and the downtown as a backdrop. Off in the far distance, was the venerable Mount Hood poking out its snowy head. Portland didn't have mountain ranges to gaze at, but the lone Mount Hood was majestic enough to hold its own.

I rolled up a joint with a portion of Wallace's gift, lit it, and passed it to Sam. Sam paused, staring at the joint in apprehension. He reached to grab it, then hesitated for a second, then took it in his fingers and put it up to his mouth. He took in a light hit before violently coughing out smoke. He got red in the face and passed it back. "Whoa, this is heavy shit!"

"Tell me about it. My buddy got it in Oakland."

Sam let his rigid body slide into the bench and he stared out at the view. "Kara doesn't smoke weed, so I haven't been doing it too much as of late."

"Does she not like you doing it?" I asked.

"No, not really." I watched Sam's face turn forlorn, then I turned away and stared at Mount Hood.

I had a flashback of coming home from college and Sam happened to be home too. We drove out at night to a lake and sat on some rocks by the shore to smoke a bowl and talk. It was summer and the night air was comfortable with a slight chill. Little floating clouds in the night sky were faintly lit up by a light source from somewhere unknown. The soft murmur of distant crickets and frogs soothed our souls.

"This lake is perfect right now," I said.

"I know!" said Sam in his (back then) normally excited tone. "I was thinking the same thing!"

"There's not a single hint of breeze."

"I think, that of all the places you would want to be in the whole world at this very moment, this place would be high up on the list."

"Agreed."

Both of us were going through the same college phase of discovery. We bounced off ideas between each other, sharing what each of us had learned on our respective life paths. Sam had such a zeal for every subject and it was infectious. I was happy to know that he was out halfway across the country and developing his own life experiences, which were paralleled to mine. We talked about finding that new appreciation for things that already revolved around us.

But I couldn't see that zeal in him now. We sat there on the bench for a while, and talked, and had a few laughs, but it wasn't the same. Every so often Sam seemed to get excited, but it was lost again, like a weak flame that flickers on, but doesn't have enough power to keep itself going, and vanishes as quick as it had come. What happened? Did Kara do this to him? Was it her to blame for the fickle nature of my friend's reluctance to help me on my journeys? Were we dealing with a classic Yoko Ono?

Once the intensity of the Cali bud subsided and it was possible again to pretend to function in society, we got up from the bench and walked (floated is a better word) down the hill, back toward where we came from. We walked along, passing bushes full of large luscious roses the size of our heads. I grabbed one and Sam took a picture of me intimately sticking my tongue inside.

"That's gross," said Sam.

"Thanks!" I didn't know at the time that I was violating a rose in "the City of Roses."

We decided it would be nice to briefly check out the downtown area before we had to meet up with the girls. We took a clean-looking bus which probably ran on electric or biodiesel, made with the tears and sweat of a female-hippie's hairy armpit. It took us down the same street we had walked on, then over a bridge which took us over the river and into downtown.

We were sitting at the back of the bus and observed the people and surroundings. Everyone looked hip except Sam and I, who were clearly falling behind in style points. *Fashion's done changed since I left on this trip.* Most of the people looked our age, or at some other point in their twenties, but I could not quite pinpoint where in their twenties they were. I think I will call them, "Twenty Somethings." Yeah! That sounds right! Tell all your Twenty Something friends that I made up a new phrase—what? That's already a phrase? Damnit, that always happens.

At one point a really cute Twenty Something girl got on the bus. She was hip, but not too hip. She had flowing blond hair that she kept a little messy and it rested down over her chest. I watched her as she stood in the middle of the bus, her face in profile calmly looking out the window. I didn't tell Sam, but I had a debate in my head. *Do I talk to her?... I should. What do I have to lose? I'm three thousand miles from home. She could be happy to talk to an exotic foreigner. She could learn a lot from me and my New England ways. I could teach her how to make maple syrup, and clam chowder, and we can make beautifully hip babies that will run around our home on the Oregon coast. We'll have a pet seal. It will be glorious.* But I had yet to see the Oregon coast and I didn't know how to make maple syrup or chowder. And I was way too stoned to talk to anyone except for my comparably stoned companion.

Sam nudged me. "Should we get off at this stop?"

I looked back at the girl and sighed. "Yeah."

We "stepped down" from the bus and found ourselves in the middle of the downtown area. Portland was no bigger standing in the middle of it then looking at it from afar. There were a few skyscrapers but none too tall to write home about. We found a map of the downtown area which highlighted the neighborhoods in different colors. There appeared to be only five or six areas and none were more than a few blocks long or wide. I felt like I was looking at the map of only one neighborhood in New York City. We walked a few blocks and entered Chinatown. There was a big red Chinesey arch with gargoyles protecting the entrance on each side. *If Chinatown was one of five neighborhoods, was Portland one-fifth Chinese?* I stood in front of the arch pondering this in my stoned brain.

Looking around I still saw mostly Twenty Somethings walking aimlessly. It was like Oregon was a big theme park and all the children wandered away from their mommies and daddies and got trapped in Portland. I had heard a statistic that Portland is the most popular city to move to, after graduating. I believed it. It looked like I was walking on the campus of a very hip college. *Was it too hip for me? Could I get along with all these hipsters? What is a hipster anyway?* It's hard to define a hipster, but you know one when you see one. There are some common characteristics: skin-tight pants, road bikes, pretentious, and monotone. I didn't fit into those pants. *Would I not fit into Portland?*

I thought about living there. Then I found myself thinking about living in all of the places I had passed through. Graduating college had thrown me out of a home and sent me drifting in space, to float by different places and try to choose what looked best. Could I live here? Are there others living here like me? Is it pretty? Are there things to do? Is it cultured? What do I really want in a place to live? *Hmm. Shit, I don't even know.* I could feel my brain forming into a Twenty Something as the days went on and the college mentality faded away. Now I had responsibilities. Now I had to make money. Now I had to prove that my twenty years of schooling were worth it. I was supposed to be a well-formed, well-educated machine, ready to tackle the world and make something of myself. Now was the time to be the person that I dreamed about being through youth... *Wait a minute, what was that again? What did I want to be? I never actually figured that out.* All I knew was that for the last year, I really wanted to drive across the country and I was doing it. Just because I was a graduate, who said I needed to rush into something that will encompass my life until I was ready to retire?

Maybe I needed to travel more. Maybe it was my destiny to not just see the continental US, but the entire world. *Or maybe I shouldn't. Maybe I do need to get back to the East Coast and get working on what I was preparing to do for my whole life: Get a job.* Maybe Gill and Wallace were right. Maybe my trip had run its course and it was time to go home. Maybe a month is too long for a vacation. Maybe I should start getting used to week-long vacations like normal people do: Two weeks a year to travel, plus Memorial Day, Veteran's Day, and Christmas. And the rest of the time is for working. Make money. Buy stuff. Stuff like expensive wedding rings, and new upholstery, and couches to match the upholstery. Maybe that is what post grad life is all about. Maybe maybe—or maybe I'm doing exactly the right thing.

"Evan? Evan!"

"What?" I turned to Sam.

"What are you thinking about?" he asked intently.

"Nothing."

"Really? Because you've been staring at that arch for the last ten minutes."

"Oh."

"Maybe not that long. Anyway, I just got off the phone with Kara. She wants to meet us somewhere and we're going to drop our stuff off at the hotel."

Shit, the hotel. I had forgotten about that unresolved issue. "Oh, right." I said. I looked down at the ground. "I guess I need to figure something out about that."

Sam took a deep breath. "It's okay, you can stay with us tonight."

My head shot up. "What?"

"Yeah," he said, "I pulled some strings."

I looked at Sam straight in the eyes. "Thank you."

"Hey," he said with a reassuring tone, "we're on the other side of the country. I'm not going to kick you out on the curb."

I smiled. My friend Sam was finally back.

We walked to a park overlooking the river, where Kara and her sister were coming to pick us up.

"I'm going to warn you though," began Sam, "Kara's sister is very conservative."

"Okay, I won't mention weed or Obama."

"And quite wealthy so anticipate emptying your wallet tonight."

<Gulp> "Okay."

We sat on a nice bench overlooking the river and neighborhoods across the way. The day was still bright and beautiful. A few West Coast Hippie Bums were lying around with the same demeanor and style as the ones in Golden Gate Park. One scraggily looking creature approached me. "Hey man, you need anything? Coke? Weed?"

"No thanks, I'm good."

He nodded and scraggelled back to his cardboard sign and mangy dog.

Kara and her sister pulled up and we hopped in the back. My scenery changed from destitution to wealth. Kara's sister was immaculate. Her hair was tied back nice and tight and she wore a black and white dress with an extra blouse to cover any cleavage, but low enough to keep her large pearl necklace in view. She was clearly older than Kara, past Twenty Something status. She turned around in the passenger seat, eyes squinting, and searched me from head to Birks. Then she smiled politely, and shook my hand. "Hello, I'm Delilah."

"Evan, nice to meet you."

"Hello Sam."

"Hey Delilah, good to see you."

That seemed to be sufficient formalities for her and she whipped her head forward and got down to business. "So we'll drop our things at the hotel," her tone turned authoritative, "and then go grab something to eat downtown. Sound good?"

<Gulp> "Sounds good." I shot Sam a glance but he remained looking forward. He looked nervous again.

We crossed the bridge back to the area we started in and traveled a few streets over to a similar street of impeccable hipness. Sure enough we pulled into the hippest looking hotel in the neighborhood called, the Jupiter Motel. It had a nouveau/fifties-style decor and everyone walking around played the part. It had a motel physique, similar to where we stayed in Eureka, but less trash and more sass. It looked fine and interesting to me, as long as I didn't have to front the bill because it also looked fucking expensive.

Delilah took out her matching black and white suitcases and we headed to the room. "Here we are," said Delilah. "They gave me two room keys. Here's the other one, Kara." She handed Kara the room key. "Sorry boys, I hope this isn't an inconvenience. If you need one, don't be afraid to ask."

"Hey Delilah," I said.

She whipped her head at me and squinted.

"Thank you for letting me stay. This is a real help."

She pursed her lips and arched them slightly upward to give a polite grin, then whipped her head back around and opened the door.

<Gulp> I walked in.

The room had hip little retro desk lamps and the wallpaper on the back wall was an all-encompassing poster of the San Francisco skyline. *Oh memories...* There were two big beds. *Uh-oh. What were the sleeping arrangements? Couples and newbies? Boys and girls? Chick swap? Put the beds together for a Turkish orgy?* The choice was obvious: Sam and me in one bed, sisters in the other. I was just grateful to have a roof over my head and a bed to sleep in. I couldn't count on these luxuries from here on out, aside from moments of luck and blind generosity.

Everyone dropped their bags and took time to arrange some things or make minor wardrobe changes before we headed to dinner. My situation was painfully simple: Drop the bag on the ground. Need a sweatshirt? Nope, too warm. I was ready before you could say, "Holy Shit! Is that a fixed gear?" I went outside to make a call to ensure that tomorrow night would not be dictated by luck.

Ring...Ring... "Hello?"

"Casey, what's happening?"

"Oh you know, living la vida La Grande. Where are you?"

"I've infiltrated your state, pillaged your metropolis, and stole your women."

"Cool. How's Portland?"

"Good. Sam finally came to his senses, his girlfriend's Republican sister hasn't stabbed me yet, and I inappropriately fondled some roses."

"Get used to that."

"What? Fondling roses?"

"No, Republicans."

"Why's that?"

"Because once you leave the little progressive Portland bubble, you're in *God's country*." He said the last part with a southern drawl.

"Really? I thought Oregon was liberal."

"Not out here it ain't. Out here it's country music and rodeos. But it's fun. I like it so far. Are you still planning on coming out here?"

"Sure am, pilgrim. I'm going to catch a bus tomorrow afternoon."

"Okay, give me a call when you know what time you'll be getting here. Like I said, it should be around five hours."

"Okay, I'll do that."

"Great, see you tomorrow."

Wonderful. Next stop would be Republicanland, Oregon. I was excited. For an Easterner like me, born and raised in liberal, democrat, peace loving, granola crunching New England, it was exotic to go to a place surrounded by the opposite. I was open-minded and accepting. One must be, or else the Republican natives will tie you up, tear your bleeding heart, out and roast it on a pike.

We drove back toward downtown. "Do you all like sushi?" asked Delilah. "I was recomended a great place."

"Sure," said Kara.

I turned to Sam with a sly smile. "I could go for some Korean. Right?" I chuckled.

"Uh huh," was all I received from Sam's deadpan face.

Is that really all he's giving me?? Who the hell is this person?

"What was that?" asked Delilah.

"Sushi's fine," answered Sam.

I turned forward and kept my mouth shut. *What's the use.*

We found the sushi place with ease and parked right in front. Portland seemed to be an easy city. Easy to get around, easy to park, places were easy to find. Easy, cheesy, bing, bang, boom. I liked it. Simple, yet lots of depth.

The restaurant was decorated in Japanese/chic/nouveau hipness. I opened the menu to see that the prices were...okay. <Gulp> *It's alright Evan, just get something small. Starve yourself. You need to lose some weight anyway. In a few weeks, when you run out of money, and your clothes are ragged, and you adopted a mangy dog, and you're living in the park, you'll need to be skinny enough to be able to successfully sell your "need money to go home" cardboard sign.* Preparation. It was all in the preparation.

I looked up from the menu and surveyed the room. A waitress across the way caught my eye. *I know that girl. How do I know her?* She was beautiful, blond, hip but not too—*wait a minute, that's the same girl I saw on the bus today!* I got flustered. Was it a sign? Either fate had drawn us back together, or this city was absurdly small. *Shit, she's coming over here. She has a pitcher of water. She's going to fill our glasses. Is she our waitress? She can't be our waitress.* I looked over at my party. They were busy studying their menus. *Should I say something? Here at the table? What do I say?* My heart beat out of my chest and fell onto the table. *Here she comes.* She was more beautiful as she came closer. She was a blond belle. *Here she is.*

"Hello." She smiled and began to fill our water glasses. Everyone else glanced up and smiled, then looked back to the menus. I opened my mouth but nothing came out. She grabbed my glass last. I looked up at her. She glanced at me and smiled. *Did she recognize me?* No, it was merely the cordial smile of hospitality with no recognition whatsoever. I was just another glass of water to fill.

"Um," I said.

"Your waitress will be over shortly," she said.

"Thanks," said Delilah.

And she was gone with the air conditioning breeze.

We ordered from a different person. I sighed and sat pleasantly. Four people we, all knowing someone quite intimately, and the other as much as they knew a West Coast bum.

Delilah sat up straight, crossed her arms, pursed her lips, and squinted out the window. "Portland's nice. Not much going on, but pleasant nonetheless." She turned to me. "So Evan," her tone of voice meant, "So complete stranger wanting to infiltrate my vacation," "what do you do?"

I didn't get this question much, so I was confused. "Um, I don't know, you mean what am I doing?"

"No, not exactly. I was referring to work, but sure, let's go with that. What are you doing?"

I wasn't sure if she was mocking me but I gave a genuine answer. "I'm on a road trip. I was with two friends but our car broke down in California and these guys picked me up and brought me here."

"And how long do you plan on staying?"

"I think I'm leaving tomorrow for eastern Oregon to a town called, La Grande."

"You *think* you are?" she asked.

"Yeah, well," I paused. *Damn, I'm letting her beat me at my own game!* "I don't really know what happens for sure until it happens. I thought I was road tripping around the country and back, but that plan has changed."

"I understand. 'Until the fat lady sings,' as they say. Isn't that a bit nervewrecking? Knowing things will go wrong?"

"Not really. I'm prepared for anything. And I don't consider it to necessarily go wrong. It just means my course will change and I'll experience something different. But either way it's new and different so both ways are fine by me. My friends and I steered off on different courses, but now I have the pleasure of spending time with you folks."

She gave me another pursed smile. She was not amused. "Well I need concrete plans in my life. Speaking of that, what are we doing tonight? I know a great movie theater we can go to and I guarantee you've never seen anything like it."

Sam, Kara, and I looked at each other, too passively intimidated to argue against this authoritative figure. We nodded. "Sure, sounds good."

"Great! Now do we *think* we are doing it or do we *know* we are doing it?"

Kara and Sam chuckled. I wasn't amused. I shot Sam a look and he stopped laughing and bowed his head.

The drive to the movie theater was only a couple minutes around the corner. I wondered if when people gave directions here, things were always "just around the corner." The theater, called McMenamins, did turn out to be quite extraordinary. It was set up more like a concert hall with a delightfully decorated balcony that wrapped around the top and extended along the sides. Instead of rows of seats, there were tables and chairs situated like a café. The concession booth was in the back of the room and sold theater staples, along with substantial food, and pitchers of beer. I had to hand it to Ms. Republican, it was a good choice. We ordered a pitcher of one of their homebrewed beers. *A movie theater with a casual setting and homebrewed beer? What more can you ask for?!*

We sat down to David Mamet's, Red Belt. It was about some martial arts teacher and his struggles in life, love, and friendship. It started strong, then quickly turned sour and melted into a pile of crap at the end. And that is my movie review of David Mamet's, Red Belt. Needless to say, the actual film was not the highlight of the experience. The beer was great and the setting was just right. I don't know why more places don't do it like this. *Maybe that's what I should do! Open up a movie theater/casual pub on the East Coast! Great, I just decided my life career. Now I can relax again.*

This ended our exciting night in Portland and it was back to the Jupiter Motel for some awkward sleeping arrangements. As expected, it was Sam and me in one bed and the sisters in the other. I was sure that this was not the first homosexually incestual encounter to go on at the Jupiter Motel. But this was it for me. There was no question I was getting the first bus out of here tomorrow and heading—oh God, it's never easy to say—*east. Don't get offended Portland, it's nothing personal against you. Hopefully next time I come, my party won't include Republicans, controlling women, and spineless friends.*

DAY 16

I was woken up by another goddamn alarm. It was twice as bad as yesterday's, since today's was one of those hotel bedside alarm clocks. Naturally the Jupiter Motel had to spice it up, so Hercules and Love Affair blasted in my ear as I rolled over in rudely awakened pain. Delilah was already up. *I knew that Witch had something to do with it.* I opened one eye and watched her bustle past me in a hideous pink nightgown. "Come on people, let's not waste the day here!" <Slam!> Went the bathroom door.

I picked my head up. *Where was I? Oh yeah, some strange, hip motel in Portland, Oregon. Who's this strange man in my bed? I don't remember bringing anyone home from the gay bar last night.* Sam sleepily rolled over on the other side of the bed.

I felt out of place in this motel with my backpacking pack, beard, and absence of cocaine. I didn't belong here, especially with these people. I needed to get back into the wilderness. That was enough motivation to get up.

I packed up my stuff, put on a new shirt, put my laundry in a plastic bag, stuffed it far down into my backpack, packed my toiletries into the top pocket, and stuffed my shoes in another plastic bag which got wedged under the top pocket. It was a travel day, which meant a Birks day. There was nothing worse then having my feet overheat in some poorly circulated shoes, when crammed into a small seat on a crowded bus. *Wow, a bus. I'm going to be on a bus today.* This would mark my first ride on impersonal public transportation on this trip (save for city buses). I needed to prepare myself for more of my freedom getting stripped away. At least in Sam and Kara's car, I could have convinced them to pull over if I really needed them to. Forcing a bus to pull over is something called, "breaking the law."

Once the whole party was ready, we went downstairs to a restaurant next to the lobby, where we ordered overpriced range-free eggs with locally grown hash browns, organic wheat toast, and grapefruit juice not from concentrate. The walls of the establishment were lined with cured, shellacked oak planks. I had a clear image of a tattoed hipster in the middle of a warehouse, dripping sweat in his tight pants, while shellacking the shit out of these wood planks and blasting Animal Collective. I pondered this while Delilah listed all the things she planned to do today. I wasn't regretting missing shopping, a garden tour, and another expensive-sounding restaurant for dinner.

We drove back downtown and parked near some bookstore called, Powells, which apparently is famous. The plan was to spend some time there, and I could leave when I wanted because the bus station was "just around the corner."

Once we got into the bookstore I didn't spare a moment. The time had come. "Well Sam, I think this is where we'll be parting ways."

Sam nodded and glanced at me, then back to a bookshelf and said, "Okay."

I waited for him to say something else, but he didn't. I gave a defeated sigh and turned to the sisters. "Nice to meet you guys, thanks for your help, you really saved me."

"Yeah, good luck." They were happy to get rid of me, I heard it in their tone. Even Sam seemed relieved. His mistresses pulled him over with their imaginary leash and they walked off without looking back. I watched Sam's cold back disappear around a bookshelf. I knew at this point we were very different people, but no matter how much people changed socially, I felt like a pure connection should've been kept with an old friend forever. I was able to get that pureness out of Sam for a brief time yesterday, but he recoiled as fast as it had come. I was hurt. What a great opportunity this was to bond in a little portion of both of our exciting travels, yet most of it was wasted by awkwardness. Just when I thought I knew someone...he couldn't even say goodbye. I took a deep breath and exhaled my woes. That was the past, on to better things. I secured my wicker hat on my head, slung my pack over my shoulder, and walked out of the bookstore, ready to tackle my next adventure.

If Eureka was hell, Sam's ride had brought me through and dropped me at the gates of the real world. But the real world is dark and scary. I couldn't just throw my lonesome self into it—unless I was fitted with some kind of chariot (i.e. the Suburu). But my chariot lost an axle and I needed to soldier on by myself. I needed a safe haven to prepare for such an undertaking. This safe haven happened to be five hours away in La Grande, Oregon.

As I walked closer to the bus station, I noticed some West Coast Hippie Bums sitting around on the sidewalk, slouched onto the sides of the buildings. At the next block, there were twice as many. "Hey man, you need some weed?" I shook my head and walked faster. But the farther I walked in that direction, the more they multiplied. Sure enough, the bus station was their mecca. They surrounded it in droves and it felt like I was wading through a battlefield after the battle, and the victors were long gone. My bright red backpack stuck out in their black and grey and some of them squinted or shielded their eyes when I passed.

Inside the station I bought a ticket for a bus departing in twenty minutes headed for my destination. A line was already forming to get on so I walked over. A few minutes after standing there, a lady walked up behind me with a small, dirty duffel bag. She may have been in her forties, but substances had made her face look twenty years older. She was hunched over with raggedy clothes and she smiled at me, showing that what little funds she most likely had, were not being spent on dental work. She was chipper today—or at that moment. I gave a small, noncommittal grin.

"Oh lord help me!" she chuckled.

I nodded, pretending I could relate to the lord helping me.

"I need to stay in here till the bus comes...too tempting out there." She chuckled again and I gave a questioning look. "And I don't mean the alcohol!" She laughed mischievously and I nodded, pretending I could relate to crack. I turned my head and she continued to mumble.

The bus driver walked to the front of the line and yelled, "Boise! Boise! Bus to Boise and all stops in between. Have your ticket ready please!" It was a long line, most likely a full bus. I put my bag in the bottom cargo hold, grabbed my nalgene and my purple notebook with the Grateful Dead sticker on it, and got on the bus.

I hoped that what seemed like a fifty-fifty chance of not sitting next to a crackhead, would roll in my favor. Most of the seats were already taken. I bit my lip and walked toward the back. The hard part about walking to the back of the bus is you're unable to walk back to the front. Once you're back, that's it. I prayed that I made the right decision. I passed a few empty seats but I refused to sit next to the crackhead, junkie, or big-ass dude who looked fucking mean. Toward the back I spotted a seat with a pleasant-looking lady in her thirties. She looked up at me and gave a friendly smile. *Bingo.* I scooted into the window seat. She looked motherly which made me feel safe.

The driver got into his seat and closed what looked like a bulletproof glass door that surrounded him. He then got on the speaker and his voice sounded like a prison guard's. "Rules of the bus: No cell phones. No smoking ESPECIALLY in the bathroom! Do not get up under any circumstances unless to use the bathroom or to leave the bus ONCE IT IS COMPLETELY PARKED!!! Any drugs or alcohol use, will result in immediate ejection. Keep all conversations to a whisper and do NOT under any circumstances, attempt to talk to the driver...Have a nice trip." He started the engine.

I looked up and saw that at the front of the bus was a camera with a sign saying, "This vehicle is under twenty-four-hour surveillance." I have taken my share of buses, but never have I felt like I was being shipped from one correctional facility to another. The East Coast would never have a glass partition separating the driver from the passengers. Then again I never saw so many bums on East Coast buses. Was there a connection?

The lady next to me smiled calmly as if she was used to this type of prison treatment. Her demeanor helped me relax a little, up until I raised my head and noticed some bus employee with my bag in his hands, walking onto the bus. *What the fuck is going on? Why is this random dude holding my bag? Oh shit! The weed! They found the weed and cookie!* I was so caught up in thinking about the crackheads, that I had forgotten about *my* drugs. They were stashed in my top pocket and easily accessible and even easier to smell. I remembered thinking quickly in the hotel that I could smell it in the bag, but I passed it off. *Is this how my trip is going to end?? Is the finale going to be in an Oregon prison? Do they give the death penalty for weed possession in this state?... Just keep calm Evan...*

The employee lifted up my bag. "Who's bag is this??"

My mouth went dry and I couldn't speak.

"Who's bag is this?!?"

Can I fake it? No, I can't. They'll find out somehow, even if I don't fess up. Not speaking up will make me more suspicious... Okay. It was time to face the music. I slowly raised my hand. The employee noticed me and everyone immediately turned to look at the culprit. The bums looked relieved. For once it wasn't *them*.

"Can you come up here please?" asked the employee.

I stood up and slowly walked to the front. *Goddamn public transportation. GODDAMN public transportation!* It was the longest walk of my life. I thought about Gill and Wallace. What were they doing right now? Much closer to home then I was, for sure. At least they had each other. All I had was Sam and his mistresses. Although it made me a tad amused to imagine them having to take more time out of their trip to bail me out of jail. I couldn't believe that out of all these bums, I was the one to get caught. I probably deserved this from talking so much smack about them. *I'm sorry bums, I'm sure you are all delightful people with families and mortgages. If you get me out of this, I promise I will never utter a negative word about you all ever again!... Did I just pray to bums?*

I made it to the front. The bus driver was still in his capsule and I thought I saw him lock it as I approached.

The employee looked at me. "This is your bag?"

"...Yes."

"Where are you going?"

"...La Grande."

"La Grande? Are you sure?"

Deep breath, "Yes."

"...Okay, I just wanted to make sure because it didn't have a tag. I'll go put one on for you."

"Um, thanks?"

"No problem, have a nice trip!" The employee walked back out, stuck a tag on the bag, and put it under the bus.

I stood there in shock. *What the hell just happened?*

I looked over at the driver who was staring at me through his partition. "Sit down please, the bus is ready to depart."

I shuffled back to my seat. When I sat down, the lady next to me turned and smiled. "Forgot your tag?"

"Yeah, I didn't know I needed one."

"Those tags are a pain in the neck to remember."

"I guess I'm just not used to it."

"Are you from around here?"

"No, I'm from Massachusetts."

Her eyes lit up. "Really! You've come a long way!"

I certainly have. I always like the feeling of being a foreigner and getting that reaction from people. I was a more interesting specimen to talk to, than the average local. "Yeah," I laughed, "I guess you're right."

She had a nice smile. Her face was young and still pretty, but her body had outgrown her once thin physique from bearing children and being the stay at home wife. "So what brings you out to Portland?" she asked.

"I road tripped out here with two friends of mine, but our car broke down a few days ago," this story had turned into my shtick, "and now I'm traveling by myself up to Washington and then British Columbia."

"Wow, that's exciting..." She gave me a concerned look that seemed genuine. "But you know you're going east, right?"

I laughed. "Yes, very observant. I forgot to mention I'm first spending a few days in La Grande with my friend, before I head up to Seattle.

"That's nice, La Grande is a great area. Dog-gone middle of nowhere though." I liked her G-rated phrases. "But beautiful country. Mountains and all, good for hiking if you like that sort of thing."

"That sounds perfect. I think that's actually what I plan to do with my friend."

"I'm sure you'll have a great time then. Are you on this trip for any particular reason?" she asked.

I paused and thought. There wasn't a simple answer to this question. And without too much thought I said, "Searching."

She smiled and nodded. "Okay." Then she paused and turned away like she was in thought. If she continued to press this question, I was afraid we would be spending the rest of this five hour ride on the subject, because that was how long a question like that needed to be discussed.

She turned toward me again. "Did you say you're heading up to Seattle afterward?"

"Yeah, that's the plan right now, although my plans tend to change a lot."

"Do you have friends in Seattle?"

"No, I don't know anyone."

"I'm from Seattle, so I guess now you know me." She smiled and extended her hand. "My name is Linda, what's yours?"

I shook it. "I'm Evan. Pleasure to meet you Linda."

"Likewise."

"Do you live right in the city?" I asked.

"I live close by in a suburb called, Tacoma with my husband and three sons. I'm going to pick up one of my sons at The Dalles now—that's a town before La Grande. He's staying with my mother."

"Oh?"

She leaned in and whispered, "He's our only biological son. The other two are adopted."

"Oh..." *Wow lady, you don't even know me and you're telling me about which sons of yours are adopted. Weird.* Or maybe that wasn't so weird. This was that typical "strangers on public transportation" situation where you can divulge anything you want to someone, knowing that there is an exponentially large chance of never seeing them again.

"What does your husband do?" I asked.

"He's a pastor. I work in graphic design." She looked past me out the window. "Hey, have you ever heard of the Gorge?"

"Hmm, I think I have," I said.

"It's the best part of Oregon. We'll be driving through it soon."

I turned and looked outside to find that we were clear out of Portland and back to a spotted landscape of evergreens, fields, and billboards.

Linda and I continued to chat. I told her more about my trip and she listened intently, seeming to be genuinely fascinated by all the things I had done. She told me about Seattle and how nice Washington State was. She was also curious about Massachusetts and the East Coast. "I've never been out that way," she commented. "I heard it's beautiful."

"It certainly is! Especially in the fall when the leaves change..."

The two of us turned into East Coast/West Coast representatives, like we were trying to sell each other real estate. "...it can get rainy in Seattle, but it keeps everything very lush. And did I mention we live between two national parks? If you like to hike, by golly you would be in heaven up there..." This was exactly what I needed: some genuine friendliness to lift my spirits and keep me engaged to forget about my confined space on this public vessel.

After a half hour of jovial chat, Linda pointed out to the driver's side windows. Outside the trees had dissipated and a large gap was forming and getting deeper with a wide river running through the middle. "Welcome to the Gorge," announced Linda. "It runs across the northern border of Oregon. The other side is Washington. *My* state," she proudly proclaimed. The northwestern-most part of the US was so close, so close I could see it with my own eyes.

The Gorge reminded me of that majestic canyon we had crossed in Idaho, although this was a bit shallower with more water, and huge evergreens blanketed the craggy sides instead of flat desert. On the passenger side of the bus was a steep, wooded mountainside. We passed a few turn-ins, where we could see tall waterfalls cascading down from so high up that I couldn't see the top. I kept getting the urge to yell out at the driver to pull over to check out a waterfall, but alas such luxuries were not given to bus users. Also I would be breaking the rules: "...and do NOT under any circumstances, attempt to talk to the driver...Have a nice trip."

We traveled for an hour admiring the beauty of the Gorge, until the road veered away heading southeast. Signs for The Dalles came up and the bus took the exit. Linda began to gather her things. "This is my stop." She reached into her purse and took out a pen and paper and started writing something. "So Evan, I'll be here for a couple days before I head back up to Tacoma. If you find your way around those parts and you need a roof over your head, our door will always be open."

"Really?" I couldn't believe what I was hearing. I never asked for this.

"Yeah, here's my phone number and email. Don't hesitate to call." She handed me the piece of paper.

"That is so kind of you! I don't know what to say—besides thank you, of course."

"Yes, well if you don't have a problem with three rambunctious boys and a dog, then we'd be happy to have you."

I laughed. "That sounds perfect."

"Great, then I'll see you in Seattle!"

The bus stopped and the driver announced, "This is The Dalles! The Dalles! Wake up if you want The Dalles. If you do not want The Dalles, do NOT get off the bus. This is not a rest stop, I will leave without you. Once again, The Dalles."

Linda got up. "Safe travels, I'm sure you'll enjoy La Grande, it's a fine place."

"Thanks Linda, safe travels to you as well. And I hope you were serious, because I'm known to take people up on generous offers!"

"I certainly am. I look forward to hearing from you. Bye!"

Linda got off with a few other people and shortly after, the doors shut and we were back on the road. I sat back in my seat and relaxed my nerves. Just like that, I secured a place in Seattle. I didn't know what I did, but whatever I did, it was right. It must have been my charming personality and delightful smile. Or was it my grungy looking beard and my smelly clothes? No, I'm selling myself short. My clothes didn't smell that bad...yet. Maybe it was because I was traveling alone. I told her my shtick and she knew I was willing to take any handout I could get. In this case it paid to be alone. Too bad I chose not to sit next to a bum. I probably wouldn't have found a place to stay, but I bet my shtick could have scored me a lot of discount crack.

I spotted a sign for La Grande, which said we were one-hundred-and-fifty miles away: Three hours roughly. *Uhg.* I shifted uncomfortably in my seat. A long distance bus ride wasn't nearly as fun as being in a car. Chatting with Linda helped me forget about the time, as well as my surroundings, but now the sounds of the bus were more prevalent. Some large individual a few rows back was snoring. Behind me a Latino man was talking loudly on his phone. *Didn't he hear the rules? No, he probably didn't even understand English.*

I felt a small object hit my lap. I looked down and saw a wrapped peppermint candy. I looked across the aisle and straight at the crackhead lady who had stood behind me in line. She was giggling. "Merry Christmas! Te-he-he!"

I cringed, but I faked a smile. "Thanks!"

She drew her finger to her mouth as if to shush me. She grabbed another peppermint from her pocket and tossed it onto the seat in front of me. There was a kid there, who looked around fourteen. He looked over at the Peppermint Crack Lady and she gave him the same routine adding, "Hehe, don't tell momma I gave you candy!"

The kid chuckled nervously. "I won't."

Her face grew thoughtful. "Is your momma here?"

"No, I'm by myself."

"Really? How brave! Where you going?"

"Boise."

"Is that where your momma is?"

The kid nodded.

"What are you doing all the way out here?" she asked.

"I just got out of juvy."

The Peppermint Crack Lady gasped and put her hand to her chest. "Oh Lord, you poor thing! Oh Lord," she looked up at the ceiling of the bus, "oh Lord help us. Lord help us and keep—" She looked back down at him. "What did you do?"

"Theft and possession."

"Oh!" she yelped up, "Oh Lord help us!" Down, "Did juvy get you straight?"

"Yes ma'am."

"Did you go to church?"

"Yes ma'am."

Up, "Oh! Thank you Lord, you saved another!" Down, "That's all you need, honey. Keep your faith in Jesus and you will lead a straight path."

"Yes ma'am."

"I tell you, when I found Jesus, my life changed. I saw the light. It was a miracle. And whenever I get bad thoughts, whenever I want to steal, whenever I want to do drugs, I reach out to my Lord and savior, and he answers." Up, "He says, 'Darla, Darla, don't do that. Put that down and put your love in me.' And I say, 'Yes Lord, I will, I love you.'" Down.

Outside it was back to barren desert. Not like Nevada desert, but throw some Nevada in a pot with some South Dakota prairie on top, mix it around, and you got whatever this was. When I imagined Oregon, I did not imagine this. But seeing as how there was nothing else in sight, this landscape must have taken up a good majority of the state. I also didn't imagine this area to be so full of Jesus freaks. Casey was right: Get out of Portland, and you've entered *God's country*. I tried to tune out Darla's pontifical prayers, but I was either listening to that, or a one-sided Spanish conversation. *Man, I love buses!* But I couldn't complain too much. I had a promising prospect for a place to stay in Seattle and that wouldn't have happened in a car with two other Easterners.

After an hour of desert, some green hills appeared on the horizon. Soon we were rising in elevation and the road weaved around rocks and mounds. Once we reached a certain elevation, the bus turned perpendicular to where we had come from and I was able to look out onto the flatlands below. It was amazing to see the phenomenon of perfectly flat earth that stopped at the edge of the mountains, like hitting a brick wall. I had seen it in Wyoming and Nevada as well. This was a true signature of the West.

Once we turned back east, the flatlands vanished and we were engulfed in hills. This was Casey country—La Grande was close. As I sat enraptured by the changing scenery, a new voice emerged behind me. "Hello? Yeah, I'm super close. Oh my God, we have *totally* left civilization, this is so weird!" It was the voice of a teenage boy with an extremely effeminate tone. "It's like, all trees and shit! I feel like I'm in a horror movie...I know! I'd be so scared! Oh my God, seriously, you have to take the next bus out here, I can't be in the middle of nowhere alone!"

I clenched my fists. *You're not in the middle of nowhere, you have full cell service, dipshit.*

"Oh my God, oh my God, I swear the farther we get from Portland, the more I can feel myself turning into a hick. I think I'm actually *smelling* cow shit. Oh my God I can't wait to get back to clean civilization. This is going to be the longest week of my life! I swear I'm going to text you every ten minutes...no seriously, I have to! I'm going to turn into a hick if I don't!...Don't laugh! I'm serious!"

I was biting a hole in my lip. I have a very low tolerance for people who don't appreciate nature. I find it unnatural for a human to be unable to identify with it. We are natural beings, not born from concrete.

It's unfortunate to meet someone that grows up in a city or urban environment, who is legitimately scared of nature. The city is much more dangerous and dirty than the wilderness. This is the most common misconception.

I had to listen to that twit carry on his conversation all the way to La Grande, but thankfully it wasn't much farther. The bus turned off the highway onto a road that was in the middle of a valley surrounded by mountains. I called Casey who told me he would be there in a couple minutes.

The bus stopped at a truck stop/gas station. "La Grande! La Grande! Get off for La Grande! If not, do NOT get off—" I wasn't going to miss that voice. I got off, along with the rurally challenged femme boy, whom I watched with disgust. He sprang off and looked around with his cell phone clutched in his hand like he was getting off the boat at the beaches of Normandy, holding onto his only form of protection for dear life. He scampered awkwardly like a frightened urban chipmunk into the gas station.

I grabbed my tagged bag of drugs and looked around. The area was mostly flat, with long stretches of road that jutted out into the valley. The mountains weren't far off, maybe ten miles out. This had to be the outskirts of town, but even so, Casey was right. It didn't look like much was going on in eastern Oregon. But I didn't expect much regardless. All I knew I needed, was a roof over my head, some old fashioned internet, and some healthy outdoors.

Then I saw that little black Honda come parading down the road like a shining beacon. It was a relief to know I would be in good hands for a few days. Casey pulled up with a reassuring grin. He didn't look any different from when I saw him last, eight hundred miles south of here, one week prior—*Was it only one week since we were having breakfast with Casey's family at a campsite in Yosemite? It could have been years ago.* I couldn't look at this trip on a time scale. I had to figure out some other kind of way to gauge it, because time wasn't working.

I threw my pack in the backseat, tossed my wicker hat on top, and climbed in the front. I looked over at this all too familiar friend and smiled. "Long time no see."

Casey thought for a second, then shrugged and gave a light chuckle. "Sure." He put the car in gear and we were off.

We headed along the streets of La Grande with Sam Cooke playing from Casey's speakers, and all was right with the world.

"How long have you been here?" I asked.

"Just a few days. I got out of the Yosemite wilderness and drove straight up."

"How was the hike by the way?"

"Fucking amazingly magical shit."

I shook my head in utter jealousy.

"I saw the sunrise from the top of Halfdome."

"You bastard!" I've said it before and I will say it again, you have no idea what a National Park has to offer, unless you hike into the back-country. "Goddamn, I can only imagine."

We were getting into what seemed like the center of town. It looked like one main street, maybe three blocks long, and nothing had been changed since 1956. There were old stores, some barely standing and some rundown. An old marquis stood proudly yet desperately in the middle block. That huge Wal Mart that we passed on the way into town was probably what did this main street in. "I hope you weren't expecting a whole lot from La Grande, because this is all you're going to get," stated Casey.

I laughed. "No, I wasn't."

Then he added, "It's going to be pretty tight quarters as well, but we'll make it work."

We turned onto one of the blocks and immediately turned into a parking lot.

"Have you started your job yet?" I asked.

"Yeah, it's actually in the same building where I live. That's where you can use the internet. They haven't reached the advancement of getting internet into the apartments yet."

"Oh yeah?"

"It's bare bones, just a small room with a tiny bathroom attached. But it's fine, I have the key to the office and we can go there any time after hours. The job is real laid back so far. There's only four other people working, all cool, outdoorsy types."

"Sounds right up your alley."

"Yeah, it's a 'work at your own pace' type of environment."

"What's it called?"

"The Devil's Canyon Preservation Society."

My eyes lit up. "Cool! Is that where we can hike?"

Casey shook his head. "No, Devil's Canyon is actually three hours from here in Idaho. I think they used the name for some added pizzazz. We deal with the canyon, but the majority of our work is close by in the Wallowa-Whitman National Forest. Those are the mountains you can see from here."

"Have you explored it yet?"

"No, not really. I figured that's what we would do."

I smiled. "Perfect."

"We'll get into the details later."

Casey parked and we walked across the street to a large stone cube. It was six stories high and had that 1930's square office design. Casey led me up five flights to his apartment, which turned out to be just as he described. The room was so small that his bed took up half of it. There was a desk that took up another third, but just enough floor space for my body to fit lengthwise, which was all I needed. I barely missed the bathroom behind the front door. Inside there was enough space to stand by the sink, and turn around to get into the tiny shower. I looked out his one window, which looked down on the main street and the mountains in the back. The low hanging sun gave them a faint orange coat. I breathed in, relieved. No more billboards, or hip lamps, or awkward friends. I turned around and Casey was giving me a "what do you think?" look. "Welcome to my dorm room," he said with a chuckle, then he shrugged. "It works." I nodded in agreement, knowing full well that it would work for someone like Casey.

"So I have an idea of where we can hike," Casey began, "but I want to talk to my coworkers, since they know these woods like the back of their hand. Come with me, I'll show you my office."

I put my bag down and we headed out the door. He turned his head as we walked down the hall. "Brace yourself, it's a long walk." We took an elevator down one flight, then walked to the end of the hall. A small glass door said, "Devil's Canyon Preservation Society."

"That's convenient," I said.

"Yeah, I don't think I'll have trouble getting to work on time. Or at least they won't have trouble knocking on my door if I sleep in."

Casey led me into a small office. It had a long hallway with a few rooms connected, and at the end of the hallway there was a big conference room. The office was silent with not a soul in sight. The walls were adorned with large topographical maps with highlighted boxes marking different areas. I pointed to them. "What's this?"

Casey walked over. "This is predominantly what we do. The highlighted areas are where we're fighting to preserve. We have different disputes with different groups. Some are with the ranchers who graze cattle, who we're trying to stop from trampling and eating all the plant life. Some are state or federal groups who own part of the land, who we're trying to stop from developing or digging. Some are ATV recreation areas, which we're trying to stop from grinding up the soil. The list goes on."

"Are you guys writing up grants and proposals or something to get these areas protected from certain groups?"

"Yeah, more or less. It's tough. The first thing they emphasized to me is that we're a small fish in a big pond. It's a classic case of a small, non-profit activist group fighting an uphill battle to save the innocent, voiceless party—that being nature."

I nodded. "Gotcha. Go you."

"Yeah, I'm excited. My job is basically to hike a lot and write a lot."

"Sounds like your dream job."

Casey shrugged. "It's good for now. Not the most ideal location, but who knows. I haven't even been here a week. I heard about a rodeo coming up soon a few towns over. I'm *very* excited."

"Really?" I asked incredulously. "In Oregon?"

Casey looked at me like I still wasn't getting it. "In case you didn't know, you're back in the Wild West. Western Oregon may be the hippie, liberal, Pacific Northwest, but you're in eastern Oregon. They might as well be two different countries."

I thought the office was empty, but a man came out of one of the rooms and joined us. He looked like he was in his fifties and gave off a relaxed attitude with a genuine smile. He was dressed formally, but I could tell he had a rugged body, probably from a healthy lifetime of hiking these mountains. "Hey Casey."

"Hey Harry, what's happening?" Casey said jovialy.

He looked at me. "I take it this is your friend you said was visiting."

"Yeah, this is Evan, he's passing through."

"Hello Evan, nice to meet you, I'm Harry."

"Hi Harry." I shook an extremely callused hand.

"Casey must be a popular guy, he hasn't even been here a week and he's already got people coming all the way out here to visit."

We laughed. "Yeah, but pure coincidence," said Casey. "Lightning won't be striking twice I'm sure."

"Where are you passing through to?" asked Harry.

"Seattle, then British Columbia." I said.

Harry nodded. "Oh yeah, beautiful country up there. Great hiking, some of the best in the world."

"Yeah, hopefully I can do some."

"As a matter of fact," Casey interjected, "I wanted to ask you about that. We're planning on going out to the wilderness for a couple days. Where do you think is a good start?"

Harry turned and thoughtfully looked over at one of the maps. "Hmm. Well you got a lot of choices, but a good start is the Eagle Cap Wilderness." He pointed to an area.

"That's where I was thinking," agreed Casey.

"There's a hunting shack about five miles in, easy hike, just be careful because the snow is still melting in spots. You can get caught in a snow pile and lose the trail if you're not careful."

"Good to know, thanks."

"Sure. And while you're out there can you check up on the cattle grazing zone over here?" He pointed to a highlighted spot on the map. "I'd like to know what kind of shape it's in."

"Absolutely!" said Casey. I could hear the excitement in his voice. I would be excited too about getting assigned a task in the wilderness by my new job.

"When are you planning on leaving?" Harry asked.

"Tomorrow morning most likely."

"Sounds fun." Harry grabbed his bag. "I'm getting out of here. Good luck boys."

"Thanks Harry."

Harry gave a nod and a smile and walked out.

I turned to Casey. "Nice guy."

"Yeah, he's great, real helpful."

"Is he your boss?" I asked.

Casey thought for a second. "I don't know. Probably. I don't get a feeling of hierarchy around here. Everyone's probably my boss in some respect. Who knows, maybe I'm theirs and I don't even know!"

This lax attitude was amazing. Maybe this was the route I needed to take. I knew I didn't want to be part of some huge office, pushing papers around in some rigid environment. A small non-profit sounded perfect. No stress, friendly and genuine coworkers working for a good cause, no eyeballing bosses. Maybe they had room for another employee. Hiking and writing sounded like a fine profession to me.

Casey walked down the hall to a desk with a computer. "If you want to use the internet you can use this."

"Cool, thanks."

"Do you need to use it now?"

I nodded, "Yeah, I probably should."

"Okay, I'll set you up and head back to my room. I still have some unpacking to do. When you're done, come back up and we'll go to the local bar for some food and drink."

"Do we have to make reservations?" I asked.

Casey shot me a dull look. "Funny," he said, and he walked away.

I sat down at the computer. It was time to figure out some sort of plan. Unfortunately without a car and a tent, I was unable to travel as freely and spontaneously as the past few weeks. I needed to know my mode of transportation and I needed to have a good idea of where I was sleeping at night. Everything else could be worked around. Transportation wasn't hard. I looked at the Greyhound bus website and checked buses leaving La Grande. The next logical place to go seemed to be Seattle. I couldn't think of anywhere in between, unless I was to take a huge detour back to the coast, which wasn't realistic. Plus, it made sense to head to Seattle since I had a fresh friend with her doors open...at least I hoped so. I took out the piece of paper from my pocket with Linda's info on it and started writing an email.

"Hey Linda, this is Evan, the lonely traveler from the bus—"

I paused. *Is it too soon to write an email? I just got off the bus a couple hours ago. Will she think I'm strange for contacting her so soon?... Wait, what am I saying? She's the nicest lady on earth, she won't mind... at least I hope so.*

> Hey Linda, this is Evan, the lonely traveler from the bus. I think I'll be heading to Seattle in a couple days like I had mentioned. I was wondering if it was still okay if I stayed with your family for a day or two. Let me know.
> Talk to you soon,
> Evan

Okay, I got that taken care of. All I could do now was hope that she was as nice and genuine as she seemed and would write me back. If not, well, I'll deal with it.

On to the next order of business. It was best to figure out the rest of my trip while I had the resources, because who knew when I would get this chance again. *Where do I go from Seattle? I should check out Olympic National Park! But how will I get there? Where will I stay? I probably needed a tent. Didn't Wallace mention having a friend who was willing to take us to the park? Yeah! And I also remember he said he lived in Seattle! He could be my backup for a place to stay!*

I gave Wallace a call..."I'm sorry, you cannot leave a message because this person's mailbox is full. Goodbye."

Fuck you, you robot whore. And you too, Wallace, clean out your goddamn mailbox already... Wait, that's right, Wallace doesn't have a phone—sorry Wallace.

I gave Gill a call. Ring...ring...ring..."Hey this is Jacob, please leave a—"

Shit. I guess I'll try later.

Who knew where those two ruffians were. Probably lounging in the Nevada hot springs with naked women and cigars. I wasn't going to rely on a call back. If I didn't get one, Olympic National Park was out of my reach.

The next logical choice seemed to be Vancouver. I was positive that buses were easy to find between the two cities so I saved that search. The challenge was a place to stay.

A hotel was my last resort. Let me repeat, my *last resort.* It was like being stuck on a desert island and chewing off my own arm as a last ditch effort for sustenance. Hotels are hospitality dungeons where people go to escape the places they are visiting to immerse themselves in stale, superficial, impersonal comforts. My goal was to always be immersed in the place I was traveling in. I wanted to eat, sleep, and breath it. Clean white linen, free HBO, and continental breakfast did not spell, "Vancouver." It spelled, "every fucking hotel in the world."

I went onto some hostelling websites, some I had used when traveling around Europe. Hostels are a bit like hotels, but they're usually cheaper and there's an opportunity to meet other travelers, as opposed to being isolated in a cell—I mean room—no, I did mean cell. I predominantly stayed in hostels throughout my travels and most of them worked out fine. I figured the Northwest must have had hostels somewhere. Not as extensive as Europe I was sure, but there had to be a few. I wasn't able to carry a tent on my back, so hostels appeared to be the only realistic option.

I searched for Vancouver and a few places popped up:

"Vancouver's premier hostel at the center of downtown!" *Okay, how much? Thirty Dollars a night?? That's crazy! What else?*

"This hostel is set a bit outside of the city. Buses run into the city periodically." *That sounds okay, I guess. Twenty dollars a night? A little better, but still not good. Maybe worth it, if it was in the city.*

There were a few other choices, all similar. My search results didn't leave me satisfied. *Are there any other options?* I hopelessly stared at the computer screen.

Maybe I should try that site that Sam's girlfriend had mentioned. What was it? The axe murderer one. Couchsurfing I think?... But Sam's girlfriend recommended it. What the hell does she know?... Fine, I'll check it out. I searched for "couchsurfing" and it brought me to "couchsurfing.org." On the homepage it prominently read: "Surf millions of couches across the world!" My interest was peaked and I clicked on the "search couches" icon. It brought me to a page with a map of the world where I had the choice to click on every continent. I clicked on North America and it listed United States and Canada—*and Greenland?? Holy shit, people live on Greenland? And I can stay on their couch??*

I had to click on Greenland. It gave me a list of cities and how many "Couchsurfers" were in each city. "Nuuk: 18 Couchsurfers; Ilulissat: 5

Couchsurfers; Kangerlussuaq: 3 Couchsurfers. I clicked on Kangerlussuaq and clicked on "list surfers on next page." It listed pictures and some basic info of three Couchsurfers. I clicked on "Kirsten" and it brought me to her profile. The profile showed pictures, personal interests, couch availability, references, and other related details. I looked at Kirsten's info. She had a picture of herself smiling with a backpack, on the top of some mountain. *She must enjoy traveling. What a coincidence, so do I.* I looked at her references. Jorg from Denmark said, "Kirsten is a very awesome host! She hosted me and my friend and showed us all around her city, then cooked an amazing meal. You are always welcome in Denmark where I will show you as many awesome places as you showed me!" Kirsten had ten other references and they were all positive. I assumed all of these people weren't chopped up with an axe and had lived to tell about how great a time they had. I couldn't believe she took them around her town and cooked them dinner. It sounded like some five star exotic resort with a personal guide. My interest was peaked twofold.

I went back to the search and clicked on Canada—*Holy shit!* Montreal: 6776 Couchsurfers; Toronto: 3292 Couchsurfers; Vancouver: 2582 Couchsurfers! *That's insane! How do this many people know about this website??* I clicked on Vancouver and got a forty-page list. I began a frenzy of browsing people's profiles, like I was a high school girl glued to Facebook. This site had similarities to Facebook but it seemed much more meaningful.

People had a wide array of couch availability. Some said they did not have a couch available but would meet for "coffee and a drink." Others said they were currently traveling. And the ones that had couches did not all have "couches" to offer. Some had futons, bedrooms, hammocks on their porches, loft space on their boat—the list went on. Most people had pictures of themselves traveling. Some stood with their backpacks on the tops of mountains, some were jumping off a waterfall, some were sitting around a huge table of delicious looking food, with a large group of smiling faces. The caption said, "Couchsurfing in Mumbai." I did not see anyone with a simple "glamour shot" picture of their ugly mug. This clearly was not the point of the website. What struck me the most from reading their info was that they all seemed like pure travelers. They got it. They shared exactly what I felt when it came to traveling. Was this site too good to be true? It seemed like the perfect way to travel and I had no idea it had existed until now. *Does it cost anything? Nope, totally free.* There had to be some catch. *Do I have to pay anything to stay on people's couches?* I could not find anything that required any sort of compensation.

My interest was peaked threefold so the next thing I had to do was to create a profile. I spent the next hour creating one for myself. I tried to put in as much helpful info as possible. The only thing I could not give was a picture, since I had no way of downloading anything from my camera. I decided to write on my profile an explanation of exactly why I couldn't provide a picture. This entailed putting down my shtick of how the car broke down, how Wallace and Gill left me for dead, and how I was "forging" the Northwest on my own. I figured that my story was compelling enough to convince some people, since it was probably hard to accept a faceless traveler. Some would think that *I* was the axe murderer. I prayed that my pershwayshive shtick would shway their opinion.

When I finished my profile I spent another hour searching for hosts and sending "couchsurf requests." I gave my phone number in my message since I knew I would have scarce access to a computer past this point. While I searched in Vancouver, I figured I would extend my search. I sent requests to surfers on Vancouver Island, as well as Whistler. Whistler only had a few surfers to choose from, and I crossed my fingers and toes as I sent the requests.

When I felt like I had sufficiently sent out enough requests, I sat back and looked up. The office was dark. I was so absorbed I didn't realize the time. My stomach came back to reality too, and gave me an awakened gurgle. My work was done for now and it was time for some Oregon drinkin, Oregon eatin, Oregon hootin, hollerin, shit kickin, wranglin and 'rastlin. Yeehaw!

I ran back up to Casey's room ready to divulge this newfound traveling tool to a fellow traveler. I found him standing on his bed, pinning up a colorful tapestry to a blank white wall. Combustication by Medeski, Martin, and Wood played softly from his computer speakers. It was like being in the dorms again during the first week of school.

Casey turned around. "Hey you're back. Did you make some headway?"

"Casey! You wouldn't believe it!" I sounded like I had found the Holy Grail. "I found the most amazing website, it's like it's tailored to people like you and me! I mean travelers. You know, like real travelers, not tourists." I was pacing around the room with a giddiness churned up in my insides that had been lying dormant for centuries. "It's perfect! It's everything you would want when traveling, and no bullshit!"

"Are you going to tell me what it is?" he asked.

"It's like when you travel to a place—what? Oh sorry, it's called Couchsurfing. So when you travel somewhere and—"

"It's like actual couchsurfing?"

"Yeah, you can search anywhere in the world and stay on someone's couch—but it's not always a couch, it can be anything, like a treehouse!"

Casey furrowed his brow and folded his arms. "And do they chop you up into little pieces while you sleep?"

I laughed. "No, that's what I thought but it doesn't look like that's the case. It looks like a site full of people like you and me. It's amazing. Let me ask you. When have you had a better travel experience? When you stayed in a hotel, or stayed with a friend?"

"A friend, of course. Is that a trick question?"

"It's obvious, right? When you stay in a hotel, you're just a foreigner in a foreign place. You leave your hotel and wander around, aimlessly figuring out what to do, or do something you read was fun to do in some dumb brochure and spend your time with all the other tourists who also heard about that 'fun' thing to do. And more often then not, it's just a tourist trap. And do you ever get the true sense of being in a place while spending time in a tourist trap or hotel?"

Casey's arms remained folded. "No, stop asking rhetorical questions. I see where you're going with this."

I ignored him and kept pacing. My mind couldn't slow down. "So with Couchsurfing, you're staying with a local, just like if you were staying with a friend! You're experiencing the true culture of that area, just by staying there! And, and, and—"

"Evan, slow down. Take a breath."

"Sorry." I didn't slow down. "And you can say, 'Hey, what's the best spot to go eat?' and they'll say, 'You've to go here, but don't go there because that's where all the tourists go.' Or maybe they'll even take you around and show you! This website holds the key to finding the true culture in where you travel!"

"Are you sure?" asked Casey. "You sound like you're their spokesperson and you haven't even done it."

I stopped pacing. "No, I'm not sure but I'm really excited to find out."

"Sounds cool though. Where are you going to do it?"

"Hopefully BC. I sent a bunch of requests. I really hope I can do it in Whistler."

Casey nodded. "That would be awesome. Just don't call me telling me I have to pick you up because you got your arms chopped off."

"I might not be able to call you if that happens, but we'll see."

"Good point, you need arms to use a phone. Hey, does this look straight?"

I looked up at the tapestry. "Sure does."

Casey stepped down from his bed. "Good. You hungry?"

"Starving."

"Let's go to the bar."

The bar was in walking distance, just a block down Main Street and a block north. There was a slight chill to the air, just enough to remind me that I had gained elevation. The walk was quiet. Any stores still in business on the main street were dark, and once we turned the corner, the block was equally dark, save for a neon sign lit up at the end that stuck out of the building. The sign appropriately read, "The End Zone" in athletic script, and neon beer signs adorned the windows. We walked into a fairly empty room, with some blue-collar dressed men sitting at a couple tables. The place was a standard divey sports bar: Long bar, grungy tables, and TV's propped up on the walls playing ESPN. Some of the men glanced up at us briefly, then continued looking at their beer or the TV. I noticed one guy shake salt into his beer: blue-collar special. "Go have a seat over there," Casey instructed. "I'll get the beers. You have to try their local brew, it's delicious."

"Okay." I sat down and observed what was around me. I noticed another guy shake salt into his beer. I had to add that to my list of questions to ask my personal La Grande representative.

Casey came over with a dark brew in each hand. "This is a tasty nut brown ale called, Snake River."

"Snake River?" That sounded familiar. We cheers'd and I sipped: Delicious. It gave off a familiar taste. *Wasn't that the beer I had in Jackson?* "Where is this beer from?" I asked.

"I think Jackson, but they consider it their local brew."

"Yeah! That's what I thought. I had this beer in Jackson. Wow, they get it all the way out here, that's cool."

"It's not as far as you think," said Casey. "All you have to do is cross Idaho and you're there." He was right. It seemed like such a long time ago that I was in Jackson and so much distance was covered in between, but I didn't necessarily move farther away from there. Heading north and then east got me closer than I realized.

"I ordered some wings, they're good and spicy here," said Casey.

I took another sip and relaxed in my chair. I was on autopilot, letting everything happen. This was a much better situation than twenty-four hours prior, awkwardly sitting in a posh Japanese restaurant.

I watched another dude give his beer the blue-collar special. "Do you know what the deal is with putting salt in your beer?" I asked.

Casey shook his head. "I've been wondering the same thing but I believe it's the Oregon way of getting the foam down."

"Oh, I see." I turned to Casey. "You remember how we do it back in the East, right?"

Casey scoffed. "Do you think I got amnesia or something?" He then took his index finger, wiped the side of his nose to grab some sweaty oil, and stuck it in the beer, swirling it around in the foam.

I laughed. "Just making sure you remembered your roots out here."

"Give me a break! I've been out West for just a few weeks. Come to think of it, I've been out West for as long as *you* have!"

"This is correct. I haven't forgotten my roots either." I grabbed myself a good swab of nose sweat and plunged it into my beer. I watched as the foam in my glass disintegrated—or did it? This ritual could have worked exclusively in our heads and the same could have been for these guys using the salt.

"So is there anything going on in this town besides men putting salt in their beer?" I asked.

"Yes," answered Casey. "As a matter of fact, La Grande is home to the Hot Shots."

"Hot Shots?"

"Yeah, ever heard of them?"

"I can't say I have."

"Have you ever seen the movie, Top Gun?"

I looked at Casey like he was crazy. "Is that a question?"

"Okay, well substitute fighter pilots for forest fire fighters. That's the only difference. These guys either hike or get parachuted in to fight forest fires. Pretty badass, but unfortunately their title adds fuel to their already inflated egos."

"They're actually called Hot Shots?"

"Yes, that is their official title."

"Wow, God help us."

After a couple more quality beers and mediocre bar food, Casey and I were inclined to head home, because tomorrow would be an early wake up to head out on the trail. As we were walking out the door, a different crowd started pouring in the bar. They were men and women, all around our age, looking well fit, and wearing mostly Abercrombie and Fitch with a western twang accessory, like cowboy boots or a camouflage hunting hat. It was like someone ordered a frat party to be delivered and they all came at once. They strutted in like they owned the place (I was sure they did) and didn't pay much attention to us. When we were outside, I heard some screams and hoots before the door closed.

Casey turned to me. "Lucky you, you got a small taste of the Hot Shots."

"I'm sorry we couldn't stay to see more," I said dryly.

"Unless you enjoy Bon Jovi and Kenny Chesney playing at full volume," said Casey, "I would not be sorry."

I laughed. "As amusing as I'm sure it would be to experience, I choose sleep."

Casey nodded. "Good choice."

As we walked back toward Casey's apartment, Casey began listing our itinerary. "The trailhead is about a forty-minute drive out of town. We need to also leave time to make a grocery run. That should take twenty minutes. We probably want to get on the trail by nine or ten. It's a five-mile hike in, and we should leave lots of time when we get to our destination before it gets dark so we can gather firewood, settle in, and most importantly, *explore*."

That word sent shivers up my spine. I knew what exploring meant with Casey.

"So we should probably wake up around seven. Did you catch all that?" he asked.

I was still envisioning getting my limbs torn off by a bear from "exploring" too far off the trail.

"Evan?"

"Huh? Yeah, sounds good."

We made the long trek back to Casey's "dorm" room. Casey turned to me. "All I can offer you is my floor to sleep on, by the way. Did I mention that?"

"In so many words, but I assumed that was the plan."

"Okay, good. Sorry about that."

I smiled. "No need for apologies my friend, you're helping me in more ways than you can imagine."

I laid in my sleeping bag on the floor, thinking about how good of a choice it was to have made the five-hour detour out to La Grande, Oregon.

DAY 17

The alarm went off at seven a.m. sharp, but this time I wasn't thinking about how obnoxious it sounded. Getting up with a purpose made it worth it.

Casey had made sure to lend me his camping pad so I wasn't lying straight on his firm, industrial carpet. These were interesting living quarters that he was given for his time in La Grande. I wouldn't have been surprised if it turned him into a zen minimalist by the time he was done—correction: a zen minimalist with an undying love for Kenny Chesney.

The two of us sat up blinking at the faint morning light of the sunrise, with a pinkish glow haloing the mountaintops. Casey reached over and turned on his stereo. The smooth, uplifting vibrations of Sly and the Family Stone eased our bodies out of bed.

Once the bathroom was used and the fluids began to flow in the right directions, I put on some shorts and a T-shirt, and began the process of converting my travel home into a hiking pack. Packing for a single night excursion was not a difficult process. The shorts I had on would last me both days, as well as my wool socks. Pack an extra shirt, along with a pair of pants and my sweatshirt for the night. I wouldn't be taking a shower, so keeping the same boxers wouldn't kill me. Just make sure to wipe well—hey! Don't judge me...Then came toiletries: toothbrush, toothpaste, deodorant—I don't care where I am, woods or city, my pits will smell good. Hardware: Knives, sunglasses, harmonica, nalgene, headlamp, camera, poncho, sleeping bag, buddha bag, and finally my Birks at the top. The extra room in my pack would be for groceries and cooking supplies. I was good to go. I picked up my pack and it felt significantly lighter, which was a very good thing. If traveling with nothing but a backpack (or living in Casey's dorm room) did not turn me into a minimalist, hiking would.

Casey and I divided the cooking supplies. It wasn't a large amount because I was dealing with the "Casey family hiking machine." We had a small stove that fit in a pouch, a couple pots that folded into each other, and a couple bowls that did the same with room inside for utensils: Done.

I looked at our packs. They looked light...*too* light. "Wait, what about a tent?" I said in astonishment. Did I catch Casey off guard? How could he have forgotten such an essential item?

Naturally he shot back an answer. "We don't need one. Harry told us about the hunting shack, remember?"

"Are you sure we shouldn't bring one just in case? Maybe the hunting shack—"

"Dude," Casey cut me off, "if Harry says we're good, then we're good." He was right. How could I second-guess those callused hands? "Okay. Let's get out of this one-horse town."

We headed to the car with our light, tight packs over our strong, young backs. The sun was peaking up over the ridgeline and the first hint of warmth brushed my face. We drove to a big chain grocery store set on the outskirts of town. It was apparent that our grocery mission would go smoothly without any delays or hassle, due to the seven-thirty a.m. La Grande grocery store traffic being at an astonishing low.

Casey and I were veterans at the pre-hike grocery store shopping routine. Throughout the years, it was often me learning from Casey about the hiking essentials. We seamlessly floated through, grabbing items like nymphs picking flowers in a familiar wood. Most of the usual suspects that we picked, were revealed in Yosemite:

<u>Essential hiking ingrediants for a single night excursion (serves two):</u>

-1 pack of flour tortillas: One of the most essential items; Light, thin, and flexible; Could fit in any crevice of a pack; Good to cook, or eat raw; Goes with all meals, even desert items.

-1/2 pound of salami slices: Light, thin, and flexible; Keeps well; Good for pan grease; Adds a mild yet robust, spicy flavor.

-1 packet of minute rice.
-1 block of cheddar cheese.
-1 red pepper to cut up for a veggie in the rice.
-1 small bottle of hot sauce—cap better fucking work.
-1 bag of trail mix.
-1 small box of instant oatmeal: The box will be left in the car and the packets are easy to slip into the packs.
-2 apples.

Menu:
Lunch:
Spicy Salami and cheese wraps, trail mix on the side.

Dinner:
Spicy Rice with pepper and cheese.

Desert:
Melted trail mix quesadillas.

Breakfast:
Oatmeal, apples on the side.

Lunch:
Repeat.

We bought some extra fruit for this morning's breakfast ride and absorbed the essential sugars and nutrients as we embarked on the forty-minute drive into the mountains to our trailhead. I got to pick the music this time from Casey's ipod. Casey had a lot of music. A lot of *good* music. A pleasant early Grateful Dead live acoustic set felt right to "ease us in" to the day. Casey nodded in agreement.

Twenty minutes of driving and we ascended from the high plains into the foothills of the Eagle Cap Wilderness. I found it funny that after covering so much ground in this country, after crossing though multiple national parks and forests and mountains, my first real hiking trip would be in a little unknown stretch of wilderness in eastern Oregon. But the mountains we were driving into, already looked mouthwateringly hike-worthy. This unsuspecting land had far larger mountains than any on the East Coast. It goes to show how much there is to see in this country. These mountains would be a highly trafficked attraction in the East. However, out here in the West, they were merely another mountain range. Harry had probably spent a good part of his life exploring these mountains and I bet he still did it, rarely retracing a step. I was as excited as Casey was. This was treading new ground for the both of us.

The road got narrow and windy with houses sparsely set apart. Most of the houses were wooden ranches with grazing areas for livestock. The occasional cows and goats stood around, chomping on a blade of grass or standing and staring at God-knows what. Then the road got narrower and dirtier with evergreens flooding our visibility, meaning we were now in the mountains. Casey decreased his speed, periodically studying the topographical map in his hand, which showed hiking trails as well as access roads. "Shouldn't be far now," he said with a reassuring tone. He may have assumed that I thought he was lost. I smiled and shrugged. I couldn't care less. Driving endlessly through these roads was fine with me.

I looked back out my side window and was startled by the sudden flash of the spotted back and bushy white tail of a fawn, as it pranced into the brush. My hair stuck up on the back of my neck. I was giddy with the thought of what other amazing wildlife would reveal itself to me. "Casey! Did you see that fawn?" I asked in a shrill tone.

"What? No, where?" Casey looked around.

"You missed out, it's long gone." I stared out at the dense woods in admiration. "God, what a beautiful creature."

Spotting an animal in the woods is like getting laid. There's usually no control over when it will happen. It could happen at any moment. But the more effort that's put in, the more likely it will happen. It never lasts too long, because they usually run away. But for that moment, it sure is awesome.

A few more miles and Casey turned onto a steep, graveled road. This road was noticeably darker from the lack of light penetrating the ever-denser forest. After a half-mile we turned into a parking lot with the classic wooden post signifying a trailhead. There were no other cars in the lot and not a soul in sight.

Casey cranked up the stereo for some pre-hiking pump-up music, as we got ready to set off. This was a common practice for us back in college, as we put our ski equipment on in parking lots of ski resorts. I was the one who originally advocated for this ritual with my group of friends. It stemmed from when my father took me skiing as a child, and I enviously admired the cool college kids who did the same thing in the car adjacent to ours. I vowed that when I was old enough, I would look that cool with my friends as we suited up. Now Casey and I were looking cool in the middle of nowhere—if some guys blast music from a car, alone in the middle of the woods, are they still cool?

Casey put on his sturdy hiking boots and then placed his Birks at the top of his pack before strapping everything down. Birks at the top for easy access means, once the campsite is reached, there can be an immediate removal of the boots and easy access to light, open footwear. I had the luxury of bringing my Birks as well, but lacked in the hiking boot department. I had to rely solely on my New B's (New Balance's). But they took me this far and I had full faith that they would pull through. <Footnote: As a matter of fact they did pull through and suited me well for my entire trip. But as soon as I got back to Massachusetts, they gave me a foot rash and I threw them away. They lasted for two wonderful years—may they rest in peace.>

We slung on our packs, tightened any necessary straps, fastened necessary buckles (especially the waist buckles which go *above* the waist to ensure the weight of the pack stays on the upper body), locked the car, and we were off.

The trail started in thick woods with a moderate uphill climb. We were no more than a quarter mile in before we could hear pure, unobstructed running water. It sounded light at first, then escalated as we continued. Some sort of raging river wasn't far off, but the woods were too thick to see the origin. We were surrounded by too many thick pines that towered over us, spritzing freshly wooded scents onto our lightly perspired faces.

A half-mile in, we came upon a wooden sign. The words were carved in with crafty precision. It read: "You are now entering the Eagle Cap Wilderness, part of the Wallowa-Whitman National Forest." Casey stared at the sign with an admiring grin. "This is my new home." I was glad we could share similar but different excitement. It was exciting for me to explore some awesome woods. It was for Casey as well, but in addition he had come face to face with an area he would be exploring for many days to come. I was also excited because the "Eagle Cap Wilderness is a sweet-ass name. I wondered what animals inhabited this land: maybe ones that flew in the sky with bald heads and huge talons? Hint, hint?

The next couple hours led us in a romp through the woods. There was some elevation climb but mostly flat traversing. A couple times we had to jump across a stream or river. At one point I had to take off my shoes and socks, throw them over a knee-deep, fast moving current to the other side, and cautiously tread across. That is often a tricky endeavor, and this instance was no different. The riverbed had loose, slippery rocks, and the water tried to force me in a perpendicular direction. But the elements were no match for our unfaltering strength and agility. The water felt nice and cool on the—yet again—warm, clear summer day.

Around noon we broke out of the woods to a large, flat meadow the size of four football fields. The trail we had followed, which had been obvious our whole way here, had disappeared. We walked out to the middle of the field, where the grass was short and there were hard, dark mounds the size of frisbees, splayed out in different spots. I scanned the whole area, seeing if an animal would be present, unbeknownst to our entrance: nothing, neither by land nor sky.

Casey surveyed the area. "Yep," he said, "this is what Harry talked about. It's a popular place for cattle grazing. Notice all the cow pies?"

Ooooh, that's what those frisbees are. I acted like I knew all along. "Yeah-yeah, the cow pies."

"I'll probably be sent here a lot to monitor this area."

"Not a bad place to hang out: in a clearing surrounded by dried cow shit."

Casey turned to me. "Speaking of cow shit, you hungry?"

I looked at him. "I'm so hungry I could eat a cow and shit a pie."

"Okay then, let's find a place to sit."

There was not a single elevated object for sitting potential in the whole meadow, so we scoured the sides where it met the woods. We soon found a big fallen tree conveniently placed at the edge, for optimal views of the meadow and comfortable shade. After we took off our packs I felt so light that I thought I could levitate. We got out the tortillas, salami, cheese, hot sauce, and trail mix. I checked my water situation. My nalgene was half full and Casey had a good amount left in his camelback. We agreed it could most likely last us through the night but we would need to find a water source the next morning to refill. I knew Casey had iodine tablets to rid the water of bacteria and make it potable. I knew Casey had *every* hiking necessity.

The spicy salami and cheese wraps were divine, and the trail mix hit the spot. The only waste was the tear away wrapper from the tortilla bag, and the cap wrapper from the hot sauce. We had brought a couple of our grocery bags along, which acted as our garbage bags, which would be carried with us for the entire hike and thrown away back in civilization. We happily munched away on our fallen log, under the shade, enjoying the view. On the other side of the meadow was a hill of dense trees, and some craggy mountaintops could be seen peaking over in the distance. Some had snowy peaks.

Casey pointed to one closer to us. "I bet our hike will end around that one."

"On the summit?"

"Maybe..."

Maybe. Maybe is a vague, scary word. But I didn't mind at the moment. My stomach was full and pumping fresh energy into all corners of my body. I was ready to tackle any obstacle—save for a bear. That would require a few more push-ups and salami wraps.

We packed back up, slung over our packs, and headed on. Like I said, the trail had disappeared in the meadow, but toward the opposite end of where we came from, an opening emerged in the wood. It was interestingly connected to a small streambed that trickled across the meadow. We safely assumed that the stream bed and the trail were one in the same.

This part of the trail drastically increased our incline and it appeared that we were heading up a ridge. There was a ravine to our left, which grew deeper and more defined as we ascended. At one point I stopped and looked over to the other side of the ravine, and my field of vision was engulfed by an ocean of fresh green pines. At first glance they all looked exactly the same size and pointed in the same direction, leaning as if a steady wind was blowing them. I had never seen such a dense concentration of pines. All I could think was, *I am nowhere else in the world, but the Pacific Northwest.*

We continued on our incline and about a half-a-mile down, we stopped. Ahead of us was what Harry had forewarned: Snow. We walked up to where the trail seemed to stop—or rather disappear. A great big mound of snow lay in front, extending thirty feet ahead. On the other side we could see that the trail reemerged. I looked forward and saw that this pattern continued on: mounds, trail, mounds, trail...

Casey turned to me. "Merry Christmas."

I turned back. "Happy Chanukah, let's do it." I bravely took the lead and stomped onto the mound. It was firm, like old snow commonly is, but alas my forging ambitions made me careless. A few clomping steps in and my foot broke the seal and went crashing down, stopping at my upper thigh. "Whoa!" I yelled.

Casey sniggered. "Thanks, I'll learn from your mistakes!"

"I'm happy for you. Shit!" It took a lot of strength to awkwardly push my body up and get my leg out. Casey walked around the mound and laughed, watching me struggle from the other side. *Goddamn snow in June.*

I made sure to be more cautious as we continued, walking around the small mounds and tiptoeing across the bigger ones. The farther we went, the larger the mounds grew in size, and it took us longer and longer to find the trail. One of us would cross a mound and realize the trail did not reappear on the other side. Then the other would find it veering toward the left or right. This was becoming more disconcerting and eventually the trail was impossible to find, leading us to walk in directions we could merely guess seemed right. Getting lost in the middle of the Oregon wilderness was not a fun thought. Who knew how far these woods went. Ideas flooded my head of getting lost for days, caught in more snow, and coming out somewhere in Idaho—or not coming out at all. My worries sometimes heightened when I was hiking. I knew that if something happened, there would be no one to call, nowhere to go for help, no hospital to get to, no provisions to be replenished, no resources, no one to hear me scream and die, and no one to know where to find my carcass. But that was all part of the excitement, wasn't it?

After some nervous wandering, we saw a clearing up ahead. When we reached the edge of the woods, we could see it was different than a simple cow pie meadow. There were snow mounds that wound around flowing green grass and patches of tall pines sprouted up in random areas. The forest bordered one side of the clearing. On the other side, a mountain shot straight up from where the clearing ended. In front of us we couldn't make out the end of the clearing because it hooked around a patch of trees. I did another animal scan: still no sign of life.

We walked around the tree bend and on the other side, nestled into another wooded patch, was a little pristine log cabin. In front of the cabin was a neat little fire pit with a neat little stack of wood sitting next to it. A big old ax stuck up from a stump.

"This is the hunting cabin that Harry mentioned, right?" I asked.

Casey shrugged. "Could be. Whatever it is, we're staying in it tonight."

We walked up to the door. A deer skull hung in the middle like a doorknocker. We opened it to find another door with a wooden lock. "Extra protection from bears," said Casey. He opened the other door and we walked in to a dark, musty room which took up fifteen square feet. The door was the only light source due to a lack of windows. Two cots were conveniently set up against one wall and the other side had a few cabinets. We dropped our packs on each cot and I walked over to the cabinets. There was a small counter with a small can of bug spray and an empty, fire-scorched aluminum can. I opened a cabinet. It was dusty and empty, save for a folded up map. The place had an eerie feel to it, a mood that had been set by that deer skull.

We walked back out and sat on some log benches by the fire pit. "We're definitely staying here tonight?" I asked.

Casey gave a questioning look. "Yeah, why?"

"No reason." I was creeped out but didn't want to show it. "Just making sure."

Casey passed it off and changed the subject. "We still have some time in the day for exploring." That was true. We did make good time.

The sun had just passed its zenith and was beginning its downward arc, giving us enough daylight to <gulp> explore.

"Sooooo," I reluctantly began, "what did you have in mind?" I braced myself for the answer.

Casey gave me his famous, "Casey shrug," which meant, "I don't know, but I also have hidden intentions of mischief." "I don't know," he said, then smiled and looked up. "But let's go over to that mountain and see what happens."

We each grabbed water bottles, I put some survival devices in my pocket, and we headed off. Without my pack, I felt as nimble as a Newfoundland in November. Some leaps over a rocky stream and wading through tall grass and we found ourselves at the base of this mountain. It was one mountain along a string of mountains that created a ridge, which spanned down the clearing, farther than we could see from this vantage point. It appeared to be a steady incline to the top, maybe a four-hundred-foot vertical ascent. There was no trail but the entire climb was visible with no tree cover, which meant a rock and dirt scramble to the top.

Casey looked at me. "So are we doing it?"

"Um, I guess we are. It doesn't look too bad." I was unsure if that was how I really felt. My emotions wavered between fear and excitement.

"Good. Onwards and upwards." Casey sprouted ahead.

From the bottom, the mountain didn't look hard. "Do you want to give a time estimate?" asked Casey.

"You mean how long it'll take us to get to the top?"

"Yeah."

"I'd say, fifteen."

Casey nodded. "Yeah, I agree."

The beginning had a mild, steady pitch. We breezed our way up and my fears were subsiding. Maybe this fifteen-minute estimate could be reduced to ten. But after five minutes, the pitch changed, *a lot*. I wasn't able to see this drastic pitch change from the base, but now it was loud and clear in front of my face. Our pace slowed and I had to push my knees with my hands to help hoist my body up. I was solely focused on each step, making sure my footing was placed in secure spots. My world became the dirt and rocks in front of me. Every ten feet I would catch my breath and look up and down to see our progress. We were still so near the bottom and the top wasn't getting closer. By the time we reached twenty minutes of hiking, I knew my estimate was way off.

"Hey!" I said panting.

"Yeah?" said Casey, panting ahead.

"I have a new estimate. We'll be lucky to make it in forty-five."

"I say an hour."

Just then, a boulder the size of my head rolled a couple feet past me, picking up speed and crashing down to the bottom. It had enough speed to knock me out and send my unconscious body tumbling down with it. I looked up at Casey. He was trudging fifteen feet ahead, absorbed in his own dirt and rock world. "Hey!" I yelled and Casey stopped and looked over his shoulder. "Be careful! You just sent a huge rock flying past me!"

"Really? Shit, sorry, I'll be more careful."

"Remember," I warned, "if I get hurt, you're dragging me out of here."

We continued and I shimmied over a few feet so I wasn't directly behind his path of deadly debris.

It looked like we had reached the halfway point, when the pitch got steeper. It turned from a hike to a climb as our hands became as equally as participatory as our feet. I had to dig my shoes in the dirt to get the right footing and choose the footing more wisely. At points, going straight up was no longer an option and we would traverse across the hill to give ourselves a milder incline. At this point looking down was like being on the edge of a cliff and the potential of tumbling down was very real. My body and mind went into survival mode and I became aware of my every movement.

Why are we doing this? We were now risking our lives just so we could say we summited this stupid mountain. Was it pride? Ego? I didn't think so. Nobody back in La Grande would care about a death-defying climb we made up an unknown mountain. The Hot Shots would laugh in our faces. Regardless, Casey and I weren't the kinds of people that thrived on boasting about such things. I believe the reason was simply the drive to explore. It was the curiosity of what would be in store for us at the top. Will we be looking out on the most magnificent thousand-mile view of snowcapped peaks? If so, we could stand there and feel proud that we were the only people experiencing it: our own private paradise. And we had earned it by scaling this treacherous mountain. Or maybe we would get to the top only to find a hidden peak on the other side, which would require more climbing to get to the *real* top. But either way, I knew that it would feel good. We would be reaching that feeling of personal success. It would be something for us to store in our memory box, and we will be able to think back on it for the rest of our lives. I could meet up with Casey in fifty years and we could reminisce about it. "Hey old buddy, remember when we were climbing that mountain in Oregon and that boulder knocked me down and you had to carry me out of the forest?" "Of course! Do you think I got amnesia or something?" We would sit back and smile, lost in the comfort of our memories. And at that point, our memories would make this mountain twice as big and twice as steep. The view at the top will be remembered as the most amazing view of the Eagle Cap Wilderness, and this whole experience would have been nothing short of amazing. At that moment as we risked our hides, we were living for our memories. Because in fifty years, I will have forgotten about how fucking scared I was and how I thought that this was such a bad idea.

These thoughts kept me occupied and before I knew it, the pitch was rounding out and we were almost at the top. It was an easy trek up to the highest point. I scanned as we walked, maybe to catch some grazing wolf off guard, or some bald headed bird relaxing in a tree. No wolves, no eagles, no nothing. The animal kingdom did not deem our arduous climb worthy enough to give us a welcome ceremony.

Sure enough, my latter theory panned out. Any kind of amazing view of snowcapped wilderness was obstructed by another taller mountain. However, laterally we were provided with fantastic views because we were able to see down both sides of the ridges. I looked at where we had originally hiked from. The cow pie meadow looked like a small patch of grass. Looking the opposite way, the ridgeline spanned down a handful of round peaks like ours, then curved around and came back the other way, which formed the valley that we would be residing in tonight.

Casey and I walked toward the end of the peak and sat where it sloped down in the direction of the other peaks. There we were, the recent conquerors, looking out at our domain. I reached in my pocket and took out my Cali bud. Casey looked over and took interest. "Oh, surprise surprise! Good thing I brought my apparati." Casey reached in his pocket and pulled out a lighter and a small glass bowl. I packed it up and we smoked as we sat on a small flat rock staring out at the ridges. The sun still beat down but had a cool, early summer mild warmth, which wasn't hot enough yet to melt the snow that cased the slope in front of us.

Casey pointed out yonder. "I think that's an animal over there."

I perked up. "What? Where?"

"Over on that next ridge, a little ways down the slope. You see?"

I squinted. "Um, oh, I think so." There was a little speck and when I squinted my glazed eyes harder, I could make out some kind of four-legged creature that appeared to be bending down. *Is it—could it be—yes, I think it's...grazing!! Holy shit stop the press, we got a grazer!* This tiny speck wasn't moving. "*Is* that an animal?" We both honed in on it for a while to see if it would move...no movement.

"It's most likely an elk," said Casey.

"Ok, but don't elks move?"

"Yeah, but he's grazing. He's in the zone."

Casey picked up a rock. "I have an idea. Let's play snow botchy."

"What's that?" I asked.

"You know botchy ball?"

I nodded.

"Well this is snow botchy."

"Oh, that explains a lot."

"Watch." Casey hucked the rock out fifteen feet in front of us. It rolled on the snow then stopped. "Now," he continued, "we take turns throwing rocks at it and whoever gets closest wins."

"Okay."

"Find three rocks," Casey instructed.

I was skeptical at first, but snow botchy quickly became my favorite game to play stoned, at the top of a mountain, in the early summer, when there is still some snow on the ground, which is conveniently placed in front of a comfortable rock to sit on.

I kept glancing over at the grazing statue across the ridge. It stayed in the same position with its head down, but I swore it was in a different spot then before. I think I was getting too desperate to spot an animal and I should have released my infatuation with this stupid grazing speck. My desperation was causing me to lower my animal spotting standards. *You can do better than fixating on a tiny speck, Evan.* I peaked over my shoulder to make sure there weren't any sneaky wolf grazers: still none. All I wanted was to get animal laid—that fawn was such a cocktease.

After a good few rounds of snow botchy, we noticed that the sun was on its way toward one of the ridges. A cool breeze crawled up our ridge and gave us the chilly cue to head back to camp. I had almost forgotten about our fun little route required to take us down. Our descent would not be as bad—meaning it was still terrifying, but to a lesser extent. Casey and I stuck closer together and didn't have to worry about boulders falling onto us. In fact we got much satisfaction in pushing a boulder and watching it pick up speed and tumble ferociously down the hill. Some would catch another rock and fly up ten feet in the air.

The sun was well over the ridge by the time we made it down, giving us an early dusk. We got back to the site and went straight into dinner-by-the-fire prep. This involved taking out all the necessary dinner food, and utilizing the ax to chop wood. Once the fire was built, Casey set up the camping stove next to it. The spicy rice with pepper and cheese was delicious (as usual). We traded the hot sauce back and forth, dousing our spoonfuls.

Even though both of us were experiencing this foreign place, I felt right at home during this whole process. If I closed my eyes and opened them again, I would have been convinced we were sitting in a campsite in the Green Mountains of Vermont or the white peaks of New Hampshire, cooking the same meal in front of the same fire. It felt like yesterday we were in New England, doing the same thing, yet it also felt like ages ago.

My college days were long gone. I was onto a new chapter of life, which involved a constant state of dream-like migration. I was traveling in an alternate dimension which caused everything around me, no matter how commonplace it all was, to seem amazing and new. The people I had crossed paths with were happy to show me this amazing newness, which to them was their normal world. I was sure that as soon as I continued on my migrant way, they returned back to their normal lives. Jenny was probably on her boat with Murphy. Becca was probably cooking a meal in her apartment after a day at the office. Wallace and Gill might have been back in Massachusetts by now, in the comforts of their homes, telling their parents all about the exciting things they saw and did as they pet their favorite cat who laid comfortably on a lap of fresh-washed jeans. I felt good knowing that I was still out here in the wild, exploring these foreign parts of the earth. I was forging my way up mountains, and so what if there wasn't a breathtaking storybook view at the top? It was something new. A constant state of exploration was where I preferred to be.

Casey and I conversed the same way we always did, while staring into the fire. Casey shook his head. "I'll take watching a fire over watching TV, any day."

"They do have similarities," I remarked.

"Like what?" Casey asked.

"Both can allow you to sit in front of them and tune out."

"That's true."

"I wonder if before TV, people would come home from a day of work and build a fire, and then just stare at it for a while until it was time for bed."

Casey nodded. "I could totally see that happening: 'Leave me alone honey, I'm watching my favorite part of the fire, when the fresh log starts blazing!'"

We both laughed, the same way we always did.

When the flame episode drew to a close, and the chill of the melting mountain snow infiltrated our weak border of warmth, we spread out the coals, poured some water on, and retired to our cabin. I passed out on my musty cot in musty content. I would have taken this dark, musty, moldy, cold cabin over the Jupiter Motel any day.

DAY 18

I figured out my future job. It will make me millions in a few months, and I could live the rest of my life traveling, drinking venti lattes, and wearing sweatpants: I am going to invent an alarm that mimics the muffled sound of birds chirping through cabin walls.

I was so pleasantly awakened until I opened my eyes and was disoriented by the complete darkness that engulfed me. The chirping birds made it a sure sign that it was morning, but I checked my watch just in case. The other life form in the room sensed my stirring and I could hear it pick up its head.

"It's eight-thirty," I said.

"Oh, perfect," a familiar voice said through the dark. Then the voice asked, "How'd you sleep?"

"Like a dried up cow pie," said a voice that sounded like me.

"Did you hear that animal last night?" asked the voice.

"No, I didn't wake up at all."

"Something was scratching the side of the cabin right around here."

"Are you pointing?" I asked. "Because I can't see shit."

I heard the rustling sound of the body moving, and then a blinding beam of light shot into my face. *God? Is that you? Oh, it's Casey's headlamp.* "Here." He turned his head to the wall next to his cot and pointed. "It was scratching right here. I'm guessing it was a coyote or something similar."

"That's strange."

"He was probably jealous. He wanted to be in the cool kids cabin."

"Yeah. That, or he smelled some cool kids that he thought could be a lot cooler in the pit of his stomach." I knew all along that there were loads of animals around. They were so sneaky, probably watching us and quietly licking their chops from the bushes as we dined by our fire last night.

I got out of my sleeping bag. The cabin was as chilly as it was dark. I walked over and opened the double doors. The colors of the world flooded through the threshold like I was Dorothy walking out of her fallen house to the new land of Oz. A cool morning breeze lingered, but it was a hell of a lot warmer than the musty cabin.

Casey and I got dressed and unpacked our breakfast supplies. Casey sat at the same spot by the fire pit and heated the stove to make oatmeal. After breakfast, we went to the river around the corner toward our newly conquered mountain, to wash the dishes and refill our water bottles and camelback. Casey took out his iodine bottles. These two small bottles were the size of thimbles and were filled with tiny pills. Each container of water required a pill from both bottles. The first pill was the iodine which would kill the bacteria. The other pill was a flavoring agent to get rid of the gross iodine taste and make it taste like normal water. All we had to do was drop the pills in, then wait a half-hour and we would have ice-cold spring mountain water, bacteria free.

We then spent some time rummaging in the surrounding woods and carried back fresh firewood to add to the pile, just as the previous inhabitants did for us. This is a common courtesy in the woodland book of codes—it's a karma thing.

That was it for the morning chores and it was time to hit the dusty, snowy trail. Going back across the snow mounds was easier. We had familiarized ourselves with the area, and we could follow some of our footprints that had been made. In no time we were back on the real trail, coasting downwards.

About a half-a-mile down, I looked up from my in-the-zone hiking trance and was startled by a living thing approaching us from the opposite direction. The startled feeling turned to excitement of an animal, which turned to fear because it was big and close to us, which turned to disappointment because it was a human, which turned to interest because I realized I knew this person. He looked at us and gave a friendly smile. "Hey boys!"

"Hey Harry!" said Casey.

We converged. "How was the hike up?" Harry asked.

"Great!"

Harry smiled. "I realized I couldn't sit around in the office knowing you two were enjoying yourselves out here."

Casey and I laughed. "I don't blame you!"

"Did you find the hunting cabin?" he asked.

"Yes we did," said Casey. "We stayed in it last night. It was great. We also hiked up one of the peaks next to it."

"Oh, you must have been on..." Harry rattled off multiple names of peaks, too many to remember. Then he asked, "Did you run into any snow?"

"Yeah, about a half-a-mile up, there are some patches, but not too bad."

Not too bad? I disagreed with that statement.

"That all should melt off in a couple weeks." Harry turned to me. "Did you enjoy our backyard?"

I nodded and smiled. "I did indeed. You have a beautiful home."

"Yeah, it's not so bad. Well, I won't keep you guys. Have a good trip back. Are you in the office tomorrow, Casey?"

"Yes."

"I'll see you then."

"Alright."

And Harry was off. We walked a little farther until we were out of earshot, then Casey turned to me. "Did I mention I'm getting paid for doing this?"

"I think you hinted at it, but I wasn't positive. That's amazing."

"Yeah, I'm fine with this." Casey looked around at his new home and gave a nod and a content smile. Three weeks out of college and the bastard found his dream job.

The hike back went quicker—like it always does. We had a similar lunch, this time on a log by the river. When we passed by the welcome sign to the Eagle Cap Wilderness, a feeling of sorrow welled up inside me. I didn't want to part so soon from these piney woods and its shy wildlife. But when we spotted our car, it gave us a nice, "welcome back to civilization" feeling, like it always does after a hike. *Good to be back,*

Civilization! "Welcome back, Evan and Casey! Boy do I have to bring you up to speed." *Really? What did we miss?* "Let's see, war in the Middle East, five new radio pop songs, a new ipod version, the list goes on." *That doesn't seem like anything new.* "Yeah, I guess you're right."

We got to the car and stripped off our backpacks, shoes, and wool socks, threw our Birks on, and got in. I put on Otis Redding to help give us a smooth, soulful transition back into society. This was partly because Casey's choice of Sam Cooke had gotten me in that soulful mood a few days prior.

Casey and I have always developed a huge appetite after a hike, and a strong desire for non-camping food. We decided on a local pizza place, got a large pie (half meat, half veggie) and a pitcher of what I later learned to be Oregon's staple, Deschutes, Mirror Pond Ale. I was in love with this beer as soon as it hit my lips. It had to have been the best beer I had so far on the West Coast—or it tasted so good because anything would have, after a big accomplished hike.

After dinner we headed back to Casey's pad. We took showers and Casey let me back into the office so I could solidify my plan of action. I checked my email first to see if Linda had responded. If she didn't, I assumed I would have to call Gill and Wallace again and pray for a miracle (something I wasn't looking forward to relying on). *Or I could send out some Seattle Couchsurfing requests.* That was an appealing idea. But they would have to get back to me tonight or early tomorrow if I wanted to be there by tomorrow afternoon. I wasn't optimistic about such a short notice reply. I held my breath and opened my email: Click...Click...Click...*She replied!*

> Hey Evan! Of course you can stay with us! I'm so glad you got in contact! I just want to warn you again. We have three rambunctious little boys and a dog. But if you're up for the challenge, give me a call and we can figure out a time to pick you up. You're taking the bus I assume? Talk to you soon!
>
> -Linda

At the bottom of the email, she left her home phone and cell number. I nearly jumped out of my seat I was so thrilled. Seattle was booked and ready to go. I shot her back an email thanking her and letting her know that I would be in touch with her tomorrow.

I figured since the ball started rolling, I would keep up the momentum and see if Couchsurfing was pulling its weight: Click...Click...*Three messages in my inbox! Oh my! People on this site actually exist! Real people! And they're Canadian too!* The first message was from Colin from Vancouver. It had a "Declined" icon next to it. That deflated me. *I can imagine what this will say:*

Sorry Evan, can't host. Good luck!
-Colin

Damn, bad start. He probably thought, "hell no," without a picture. I should have figured out how to get a picture on here... That was stupid, Evan. Try harder next time.

The next message had a "Maybe" icon. It was from Dan from Vancouver Island:

Hey Evan, I normally don't accept couch requests from profiles without a picture. But your story is pretty cool! You're welcome to stay, just let me know exactly the dates you plan to be here and I will give you a definite answer.
Cheers!
Dan

Okay! Not all hope is lost. The next message was another maybe, from Vancouver. It was troublesome to not have any definite answers, and worse to have received nothing from Whistler. I decided to hold out on replying to the messages, to wait and see if I could get more definite replies in the next few days. But a beam of hope hit me with the thought that I potentially had places to stay in British Columbia. And it would be with real live people who were opening their homes to me. I was optimistic. Things looked like they were working out. Just a few days ago, I thought I was lost and alone in the middle of the Northwest. This was no longer the case through the immediate kindness and openness of people. I had forgotten that people like this had existed in this world.

I marched back to Casey's room and told him about my responses.

"Really? That fast?" He was just as astonished.

"Yeah!"

"That's amazing! I really need to check this site out."

"Do yourself a big favor. You won't regret it." I was becoming a Couchsurfing salesman too soon. I had to remind myself that I had not yet done it.

Casey and I laid low for the rest of the night. I showed him the pictures from my camera of my road trip so far, which was followed by him showing me the pictures from the Yosemite backcountry. I had a fit of jealousy when I saw him standing at the top of Half Dome with the sun rising behind him. But I could tell that he was equally jealous by my pictures. We were two avid travelers yearning to walk over every inch of this great earth. It was good to know that we were both putting out the effort.

The detour out to La Grande was a success. I felt like I was back on my feet. I had a foreseeable plan of action (until something out of the blue happened but I was prepared for that as well). And spending time with a likeminded soul gave a boost of strength to my traveling desire. Tomorrow I would be heading to Washington State. This was the last point to hit in the US and from here on out, I was completely, utterly, beautifully, frighteningly on my own. I was back at the bottom of the mountain, staring up at the top, and that same combination of fear and excitement was what ground my thoughts into sleep.

DAY 19

I woke up initially to Casey's alarm, but I knew it wasn't for me. Casey had to get up early to make his long commute to work. We had discussed the plan last night. Casey would go to work, then skip out to drive me to the bus station in the early afternoon.

I woke up later on my own by my trusty internal alarm clock. The sun pointed straight into Casey's empty room. Outside I heard nothing from La Grande's not-so-bustling downtown. I got up, cleaned up, then took the liberty to use Casey's electric razor, and shaved. This was the first time that had I shaved since I left on the trip (in case there was any wonder about what I looked like up to this point). I felt like I needed to start anew for the path ahead.

My bag had to be turned back into a travel home from a hiking pack. I stuffed my laundry at the bottom and put on a fresh T-shirt. As I looked over my accessories, I decided I should no longer hold onto this bag of weed. It looked like I was going to be staying with a nice family in the suburbs of Seattle and I wasn't going to rely on these "three rambunctious boys" to participate in helping me smoke the rest before crossing the Canadian border. I left it on Casey's desk and considered it my thank you gift. I kept the ganja cookie though. I knew that would come in handy.

As I finished packing, Casey popped in the door. His work clothes were no different than his regular clothes, unless this company's dress code required wearing T-shirts of the band, Phish.

"Good morning!" I said.

"Good afternoon to you," said Casey. "Are you all packed up?"

"Just about. Here." I reached over and handed the buddha bag to Casey. He looked at me with a smirk. "Is this your parting gift?"

"Yeah, it's the least I can do for all your help. Also you'd be helping *me*, since I can't take it over the border."

"Nothing says thank you like a bag of drugs!" Casey took the bag and threw it on his bed nonchalantly. "I figured we'd grab a quick bite before I dropped you off. There's a funky, local fast food chain on the way with good rotisserie chicken."

I perked up. "Like Boston Market??"

"Pfff!" scoffed Casey. "Of course not! And thanks for putting that idea in my head. Now I'll be dreaming about it for the rest of the day." You can take the kid out of the East Coast but you can't take the Boston Market out of the kid.

The rotisserie place was okay, but it couldn't hold a candle to Boston Market. If places like this, along with pizza, and bars with hot wings were the scope of what La Grande had to offer for out-of-home dining, I wished the best of luck to this poor child.

Then it was back to the little bus stop at the gas station. It felt like I was just there, getting into Casey's car—then again I had stayed longer at this place, then every other place on this trip other than San Francisco. I grabbed my big red pack out of the back seat, slung it over my shoulder, fitted my wicker cowboy hat back on my head, and walked over to Casey's side.

He rolled down the window and gave me a firm handshake. "Be careful out there. Keep your wits about you."

"I will. I can't thank you enough. This was just what I needed."

"No problem, I'm glad I was able to help out at an opportune time. Good luck with that Couchsurfing, I'm interested to hear about it."

"You'll be the first one to know if they start axing my limbs off."

"Cool, I can't wait. Okay then, back to the ol' nine to five. See you later."

And then my only friend and lifeline in the Pacific Northwest, drove off. As I stood watching the little black Honda drive into the great blue yonder, I wondered when "seeing Casey later" would be. Weeks? Months? Years? There was a possibility that I would never see him again. We were no longer college neighbors. He was living in a little podunk town in eastern Oregon and who knew where I would end up. I figured that I would have to get used to the idea of seeing less and less of old friends, that is if I was to see them at all. Was that a tell tale sign of getting older? What a horrible concept that was. I turned my back to the thought. It was time once again to move on.

I walked over to the bus stop to buy my ticket and wait for my bus to arrive. That bus would go an hour northwest—*ahh that sweet word, "northwest", like the song of an angel*—to Pendleton, where I would switch buses to Seattle, another six hours away. Outside the bus stop, a man was sitting and waiting on a bench. He had a *real* cowboy hat on with the whole outfit: boots, jeans, and a leather jacket. A stuffed duffel rested by his side. As I sat down next to him on the bench, he glanced over to me briefly, focused on my hat, then looked away.

While I waited, I decided to dig out Linda's number and let her know my status.

Ring...Ring... A familiar motherly voice answered. "Hello?"

"Hello, is this Linda?"

"Yes it is."

"Hey Linda! It's Evan, from the bus!" I made myself sound extra friendly.

"Hey Evan! I was expecting your call. How are you? How was La Grande?"

"It was great! Really beautiful, just like you said!"

"Awesome! So do you think you're going to make it up to Seattle?"

"Yes! I'm actually waiting for the bus as we speak! Is it still alright to stay with you?!"

"Of course! When will your bus be getting in? I can come and pick you up."

"It should arrive at um, the greyhound bus station at six-thirty tonight!"

"Great! I'll pick you up then. Do you like meatballs? That's what I'm making for dinner."

I have dinner plans? "Oh, um, yeah! That sounds great!"

"Okay, have a nice trip, see you at six-thirty!"

Meatballs for dinner. I had dinner plans in Seattle, Washington for a meatball dinner. I couldn't believe it! I didn't realize I had such a big grin on my face and I looked over at the Cowboy who was looking at me with a blank stare. "I'm having meatballs for dinner!" I announced. The Cowboy stared for a few more unamused seconds, glanced back up at my hat, and turned his head away.

Eight minutes and twenty-two seconds more of awkward silence, and the bus rolled up. The sign in front said, "PORTLAND." The bus driver walked out and took my bag and ticket. He looked at me but not quite at me, more off to the side. "Transfer at Pendleton." I nodded and walked on the bus with my nalgene and purple notebook with the Grateful Dead sticker on it. The bus was near full capacity and I didn't find an empty seat/non-junky-looking seat buddy until I got to the back. I sat down next to a lean white male in his late twenties. He had on a plaid shirt and jeans, and a blond shaved head. He could have been a white supremacist so I kept my guard up, but he gave me a friendly nod and a smile as I sat down, which eased my worries about any desire for him to hang my Jewish head from a stake. The driver got in his bulletproof capsule and decided to spare me the prison bus speech. We were off.

My seat buddy turned to me. I was looking forward but I could tell that he was looking at my hat. I took it off and put it on my lap. "That's a nice hat," he said. "Where'd you get it?"

I turned to him and was eased by his smile but still wary. "Um, I got this a few years ago, down in Florida."

"Oh, that's nice. I got one similar to that, 'cept not in Florida. I got mine in Eugene."

"Cool."

"You from Florida?" he asked.

"No, Massachusetts."

He nodded, seemingly intrigued. "Okay, just as far. What you doin' out here?"

"Well hmmm..." *How much do I divulge to this man?* "I'm heading up to see a friend in Seattle."

"Seattle's nice."

"Where are you going?" I asked.

"Eugene—well, a town near Eugene. It's out in the country where the *real* Oregon is." He chuckled.

"Is there a fake Oregon?" I asked.

"No, I was just jokin'. I was talkin' 'bout Eugene and Portland, which're a hell of a lot different than the rest of the state. You know, like the *Left*."

"Oh," I said, "I get it. I came from Portland before La Grande, and they seem like pretty different places."

"Yeah, that's for sure. But I guess that's what makes this place so dang interesting isn't it? Can't have one side without the other, right?"

I cracked a smile and shook my head. "No sir." I was beginning to like this guy.

"Are you from Eugene? I mean, the *real* town outside of it?" I asked.

"Yeah. I grew up there and I'm goin' back to visit my wife and boy."

"You're just visiting them?" *Evan, what are you doing? That's a personal question... Oh I forgot, we're "strangers on public transportation." Ask him what kind of underwear his wife wears—wait, don't ask that. Don't ever ask that.*

He nodded. "I work on a horse ranch in Colorado. I come home 'bout once a month."

"But why doesn't your wife and kid move out there? Or why can't you find a job in Oregon?" I was pushing my boundaries but he rolled with it.

"It ain't that easy. It's a good gig, but the living quarters ain't fit for a family. And she don't work, so I gotta send back all the money to take care of the kid. I get free room and board plus benny's, so it works out for the time bein'."

Benny's? What the hell? He get's free Benzedrine for working? "Benny's?" I cautiously asked.

"Benefits: health care, 401K, and shit."

I nodded. This was a new term to put in my "real world vocabulary."

He told me more about the horse ranch and his ranching duties. Not only did it sound strenuous and lonely, but I couldn't wrap my mind around the fact that he was forced to travel across half the country to work, while his wife and kid sat in a little town waiting for his checks to arrive. This was a different world that my post graduate Massachusetts mind could not comprehend. Were people desperate enough to take a job halfway across the country *just* so they could receive healthcare and a retirement plan? I couldn't begin to imagine myself doing such a thing.

What I did know was that life changes with the addition of a wife, and exponentially more with a kid. There would be no getting in the car and joy-riding across the country—unless it's to some job on a ranch shoveling horse shit, so my baby can have pampers and I get "benny's."

Hearing this man's interesting alternative to life burned through the time and before I knew it we were pulling off the highway to a gas and food stop. The driver got on the speaker. "Pendleton! Transfer here for Seattle." Sure enough there was another bus waiting there with a sign that said, "SEATTLE." "We will be taking a fifteen-minute break. Please be back on the bus promptly because I *will* leave without you. Pendleton!" We parked next to the Seattle bus and the driver got out and walked to the side of our bus.

People were moseying out and migrating toward the convenience store and fast food restaurant. I was still full from fast food rotisserie, but a little snack sounded enticing. *Maybe Oregon has their own version of tasty jerky.* "I'm going to see what that convenience store has," I said to the rancher. He nodded, I nodded back, and then I got up and never saw him again in my life.

As I exited the bus, I looked over between the two buses where the driver was pulling out the bags that needed to be transferred. I turned my head and kept walking, but slowed my step. *I don't think I saw my bag pulled out... I'm sure it's fine, he just hasn't gotten to it yet.* I kept walking—*But maybe I should go back and watch, just to make sure he transfers it... Do you really need to do that Evan? You don't trust this bag moving professional?... I guess—well, I don't know, maybe not.* I backed up and watched. The driver pulled out a half-dozen more bags, shut the side door, and walked past me, into the fast food joint. *Are my eyes deceiving me?* I scanned the pile of bags. Mine was definitely not there.

The other driver got out of the Seattle bus and opened his side doors to put the bags in.

I walked up to him. "Excuse me?"

"This bus goes to Seattle," he said as he grabbed a bag.

"Yes, but—"

"We leave in ten minutes."

"Okay, but—"

"What is it??" The driver stopped loading the bags and looked at me like I had breached the two-question limit and now I was cutting into his valuable time.

I stood defiant. "I am transferring onto *this* bus and *that* driver did not take my bag out of *that* bus." I pointed straight at the bus next to us so there was no confusion.

The driver screwed up his face like I had short-circuited his automated response system and human empathy was slipping out of the cracks. "Really? Are you sure?"

"I'm positive. I watched him take out every bag. It's not here."

"Sorry about that sir. You're going to have to talk to the other driver though. He's the only one authorized to operate devices on his unit, like the basement doors. I believe he went inside so you can let him know."

I gave him a firm nod. "Okay, I will go talk to him and I *will* be back."

"Really sorry about the confusion sir."

I about-faced and marched to the fast food joint.

The other driver was sitting alone at a table and scarfing down a burger.

I walked up to his table. "Excuse me—"

"Bus leaves in eight min—"

"I know!"

He stopped chewing and looked up at me.

"I am transferring to the Seattle bus and my bag is still sitting in yours."

"It is??"

"Yes."

"Are you sur—"

"I am Positive. I watched you take out every bag and you neglected to take out mine." I made sure to sound as serious and direct as possible, in case my wicker hat did not command enough respect.

"Really, I apologize for that sir, I will get it right away." He wrapped up his half-slobbered meat sandwich and shuffled out to the parking lot.

I perched over his shoulder like a persistent parakeet and watched as he grabbed my bag—my home—and passed it to the other driver who put it in the other bus. "Sorry about the mix up sir," said the drivers in unison.

I walked onto the new bus, took a seat by myself and let out a gasp. I wondered what the trip would have been like if I had never stopped and walked back to watch this folly. I envisioned many phone calls and a boatload of time wasted. Instead of enjoying Seattle, I would have been holed up in Linda's house, working out all kinds of logistics and eating meatballs. *Mmmmm.* The meatballs made it sound more pleasant, yet burdening Linda's poor family while I worked out my problems, would have sucked (for both parties). A feeling of nostalgia hit me and I thought about Wallace and Gill and the lemon Suburu. That shit-stick may not have worked, but at least I knew where my bag was! Putting that extra effort in caution was necessary when flying solo. Losing sight of my possessions meant losing sight of everything I had.

The majority of the six hours across Washington State was wildly uneventful. We crossed through grey desolate plains with nothing in sight but wire fences and occasional cattle, who bent down to lick dust. Was this all that central Oregon and Washington had? Was I missing anything? Yes. I knew exactly what I was missing and that was the Pacific coastline. I imagined blasting Pearl Jam, Ten, through that pulsating subwoofer as we weaved through evergreen forests and rocky cliffs, Wallace at the helm, Gill and I laughing and—*Meatballs. Keep thinking about the meatballs, and exploring a new city, and Beautiful British Columbia after that.* I shut my eyes and forced myself to fall into partial bus sleep.

I opened my eyes to a radically different landscape. Trees, rocky cliffs, and towering mountains meant we had reached the Cascades. Extreme pitches of ravines and valleys cut into the sides, with vast, emerald-green brushstrokes painted from the ground to the sky. We passed by a mountain with long wide lines that snaked from the peak to the base, and at the bottom were some buildings with alpine-style construction. This was Cascade ski country. The skiing out here wasn't known for its large resorts, but what they lacked in acreage, they made up threefold by their gargantuan dumps of fluffy powder. I had heard people say, "When it's raining in Seattle, it's snowing in the Cascades," and from all I've heard, it is *always* raining in Seattle. However, in forty-five minutes I would find out if that was true.

The pass we traveled through did not last long and we were down from the Cascades as quickly as we entered it. This journey through Washington was a journey through multiple climate zones. We had hit plains, desert, forest, alpine, and we were about to enter the next and final climate zone: suburbia. Wealthy homes littered the hilly country and billboards offered the best cell phone deals ever created in the history of mankind.

We crossed a bridge over a beauteously blue bay. The road curved over one last hill and the skyscrapers of downtown Seattle welcomed us on the other side. The buildings glittered under the sun and clear blue skies. Seattle wasn't so rainy after all. I looked at my watch. We were on time, *with* my bag safely stowed under the right bus.

We headed straight toward the skyscrapers and soon we were engulfed by city streets with shops, cafés, Starbucks, bikes, newspaper stands, Starbucks, bums, and more Starbucks. We pulled into the bus station and I called Linda. She picked up and told me she was already there waiting, as if I had a prompt car service. I still didn't know what I did to deserve this.

Stepping out of my confined, sterile capsule to the Seattle air was like night and day. A cool, subtle oceanic mist was mixed with the sun's warm comfort. The stuffy bus environment made the outside air smell especially fresh. It was a grim reminder of how harsh public transportation could be on the olfactory senses.

Linda gave a smile and a wave as I approached her silver, state of the art, soccer-mom minivan. "Hey Evan, you can put your bag in the trunk and get in the back seat." I noticed there was another woman sitting in the front passenger seat. She looked like a dark haired version of Linda: thirties, plump, with a nice face. I threw my bag in the back, put on my shin guards and cleats, and hopped into the soccer mobile, managing to find the only seat that didn't have a child's safety seat attached. I caught a strong waft of diapers and fabric cleaner.

The two women turned around and I sensed some polite nervousness. "This is my friend, Kat." Kat extended her hand and I shook it with a smile, which she nervously returned. I was getting the idea that Linda had brought her friend along for a cautionary measure, in case meeting me on a bus was not enough affirmation to rule me out as a serial rapist sociopath. That was fine by me. I had enough bullets in my gun to kill both women and enough space under the floor to hide two bodies. It would be a cozy fit, but I would just need to move some things around.

We pulled out and headed down the Seattle streets. "Thank you for picking me up," I said in my excited, friendly tone, "this is great!"

"No problem. How was the ride?"

"Okay, a bit long."

"Any highlights?"

I laughed. "Yeah, the bus driver almost lost my bag."

"Really? How?" <Proceed to tell Linda and Kat about the amazing bag story and how Evan swooped in, killed the bad guys, and saved the poor bag> "Wow, that's so lucky you caught that!"

"I know," I said, "I don't know what I would've done."

Kat turned around. "Do you want some coffee Evan? We can stop."

"No, thank you. I don't really drink coffee."

The two women gasped. "You don't?"

"What are you going to do in Seattle??" said Kat facetiously.

Linda giggled. "Stop that Kat, you're going to scare the poor man out of his wits."

"Heck, I'm still buzzed from that cup from before."

"I know, me too."

"I love that place. I don't go there enough."

"Yeah, it's a bit out of the way but well worth it."

"Ooooh, have you been to that new place on Ninth Ave?"

"No! I heard it's great! How is it?"

"It's good. I got a macchiato and they brewed it extra strong, which I don't normally like, but it was still good..."

The two plump bodies continued to chat about coffee at a constant thread until we got out of the city proper. Then we were back in suburbia and their conversation switched to suburban topics. "I have to remember to get that specific cough medicine for Zebadiah."

"He's still coughing?"

"Only at night. It's not nearly as bad as it was before. Adam took him to the doctor last week and he said it's on the decline, but the medicine will help a lot."

"That reminds me, I need to talk to Adam about what I should bring to the pot luck next week."

"I already said that cookies or some other desert is fine."

"Yeah, but Cathy was talking about cookies and Adam will know more about who's bringing what..."

The incessant housewife suburban chatter continued for our ride through anywhere suburban USA: neighborhoods, shopping complexes, rich houses, Starbucks, middle class houses, etc. I wasn't sure what I was getting myself into. The normalcy of suburban life was foreign to me—then again foreign-uncertainty was my middle name.

We drove along another bay and the road curved around it with hills of modest homes on the opposite side. "This is Tacoma," announced Linda. "We're almost home." We took a turn away from the bay and headed up a steep hill, into the neighborhood. A few more turns and we pulled into a two-story, middle class house built circa the 1980's (the surrounding houses played a similar role). Kid's toys littered the front lawn like a minefield. Everything looked safe and comfortable, filling me with the desire to take my bike out of the garage and meet up with my neighborhood buddies before I had to be back for dinner.

Linda led me into the house (Kat took up the rear). A happy, wagging shepard greeted us. "That's Toby. He'll smell you first, but he's harmless." I reached my hand out in offering to the animal. Toby looked at it, paused, sniffed, then wagged again. Their house was neat and modest: simple living room, plain flower paintings on the walls, clean, freshly vacuumed carpeting. "I'll show you your room in a little bit," began Linda, "but I need to start dinner first. I'm sure your hungry, as well as everyone else in this house—boys!" she called up the stairs. "Boys! Mr. Evan is here! Come say hello!"

Mr. Evan?

Linda led me to the back of the house to the kitchen, with a connecting living space that had a couch, TV, and kid's toys scattered like landmines. A screen door led out to a small fenced-in yard with a swing set, along with outdoor toys that I wished were mine. The upper halves of neighboring houses peeked over the perimeter. I had finally done it. I had reached the suburban core. *If only I could find the reactor...*

Then, like a prepubescent explosion, I heard yelling and scampering of multiple pairs of small feet tumbling down the stairs. Three young boys of different ages and ethnicities came running in. "Boys," said Linda, "this is Mr. Evan. He'll be staying with us for a couple days. Say hello." One boy said hello as he ran by. Another just barreled past me and out the back door. The third followed, laughing. Linda pointed, "That's Jessie, the oldest, he's five. The middle one is Asher, four, and Zebadiah is three."

"I see you've got your hands full," I said.

"Yeah, they keep us busy," said Linda casually.

Kat walked out back. "Hey Zeb!"

The youngest one turned around. A cute little guy, maybe of Caribbean decent, like Dominican or Haitian.

"Where's my hug?" asked Kat with her hands tightly fastened onto her lovehandles. Zebadiah gave a shy smile and scampered up giving Kat a hug. Kat's white lips kissed his mocha forehead, then she freed him and walked back inside. "Okay babe, I'm outta here. We'll be in touch about the potluck. Nice to meet you Evan!"

"You too!"

"Bye Kat!" Linda said with her back turned to us. She was shuffling along the kitchen counter already busy making progress on the meatballs. Kat let herself out. I assumed she had finished scanning me and I was given suburban security clearance.

As Kat closed the front door, another racially diverse member of the Linda clan entered the kitchen in a seamless transition. This tall black man approached me with a warm, welcoming smile and extended his hand. "You must be Evan."

"Yes, hello." I shook his warm, welcoming hand.

"I'm Adam, welcome. I've heard you've had a long, interesting trip!"

"Yes, I have. Thank you so much for letting me stay. This is a huge help."

"Of course, it's our pleasure. I just hope you can handle three boys because they won't let up, I can assure you!" His laugh was no less warm and welcoming.

I politely returned a laugh. "That's no problem, they seem like a lot of fun."

"Yeah, at times. We're still getting used to the three of them. We've only had Asher and Zebadiah for six months. Did you explain that yet, Linda?"

Linda's upper body was swallowed by the fridge. "I may have mentioned it hun, but I didn't go into detail." She was then spit out with handfuls of hot dog buns.

Adam turned back to me. "We took them in because their biological mother was having a rough time. Finances," he leaned in and whispered, "drugs, that sort of thing. We're taking care of them until she gets back on her feet, or we see fit that they're ready to go back." I nodded and soaked it all in as he continued. "It's doubtful, but hey, the Lord works in mysterious ways." I kept nodding. Adam smiled and looked out the window, admiring the three tykes. "Jessie is our biological son."

Linda walked up and handed me a plate with a big meatball sub and a side of cooked frozen vegetables. "Here you go Evan, feel free to start, we're pretty informal around here. Let me know if it's warm enough, I'll stick it back in the microwave."

"Thank you so much! This looks great!" The food actually looked bland and cheap, like she had raided the fridge of the frozen foods section of the discount supermarket—but I was gratefully starving.

"Hey Asher!" Adam yelled out the back, but his voice stayed even and calm. "You need to share that shovel buddy. If I see that again, you're going in timeout."

"Okay," said a tiny voice, and he let go of the shovel immediately, as if a higher power had done it for him.

"And that goes for the rest of you guys." All three boys nodded obediently. Adam turned back to me. "So Evan, have you been to Seattle before?"

I shook my head, mouth full of meatballs. The food tasted as bland as it looked but it hit the spot in that hearty, wholesome kind of way. "No, I was planning on checking it out tomorrow."

"Anything you had in mind that you wanted to see?" he asked.

"No, I'll probably just walk around and take in the sights."

"There are some great coffee shops to check out."

I opened my mouth but Linda spoke first. "Adam, Evan doesn't drink coffee, can you believe it?"

Adam laughed. "Good for you! She's kidding. I didn't drink coffee before I moved here, but it's tough not to. I try hard to limit my intake."

"I guess I'll have to try it," I said. "Just for the sake of it, since I'm here. Are there any other places I should check out?"

"I would recommend downtown, Pike's Market. That's always fun for visitor's."

"I've heard of some rock n' roll museum that sounds cool," I said.

"Oh yeah, that's by the Space Needle. You can probably walk there from downtown. It's not too far. Linda, don't we have a map of the city that we can give him?"

"Yeah, it's upstairs. I'll get it in a bit," said Linda. She was showing no signs of slowing down.

"Wow, that would be great, thank you," I said.

"And if you don't have plans tomorrow evening, we're doing a barbeque with some people from church across the street. Linda, did you mention what I do?"

"I don't think so hun."

"I'm a pastor at the church around the corner."

I had forgotten that Linda had mentioned that little tidbit on the bus. I was getting a full picture of the situation: the friendliness, the help, the adopting, it was all making sense.

Linda yelled outside. "Boys! Dinner!"

The three bambinos ran in and crowded around the table. "Excuse me!" proclaimed the matriarch. "I don't see any clean hands here! Bathroom, chop-chop!" Out of the room they stampeded and there was a thirty-second calm that Linda took advantage of. She sat down and let out a deep breath.

"You weren't kidding!" I said.

"What's that?" asked Linda.

"About your three rambunctious boys."

Linda shook her head and smiled, "No sir-ee-bob!" She looked tired but her smile showed her unrelenting love.

Then the boys flooded back in. Zebadiah ran up to me with an adorable look like an eager puppy. "Mr. Evan, can I sit on your lap?"

"Zeb!" said Adam.

Zebadiah looked at his surrogate father, then back at me and smiled. "Pleeeeeaaase?"

How could I refuse such a request? "Sure Zebadiah, come on up." The three-year-old extended his hands to get ready for liftoff and I picked him up by his armpits. My backpack had to have weighed twice as much as this tiny human. I plopped him on my lap and he wasted no time to dig into his meatballs.

I observed the happy Christian family eat. "Is Joe here?" Linda asked Adam.

"No, he won't be back till late." Adam turned to me. "Joe is staying in our extra bedroom. He'll probably be at the barbeque."

Wow, another informal member of the family. This place was a revolving church door.

I looked over and noticed Jessie looking at me. He was as cute as the other two, but I could tell now that he had his mother's nose and chin, dark hair like his dad, and tomato sauce smeared across his face like his meatball sub. "Mr. Evan?"

"Yes Jessie?"

I was already used to my formal prefix. In fact I already felt like the seventh member of the family—or the fourth informal member.

"Have you ever played Lego Wars?" the child asked with all the seriousness that could be mustered inside of a five-year-old.

"Here we go," said Linda.

"No Jessie," I said, "I don't believe I have."

"Well, um, it's um, a really cool video game and um, I was wondering if you want to play later."

"Sure Jessie."

His face lit up like the Lord had answered his prayers.

"Jessie, remember, only after you've gotten ready for bed," said Adam. Jessie nodded profusely. I felt like I was stuck in a Christian family values TV show. They were too perfect and well behaved.

After dinner, Linda did the dishes and rushed Asher and Zebadiah off to sleep. Jessie did exactly what he was told and got ready for bed. In the meantime, Adam sat down with me and was showing off the map of Seattle. "Here's where the bus will drop you off and here is Pike's Market. Great views of the water and if it's clear, you'll get a good peak at Mount Rainier. And I would recommend lunch right around here. Lots of good cafés—

"Mr. Evan!" Jessie burst in with his Veggie Tales pajamas on, and jumped on the couch. "I'm ready to play now!"

"Hold on Jessie," said Adam, "Mr. Evan and I need to finish talking."

I butted in. "Oh that's fine, I promised Jessie I would play." I shot Jessie a serious look. "Did you brush your teeth?"

"Yes Mr. Evan, I did."

"Okay, then let's do it. Thanks for the map Adam."

"No problem, the city isn't very large. You'll be fine. Anyway, I'll leave you two to the real business at hand." Adam shot Jessie a seriously serious look. "Jessie, twenty minutes and then time for bed." Jessie nodded excitedly and rushed to the gaming system.

For exactly twenty minutes I played vigorously alongside a five-year-old. Once the idiot-box had come on, the young, impressionable, god-fearing child was transfixed. I tried to sound and act engaged, but I realized that it wouldn't have mattered if I put the controller down and sat there, or even walked away. I no longer existed to Jessie; the television had him now. I was once like Jessie, but that evil spell had passed long ago.

At minute twenty on the dot, Linda walked in. "Okay Jessie, time for bed."

...No answer.

"Jessie, come on, you've had enough game time with Mr. Evan."

"Just a little longer." Jessie half slurred, eyes glazed over. The game still had a firm grip on his soul.

Linda walked to the TV and shut it off, thereby exercising the demons out of the child and bringing him back to reality. Jessie got off the couch. "Say goodnight to Mr. Evan and thank him for being generous enough to play with you."

"Goodnight, Mr. Evan. Thank you for playing with me."

"Any time, kid."

And the obedient little boy scampered off to bed.

I turned and watched Linda. She was picking up toys from the ground and putting them in baskets and cupboards. She looked exhausted now, but maintained that tireless smile of motherly endurance and looked at me. "Do you need anything Evan?"

I shook my head. "No, I'm okay." Then suddenly I got a similar urge that Jessie likely had for video games, but mine was for Couchsurfing. "Actually um, I was wondering um, if I could use a computer for a few-um-minutes."

"Sure, you can use mine in my office. Follow me."

She led me upstairs to a quiet hallway with multiple doors. I followed her to her office where she set me up at her desk. "Stay as long as you want. Also I had brought your bag up to your room. It's the kid's room, two doors down. The top bunk has fresh sheets on it."

Bunk?

"I'm going to bed, I'll be waking you up at seven if that's okay—I figured you'll want breakfast before we take you to the bus."

I nodded in complete approval. "Wow Linda, I really can't thank you enough."

"No problem. If you need anything, we're three doors down. Just knock. Goodnight!"

I settled in to the chair and Toby walked in and plopped himself next to me on the floor. I scratched my informal dog's head and logged into Couchsurfing.

Click...Click... *Two new messages in my inbox!* The first was from Dave from...*Whistler?? Oh my God!—Wait, shit.* There was a simple "Declined" icon with no message. That decreased my odds for Whistler by fifty percent.

The next message was from a girl named, Devina from Vancouver. It had—*Oh my God are my eyes deceiving me?*—An "Accepted" icon.

> Hey Evan, you're welcome to crash. Just so you know, my place can sometimes seem like a hostel with people coming and going. Here's my cell, give me a call when you get in town.

I've been accepted! I wanted to jump out of my chair as if I had opened my first college acceptance letter. I wondered what she meant by her place being like a "hostel." I checked her profile. There was no picture of herself and in its place was a crude drawing of a stick figure girl. *That's strange.* Although I didn't have any kind of picture, so who was I to complain? I checked her references. She had lots of them, all positive. I decided to wait until tomorrow to make any decisions, in case someone else replied last minute and I could weigh my options.

I signed off before the urge to search more profiles around the world became too strong. I needed to get some sleep for an early wake up/day in Seattle/potential Tacoma evening church barbeque.

I walked into the kid's room to find my bag resting next to a bunk bed. The top bunk invited me in with folded sheets, like Linda promised. The room had a distinct theme: murals of an ocean and ships painted on the walls, lobster and fish stuffed animals, and the bunk bed wasn't actually a bunk bed, it was a pirate ship. I turned around to look at the mural on the opposite wall. It was of a torn, unrolled scroll, but instead of a treasure map it had a list. On the top it read, "The Pirate's Code." Under that was a list of ten phrases: "Ye shall have no other pirates before me. Ye shall respect the ship's captain. Ye shall respect a pirate's mommy and daddy..." *Oh my god, I'm reading the pirate's ten commandments.* I had to cover my mouth, not to let out an uproar and wake the house.

I got ready for bed and climbed into my pirate ship. From a musty cot of a cabin, to a tough, cramped floor, to the top bunk of a child's bunk bed/pirate ship. *Where else will I find myself sleeping in the Pacific Northwest?* Not to mention that they were kind enough to hand over the kid's room to me. How I ended up in this situation was still unclear, but I was more than happy to go along with it. I fell asleep comfortably on the swarmy seas that the good Lord—I mean captain—made for me.

DAY 20

I woke to a knock on the door and a strangely familiar voice. "Evan, time to get up, breakfast is ready." It sounded like my mother. *Was* it my mother?

I don't want to get up Mom! I'm too comfortable in these warm sheets. This lobster stuffed animal I'm hugging is so soft. I'll never let go. Never! I had such a strange dream last night.

<Knock, knock> "Evan? Are you up?"

"Wha? Oh, yeah, yeah I'm up. Be right down!" I opened my eyes and I could see that my dream was reality: I was still in a child's pirate ship.

I got up, took a shower, put on some fresh shorts and a T-shirt, and walked downstairs. Light was flooding into every window, and blue sky was what the outside world offered. Toby walked up to give me a morning greeting. I patted his head and he followed me into the kitchen.

The three boys were at the table absorbed in their doily-trimmed cereal bowls, while Linda was bustling about making bagged lunches. She turned and gave a start to see me standing there. I must have broken her kitchen zen. "Oh! Good morning! Boys, look! Mr. Evan is up. What do you say?"

Three adorable faces turned to me and smiled. "Good morning, Mr. Evan!"

And the Lord smileth unto all of his children. "Good morning boys. Thanks for letting me sleep in your pirate room, it's pretty cool."

"You're welcome."

I sat down and Linda put a bowl and spoon in front of me. "Are Alpha-Bits okay?" she asked. "If not I have shredded wheat."

"No, that's fine, I love Alpha-Bits." I grabbed the cereal box on the table. I couldn't remember the last time I had sugary kids cereal, let alone sat with three toddlers while eating it. In fact I did not remember the last time I had cereal, period. Morning routines weren't common in college.

"I'm taking Asher downtown in twenty minutes," Linda said, "and I can drop you off at the bus station. Do you think you'll be ready to go?"

"Yeah sure, I just need to grab a couple things from my bag."

"Good. By the way, I didn't make you a lunch to take, but I can if you want. I held off to ask you, figuring you may want to eat somewhere in the city."

This woman is too much. "Yeah, I'll get something in the city, but thank you anyway!" I wondered how many times I would say "thank you" before I left this family.

I thanked Linda for the cereal and went up to the pirate ship. I didn't have a daypack, but I did have cargo shorts on, equipped with large cargo pockets. These pockets may have seemed dorky (Portland would have been appalled), but they always came in handy when the time was right. I threw in my sunglasses, my camera, and my—wait, close the door—and my weed cookie, and I was good to go.

I followed Linda and Asher out of the house. The temperature outside was perfect: clear skies, high seventies, no humidity. And that deliciously mild scent of sea salt mixed with fresh pine, still lingered in the air. "You picked a great day to walk around the city," said Linda. "We've had a string of bad weather, but that cleared up a few days ago and this should last for a while."

"That's great, it's beautiful right now. Right Asher?" I looked down and Asher gave a shy smile. *Cute little guy.* The middle child is always the quiet one.

With Asher strapped in and me in the passenger seat, the soccer transport lifted off and we were back on the suburban streets. "Okay Asher," said Linda excitedly, "are you ready to sing?"

"Yeah! Yeah! Yeah!" squealed the bouncing child.

Linda pushed a button and a mild rock-alternative song started. "Okay Asher, repeat after me. Evan you can too, but it's optional. The verse was coming around and I could tell where this was going. "Ready? Here it comes!"

2,3,4,

Linda: You are holy!
Asher: You are holy!
Linda: You are mighty!
Asher: You are mighty!
Linda: You are worthy!
Asher: You are wordy!
Linda: Worthy of praaaaaise!
Asher: Wordy of praise!
Linda: I will follow.
Asher: I wiw fowow.
Linda: I will listen.
Asher: I wiw listen.
Linda: I will love you!
Asher: I wiw love you!
Linda: All of my days!
Asher: All of my days!

The duo sang Christian songs to each other all the way to the bus station. I sat quietly and smiled, amused by the novelty of hearing Christian rock sing-along's. As long as it stayed a novelty, I would enjoy it. Any more and I would have thrown myself out the car.

Linda pulled up to the station and turned down the jams. "Okay Evan, give us a call when you're ready to come home and we can direct you toward the right bus. Do you think you'll be joining us for the barbeque tonight?"

I imagined the sing-along situation in this car but multiplied by thirty people with hot dogs and fruit punch in their hands. I cringed at the thought, but how could I refuse? I had to accept the fact that this would be my Seattle experience. "Yeah, I think so."

"Okay, that's happening around six, so plan to get back by then."

"Okay Linda, thank you so much for the ride! Bye Asher!"

"Bye-bye Mr. Evan!"

I got on the bus and headed into the big city. This was a suburban commuter bus (as opposed to the Greyhound), so most of the passengers wore business suits and did not smoke crack, let alone knew what it meant. No prison guard bus driver either. Just a smooth ride to...

Seattle. I didn't know much about Seattle. I did know grunge. If San Francisco had culturally shaped the sixties, Seattle had done it in the early nineties with Nirvana, Pearl Jam, Alice In Chains, plaid, and ripped jeans. Just like in San Francisco, I was hoping that when I got off the bus, I would be surrounded by this style that had shaped the city's history. But that was just it: history. When I got off the bus, everyone looked normal. Actually most people were in business suits, but that made sense since I was dropped off downtown. Not much grunge happening in Seattle's financial district.

What I first noticed was how immaculate the streets were. A city bus breezed by on what looked like a railroad track. It made a humming sound, reminding me to switch to electric energy and stop burning gasoline. I liked cleanliness. I liked the environment. I liked that Seattle liked a clean environment. In fact all of the West Coast cities I went through, seemed to share this progressive view. I liked that.

I looked around. Down the hill at the end of the street I was on, I saw water. Adam had mentioned that the waterfront was worth checking out, so I walked down. In front of me was Pike's Market, where a bunch of tourists stood around watching animated men in white aprons yell and throw fish. Across the street was the location of the original Starbucks, where a bunch of tourists went to take a picture of themselves drinking a cup of coffee, after taking pictures of men throwing fish.

I eagerly made my way out of this area and found a nice quiet spot overlooking the water. I did my own fishing through my pockets and caught a special cookie. I went to unwrap it and noticed that there was a small sticker on the back that said, "Medical use only: Keep out of reach of children and pets." Alas, it did not specify excluding "lone individuals consumed by wanderlust," so I was good to go. I was about to throw the wrapper away, when I stopped myself. *Wait a minute, this sticker is too good to toss. I think I have a good place for it.* I put the crumpled wrapper in my pocket and continued on, munching on my delectable edible.

I then walked into an independent coffee shop that jutted onto the water. I grabbed a seat outside on the back porch overlooking the water with an independent cup of coffee to sip on. I was looking out onto a beautiful bay and in the distance I could see a range of jagged mountains. Once I was able to familiarize myself with my sense of direction, I knew that I was looking west, out at Olympic National Park. I thought back on the Google Images I searched for back in Amherst. Now I was staring at this mountainous rainforest, yet it still felt so far away. Would I be seeing those mossy trees and secluded beaches up close? I wasn't ruling it out yet...

I left the coffee shop buzzed, and a little floaty from an early start to the cookie high. I floated down the block along the water and out of the downtown area toward the Space Needle. The Space Needle is the distinctive symbol of the Seattle skyline. It's up there with the likes of the Transamerica Building, the Sears Tower, the Empire State Building, the Eiffel Tower, and Big Ben. You architectural marvels tell us, "Hey! You're in this city! And there's no mistaking it!" And people come from all over the world to see you and say, "Hey! I'm in this city! And there's no mistaking it, because look at that building I'm pointing at behind me!"

I walked up to the base of the Space Needle. There was a park surrounding it and on a raised area so I could look out on the rest of the city. I got a better view of the Olympic Mountain Range with its succession of distant snowy peaks. I looked to the opposite side of the city facing southeast, and there was a single giant peak out in the distance. It rose up into the sky above the clouds with nothing else visible around it. May I present, Mount Rainier: the tallest mountain in Washington and the highest prominence in the continental US. It was the mountain's prominence that made it amazing to look at, since so much of it was visible without obstruction. Her Majesty had a frosty top that perfectly rounded off and gradually disappeared in some form of mist that could only be romantically concocted by Mother Nature.

I was fascinated that Seattle was sandwiched between beautiful, completely separate mountains ranges (Cascades included). I don't know of any other city that could boast about such a trait. There must have been endless outdoor options for these coffee-crazed, environmentally clean, city dwellers. I would have loved nothing more than to explore these options, but alas traveling alone without transportation made it tricky. It would require ingenuity. I needed to find a jet pack to easily propel me into the Olympic forest. *No, jet packs don't exist yet, or if they did, they might be* just *out of my price range. If only I was rich, then I could buy my way to anywhere I wanted.* Welcome to the trials and tribulations of a poor, car-less traveler. Twas a hard life I led, a hard life indeed. My mind kept grinding. *Maybe I should take a bus right now, and head out to the mountains!* No, my backpack was in Tacoma, held hostage by the Jesus Pirates. *Maybe I can go on a covert mission to sneak into the pirate ship and snatch my bag unnoticed—... Evan, stop.* The cookie was getting to my head. I shook it off and marched on.

Down the hill I stumbled upon a peculiarly colorful building. It looked like different pieces of giant foil that were oddly glued together. This strange structure had an entrance so I walked in. A large sign read: "The Experience Music Project." Posters adorned the walls of Jimi Hendrix and Kurt Cobain. This was the rock museum I had asked Adam about. I debated on going in, and decided that if I was going to add a museum to my road trip itinerary, this was probably the best bet (being slightly stoned helped too because everyone knows that weed and museums are a match made in heaven). It ended up being right up my alley. They had multiple exposés on different rock bands and artists who I had grown up with and worshipped. I became so absorbed that it wasn't until an hour went by that I realized the time, and pried myself away to leave time in the day for other things.

As far as the rest of my day in Seattle went, I walked around, ate at a café, checked out some bookstores, bought a Chuck Palahniuk book (thinking that buying a Chuck Palahniuk book in Seattle was an appropriate act of assimilation), and drank a beer at a bar while watching a Euro Cup soccer game. None of this was worth going into a twenty-page disquisition about. Seattle is a fine, clean city and I was grateful to walk around it—but my mind was on other things. I looked east and saw a towering mountain I could not climb. I looked west and saw majestic rainforests I could not explore. But when I looked north, I saw hope. It was where I needed to be as soon as possible—except first I had a Christian barbeque to attend.

Near the bus station I found a bakery and bought an apple pie to bring. Who can turn down an apple pie? That's right, nobody. Especially not a gaggle of Christians.

I caught the bus and made my third trip through suburban America—and no, the third time was not a charm, it was exactly the same. I was picked up again by the soccervan, but this time Adam was at the helm with Zebadiah strapped in the back seat. "Hi, Mr. Evan!"

"Hey Zeb, what's shakin' buddy?"

"What?"

Adam chimed in. "Mr. Evan was asking how you were doing and how your day was."

"Gooood. I went to Play Zone and ate a Snickers."

"Oh really?"

"How was the city?" Adam reverted our conversation just as it was getting good.

"It was good, I…" <proceed to tell Adam about my aimless walking excursions while floating on a weed cookie, minus mentioning the cookie.>

"Cool," remarked Adam, "the city's nice like that. It isn't too big so you can walk to a lot of stuff. Plus, I don't think you can argue about how clean this place is."

I shook my head. "I will not be the one to argue that."

"Are you hungry?" Adam asked. "We've started the barbeque."

"Yes I am. I brought an apple pie."

Adam drew a wide smile. "Oh! That's so nice of you! Now you'll be accepted with open arms!" He let out a laugh that was coated with irony, implying that I would be accepted with open arms no matter what, even if I brought a steaming turd on a platter. We're talking about Christians here.

When the soccership landed in it's suburb-pod, we got out and Adam led me to the house directly across the street. He filled me in on the short walk. "These are good friends of ours and fellow church members, Bob and Marie. Marie just came back from Africa, working with a church affiliated organization. She has some neat stories to tell. Ask her if you get a chance."

We walked into a drab home with very little decoration, not unlike the house across the street. A group of unscandalously dressed adults stood in the kitchen with big smiles. Zebadiah ran out the back door where Jessie and Asher were playing with an African boy of similar age.

Linda was in the kitchen doing her usual thing, but she stopped bustling and turned to me when I walked in. "Hey Evan, this is Marie."

A wide grinning woman walked up to me and I sensed an uncharacteristically high amount of energy. "Hello Evan!! Welcome!! I'm Marie!! What's that??" She pointed to my pie.

"This is an apple pie I brought."

Her eyes popped out of her sockets. "Oh wow!! That's perfect!! Thank you so much!!"

"You're welcome, thank you for having me."

"Our pleasure!! I've heard you've come a long way!!"

"Yes I have."

"Where exactly?? Pennsylvania??"

"Massachusetts."

"Wowee!! Well congratulations on your journey!!"

"Thank you."

A man with a tacky, tucked in Hawaiian shirt and khaki shorts walked up to me. "Hey Evan! I'm Bob. I hope you're hungry. We could feed the whole darn town with all this food!"

"I sure am Bob!" I was learning to use my exclamation points. "Thanks for having me!"

"Sure thing, help yourself to anything. There's a beer cooler on the back porch."

A few more overenthusiasticly formal exchanges, and I made my way out back.

Toby was running around a small suburban yard with a labrador, and the kids were chasing them. Beyond the yard with no obstructions in between, stood a simple brick building with a white steeple. Two intersecting beams that resembled ones that a famous guy was nailed to, rose proudly on top, reaching toward the sky. These lucky folks had direct access to God's house. Adam wasn't kidding either. His office was right around the corner.

I opened the beer cooler and my heart sank. I had heard that Seattle held its own when it came to microbrews. If that was true, I wouldn't have known by this cooler, because they were making a strong case against it. Let's just say that the most exotic beer I saw, was a Bud Light with Lime.

I cracked open an all-American-cold-one and walked up to Kat, who was standing on the porch with a tall, jacked, blond dude sporting a crew cut. *I smell something in the air.*

"Heyya Evan, how was the city?" asked Kat. Not only did everyone at this party know my name, but they all seemed to track my every move.

"Seattle was good. It was a really nice day to walk around."

"Did you get yourself any coffee?"

"Yes, I caved in and got a cup."

"Hey Evan," the big dude extended his big hand, "I'm Joe, I'm staying in the room next to yours."

Ah yes, the sixth member of the family—or third informal member. "Oh, okay, nice to meet you."

"I got home pretty late last night so we didn't get a chance to meet. The police force keeps me late sometimes."

I nodded, "Oh." *I knew I smelled a cop.*

Adam popped his head out. "Hey guys, the food's almost ready. We're going to gather in here for prayers. Jessie! Boys! Come inside, it's prayer time."

We all walked in—the boys raced in, like the new Lego video game had just hit stores—and a circle was formed in the middle of the kitchen. We completed God's circle by holding hands and bowing our heads. Adam spoke in his calming, confident voice, required for Pastor's to help them communicate with the heavens. "Dear God, we thank you for this bountiful day and thank you for this heavenly weather that you continually feel compelled to bless us with at this time of year. Thank you for this food and giving us a chance to share this day with these people. And thank you for our guest you so graciously bestowed upon us."

I think that's me.

"And with that we say," in unison the flock found their cue, "Amen."

Baked beans were being served from a crock-pot, cornbread was taken out of the oven, and Bob went outside with a large platter of meat to man the grill.

Marie brought the African child up to me. "Evan, this is our son, Enenius."

"Hey man, what's shakin'?"

The boy looked up at me with shy, confused eyes. "What?"

"Nice to meet you," I said.

The boy scampered off and Marie watched him adoringly. "I adopted him after finding him in a village on one of my mission trips to Zimbabwe." She shook her head. "Wow, that was already five years ago. It feels like yesterday!!" Then she turned to me. "Do you hold any church affiliation?"

"Me? No, I'm Jewish." I felt a slight pause in the room, like the world had froze for a second, and then went back to normal. *Shit, what was I thinking?*

"Oh, okay!" Marie smiled. "That's nice!"

"Yeah," I shrugged. I didn't know what to say. But I was relieved that these were the accepting kinds of Christians. This barbeque didn't need a trip down to the river for an emergency baptism.

The truth of the matter is, I am not "affiliated" with anything. I'm Jewish by blood and was raised religious (had a fucking sweet Bar Mitzvah), but I haven't practiced for many years. As far as identity is concerned, I do not like to give myself a religious/political/national affiliation. I like to consider myself an international citizen. When I travel, I approach things as an open-minded individual with no bias, which has helped me in many instances. Affiliation has the potential to create restrictions when traveling.

Along these same lines of affiliation, I do not hold any dietary restriction (whether it's for health reasons or religious/personal preference). The last thing I would want to do is insult someone because they did something like, graciously offer me a plate of food and I turned it down because I was "Kosher" or "Vegetarian." I have no reason to restrict myself and stay in my comfort zone (unless I'm being dragged to get baptized). In fact I find comfort outside of my comfort zone. Maybe that is why I love to travel.

The Seattle evening stayed warm and mild, holding its breath without letting a single gust hit the perfectly still evergreens. I filled my belly with beans and hot dogs, and took part in some lawn games. As the sun dipped into a turquoise sky, I savored my slice of apple pie: Just another backyard summer barbeque in America.

I was talking with Adam and Bob about the Euro Cup when Linda walked up. "Hun, I'm heading back and taking the kids with me. I'll get them ready for bed."

"Okay, we'll be back in a little bit," said Adam.

Linda turned to Bob. "I was begged to let Enenius come over for a sleepover, so if you're looking for your son, you'll know where he'll be."

Bob laughed. "Okay, fine by me! Hope they're not too much of a handful."

Linda gave a casual shrug. "What difference will one more make?" She said it with an air of confidence that only a professional mother could obtain through years of experience.

Bob guffawed. "God bless you! You cease to amaze me!"

"Yeah, well if I could learn how to fix simple things like the drain on the tub, then I'd be *really* amazing."

"Oh yeah!" said Bob. "You're still having trouble with that? I'm still planning on coming over and taking a look at it on Saturday."

"That would be great," said Adam.

"Thanks Bob," said Linda, then she turned to me. "Evan, you're welcome to stay here. Come back over whenever."

"Okay," I said, "I figured I would hang out a bit longer."

"Alright then gentlemen, enjoy!" Linda turned with a smile.

These were pleasant people. Easy going, inquisitive. I couldn't help but admire them for their strong sense of community (Lord knows the church is good for that). Their meatballs may have been bland and their beer may have been as boring as their khakis, but their community was as bright as their smiles. I respected this type of living which was so distant from mine. I could relate it to my "college days" when all of my friends were close by. Friends become family in that environment.

I brought myself back to the moment, and took the opportunity to step back and realize where I was and what was going on. Stepping back often helps to ignore the jumbled thoughts and complications, and simply lays out reality. Sometimes it can be important to help appreciate the significance of a situation such as this: I was in Tacoma, Washington, at a backyard barbeque, drinking beer with a bunch of people who were radically different from myself, whom I met within the last couple days. I realized that I did not have to venture out into the mossy Olympic wilderness to be as content as I was at that moment.

As the light left the sky, the party wound down. I thanked Marie and Bob and they thanked me profusely for the pie. "It was so nice to meet you!! Best of luck!! Come visit us any time!!!!!!!!!!!!"

Adam, Joe, Toby, and I walked back across the street. When I walked in the door, Jessie was there to greet me in his pajamas, sporting a hefty grin. I crossed my arms and nodded. Time for the final round of Lego Wars. This was for all the marbles.

We were able to defeat the evil Trogdor before Linda cut the cord. "Okay Jessie, let's go. What do you say?"

"Thank you Mr. Evan for playing with me and helping me defeat Trogdor."

"You're welcome kid. Sweet dreams."

I petted Toby on the couch for a few silent moments, then headed upstairs to check on the Couchsurfing updates. There were no new messages in my inbox, which meant that Devina with her so-called "hostel" was a go. No new messages also meant more discouragement on the Whistler front, but I needed to focus on Vancouver for now. I sent Devina a reply, confirming tomorrow's arrival, then I took down her number and signed off. All that was left to do was to get a bus ticket for tomorrow's ride north.

As I signed on to the Greyhound sight, Adam walked in and sat down. "So what are your plans for tomorrow?"

"It looks like I got a place to stay in Vancouver so I'll try to catch a bus in the morning. I'm looking at the buses now. I assume there's one direct from here to Vancouver?"

"Yeah there are plenty of buses," began Adam. "There's also a nice boat ride you could take, which I recommend."

I nodded calmly and looked at him, but inside I was perked up like a curious meerkat.

"It takes longer, but you go through the San Juan Islands, which are worth checking out."

"Really? That's great! So it leaves right from the city?"

Adam frowned. "That's the detail I would need to look at. I'm not sure. Hey Linda!"

Linda walked in on cue. She sat down in a chair with a sigh. It must have been the first time she relaxed all day.

"Where does that ferry leave from that goes through the San Juan's to Vancouver?" Adam asked.

"I believe it's from some port north of the city," she said.

"We may have a boat schedule in the travel drawer," said Adam.

Linda nodded. "I think you're right." That gave her a nice twenty-second break before she stood back up and walked across the room to a bureau. She opened a drawer with maps and brochures inside, fished around, and pulled out a fold out brochure, containing lists of times. She studied it, then nodded. "Yeah, it's where I thought it was. The port is in Anacortes, about two hours north of the city."

My heart sank. No boat excursions for Evan. I nodded and turned back to the Greyhound site. "Okay, I'll look up the bus times and try to shoot for the morning—"

"No, no," Adam interrupted, "you can't miss this boat trip, it's a fantastic opportunity."

"Yeah, but—"

"Don't worry about it, I'll drive you in the morning."

"What? No." I shook my head. These were giving people, but this was too much to ask. "I can't—"

"Trust me," said Adam, giving me the most seriously genuine look I had ever gazed upon in my life, "it's worth it for you to experience this."

Was I hearing this right? Was he offering to drive two hours (making a grand total of four hours) out of his way, so *I* can have a good experience? I pleaded with them. "This *really* isn't necessary. I mean, thank you so much for the offer, but *really*—"

They wouldn't budge. The words, "you" and "experience" rang in my head. They were attempting to commit a first-degree act of pure selflessness. And there were no strings attached. Nothing was asked in return. They didn't even ask me to take a trip to the river.

What possessed them to do this for me? Why did they offer to take me in in the first place—and feed me, and drive me, and fix me up in their child's pirate ship? If it was from pure Christian intentions, they excluded any ulterior motives to attempt to convert me. These were not Jesus freaks, these were good Christians. In other words, they were good people, reaching out of the kindness of their hearts. And it was as simple as that. Their actions did not make me want to convert, they made me want to be a good person.

I tried a little harder but I couldn't make them budge, and it was settled: Tomorrow morning, Adam would take me to the boat launch. I thanked them for the two-thousand-and-fifty-first time, before we bid each other goodnight.

Back in the pirate's cove, I sat on the floor and rearranged some things to prepare for the days to come. I emptied my pockets and pulled out the weed cookie wrapper. I stared at it with a smile. Then I took out my purple notebook with the Grateful Dead sticker on it. I peeled the weed warning sticker off the wrapper and stuck it to the back cover of the notebook. It fit perfectly.

I put the notebook away and fished in my bag for another important item. My hand reached the familiar object and I took it out. My ticket to explore the earth rested lightly in my hand. I admired the metallic eagle that was proudly spreading its wings over the navy blue laminate of my passport. *Tomorrow you're going to prove your worth, my little friend.* I remembered back in Amherst trying my hardest to remind Wallace and Gill in every message I left them, "Pack your passport!" I was never sure if they ended up remembering, but it wasn't like they needed them anyway.

The countdown to British Columbia had begun. I got in the pirate ship and thoughts of the not too distant future swirled in my head. I lay awake in bed clutching my lobster for an hour of anxious excitement, before my mind permitted me to rest.

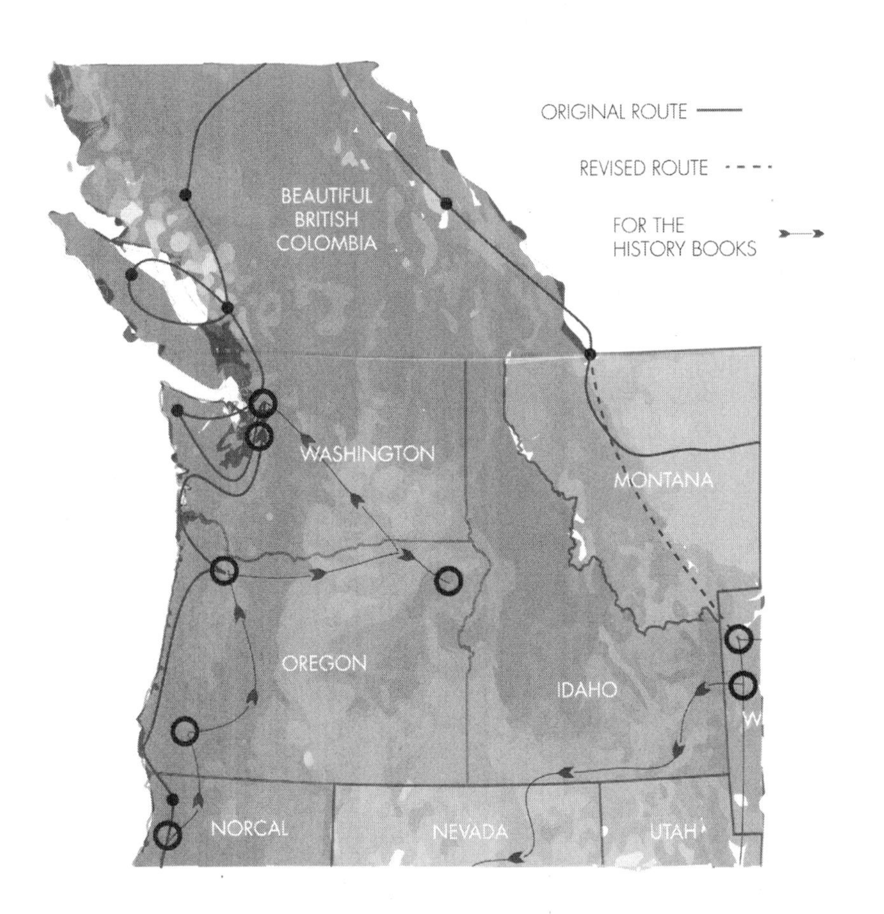
ORIGINAL ROUTE
REVISED ROUTE
FOR THE
HISTORY BOOKS
BEAUTIFUL
BRITISH
COLOMBIA
WASHINGTON
MONTANA
OREGON
IDAHO
NORCAL
NEVADA
UTAH

PART III
TWO GUIDES

ORIGINAL ROUTE
REVISED ROUTE
FOR THE HISTORY BOOKS

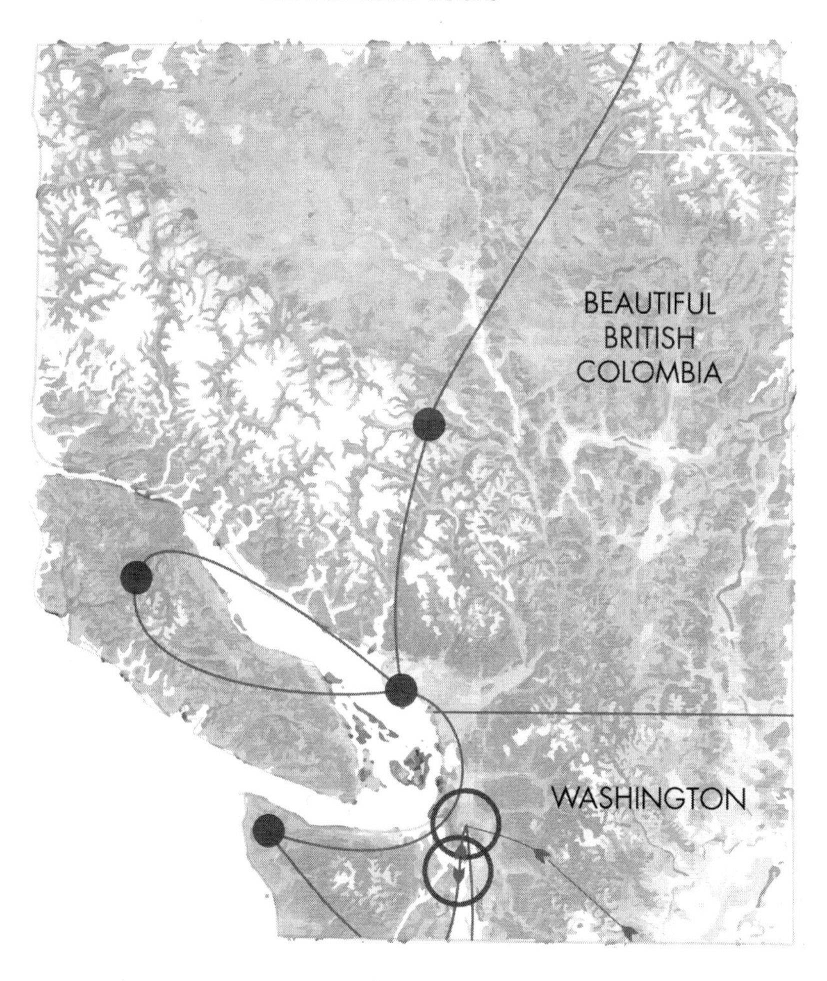

DAY 21

I woke again to a knock and mother's voice. The disoriented feeling of being fifteen years younger and inside a pirate ship lasted less time and I got a grip on reality:

I'm going to Vancouver.

I shot up, washed up, packed up, and headed downstairs with my pack, ready to go. The whole family—adopted and all—was in the kitchen munching away at their cereal. Out the window, the sky looked different. There was no blue to speak of. In its place was some strange layer of grey and mist. I learned later that these were called, "overcast clouds." That concept sounded so familiar, like I had seen this before, but not for a very long time.

"Hi, Mr. Evan!" said a shrill voice from somewhere below my eyeline.

I looked down. "Hey Zebadiah, what cereal do you have there?"

"Flleeeriooooossh!"

"Zeb! Don't talk with your mouth full!"

I sat down and Linda passed me a bowl and a spoon. Adam was sitting, reading the schedule for the ferry. "If we leave in the next twenty minutes," he said, "we should have more than enough time to get to the ferry by ten fifteen."

"Are you going on a ferry boat Mr. Evan?" inquired Jessie.

"Yes I am."

"Why?"

"Because it's going to take me to Canada."

"What's that?"

"Excuse me Jessie," interrupted Adam. "So the boat is going to take you to one of the San Juan islands. Then it looks like you have an hour layover before you get on another boat that will take you to a town called, Sidney, on Vancouver Island. Then you take a short ferry ride to Vancouver." I nodded, but Adam frowned. "Are you okay with all of that?"

I laughed incredulously. Did he actually think I would not have enjoyed such a varied itinerary? Before last night I thought I was taking a shit-ass jail bus, non-stop from Seattle to Vancouver. Now I was upgraded to island hopping on multiple boats. "Yeah! It's perfect!"

"Okay then, when you finish breakfast we'll hit the road."

I made one last attempt of polite, passive coercion. "Adam are you *sure* you want to do this? You *really* don't have to—"

Adam interrupted with a dismissively reassuring smile. "Evan, Evan, don't worry, you're going to have a great time!"

I quit.

After breakfast I gave a big hug to every family member—adopted and all—and thanked each one for all their amazing hospitality and video games. "And boys, really, thank you so much for letting me use your pirate ship. It's the coolest pirate ship in the world."

"I know, it's the bestest! Want to go up and play pirates and sharks?"

"Sorry buddy," said Adam, "Mr. Evan has to go now."

Damnit Adam, you're great, but you know when to ruin all the fun.

Linda came up and gave me a warm hug. "Good luck Evan. I hope you have a great time and find what you're looking for."

I smiled and looked at my surrogate Seattle mother. I wasn't sure what Linda meant by that, but I also knew exactly what she was talking about. "Thanks for everything Linda, I'll be in touch!"

Adam threw on his classic Pacific Northwest, light windbreaker, which was exactly like the one I saw the morning in Mendocino. "Are you ready?" he asked.

I slung my pack over my shoulder and plopped my whicker hat on my head. *The question is, is Canada ready for me.* I turned my back to my Pacific Northwest-suburban-Christian-surrogate family and followed Adam out the door to the soccer-dad minivan.

The suburbs crept in and out of the grey mist and soon we were on the highway heading north. A dense fog was over the bay and Seattle was barely visible. I felt like I was appropriately seeing this city for the first time. I thought about living in a place that probably looked like this for the majority of the year. That did not settle well with me, but I was also given a taste of how good it was when the sun did come out. You couldn't ask for a more perfect temperature mixed with such a bright, yet mild sun warming you just right, over the bluer than blue skies. But was that perfection worth all the grey I would be getting?

Once we were past the northern suburbs, dense pines lined the road and grey and green were the only visible colors. After some peaceful silence, Adam spoke up. "I remember Linda and I took a road trip when we first moved out here."

"Where did you come from?" I asked.

"Minnesota. I was in school when we met and got married. I always had a fascination with the Pacific Northwest, and Linda has family out here, so I applied to some jobs and landed one. Before I knew it, we were packing up as much as we could fit in our little Suburu—" *How appropriate.* "—and made the trip out. Everything that we couldn't fit we sold." I looked over and Adam had a nostalgic grin on his face. I imagined myself telling stories of this trip years later, with the same fond feeling.

"We had some car trouble too," he continued.

"Where was that?" I asked.

"Um, hmm, golly where *was* that?" Adam squinted his eyes, reaching into his memory bank. "Oh! Right, Ritzville, Washington: Smack dab in the middle of the state. It wasn't a serious problem, but the car needed service for a day. And man, we were stuck in the middle of nowhere!"

"Yeah," I agreed, "I got that feeling coming up from Oregon."

"East of the Cascades, you're in no man's land." Adam paused, then grew another nostalgic smile. "But I have to say that some of my fondest memories were from that day of doing nothing—I mean, we did something, we walked around this little town and you could literally see the 'outskirts' so to speak, where the town ended and the flat prairie stretched as far as we could see. And Linda and I, we kept walking and walking and I don't remember stopping, except to eat. And we talked. We talked endlessly, mostly about things we had never talked about before. I think it had to do with being in this strange place, but something about it made us completely open up to each other, and it was then that I knew we were destined to be together."

"Wow, that's great," I said.

"And that evening we watched the most beautiful sunset I think I had ever seen to this day. The prairie is good for that kind of stuff."

"Yeah I agree," I genuinely responded. Before a couple weeks ago, I wouldn't have been able to agree. Now I could. The prairie *was* beautiful.

"That's what is so fantastic about this great earth. No matter where you are, God seems to give it its own unique beauty. Even when it's not in front of your face, He will find a way to show you."

We sat silently for a while, both calmly looking forward, absorbed in our own thoughts and memories. Adam and I may have held different views about our beliefs, but we came to the same conclusion. I could not agree more that beauty could be found anywhere.

Adam spoke up again. "We were so rushed for that trip. We were so anxious to get out here. Then our car breaking down allowed us to sit back and take everything in. I tell ya, it's harder to do that nowadays with the kids running around all the time, along with my job, and helping out in the community."

Hearing this made me feel worse about this four-hour detour he had to take. "I can understand how busy you must be. I'm sorry if this is tearing you away from it."

Adam laughed and shook his head. "Evan, first of all, I appreciate where you're coming from. You're clearly a thoughtful, sensitive person. But what you should understand is that a big part of my job is to help my community—it's probably what I love the most about it. Helping you is just another part of my job."

I had no response to that. All I could think was that I had found the kindest, most helpful family (community rather) to stay with in the Pacific Northwest. This gave me a nervous feeling that Couchsurfing was going to be the opposite. Adam's family was motivated by God to do such kind acts. What were Couchsurfers motivated by? This question would be answered soon enough.

We turned off the highway and traveled through flat, open terrain. Before long our two-hour trek north was finished at the ferry launch in Anacortes. Adam walked in with me to make sure I had the ticket sorted out. I bought a ticket for the next ferry set to leave at ten-fifteen, just like Adam had said. It was currently ten o'clock.

"I think you're all set here," said Adam. I was at a loss for words. Adam extended his hand. "Best of luck my friend. You're welcome back any time."

"Thank you Adam, for the millionth time, thank you. There are so many other things to say, but I will leave it at that."

Adam smiled. "Okay then, God bless." And he turned and walked out.

Any sense of comfort was gone when Adam left, like a security blanket that was covering me was ripped off in one fell swoop. I was no longer in God's hands. In fact this was the first time on the trip where I felt completely vulnerable. I was nervous heading away from Casey toward Seattle, but at least I had already met Linda and had a good idea of what I was getting into—save for pirate ships. All I had now was an email, and a profile with a picture of a stick figure to work off of. Maybe I would get to Vancouver and this so-called "Couchsurfer" would decide not to help and leave me for dead. *Shit, I should've contacted another person for backup.* My stress and anxiety meter shot up a notch. My senses became more aware, the hair on my arm stood at full attention, ready to detect any foreign feeling. I had entered the game of survival. It was funny to put the words "survival" and "vacation" next to each other. *Wait a minute, why am I psyching myself out? Stop psyching yourself out. Go relax over there by the brochure stand.*

Up until last night, I did not know that the San Juan Islands existed. They are a string of islands not far off the coast of Washington. By the looks of the brochures, I could tell they were mostly geared toward tourism and summer home communities. I saw brochures for sailboat rentals, bike tours, restaurants, inns, real estate firms, kayak tours—*oooh, kayak tours!* I grabbed that brochure: "Take a guided group kayak tour around the San Juan Islands! See the local wildlife in their natural habitats, including killer whales who are known to congregate around the islands!" *Kayaking? Killer whales? I'm in.* Although I had to remind myself that I only had an hour layover and I should practice my general rule of traveling with reason, as opposed to simple impulsion. But I also reminded myself of my general rule of never knowing what would happen, and I stuffed the brochure in my pocket.

The announcement was made and I walked with a group of people out the backdoor where I was met by the backside of a ferry being loaded with cars and people. The grey water calmly lapped against the wooden walls of the launch. I looked out past the ferry to the ocean, where misty chunks of land loomed in the distance. A chilly breeze whipped up from the water and forced me to zip up my sweatshirt.

I walked onto the ferry and up some steps into a large, open room with big windows on all sides. I sat down by a window that overlooked the side of the ship. Was it the starboard side? I don't know, don't ask me for technical seafaring terms.

What caught my attention first was a mural that was plastered on the wall at the other end of the room. It was a large circle with a beautifully drawn depiction of a whale, with thick lines of dark greens, maroons, and blacks. I had seen this artwork scattered around Seattle, mostly depicting whales or birds. What I was looking at, was the classic artwork of the Native Americans of the Northwest. The modern Northwest had adopted this style as part of their regional signature and culture.

The ferry launched out making a U-turn, then we were full speed ahead heading west, out into the deep grey sea. I didn't think that I would be able to go farther west than the coast on my trip, but when I started planning for this, I did not factor in being on a ferry in the Pacific Ocean—or going south in Wyoming, or La Grande, or hot springs, or a broken down car, and on, and on, and on. This will have been one of the farthest points west that I had ever gone in my life. I was breaking this record every other second of this trip, but leaving the coast added more significance.

A good idea popped into my head for anyone to do—that means kids too! *That's right, even you can do it, Jessie.* "Really?? Thanks Mr. Evan!"—Get a hold of a map of the world and pin it up on your wall. Then take four pins and put them on the farthest north, south, east, and west points that you have ever traveled. Continue to move the pins outward accordingly. You may be able to take a step back and realize, "Wow, I'm a pathetic loser who hasn't traveled anywhere!" Or, "Wow, I'm a well seasoned traveler. I deserve a medal!" It could make for a good conversation piece. Also, seeing it would be a motivator to keep that pin moving. I couldn't wait to get home and put my western pin into the West Coast. However, I wasn't done with the trip yet. My pin was going to end up in New Zealand at this rate.

A group of seniors sat down close to me, who looked like two couples traveling together. "Carl, did you remember to pack the prunes?"

"I already told you, we would get them at the market on the island."

"Okay, but you know it closes early and we need them for dinner tonight."

"Don't worry Rose, we have lots of time."

Rose turned to the other elderly couple sitting across from them. "I can't wait to show you our view from the dining room."

"I can only imagine Rose!" responded her female counterpart.

"Carl just had the wraparound porch redone. It looks gorgeous!"

"Oh Rose, I can only imagine!"

Rose turned to me. "A bit overcast but not bad!"

Was she talking to me? I turned and looked at a shriveled smiling face with too much blush application. "Yeah," I responded, "very nice."

Her eyes wandered down to the ground. "That's a big bag you got there. Are you traveling somewhere?"

"I'm heading up to Vancouver."

"Oooh, that's a beautiful city. And you decided to take the ferry through the islands? That's a bit far out of the way."

"Time isn't exactly an issue for me," I said.

Rose turned to Carl. "Did you hear that, Carl? This nice boy is going to Vancouver."

"I did hear him Rose," said Carl. Then he turned to me. "You made the right choice son, the San Juans are beautiful. Where are you coming from? Seattle?"

"No, Massachusetts."

A resounding geriatric "Oooooh!" traveled through the crowd. "You're a long way from home, son!"

I noticed while we were talking, that a woman sitting in the row behind me was staring at me like I was some strange, interesting, possibly mate-worthy specimen. She looked to be in her late-thirties, but youthfully attractive for her age. I glanced over and smiled. She kept staring.

"Well I wish you the best of luck," continued Rose. "Vancouver's a fine city. Nice people too—the Canadians that is."

"Thank you."

"Massachusett." The staring lady spoke up. "Near New York, ja?" She had a foreign accent, of the European persuasion.

"Yeah, have you been?" I answered.

"No, I have never. This is my first time to de United States."

"Where are you from?" I asked.

"Svitzerland."

"Oh, wow. I've been there."

"Ja? Vhere?"

"I went skiing in Zermatt and Grindelwald."

She gave a pleasant smile like I was speaking her language. "Oh ja, very nice."

"Do you ski?" I asked.

"No, I don't like it."

I furrowed my brow in confusion. *How does someone come from Switzerland and not ski?*

"I used to ski a lot, but I got sick," she said.

I wasn't sure if she meant physically sick or tired of skiing. I didn't question her, but I hoped for the latter.

She looked down at my mobile home. "Dat is a nice pack you have. Did you buy it at Valmart?"

"No, I hate Walmart."

She sat up straight with incredulous eyes. "Vaaat?" Valmart is a great store! Everysing is cheap. How can you hate dat?"

Damnit, do I really have to get into this discussion? How could this European love Walmart? I thought Walmart epitomized what other highly developed countries hated about us. "Us Americans vith our cheap goods and big cars." Maybe I was giving our neighbors across the pond too much credit. Maybe they weren't as forward thinking as I had thought.

I tried to veer the conversation away into more familiar, less confrontational territory. "What brings you out on a boat into the San Juan Islands?"

"I vant to see killer vales."

I had to hold in a laugh. Her accent amused me in a humorous and admittedly sexy way.

"I heard dey are common out here."

"I heard that as well," I said. Then I added, "I might do a kayak tour to see some whales."

She grew a smile of apparent intrigue. "Jaja, I want to do dat as well."

I smiled back. She then gave a strange smirk and slowly turned her head away. Was this conversation done? I wasn't sure.

I looked out at the passing ocean as we crept by foggy land masses. I looked down at the water. Suddenly without warning, a school of twenty dolphins were jumping in and out of the water, racing with the boat—

Just kidding, that didn't happen—only grey water lapping up against the sides. Peculiarly attractive Swiss women, geriatrics and grey waters. This detour into the Pacific was off to an odd start.

We were getting closer to a particular land mass. Eventually I could see the large oceanfront houses, which must have been the vacation homes to the rich Seattleites. I was looking at multi-room mansions with personal docks and boathouses. It was too bad that traveling wasn't a full time job that paid a lot to let me come home and rest in my island mansion. Then again if it was, everyone would do it.

The ferry slowed down, made another U-turn, and docked into the launch. We were set down in an inlet with land protruding out on both sides. Seagulls flopped up and down the coast and little cars and people on bicycles rode around the narrow roads that seemed to follow the island's perimeter. The "island vibe" was in full force, meaning it was time to blast some reggae and get out the bong.

When I stepped outside, I could smell the fishy, windy island air and I could see that the grey sky was starting to open up with blue cracks. I had a brief hour to enjoy the island vibe before my next ferry departed, so my time would most likely involve getting lunch and taking a short stroll.

I was standing at the bottom of the ferry ramp pondering, when I was startled by something grabbing my arm. I turned and saw the Swiss Woman. "Maybe I vill see you later," she said in a soft voice as she let go of my arm and brushed by. I stood there frozen, watching her walk off.

Do I follow her?... No, she said she vill see me later... Maybe she means at the kayak rental?... You should follow her... No. Not worth it. No time... Are you sure??... Okay, I'll think about it.

There was a small town set up around the boat launch. Touristy shops, bars, restaurants, and action/adventure offices saturated my field of view. As I walked through this little island town, I looked past the flashy, tacky tourist signs, and noticed the styles of architecture. Shingled layers of tan beachwood covered the outer walls. I have seen this same style in one other place on earth: Cape Cod. Waspy islanders must have been the same no matter where you went. Or maybe it was the similar northern hemisphere, above-tropical area that both places shared. I imagined these houses could withstand more of the colder temperatures. This Waspy style didn't exist on tropical islands. For those southern places to achieve this, they would need to sell off their Rastafarians in exchange for Wasp's. <Disclaimer: Even though it sounds like it, this book does not support colonialism.>

I stuck with my original plan and found a place to eat. It was a typical island "crab shack" restaurant, with a typical menu of deep fried fish that would be served in a basket with red and white checkered wax paper. Typical "seafaring equipment," like thick rope and buoys, were used as wall decoration. I sat down at a table and in front of me was an oversized paper placemat, depicting a map. It was the classic cartooney map that depicted the town we were in, with raised buildings and colorful denotations of notable landmarks for my touristing pleasure. Around the perimeter of the map, were boxed adds for establishments of touristing interest: restaurants, real estate, hotels, etc.

My table was outside and I had a wide view of the bay. I ordered a fried oyster platter and a side of chowder from a bright-faced college-age girl with a big tourist-friendly smile. She was home for the summer to make those tips so she could afford to buy books for the fall semester. I knew she would do well. Her flirtatious smile was sure to bump up that twenty percent tip to twenty-five. Depending on my mood and her service, she would be getting my money or my number on a napkin.

After she took my order, I relaxed and looked out at the water, trying not to look down at the placemat eyesore that competed for my attention. I watched my old ferry float out of the bay, which rendered the launch vacant for any interested Canadian vessels.

It was a calm day. Traffic seldom traveled through the town. I noticed the pair of geriatric couples walking by. Rose smiled holding her bag of prunes. I envied their retired life. It led me to imagine what it would have been like to own a summer home here, or have a "family cottage:" a special place our family would all go to each summer to relax, eat prunes, drink wine, play with the kids, and look over my stock options. As I watched the couples, I planted fake fond memories in my head:

Evan's Account of Fake Fond Memories Entitled:
Summer in San Juan

-Get out of my last day of school with the pent up excitement for what I know awaits me on the island.

-I cannot stand the boat ride there that seems so long, dying with anticipation, jumping hysterically as mom pleads, "I know you're excited sweety, but you have to calm down."

-I watch my older brothers take out the family boat and feel the jealousy because I'm not old enough to hang out with the "cool" kids.

-I have a group of island friends who live down on Orca Lane. I only see them during the summer and it's a special relationship because it's a different dynamic then the relationship I have with my school friends. Something about it seems more open and free.

-I have my first kiss down by the "secret dock" that I find out from my older brother who goes there to drink and smoke with the cool kids.

-I have big, delicious family meals that my mom cooks every night on the screened in porch overlooking the ocean with the sun setting (when it isn't overcast).

-The weeks fly by, and by late August I have to wear a light jacket because the days are already getting noticeably colder and shorter.

-And finally that horrible feeling of the boat ride back at the end of the summer.

-Back to school, back to work, back to the real world.

I snapped out of my fake past and reminded myself that I was still "on the island." Summer wasn't over and I didn't have to go back to the real world yet.

The bright-faced college girl arrived with my food and I looked up and smiled. "Thanks."

"Do you need anything else?" she asked.

Besides you? "No, thank you."

"Okay, just let me know."

She walked off and I checked my watch. I had forty more minutes in America before my ship set sail for the new world. *Or, I could not get on the boat...* My thoughts of the fake past switched to thoughts of the potential future: I could finish my meal, take a kayak tour, then find a place to stay for the night. Tomorrow I would look for a job. Some tourist job downtown would do. Something like, pawning placemats—anything to keep me afloat. Get a small place, maybe rent a cheap room in someone's house. Get on my feet, meet the locals, get in with the cool, rebel kids. Marry the waitress and make a life for myself on the island. What was stopping me from choosing this path? Nothing. I poured hot sauce on my chowder and dug in. I had forty minutes to think over my life.

I looked up from my chowder and noticed that, who else but the Swiss Woman was walking by. She looked lost, holding a placemat. I considered getting her attention and offering her a drink, then including her in my plans to kayak. This would seamlessly lead into finding a place to stay, with a warm bed for two warm bodies to share. She looked up from the map and began to walk away. I had to make a decision. Behind her, I could see the other ferry pulling in to the port. *What's it going to be Evan? Canada, or a Swiss woman on an island?* I looked over at the ferry, then at the Swiss Woman. I imagined riding along the coast on a Vespa, my Swiss love latched on back and holding onto me, whispering sweet German phrases into my ear. Then I looked down at my greasy basket of fried oysters. They looked unhealthy. I popped one in my mouth and chewed...It was, okay. I forgot I didn't really like oysters or seafood in the first place. I looked up and there was no more Swiss Woman. The ferry was slowly docking on the launch and I cringed as I gulped down the greasy sea creature.

I decided to forfeit my life plans to live on this island. I didn't think I could be an island bum anyway. A ski bum would have been more my style. Maybe a place like...Whistler. Determination set in. I had to get off of this damn rock and head north.

The new ferry looked like the old ferry, except it sported an American, as well as Canadian flag decal. The flags peacefully rested side by side like the two happy neighbors they were. I walked up to the entrance and realized that I couldn't simply stroll onto the boat, like I did in Anacortes. Metal corrals led me to the side and into a small shack. A sign outside had another decal of our two nation's flags and under it, it said, "United States-Canada Customs Office." Below that it said, "United States of America." Below that it said, "Government of Canada." Below that it said, "Gouvernement du Canada." I stopped before I walked in the door and held my breath. *Did I get rid of all the naughty things I did not want to bring over the border?—Shit, the weed! No I gave that all to Casey—Shit, the cookie! No, I ate that in Seattle—Shit! The WMD'S! No, they were safely stashed in my rectum.*

I probably would have been okay with the weed. I was heading into the weed capital of North America. They would have taken my weed out, laughed at it, and thrown it away saying, "You call that weed? That's dirt. You just wait. Welcome to Canada." Someone once told me that weed was one of British Columbia's largest exports, only second to logging.

I walked into the shack and was in an empty room with a single window counter on the opposite side. I approached the window where an authoritatively attractive woman stood, with a tied back ponytail, dressed in a red security outfit. She greeted me with a smile that seemed to be stern from maybe a Canadian's perspective, but plane-old friendly from mine.

"Traveling to Sidney?" she asked.

I gave her a dumb look. "Huh? Um, Canada?"

The woman could sense my confusion and chuckled. "Yes, Sidney, Vancouver Island, Canada."

"Oh, right."

"Passport?"

It was finally time to shine for that little piece in my luggage. I had to take my bag off my back and dig through the top pocket to find my passport. It took me a minute to dig through, past my knives, toothbrush, maps, and WMD detonator. I fished out the passport and handed it over.

"Thank you." She opened it for no more than five seconds, closed it, and gave it back. All of that worrying and effort for a few measly seconds of recognition. It was funny how that worked.

"Destination?" she asked.

"Vancouver," I answered.

"Pleasure?" she asked.

I looked at her. "What?" *Pleasure? Why are all of these seemingly easy questions tripping me up? Am I getting hit on? Am I hearing what I want to hear? Am I having a border crossing fantasy?*

Her face grew more stern. "Are you going to Canada for pleasure or for work? Based on your backpack and the straw hat on your head, I'm assuming pleasure, but I'm not one to judge."

I chuckled. "Yes, yes, I am going for pleasure."

"Okay, you're all set. Walk out that door back there and wait at the gate. We will be boarding the ferry shortly. Enjoy your stay in Canada." She smiled and I couldn't help but feel warm and fuzzy inside, like I was being welcomed back into my long lost home.

I stepped out of the "high security" customs shack, followed the corral up to the ferry, walked up the stairs, and crossed through the gate that would lead me to the promised land. I'm sorry that I'm making such a big deal about going from the US to Canada. You'd think that I should get over myself. It wasn't like I was crossing the pearly gates of heaven. But in truth, I'm not sorry at all. I drove across the country to get to the Pacific Ocean, and it took me three weeks and a broken down car to get to here. I earned it. So without apologies, au revoir America, and ciao Canada!

The ferry was similar to the previous one on the inside as well. There was even another Native American art piece on the back wall of the upper deck. This particular drawing looked like a depiction of a beautiful eagle. It was a reminder that I may have been crossing political borders, but these borders did not always exist. The Native American art wasn't going to change from America to Canada.

The boat set off in the opposite direction around the island from which I came in on, leading us to travel through a narrow pass between two peninsulas. In the distance were glimpses of mountainous land, still dim and foggy through the Northwest mist. There were so many islands and channels that we were weaving through, like an intricate sea highway. No signs of life could be seen on the islands we passed, only rugged wilderness that filled the land and stopped abruptly on tall, steep cliffs. I squinted into the wilderness. *Any animals? Bears? Eagles? Fucking squirrels?? Nothing.* I looked back at the eagle painting on the wall. Looking at that was good enough for me. The round curves and mellow colors calmed my soul.

I was also squinting and searching the horizon for any sign of the sun. There was no end in sight for the chilly, overcast skies. The grey water lapped onto the sides of the boat with frigid-looking frothy suds spraying off. I tried to imagine jumping dolphins again, but it was useless. I got a bad feeling that I was heading into another prison of shitty weather. I envisioned sitting in this Couchsurfer's apartment in Vancouver, grey and rain outside, nothing to do, nothing to see. That was a thought to avoid. I looked back over at the eagle and let out a deep breath.

It wasn't long before I could feel the ferry slow down and saw that it was heading toward an island that showed signs of life. This was more of a continental landmass than an island called, Vancouver Island. When looking on the map, it is so big that it could be mistaken for a country. It is long and thin, spanning up the coast of British Columbia. There is supposed to be a spectacular rain forest to hike through, along with all sorts of mysterious surprises. I felt giddy pricks getting sent up the nape of my neck. Finding myself in this magical place was still very much a possibility after leaving Vancouver.

We pulled up to a port which looked like it catered more to commerce and industry than tourists. There was no quaint, Waspy town to meet us and no mansions to mock us. The boat docked and we shuffled off. I was instructed to take a shuttle bus that was parked across the street from the launch, which would take me to another port on the island, where the last ferry would take me to Vancouver. As I walked out of the gate, a large blue sign said, "Welcome to British Columbia, the greatest place on earth."

The shuttle took me on a short ride through a plain suburban neighborhood. There were rows of small houses, none looking vastly different from any other. Everyone on the bus was quiet, with pleasant grins on their faces. If their general vibe spoke to me, it would have said, "We are all happy and content with our grey skies and plain houses—at least we have our health (paid for by the government)." I, on the other hand, being a young, ambitious, thrill-seeking American, had extravagant dreams. This mediocrity was killing me. But this place was claiming to be the "greatest place on earth." Maybe they were referring to something deeper, like a state of mind. It was the greatest place on earth because everyone was content. There were no unfulfilled ambitions. Nobody was creating unrealistic goals and setting themselves up for disappointment. Then again it wasn't fair for me to jump to such conclusions about an entire country, within the first five minutes of setting foot on its soil. However, it is human nature to do that with first impressions—or maybe it was American nature...

We reached a similar port: plain and industrial. I got off the bus with the remaining bus patrons and we headed onto the ferry. It was crowded, but I managed to find my regular seat by the window.

This boat set out straight eastward toward the continent. I could see numerous mountainous islands ahead of us. They looked stacked onto each other, each one slightly larger than the one in front. At the bottom of every island, a dramatic cliff fell into the sea. We slowly weaved in between these island mountains like passing through valleys. It would have been a remarkable sight, if only the grey skies could have subsided.

I was so fixated on the islands, I hadn't noticed a couple that had sat down across from me. They were middle-aged with youthful expressions, looking out at the passing scenery with a pleasant "Canadian grin," like the people on the bus. The man looked over at me and smiled. "You look like you're on a trip there, young man." His voice was cheery and welcoming.

"Yes I am."

"Where are you coming from?" asked the woman.

"Originally Massachusetts."

I got the most wide-eyed, gaping mouthed look I had gotten on the trip thus far. Maybe my distance from home was directly proportional to how wide people's eyes and mouths grew when they heard where I was from. "Oooh! Down in the States there! That's over on the other end, say below Montreal, eh?"

Oh my lord, did I just get my first "eh??" "Yeah, it's a few hours south of there."

"Oh yaah. We've never been over that way, but hear it's nice."

"Yes, very nice."

"Are you headed to Vancouver?" asked the woman.

"Yes I am, I've never been before."

"Oh yaah," they said in unison. "You're going to love it. Lots of great things to do for young people especially."

"Yeah I can't wait."

"Yaah."

They proceeded to give me suggestions on all the good places to go and see. "...and Stanley Park, you can't miss that. Rent a bike and take it along the water." I nodded, trying to take in as much information as I could. I hoped that when I was their age I would be as nice and genuinely helpful to travelers. There was a kindness about them that was distinctly different. It was more natural and at ease than what I was used to.

We talked as the ship rolled through the mountainous valleys. The couple told me that they just came from Vancouver Island where they were visiting their son. "He made a trip down to Yosemite National Park when he was your age," said the woman. "California, now that's pretty country."

"Yeah I agree," I said. Before a couple weeks ago, I wouldn't have been able to agree. Now I could. California *was* pretty country.

The land we were passing was turning inhabited again and the boat was slowing down. The couple got up and gave me a parting smile. "Good luck in the city. Don't have too much fun, eh."

"I'll try. Thanks for the advice."

We pulled into a bigger and more industrial port than the one in Sidney, but no buildings to speak of. *Is this Vancouver? Just a pile of industrial waste? This isn't what Google Images showed me.*

I got off the boat and was again directed toward a bus which I was told was heading downtown. I fished out Devina's number from my pocket. Holding my breath, I dialed. <Residual #1 from this trip: foot

fungus from my shoe. Residual #2 from this trip: the expensive phone bill that I racked up from making calls in Canada. I was completely ignorant at the time, as to what I was doing to myself. Residual #3: severed my—oh wait, we haven't gotten to that part yet.>

Ring...Ring...Ring...Ring...Ring...Voicemail. It was one of those generic automated voice machines telling me I had reached the voice mailbox of the number I had just dialed, and to please leave a message for the undisclosed recipient. I hung up and stared out into this strange, grey land with nothing but frustration and contempt frothing inside me. *I knew this website was a scam—some bullshit ploy, to send people around the world thinking there is somebody waiting for you to hold your hand and be your little tour guide.* I brought my scornful mind back to reason and considered my plan B. It was time to break out the emergency funds and book some cheap-ass motel, sit around rainy grey Vancouver for a day, then head on home, back to Massachus—

Ring...Ring... I grabbed my phone and stared at the same mysterious number calling me back. "Hello?"

"Hi," said a young woman's voice. She sounded friendly, but stern. "I just got a call from this number."

"Um, yeah, I just called. Is this Devina?"

"Yes it is. Would this be Evan?"

I could feel my inner organs untwist and fall back into a comfortable position. "Yes! Yes it is. From Couchsurfing."

"Did you make it into town?"

"Almost I think. I'm on a bus that's apparently heading to the downtown area."

"Great, I'll meet you there..." She told me to tell the bus driver to drop me off at a certain place, and "don't worry, they're very helpful to newcomers." I hoped so. I still had inner scars from being yelled at to "step down."

"Okay, I'll do that. See you soon!" I hung up and walked to the front of the bus. There was no bulletproof glass partition separating me from the driver, only a thin veil of Canadian comradery. "Excuse me?"

"Yes sir?" said the driver.

I gave him the newcomer spiel that Devina instructed me on.

"No problem there sir. Just stay toward the front of the bus and I'll be sure to let you know."

This seemed too easy so far. It was as if Devina and the bus driver were working for the same hospitality agency. The way they operate is: The driver drops me off, at which point my guide rendezvous' with me to take me to my living quarters. It was like some exotic paid vacation that was voluntary and run by everyday people.

As the bus ran along suburban streets that were becoming gradually urban, I noticed the sun dipping under the clouds and peaking out for a short time, before hiding under some unknown, craggy horizon. By dusk I could see outlines of tall buildings up ahead that were brilliantly lit. Five more minutes and these buildings were above us, as we traveled down a busy street. People were out, shops were open, lights were bursting: It was suppertime in Vancouver, or as Canadians call it, "dinnertime."

It looked like we were in the center of it all when the driver pulled to the side and glanced over in my direction. "Here's the stop you asked for, sir." I thanked my driver as I stepped off. "Hey!" yelled the driver as I got onto the street.

Oh no, what did I do now?? I stepped off right, didn't I?

I turned around to see the driver looking at me in earnest. "Are you sure you know where you're going?" he asked.

I smiled and nodded. "Yes, I think I do. Thank you!"

He nodded and the doors closed.

I looked for a street sign and saw that I was at the precise corner where Devina told me to be. I stood looking around, blinking like a mouse coming out from a newly discovered hole and familiarizing itself with its foreign world. I was admittedly a tad underdressed, with my wicker hat, thift store T-shirt, cargo shorts, and Birks. The Vancouver dinner crowd was putting me to shame. Not only were these people dressed to impress, they were also beautiful. This applied to both men and women alike (with the occasional destitute fellow in between, but even *they* dressed more appropriate than me). But no matter who it was, no one paid the least bit of attention to me, aside from stepping to the side if they were walking in my path. I was like an inanimate column that needed to be navigated around in the middle of the sidewalk.

I shifted my attention to sights around me. There weren't many indicators to show that I was in a different country. People spoke English as they walked by; The destitute guy on the corner was asking for change; Sedans and SUVs and Taxis cruised the streets. What I did notice was an occasional neon sign of a bank that I had never heard of. Additionally, instead of the red, white, and blue, the red and white stripes with the great red maple leaf, hung proudly from various buildings and storefronts. Besides that, I might as well have been in America. *What were you expecting from Canada, Evan? Rickshaws and sheepherders?*

Twenty minutes had gone by before I snapped out of my bewilderment and realized that there was no sign of Devina yet. *Should I call?... No, Not yet. I don't want to be hasty. I want to be a nice, patient guest. Maybe I'll call at the half-hour mark. That's appropriate.* A half-hour call says, "Hey, I've been waiting, and I deserve some sort of update so I know to wait longer before giving up."

At thirty minutes I reached in my pocket and fondled my phone. At thirty-five minutes I took it out and called. Ring...Ring...Ring...Ring... "You have reached—" *Back to that fucking automated voicemail! You devil woman! I fell straight into your trap! You led me to the center of Babylon before leaving me for the sharks to swarm. I'm going to buy a sharp object and find the founder of this website and—*

"Evan?" a soft voice came from behind me.

I turned around and faced a girl. She looked a few years older than me, had dark hair and glasses, and gave off a pretty smile that looked friendly, but strong and confident at the same time. I smiled back.

"Welcome to Vancouver." She extended her hand. "I'm Devina."

I shook Devina's hand and any frustration or stress in my body was swept away like wind to a loose maple leaf. "Hey Devina, nice to finally meet you."

"Likewise. Come on, I'll take you to my place."

Already?? This person didn't know a thing about me, and after a couple words she was taking me back to her home? Who was I? Just some stranger she met on a website. Especially as a female, I couldn't believe how quickly she was taking me under her wing. Where was this trust stemming from? Human beings weren't supposed to trust each other like this—at least in this day and age.

I followed my new host across the street and we turned down a side street. "How was your trip?" she asked. "Did you take the bus from Seattle?"

"No, I took some ferries through the islands, but I started from Seattle."

"Oh, cool. That takes a lot longer, but a good ride. Worth it for the views, eh?"

"Yes, it was really nice. A bit overcast though."

She laughed. "Welcome to the Northwest."

Northwest? I assumed that Canadians would have called this the *South*west. After all, we were in the southwest corner of the country. I guess they've generally accepted that they are pretty far north.

Devina continued. "But I think the weather is supposed to clear up tomorrow."

"Really?"

"Well, who knows. We have to see it to believe it around here. Then she spoke under her breath. I thought that she said, "I hope it clears up for Critical Mass."

Critical Mass? That name sounded so familiar but I couldn't remember why.

"Is this your first time here?" she asked.

"Yes."

"Great! I'm sure you'll love it."

We stopped at a bus stop and she turned to me. "By the way, I have two other Couchsurfers coming in tonight. I think they're from San Francisco and they biked here. I'm pretty sure they aren't coming in until later."

"Oh?"

"You don't have a problem with that, right?" she looked at me and smiled, assuming I had only one answer.

"Um, no, not at all."

"Cool. You actually came on a quiet night."

"What?" I was confused.

She looked down the street. "Oh, this is our bus."

We hopped onto the bus that pulled up. It had a similar electric hum like its southern counterparts. We were part of a diverse group of patrons. All shapes, sizes, creeds, colors, rags, and riches, all sitting quietly with pleasant grins.

"What I meant was," Devina did not skip a beat, "three surfers are quiet for me."

"Surfers?" I asked. "I thought you said that they were biking here."

Devina paused and looked at me, then she laughed. "No, no! I mean *Couch*surfers!"

"Oooooh!" *How thick headed could I be? Of course she called Couchsurfers, "Surfers."* "Right, I'm sorry. I'm an idiot."

She laughed sympathetically. "That's fine. I forgot, this is your first Couchsurfing experience, right?"

"Yeah," I gave a shy nod, "I'm a virgin."

"I remember you mentioned that in your message. Sorry, I get so many damn messages that they get jumbled in my head sometimes. Anyway, speaking of messages, do you remember what I said about me kind of running a hostel?"

"Yes I do. I wasn't sure what you meant."

"I meant that I average twelve to thirteen Surfers a night, and that's why tonight is atypical."

My eyes grew wide. "Really??"

"Yeah," she nodded casually, "I probably have three days per month when my house is empty. I hate empty houses—too much unutilized space."

"That's amazing. Do you get privacy?"

She shrugged, "I have my own room."

I was afraid to ask the next question that popped into my head, but it came out before I had time to second guess. "Have you ever had any issues?"

She gave me a peculiar look. "Like what?"

In my head I was thinking, *has anyone ever tried to hack off your limbs?* But I chose to rephrase it. "Um, does anybody ever, I don't know, suck?"

Devina looked at the ceiling and raised an eyebrow like she was thinking through her presumably hundreds of past Surfers. "Mmmm, not really. Everyone's generally pretty cool. Besides," she put on a stern, confident face, "there isn't a situation I can't handle." She said this in such a matter-of-fact way that I had to believe her. Devina carried an air of confidence that permeated behind her openness, and I already believed that she could handle anything that was thrown her way. In other words, she was a tough broad.

The bus rolled out of the downtown area and we were passing low rises and storefronts. It wasn't as bustling as downtown, and some stores were dark. Night had hit Vancouver's outer limits.

Devina and I kept the conversation rolling. I told her about my trip and its peaks and valleys. She listened intently and seemed to be genuinely interested in everything I was saying. She traded back some cool traveling stories, like hitchhiking across Texas and into Mexico. She said she spoke Spanish and apparently had many Mexican friends. "You'll meet them I'm sure. They're a trip."

She went on about Mexico. "I love it. I might be moving to Mexico City soon."

"Really??" I asked incredulously.

"Yeah, why? Are you surprised?"

"No! Well, a little I guess." I couldn't hide my prejudice. "I just hear about Mexicans moving here—by here I mean North America. But I don't hear about many people from here, with the desire to move south."

Need I mention that Devina was clearly a "gringo." I found out that she hailed from Calgary, Alberta (an optional stop in my original route at the bottom of Jasper National Park). She had moved to Vancouver a couple years back.

"People are too uptight here, too stuffy," she began. "Central and South American countries are loose and free. And I have a lot of connections in Mexico, so it's an easy place for me to start. Then maybe I'll move south from there." I could tell that she had the traveler's gene, which was something I could relate to. Then she said something that I could not have said better myself: "Anyway, who cares? If I don't like Mexico City, I'll move. If anything, it'll be another experience."

With that simple statement, Devina was able to encapsulate the essence of traveling: It is an experience. And experiencing is what we do to keep our hearts beating. Certain people do not want to experience new things out of fear. Some might say that it is out of disinterest, but that is a lie. It is fear that keeps someone from traveling, or letting a stranger stay in their home, or trying a new food, or climbing a mountain. "What if I'm put in an uncomfortable situation? Or poisoned? Or fall off a cliff?" These concerns are legitimate, but they will not stop someone like Devina, because she knows that she is more likely to make a new friend, or eat something delicious, or see an amazing view. And if it turns out bad, then it is dealt with and you leave with a memory and a good story. This is what it means to experience. I felt good about staying with Devina. She was a fellow traveler and that made all the difference.

When we got off the bus, we left the main drag and turned onto a smaller, poorly lit street. There was an empty, overgrown plot of land on one side of the street, and a few dingy low rises on the other. We turned into the fourth dingy building down the block. From the outside it looked like a big, ugly box. In fact, not one piece of architecture had stood out to me yet, in the entire country of Canada.

We walked into a dingy hallway with a separate apartment door on each wall. Devina opened lucky door number one, on the right wall. My first impression when she opened the door may have come off as rude. This was because I stood in the doorway, visibly shocked with my mouth slightly agape for an elongated period of time. What I saw (and smelled) was a grimy room. A dirty, old, off-color couch lined one wall, with Indie punk band posters carelessly placed above it. A crappy, small TV was at the head of the room, with an original Nintendo system under it, and controllers strewn on the marked up wooden floor. A big window on the opposite wall looked out to the street that we had just walked down. One could stand on the sidewalk and dive through the window with ease. Some old bookcases on the other wall had books and VHS tapes that were carelessly thrown in, without a shred of organizational effort. In summation, every piece in this room could have been freshly dragged out of a thrift store, or tag sale, or better yet, the dumpster in an alleyway.

This was an abrupt wakeup call, from subconsciously, wrongfully assuming that a Couchsurfer's home is a hotel with set standards to accommodate the paying patron's personal needs. The reality was that I was the guest who must conform to this person's style of living, whom hath graciously opened their home to me, free of cost. In other words, beggers ain't fucking choosers.

I didn't know what I was expecting, but I wasn't expecting this. *Maybe I should bail now, before I get too far into it. I'll suck it up and get a hotel. I'll choose comfort and isolation over—well, over whatever this is.*

Devina turned around and smiled, unaware of my inner dillema. "You can take the guest room if you want. I can show you, it's back here. Or you can take the couch—"

"Guest room!" I blurted, then checked myself. "I mean, I'll take a look at the guest room." *Wait a minute, do I want to see more of this crack den? Just turn away Evan, you're closer to the door. Say thanks, and walk away. Don't look back and you'll never see her again—*

"This way Evan!"

"Coming!"

I reluctantly followed my gracious host to the other end of the living-crack room and turned a corner. Ahead of me was a small, messed up kitchen. Dirty pots and pans were piled high in the sink and covering countertops. "Sorry, we had a pasta party last night with a group of Italian surfers."

"Uh huh," came the sound out of my gaping mouth.

We turned another corner and she opened a door. It was a bare room with nothing but a bed, but the eerie emptiness was more inviting than anything else I had seen thus far. "My roommate moved out a week ago, so I'm letting people crash in here, until I find someone new. She pointed across the hall to another door. "There's the bathroom."

"Uh huh," came the sound.

"So, do you want to take this room?"

I bit my lip and forced a smile. Who knew who had been in that bed. The choice had to be made. Crack bed or crack couch—or run and jump out the window, onto the street. "Um, um," *Crack bed or crack couch? Crack bed or crack couch?* Devina stared at me. *Crack bed or crack couch?*

Then a voice emerged from inside me. *Remember Evan, it's an experience. Think about it, there's no immediate threat or danger.* This uplifting feeling sparked a good solution. *I know! I'll wait for the other Couchsurfers to come. Maybe they'll give me a new perspective. Experience...Experience...* I repeated it in my head like my new mantra. I took a deep breath. "I'll take the bed!"

"Cool!" and she turned around and walked out. The big life decision I just made seemed to have zero effect on her. Why would it?

My bag dropped on the barren floor and I stood in silence. I could hear Devina in the other room, talking on the phone. I looked over at the crackbed. It didn't look that bad. I was psyching myself out. *So what if her living room is grungy?* Sometimes there can be a fine line between knowing when to get out of a situation, or choosing to stick with it. I assured myself that the real warning bells had not been set off yet.

All of this excitement had pushed back my desire for food and it was now coming back in full force. I walked out of the guest-crack room and into the kitchen. Devina was in her bedroom, which was connected to the kitchen. I peaked in. Her room was by far the cleanest, most well put together part of the house. There were nicely framed posters on the walls, a big comfy looking bed with a crisp, white comforter, and an Apple computer monitor in the corner that was large enough to swallow the living room crack TV whole, while arrogantly insulting it because of how outdated it was. Devina was right. There was her hostel, and there was her *own* room.

She hung up the phone and turned to me. "That was the other Surfers, they should be here pretty soon."

I nodded. "Okay, cool. I was thinking about going to get something quick to eat now. Are you hungry?" *Evan, you should treat her to dinner. That's the least you can do for her hospitality.* "Um, can I treat you to dinner?"

Devina shook her head. "No thanks. I ate earlier. But if you're looking for cheap and fast, there's a good falafel place on the corner." She was a mindreader.

"That sounds great."

"Here," she threw me her keys. "The big key is the front door, and the smaller one is for my apartment. Take your time. I can call you if we're going to leave and you're not back yet."

I looked down at my hand holding the keys to this person's house. "Okay," I said in obedient shock. She smiled and I walked out.

First she took me to her place with no reservations. Now she was entrusting me with her keys? I could have run off, waited for her to leave, and terrorized her home at my free will. What I needed to do was to get out of the mindset that there was some preconceived notion that I was a violent, vindictive, selfish psychopath, who will take evil advantage of these numerous opportunities, until proven otherwise. I blamed this initial impulse on my societal upbringing. "Do not trust strangers, they will *kill* you," they said. "Do not open yourself up and make yourself vulnerable to anyone you do not know by *any* degree of separation," they said. "They will take *advantage* of you," they said. "The world is a cruel, dark place." Couchsurfing appeared to be saying the opposite. All Surfers were presumed to be genuine, trustworthy, sane people who had no intention of taking their host's services for granted, until proven otherwise. And why fight this radical assumption? Is it not a beautiful thing to put trust in your fellow man?

I think I had just answered the big question from before. Adam's family was motivated by God to do such kind acts. What were Couchsurfers motivated by? It seemed to be a combination of trust, and the innate desire to experience, via meeting and hosting fellow travelers. Holding Devina's keys in my hand had dropped the weight and anxiety from this living situation and I felt like I was walking on air as I left her apartment onto the street.

I walked toward the main drag, starstruck by this new concept of trusting in your fellow man. There was a skip in my step and a song in my head, something to the tune of The Carpenters, or Sonny and Cher. It was nighttime, but the sun was beaming bright, down on my fresh, young face. I loved my fellow man and everything was okay.

On this delightful path, I heard someone speaking to me. "Hey, hey man." I looked over and a gentleman was sitting on a stool between two of the buildings, close to the sidewalk.

I stopped and turned to him. "Hey, how's it going?" I said to my fellow man with a smile.

He grinned. "Pretty good man, hey, you want to buy some heroin?"

The smile could not have been wiped off my face any quicker. He might as well have reached his hand up and smacked it off.

"No thanks," I said as I turned and sped away. *Correction: Do not put your trust in* all *of your fellow men, Evan. Let's start with Couchsurfing and work from there. But thank you, Heroin Man, for that sobering reality check!*

Around the corner I found the small but tasty-looking falafel joint. I got my spicy falafel kebab and took it back to Devina's house. The skip in my step was lost and I strode forcefully back, so as not to be confronted again by the heroin store in between. To think in less than twenty-four hours, I was being asked to play video games by a child, and to buy heroin by a junky. *Experience...Experience...*

I went in to Devina's kitchen and set her keys on the table. She was on the phone in her room and without eavesdropping too much, I could tell that she was giving directions. I sat quietly on the tiny, stained table and munched on my falafel.

Devina walked out. "I see you found the kebab place okay. Do you want a drink? The tap water is totally safe."

I nodded. "Please."

She grabbed a (hopefully clean) glass out of the sparsely populated cupboard and filled it up. "Sorry, I would offer beer but I don't keep any in the house."

I made a gesture like that was fine, while my mouth was full of falafel, and I took the water. *I should buy some beer later and remedy that! It could be a great contribution for her hospitality.*

Devina walked over to the kitchen counter where her phone was placed. She looked at it, then picked it up and made a call. "Hi, sorry I missed your call..." I could see that I was not the only person who she did not pick up the phone for. Front desk service at this place left something to be desired. "...Oh, you're out front? Cool, I'll let you in."

Devina walked out to the living room and opened the door. I arched over in my seat and saw two tall, bearded gentlemen with helmets on, walking their bikes through the door. Stuffed saddles hung off the backs of their bikes. I heard short introductions and instruction on where to put the bags and bikes down. Then they walked into the kitchen as my face was stuffed inside a falafel bite. "...and this is the other Couchsurfer, Evan. He's also from the states. Massachusetts, right?"

I shook my head, took a big awkward gulp, and stood up. "You are correct. Hello Couchsurfers."

We shook hands. "Hey Evan, I'm Doug, this is Ian."

"Hello," said the other bearded fellow, and I shook his hand too. They looked like two weary travelers who had worked and sweat many-a-mile to be here. They were relieved and relaxed to be at their destination, and excited to meet the people who would be occupying the same space as them for the next couple of days. So was I.

We naturally set off on a traveling conversation. They were from San Francisco and had taken a coastal bike trip up here. After a few days spent in Vancouver, they would be off to Vancouver Island.

"Goddamn, I can't be more jealous!" I said. "I would kill to do what you guys are doing."

Doug nodded. "Yeah, I'd be lying if I said that we weren't having an amazing time."

"Why Vancouver Island?" I asked.

They both shrugged. "Just because."

I smiled in agreement. *What a fantastic fucking answer!* It was hard not to like people off the bat, when I knew that they were experiencing something that I had dreamt about doing, especially because they were doing it for no other reason than to do it.

I followed by giving them some details on my trip.

"Oh man!" said Ian excitedly. "I've always wanted to do a cross country trip!"

"Same, said Doug. That sounds awesome."

The three of us were off to a fantastic start of a relationship. Both parties had equal feelings of jealousy and admiration for the other. We were like a group of fanatics at a trade show, sharing our common love of our hobby. I could imagine this same situation in a different context. "Whoa! Is that a 450-CC engine with duel-combustion capabilities? Goddamn, I can't be more jealous!" "Yeah I got a good deal too. But I've been searching high and low for those chrome-alloy-muffler-spoiler-spark plug-wheels you got on that puppy." "Yeah, you wouldn't believe how I found them." "Oooh, do tell!"

"Sounds like you all have some good stories to swap," interjected Devina. "Shall we take it to a bar?"

We looked at each other and nodded in agreement. We had taken different paths, through trials and tribulations, up hill and down dale to be here: It was time to celebrate.

Our fearless leader led the three of us out to the main drag and we got on the next bus heading back downtown. The conversations on the bus were similar to the ones on the previous bus ride, except now there were four travelers swapping stories. Ian and Doug told us about biking through the Oregon coast. I made sure to tune in to every detail about what my *original* route would have been like. "...and a lot of funny looking seals on the beaches," said Ian. "They laid there and picked up their heads every so often to stare at you." Envy was added to my list of feelings toward these guys. *You bastards got to see my seals!*

We got off the bus somewhere downtown and were led down an old cobblestone street. After a couple blocks, we approached a neon sign that said, "Hostel" on the front. How appropriate it was to have found the place where I would have most likely stayed, had I not been diverted in another direction. A group of travel-weary Twenty Something's stood out front, laughing and yelling in languages that differed from my own. We walked past them and at the end of the block we rounded the corner. In front of us was the door to a large, open-spaced bar. The inside sounded like the front of the hostel, but amplified tenfold. This was where our leader stopped.

We walked past the big, pleasantly grinning, Canadian bouncer, who gave a familiar nod to Devina. The room we walked into looked like someone had taken a huge dancehall and put in a bar, along with long wooden tables, then defiled the once plain, dignified walls with neon beer signs. American eighties rock was blaring and most of the patrons were standing and cheering. The packed crowd directed their attention to the center of the room, where up on a table, a man was standing with a microphone. Next to him was a young, attractive, clearly inebriated lass. "C'mon! C'mon!" said the MC. "We need at least two more ladies up here before we can start!" Through the crowd I could see a girl being pulled by her hand toward the center table. She half resisted and half complied as she drunkenly laughed and staggered.

"This is called the Cambie," said Devina. Her voice switched the three of us out of our mesmerized trance and we turned our attention away from the center of the room. "It's situated right below the Vancouver hostel, so the clientele stays new and rowdy, as I'm sure you've noticed."

I felt like this was another good opportunity to show my gratitude. "Hey Devina," I said, "what are you drinking? This one's on me."

Devina shook her head. "Thanks, but I don't drink." I looked at her like she had two heads. "What would *you* like?" she said to me. "I know the bartender." *What kind of person knows the bartender, but doesn't drink?* Devina was an enigma.

We pushed our way to the side of the bar and Devina waved down one of the specific bartenders. When she caught the attention of the intended gent, he immediately acknowledged her and walked down the bar toward us. He sped past the multitude of eager patrons piled on the other side of the bar who were competing for his attention, and gave Devina a high-five. "Hey sweety, how you been?"

"Hey Gus."

Gus nodded toward us. "Fresh batch of Couchsurfers, eh?"

Devina nodded. "Three Granville Islands, please."

"And the Devina special?" he asked.

She nodded again.

"Sure thing sweety." Gus turned and in the blink of an eye, came back with three beers, an empty pint glass, and a pitcher of water.

We all reached for our wallets and Devina shook her head. "The first one's on the house." The three of us looked at each other. "If you want more, just flag down Gus. He'll give you a discount. Tip him well, that's all I ask." We nodded in obedient shock. Our leader was also our VIP drink hook up. I was still mulling over the thought of why I deserved any of this.

We found a table by a wall where we all fit. We also had an excellent view of the performance, which was about to start. They had found three volunteers who were standing on the table, trading shy giggles. The MC had a pitcher of water in his hand. "Ladies and gentlemen, please give a round of applause to our three beautiful contestants!" Everyone cheered. "This is," he pointed, "Shauna, Jess, and—what? Angel! Give it up everyone!" More cheers. "Music please!" yelled the MC.

The music faded and was traded with disgustingly echoed sound waves of arena rock, from the start of a Motley Crüe song. Each girl began to gyrate as he poured the pitcher over their chests. As this happened, another girl jumped on the table and stole the limelight by doing a very outgoing dance, which involved lifting up her skirt and showing us her skimpy undergarments. Nobody in the audience seemed to care that she was breaking the rules by interrupting this official contest.

"Look at that, ladies and gents! We got ourselves a wildcard!" shouted the MC, to which the crowd chanted, "Wi-ld Card! Wi-ld Card!" Ms.

Wildcard was encouraged to dance raunchier, which prompted Angel to lean over and stick her tongue in her mouth. The crowd *hated* this. Rules were getting broken left and right in this once orderly contest. This situation did not seem right. I was put in the middle of some American eighties movie.

I looked over at Devina who held an unaffected expression. I was sure that she came here so often that she had seen more than her share of debaucherous events. She pleasantly sipped her water from a pint glass: neither shaken nor stirred, straight, no chaser. She looked content, although I couldn't understand why. She did not drink, did not like soaked breasts, and did not fit in with this rowdy crowd.

I leaned over. "Do you always order a pitcher of water when you come here?"

She nodded. "I quit drinking a few years back. It saves me a ton of money."

"I don't doubt that!" said Ian.

"Do you enjoy coming here?" asked Doug.

She nodded without hesitation. "I like sitting back and observing. And since it's connected to the hostel, you always get a fun crowd—usually internationals." She took another sip of her drink. "I've met a lot of good people here."

We all nodded. Those were legitimate, sober words.

"Plus," she added, "most of my surfers seem to have a good time."

None of us were going to argue with that. But as entertaining as it was, my mind couldn't break away from the idea of biking up the coast. I turned to Ian. "How long did it take you guys to bike up here?"

"We've been on the road for two weeks now, averaging about seventy miles a day and spending a few days in certain places."

"And you've only gone along the coast?" I asked.

"Yeah, all on the coast."

"How long are you going to spend on Vancouver Island?" asked Devina.

"We'll spend a week biking around the entire island, before we head back down."

"It's hard for me to imagine doing all of this on a bike," I said. "To be honest, the thought of it feels overwhelming."

"It's the only worthwhile way to go if you ask me," said Doug confidently. Ian nodded in agreement.

"Why do you say that?" I asked.

"There are a million more things to see when you're traveling at that speed. It's mostly the simple stuff that you would pass by in a vehicle, like a big, beautiful tree, or a whale." Doug turned to Ian. "Remember those whales in Washington?"

Ian smiled. "Of course."

"Granted a car is better then say, a plane," continued Doug. "And walking has its benefits over biking, but that's an even larger undertaking."

"People do it though," said Ian. "The Pacific Crest Trail is good for that."

My ears pricked up like a fox. "The what?"

"It's a hiking trail that runs from Mexico up to Canada, hitting just about every single ecozone in North America along the way."

"That sounds amazing!" I said. "Where is it? On the coast?"

"No, it's far inland," explained Ian. "It goes along the Sierras mostly."

"It's the West Coast version of the Appalachian Trail," said Doug.

"Ooooh," I said. Now they were speaking my language. "I need to look into that."

"Yeah, it's awesome. I haven't done the whole thing but I've section hiked some of it, like in Tahoe," said Doug.

"What do you mean by 'section hiked?'" I asked.

"It means you only hike a part of it. Some people don't have three months to spend hiking the entire thing, so they'll section hike a part for a few days at a time."

"And you section hiked Lake Tahoe?"

"Yeah, the trail runs along the western side of the lake. I don't know about the rest of the Pacific Crest Trail, but I would be surprised if Tahoe wasn't one of the best parts."

This comment triggered a yearning and regret, like we should have gone to Lake Tahoe when we had a chance. I had to remind myself that Yosemite wasn't the worst substitute—but it still hurt.

This empty, helpless pain I was getting, was the feeling of addiction. Traveling is a drug. Just because I was getting some, I knew I did not get it all and I was insatiably fiending for more. I was a "crack-traveler." *I should go back to that heroin guy and ask him if he has any plane tickets.*

"If you can find a bike in the next couple days," said Doug, "you can come to Vancouver Island with us."

"Whoa," I said, "that's intense! I'm not sure if I'm prepared for that."

Ian raised his glass. "If you can find a way, the offer's on the table."

We cheers'd and I thanked them. I stored the option of biking around an island with two awesome dudes, in the front section of my mind.

"I have an extra bike," spoke up Devina.

We all shot piercing looks in her direction. "What?!?"

She held up her hand and laughed. "Wait, don't get too excited yet. That bike isn't made to tour long distances. It's more of a town bike." Then she turned to me. "But if you're interested Evan, you're welcome to borrow it tomorrow for Critical Mass."

I knew I heard her right. "That sounds so familiar," I said, "but I don't remember what it is."

"It's a biking event through a city, where the bikers shut off the streets. It happens once a month," she said.

It all came back to me and I clapped my hands together. "That's right! My cousin in San Francisco told me about it! But I thought it happened down there."

"It was started in San Francisco," said Ian, "but it's spread to a lot more cities."

"That answers my question, Devina," said Doug. "I had meant to double check with you if it was happening tomorrow."

"Yeah, it's definitely happening," answered our event organizer. "If the weather holds up, there should be a good turn out. I thought I'd already mentioned it to you, Evan."

"I heard you briefly mention it on the bus, but I forgot what it was."

"Like I said, you're welcome to borrow my extra bike and come."

"I—I—uh—" I was at a loss for words.

"Okay," said Devina, "I'll take that as a yes."

I automatically reverted back to my bad habit of playing the polite card. "Really, you don't need to do that."

Devina quickly dismissed me. "Don't sweat it. It'll be a cool way to check out the city."

These new ideas got me excited enough to buy everyone a shot. Devina humored me and took a shot of water. We drank and laughed for a while longer, absorbed in each other's company, as if we had all been old friends. And if we wanted to take a quick break from conversation, we could simply look up and watch the novelty of jiggling, wet, mammalian protuberances. At first glance, this place gave off the impression of a bar somewhere in a crazy college town in the American Midwest. The ironic part was that I had never experienced something like this in America.

The three Couchsurfers stumbled home, led by our humble host/fearless leader/sober tour guide. Ian and Doug stayed in the living room, and I didn't care as much as before about the sleeping arrangements in my current state. However I did take a sober precaution and laid out my sleeping bag over the sheets and used my sweatshirt as a pillow. I slept like a rock that drank five beers and three shots.

DAY 22

I woke with a groggy pain. I picked my heavy head up and a mild spinning motion tried to turn me in awkward directions, but that feeling was brief with little suffering. This was a good sign of the day, meaning I most likely had a mild hangover that wouldn't last long. I laid back and listened, but nothing stirred outside the empty room. A soothing warmth could be felt on my head, coming from behind me. I pushed my bowling ball of a brain around and tilted it up. The room had a small window above the back wall, with a view of the plain, Canadian brick wall of the adjacent building. However, above the building there was enough room for the radiant rays of the sun to creep in and share some warmth. Devina's cautionary weather prediction was right. It was two nights and a day since I felt the sun, but it felt much longer then that. Cloudy days are long days—although yesterday was long for multiple reasons.

I got up, crept from my room to the bathroom, got dressed, and walked out to the living room. Ian and Doug were gone, along with their bikes, and their bags were neatly packed into a corner. I smelled something in the air... A Couchsurfer was sneaking up behind me. "Ian and Doug are going to meet us at Critical Mass later."

I turned around. "Good morning!" I said to my host.

She smiled. "Good morning! Sleep well?"

"Like a rock."

"I'd be surprised if you didn't."

I laughed nervously. "I hope I wasn't out of control or anything last night." I tried to think back on any less-flattering moments. I thought I behaved myself.

Devina shook her head. "You guys were fine. A splendid group of drunk gents."

I laughed. "That's the best kind!"

Then the golden opportunity popped into my head again. "Hey, are you hungry?" I asked.

"Um, yeah, I could eat something," she said.

"Do you know of a good breakfast spot?"

"Of course. There are lots of great places around here. There's one right around the corner with delicious maple-smoked bacon."

"Awesome!" I clapped my hands together. "Let's go, my treat."

Devina shook her head and looked at me like I did not know when to quit. "No, no, you don't need to offer that." She was trying to use my own evasive, polite tactics against me, but I was impenetrable.

"Devina, I owe you *something*, and if I can't fill your belly with alcohol, I know I can treat you to food."

That got her to crack a smile. "Oooookay."

She took me up the street toward the main drag. I noticed that the heroin store was closed for the morning (they generally have p.m. hours). We turned the corner and walked past the kebab joint, then strolled by other neighborhood staples, like a launder mat, convenience store, pawn shop, ladies boutique, and bar, before we entered a hip, bohemian café. It had big windows in the front, exhibiting colorful art paintings of tigers snuggling with unicorns.

The place was packed with hip Twenty Somethings. They were exactly like the hip cats in Portland, except everyone carried around a hockey stick (just kidding, they weren't hip). I let my culinary guide order for me. She got me a swiss, artichoke, and tomato omelet with maple-smoked bacon on the side. Everything was delicious and the bacon's greasy texture helped with my hangover.

For all of the novice drinkers out there, a greasy morning meal will soak up that lingering alcohol, making you feel right as rain. Remember Pat's Hubba Hubba (the gateway to the Northeast)? The delicious grease from their chili is like an injection of an anti-hangover serum, straight to the heart. Disclaimer (read in a sped-up voice): Pat's Hubba Hubba grease serum excludes all liability toward the clogging of arteries. Do not take Pat's Hubba Hubba grease serum if you have high cholesterol or high blood pressure. Flatulence and high contents of diarrhea are common with Pat's Hubba Hubba grease serum. If you experience diarrhea lasting longer than seventy-two hours, please consult your physician, or just go back to Pat's Hubba Hubba. It will make the problem worse, but it will taste really really good.

My meal was no Pat's Hubba Hubba, but needless to say it was deliciously proficient and even though Devina stayed persistent with resisting my offer to pay, I was persistently obstinate and she desisted. "Thanks for the breakfast," Devina said shyly.

"My pleasure, it's the least I can do." *I would much rather put my money toward this, then a crappy hotel room.*

Devina looked at her watch. "We should go. Are you still interested in biking?"

I gave a confident nod. "Absolutely."

"Okay. We're going to meet my friend Rosa downtown and probably bike around Stanley Park before heading to the start of Critical Mass."

Stanley Park... I thought that was the park that the couple on the ferry recommended to me. This meant that everything was right on track. Too many elements were coming full circle, like I was spinning in kaleidoscopes of plots that were connecting on every step I took forward.

We got back to her house and when we walked in, Devina turned behind the door and sure enough, there were two bikes sitting side by side. They were classic town bikes, with fixed gears, minimum tread, and cute little baskets fastened to the front for your flowers and baguettes. I tried hard to imagine taking one of them around Vancouver Island for a week, but the thought was futile.

I switched from my Birks to my shoes, grabbed my sunglasses, put my camera in my front pocket, and we were off. I followed behind my personal outdoor excursion specialist, who led me down the main street toward downtown. The sky remained a singular shade of turquoise from horizon to horizon with not one cloud ruining its canvas. It must have been roughly seventy-eight degrees (Fahrenheit that is—twenty-five degrees Celcius for all you curious Canucks). Ahead of us, the downtown buildings beamed bright. They absorbed the turquoise color from the sky, giving Emerald City a run for its money.

To my right was a harbor, appropriately named, the Vancouver Harbor. Across the bay looking north, was a smaller city appropriately named, North Vancouver. Behind the city loomed a tall mountain with cut out trails, and lights lining the sides. Some lingering patches of snow could be seen at the tippy top. This was Grouse Mountain: the local ski spot. I imagined myself up on that trail, skiing down while observing the entirety of Vancouver below. For a second I forgot about the perfection of our current weather and yearned for frigid temperatures and a white substance covering the ground for me to lay my skis on. But that feeling faded fast, as I felt the warm air wisp through my hair while gliding along on my two-wheel vehicle.

Devina pedaled fast and focused, never looking back once. I almost lost her at a stop light, when she blew through a yellow light that I barely skinned my way through, which a few cars had something to say about. Before long we were downtown and I was weaving around cars and people, around corners, through alleyways, up, down, and around. Devina never stopped, never looked back.

We made a succession of right and left turns which I noticed was bringing us closer to the water. Soon we were cruising along the bay, where I could see that the color of the water matched the sky and buildings, completing the cerulean perfecta trifecta. We passed marinas with enormous yachts and sailboats, where people were taking advantage of this weather. They were fixing sails, or scrubbing decks, or sitting and enjoying a wine spritzer—or whatever-the-fuck yachters drink. Everyone we passed was sporting a smile, which was heightened from yesterday's national grey-weather grin.

Up ahead the marina ended and a peninsula began. This piece of land was the only place around which wasn't brilliantly blue. Instead it was a gloriously green park with dense trees and a field of grass by the water. I could spot frolicking dogs and their human counterparts. There were multitudes of other two-wheel vehicles, as well as eight-wheel vehicle's (those are roller blades) that were traveling along a path which ran next to the water.

As we got closer, I was hardly paying as much attention to the road ahead, as I was to this gorgeous park, when Devina stopped. "Whoa! Evan! Stop!"

Screeetch! "Oops, sorry." I looked at my immediate surroundings. We were close to the park and the water was next to us. Between us and the water was a bench, where a fair, darker skinned girl with jet black hair, sat giving Devina a familiar, friendly smile. She was fitted with her own town bike that rested next to the bench.

"Ola Hermana!" said Devina.

"Ola!" said the girl, and she got up and they hugged.

Then a few more Spanish phrases were exchanged which I couldn't repeat, although I thought that I caught "Couchsurfer" in the middle. "Evan, this is my friend, Rosa."

"Hello!" Rosa extended her hand, and I shook it.

"Hello Rosa."

She spoke slowly in a thick Spanish accent. "Nice-to-meet-you." Then she turned back to Devina and asked a Spanish question—*what do you mean a "Spanish question" Evan? Do you mean something like: how many tapas can a matador eat?* –I meant, a question *in* Spanish.

"Si!" replied Devina and she turned to me. "Evan, we're about to bike into Stanley Park. We have just enough time to do the seaside route, which will be a few kilometers. Then we'll make our way to Critical Mass. Sound good?"

I knew nothing about Stanley Park. I had no idea how far a "kilometer" was. I did not speak Spanish. "Sounds great!" I said.

"Okay, vamanos!"

Devina led, with Rosa behind, and I took up the rear. We followed a well-maintained bike path that steered us in a direction which was perpendicular to the direction we had gone from Devina's house, meaning we were biking straight out into the bay. The land veered right for a few football field lengths (or a half-dozen hockey rinks), then curved to the left around an unforeseen bend. Before we rounded the bend, Devina stopped, turned around, and pointed behind us. I turned around and there was a magnificent view of Vancouver, with the harbor in front and the park to the side. I fumbled for my camera and took some shots of the Turquoise City.

We then rounded the corner and a whole new world was introduced to me. I was looking out at a body of water called, the Burrard Inlet, with a succession of island mountains looming in the distance. They were infinately clearer then yesterday's mountains on the ferry. In the not too distant foreground, a great green bridge towered over the bay, connecting North Vancouver to Vancouver. It looked like a smaller, green, Golden Gate Bridge. "That's the Lion's Gate Bridge!" yelled back our tour guide as she pointed up.

We biked along westward which led us under the bridge. The path stayed along the water with a dense hill of greenery on the other side. There was a light breeze from the sea that added a perfectly refreshing chill to compliment the beaming sun. The path rounded another corner and I was hit with a feeling of complete separation from my urban environment. All I could see were trees on a hill, a path, and ocean. The path snaked along and went farther out to the sea, where a lone rock monolith stuck up out of the water, and a lone tree had bravely sprouted itself at the top. I tried to think of metropolitan areas I have been in, where you could be in a place without a single sign of human life: This I had trouble finding in my memory bank.

Once we advanced around this picturesque bend, the city reintroduced itself to our left. Up ahead to our right was a long beach—*A beach! In the center of the city? With sand and all?* It was filled to the brim with people lying out and soaking up the oh-so needed rays. I heard that that glowing orb up there didn't come often around these parts. After all, this was still the Pacific Southwe—I mean Northwest. Across the street from the beach, the high-rises of downtown began again. I had trouble wrapping my mind around the fact that I just looked out at some enormous mountains with glistening snow at the top, and I turned a corner and was twenty paces from dipping my feet into soft, warm sand. Vancouver: the town with mountains and beaches in its city limits. That was something to brag about.

"That concludes Stanley Park," said Devina. "Not bad, eh?"

I shook my head in disbelief. "You guys have beaches here too??"

"There are a few. I can show you some others, but now we should go. We don't want to miss the start of the Mass." Devina turned to Rosa. "Vamanos?"

"Si, vamanos."

We turned left and plunged back into the city streets. Our pace got faster. I huffed and puffed to keep up with Devina and Rosa, who were weaving in and out of lanes and dodging people, strollers, and vendors. As we rode, I noticed a group of riders following behind me. I looked back and I was staring at a bear on a bike. I had to give a double take, and narrowly avoid a stroller, before I realized that I wasn't seeing things: A bear was riding a bike behind me. Its head looked forward with no expression, but it seemed to notice me admiring and smiling, to which it gave a friendly wave of its paw. I waved back and kept riding.

I nearly missed Devina and Rosa turn a corner. When we did, a throng of people and bikes appeared in front of us, numbering in the thousands. Each person stood around holding a bike, chatting, smiling, and laughing. The bear rolled past me and disappeared into the crowd where it fit right in with all the other amazing costumes that people had adorned for this joyous occasion.

We were congregated in front of a large, Roman-style building. Banners on poles advertised what appeared to be science exhibits, which appeared to be on display inside the building, which appeared to be a museum. Great stone steps led up to the entrance. In front of the steps was a big courtyard/terrace with a fountain in the middle. People were everywhere. In the fountain, on the stairs, climbing up a statue next to the stairs—like an infestation of funky-clad insects.

Doug and Ian seemed to have spotted us, whom I noticed were making their way through the crowd in our direction. I was relieved to see them, like I had found my long lost friends. We swapped joyous summaries of our day so far in Vancouver. "You guys need to check out Stanley Park when you get a chance, it's amazing!..." "...If you want some delicious Chinese food, do yourself a favor and go to that place that Devina recommended to us..." And so on and so forth.

A trio of gentlemen walked over to our group, all sporting variations of Mexican wrestling masks. Devina jumped up and hugged them giddily with an enthusiasm that I had not yet seen from her. "Ola! Ola! Como Estas?"

"Ola Devina," said the wrestlers, "bien, bien." They turned to Rosa. "Ola Hermana!"

"Ola," said Rosa, and they hugged as well.

One took off his mask and turned to me. He was of South American decent with a great-big smile. "Hello, eh, Couchsurfer?"

I nodded. "Yeah! Couchsurfer. I'm Evan." We shook hands.

"I am Carlos. Nice-to-meet-you. Bienvenidos a Vancouver!"

I laughed. *Now* that's *a sentence I would never have expected to hear.*

I met the other two who kept their masks on. They called themselves Juan and Benicio (Ben). We were now a legitimate posse (the wrestling masks made it official). I never thought that being on my own in a new city would lend me so quickly into a posse, but that seemed to be the way the magical Couchsurfing cards were dealt. Need I also mention that any feeling I had of prior nervousness and discomfort with embarking into uncharted territory with no safety net, was relinquished a long time ago.

A bullhorn was heard, coming from the steps leading up to the museum. At first it was hard to tell where inside the mass infestation the sound source was coming from. Then I spotted a man, dressed in a red and white striped shirt and a black cape and mask over his eyes. He looked liked Where's Waldo called up his homie Zoro, and borrowed some accessories. In his hand was the bullhorn, which was held up to his mouth. "Hello Critical Mass!" He was heard loud and clear. Everyone turned and a resounding cheer rumbled through the crowd. The hair stood up on my neck. "Wooohoooo!" I yelled, but I couldn't hear myself. Waldo-Zoro then spoke like he was giving instructions. He said things like: "We will move together!" And, "The people in front will stop at the following intersection!" He spoke one sentence at a time, and after each sentence, he would pause, and the crowd would repeat his sentence. <This act of sentence-to-sentence/speaker-to-crowd repetition was repeated three years and three months later at Wall Street, when the Occupy movement came to be. And believe me, it was the same crowd.> Waldo-Zoro's speech was over when everyone cheered again, this time inside a symphony of bike bells, horns, drums, and any other creative instruments of noise.

We suited up. Carlos put his mask back over his face and mounted his bike. The mass started to lurch forward, and eventually gained enough motion for us to get on our bikes and spread out.

We started in the direction that we had come from, then veered off farther into downtown. When we passed an intersection, I could see that on either side of the cross street, a line of defiant bikers stood blocking the road. Behind them, a line of not-so-defiant cars sat quietly. Our heroes blocking the cars would throw themselves under these "gas-guzzling CO_2 pollutant machines" before letting them disturb our parade of "friends of the Earth." I wondered how long these cars would be sitting for, before this jam would let up. We were closer to the front of the crowd and there were surely a few thousand bikers yet to cross behind us.

This event was deliberately (and obnoxiously) done at rush hour on a Friday, to send a message to the drivers about their auto use. And apparently there was a deeper message about the ability to dress like a bear, or a Mexican wrestler, if the choice was made to ride a bike to work. Cars were for boring people with business suits.

A bike passed me with a small trailer hitched on the back. It had a little tent that would have normally secured one's baby inside. But if there was a baby in there, it wasn't normal. Instead of "goo-goo" and "ga ga", it spoke loud, bumping drum and bass sounds. Through the tent flaps I could see a large boombox. People cheered and bobbed their heads as he passed by.

We turned another corner and headed up a bridge which I believed to be the same bridge that the bus took last night, carrying me for my maiden voyage into the Turquoise City. The bridge went over a small island called, Granville Island (hence the name of the beer we drank). At the top of the bridge, I had a vantage point of multiple things. I could see the city in its entirety, still shining from the bright sun. I could see the Inlet with the island mountains. I could see the northern mountains behind North Vancouver, with the sprinkles of snow at the peaks. And ahead of me, as well as behind, I could see the Mass in all its glory: a beautiful sea of people on bikes in the thousands, all smiling, jamming, and funkifying. Devina said this was a cool way to check out a new city. Cool? I could not think of a more perfect way to do it. I was touring around, getting active, and not spending a cent in the process. Devina was a fantastic tour guide, but she admirably passed the job onto thousands of bikers, whose simple job was to bike, and I follow.

Once over the bridge, we turned right, and headed a little ways up a street, before we turned onto another bridge, which took us back to the downtown side. I looked at the original bridge across the way. It was still filled with bikers, with no end in sight. Once back over, we veered toward the water and biked along the bay, which I presumed was close to where we had been earlier when we exited Stanley Park.

Biking along the beach made me feel like I was in some tropical seaside town. Many of the buildings across the street were tall apartment buildings, each floor equipped with its own wrap-around porch overlooking the bay. I never found these kinds of buildings to be aesthetically attractive. They all looked the same and could be found on the coast of every beach town around the world. But their main function was to give optimum aesthetics for the inhabitant. Your own personal wrap-around view of the Vancouver landscape from a high vantage point could not be beat. Although the most amazing part to me, was still the fact that we were riding along a beach—*a beach!*—in northern North America. I would have expected this setting in Miami—but Vancouver? The idea felt unnatural, but being there felt as natural as anything else, like tropical colored Michigan lakes, and prehistoricly large Californian Sequoias.

I was cruising at a steady pace, nothing strenuous, simply taking in the sights and sounds. Devina passed by on her bike. She smiled and nodded, then looked forward again with a content grin like she was inside some happy dream. All of this was a big dream.

It was at that appropriate moment that a man biked past me. He wore a jacket that was decorated with various pins, all carrying a common theme of activism. In fact he carried this theme throughout his whole demeanor, from his dark, overgrown beard, to his patched together pants that looked like free-trade materials, most likely of the hemp variety. What caught my eye was the largest pin set smack in the middle of his back. In white block letters over a black background it said, "ALARM CLOCKS KILL DREAMS." It hit me like the glass board in a hockey rink. *What a profoundly true statement!*

I rode steadily behind him and read that line over and over, until I was compelled to yell it out. "Alarm clocks kill dreams!"

The man perked up and turned his head. "Alarm clocks kill dreams!" he yelled back. Then he raised a fist in the air like a Black Panther.

I biked up to the side of him. "That's a very true statement. I've never put it in that perspective."

"The truth is undeniable, brother," he replied. "We live in a society that works entirely too much. We could be equally as productive if we all worked half as much as we do. And we can employ twice as many people, which would create more jobs. Then people can work half the time, which gives them more opportunity to dreeeeaaam!"

"Amen!" I yelled.

"Amen!" yelled a few others.

He gave a smile big enough to breach his beard and rode on.

Up ahead it looked like we were heading toward Stanley Park. The Mass veered toward the right, away from the beach and into a thick patch of forest. That euphoric feeling of immediate departure from an urban environment hit me once again, and we climbed up a country road in the evergreen wilderness. The city sounds faded and the silence of the forest growth had trapped us in. This newfound absence of sound was replaced by wooping and hollering from the Mass. "Owwooooo!" I heard, and their voice resonated through the trees. It was darker in all of this growth, but the sun crept in, creating slivers and shades of light on the road and people. Up we climbed and louder we howled.

We turned a bend and were on a straight road with a steady incline. I was able to see an opening to the woods far ahead, but I couldn't make out what we were heading toward. There was a line of stopped cars pointed at the opening, and I watched one biker riding close to them. When he passed a car with their engine on, he would yell to the driver, "Turn off your damn engine!" Playing the devil's advocate, I imagined that the driver's blood had to be boiling from this obnoxious, tree-hugging son-of-a-bitch on a bike, telling him what to do in his car. I could see some driver flinging their door open so this biker would hit it, stopping the bike and sending him flying. Score one for the cars. But none of this happened. The cars were lifeless objects, patiently waiting their turn, while we basked in ours. Maybe it was the easygoing Canadian way: to sit patiently and let it all pass, knowing that they couldn't do anything about it anyway.

Up we climbed and I could start to make out a large structure at the opening of the woods. *Is that a bridge? Yep, definitely a bridge.* When the details emerged, I could see it was green. *Could it be? No. The Lion's Gate?*

We made it out of the woods and sure enough we were biking up the iconic Lion's Gate Bridge—the same I had biked under, merely a few hours prior. And if I thought that I had seen some great views around this city, well they could all get thrown off the bridge, because what lay before me was a spectacle like no other.

The Japanese are famous for their delicately detailed gardens, with a specifically designed method to viewing and enjoying them. Often there are various vantage points where one can walk to, to admire the same setting, but from different angles. There is a firm belief that one will gain an entirely different perspective by looking at the same objects from different vantage points.

This philosophy had held true here. I was seeing the same views as before: west to the mountain islands, north to the snow capped peaks, southeast to the Turquoise City. But everything looked infinitely more spectacular from atop this erected pile of steel. The Burrard Inlet gleamed and glinted from the everlasting sun.

At the top of the bridge, the Mass had stopped and people were stepping off their bikes. A line of cars spanned down the other end and over to the north side. I was part of the first few hundred people to make it to this point, and behind me I could see the thousands more, creeping out of the darkness of the wood. The funky insects were taking over the Lion's Gate, climbing up the wires of the suspensions and railings. We cheered as these select daredevils took this bridge occupation a step further.

I was in plain shock of the situation. It sure was nice of them to close down the Vancouver streets for me, but to close down the bridge?! I couldn't imagine finding myself in such unique opportunities as this very often. All I could do was to revert back to my old road trip saying: Shit just happens.

I thought about this as I stood over the railing looking out at the bay and the city. We were so high up that I felt like I was admiring this landscape from the heavens. Devina came up next to me. I was glad she found me because I had lost track of my Vancouver posse during the ride. We enjoyed the view together for a few moments before she turned to me. "Not bad, eh?" When I looked at her, she laughed at the smile on my face that stretched from ear to ear. I could see that she was happy because I was happy. If I was in her position, I knew I would have felt as good as I did, knowing that I was able to show my host such a new and unique experience. This must have been the true reason for why she (along with all Couchsurfers I presumed) was motivated to host people. And if it wasn't for instances like this, there must have been some other reason which brought Devina joy, because you couldn't host strangers like this, if you didn't enjoy it. I felt that I could easily do the same thing as her (hosting people that is, but maybe not at a hostel-worthy volume).

I realized that I naturally take a lot of joy out of showing people things that I love. When they are happy, I get vicariously happy as well. Like if I showed a visiting friend my favorite swimming hole back in Massachusetts. Even though I would have gone to swim there many times before, I would be excited to know that my friend's reaction to this special place, was a positive and new experience. Being a Couchsurfing host fulfilled that pleasure of showing something special to someone new. Even though the website never spelled this benefit out, all it took was to experience it to know exactly what was going on. The website was an avenue for gaining experience, as well as giving it to someone else. It was a social network...with a purpose.

The Mass congregated on the top of the bridge, and before long, the entire southern half of the Lion's Gate was full of funky insects. When it appeared that the entire mass had made it onto the bridge, everyone cheered. Cowbells and horns went off, boomboxes blasted—it was a celebration of life, and getting funky, and pissing off drivers. I had my own reason to celebrate: I made it. I crossed the country, took the cars, and buses, and boats, and got to see what was over the ridge. And yes it was as amazing as I had intended it to be. But was I finished? Absolutely not. The crack-traveler is never satisfied. I knew full well that even though I made it over this mountain and basked in its awesomeness and glory, I could still see an even bigger mountain in the distance that needed to be conquered. This metaphor had literal connotations, since it was actually a mountain that I had my sights on. It was called, Whistler, and as I looked toward the north, this dream that I had for so long was only a few peaks past that to becoming a reality. I had to go to Whistler.

Our posse had congregated back together on the bridge, and we moved as one Mexican/American/Canadian/badass unit, back down the hill through Stanley Park. After holding out long enough, the sun decided to start its decent and cast its milder rays horizontally through the trees, painting each tree trunk with a shade of gold. When we made it into the city, the Mass visibly shrank as we continued on, with groups splintering off at different streets.

"Where does Critical Mass end?" I asked Ian as we rode.

"There is no end. It kind of fizzles out as they're riding, until there are no more people to make a Mass."

Eventually our fearless leader took the reins and we veered away and back to her home. When our posse arrived at Devina's, the Mexicans said goodbye to us gringos, and each gave Devina a kiss on each cheek before riding away. When they left, our host turned to her three guests. "The Hermanos are going to come back to my place a little later with drinks, and we're going to have a party. Sound good?" The three of us looked at each other like, what could possibly not sound good about that statement? "Also," added Devina, "I have to double check, but I think that there's a group of French surfers coming in tonight, so it's going to be a packed house." The three of us looked at each other like, what could possibly not sound good about that statement?

We all agreed we were hungry and wanted to keep it cheap and simple, so I took it upon myself to lead the group back to the falafel joint. I also knew that I had to take care of some logistical business before the night started, so dinner had to be quick.

When we got back, I nervously turned to Devina. I needed to use her computer, but I didn't know how to ask her about invading her sacred, untarnished bedroom. I was the dirty Couchsurfer who belonged in the confines of the hostel. "H—Hey, Devina?"

"What's up?"

"Um, so, I wanted to find out if I got some other Couchsurfing requests for tomorrow night. Um, do you think, um—"

"Yeah, you can use my computer. Just hold on a sec." Devina went into her room and closed the door for a minute before coming back out. "Okay, it's all yours."

"Thank you, thank you!" I said. I wasn't sure if I was breaching some sort of Couchsurfing privacy code. Devina didn't seem to mind, but I was also never sure what was going on in that head of hers.

I signed on and found a few new messages. There was a decline from Vancouver: "Sorry Evan, got your request late. Can't host you." *Thanks.* A maybe from Vancouver Island: "I might be able to host in a couple days. Get back to me." *Thanks for nothing.* I scrolled past a few more declines or maybes but there was nothing accepted. *Is there a maybe from Whistler?* I couldn't tell from the mess of messages. I clicked to filter them and studied the list of maybes: Vancouver, Vancouver Island, Vancouver Island, Vancouver, Whistler, Vancouver—*wait! A Whistler! There's a Whistler!* I clicked on a message from a guy named Patrice Kirouac:

> Hey Evan! Sounds like a great trip! I would be happy to host you, although I am going up north to hike for a few days, but I will be coming back on Saturday. So if you are coming then, I should be able to host you. Here is my number. You can give me a call when you arrive.
>
> Cheers!
> Patrice

I fumbled with the mouse to give an immediate reply, as if these next few seconds would make all the difference:

> Hey Patrice! I am coming up Saturday, probably late afternoon, so that could work out! I will be sure to give you a call when I arrive. Have a fun hiking trip!
>
> Evan

This sounded frightfully promising, although it was not a one hundred percent confirmation. But it was enough—in my eyes—to warrant making the trip up there. The decision was made, I was going to Whistler. *What if he ends up not being available? Then what are you going to do?... I don't care. I'm going to Whistler... What about impulsive decis—... Shut up.*

I poked around Patrice's profile. With all the profiles I had been reading in the past few days, I couldn't clearly remember what Patrice's was like. His picture was a vague, far off image of him on some beach. I clicked on his pictures and he had one other of him at a dinner table with an African man, smiling and holding up drinks. I clicked back to his profile. He was thirty years old, born in Quebec City, Quebec—*A French Canadian. How exotic.* An interesting name too: Kirouac, spelled slightly different than the late Jack. I made a mental note to inquire about this. His descriptions were travel oriented, with phrases like: "I love to see as much as I can in the great world we live in." Or, "I want to always meet new people and hear their stories." And the couch situation? "I live in Whistler Village, very close to the base of Whistler Blackcomb ski resort. I live with another man who is still unsure of Couchsurfing, but he is really nice and if you are nice, then it will be fine I am sure! We have a couch in the living room, very comfortable..."

As I was reading up on my next potential host, Devina interrupted. I had forgotten that she was generous enough to let me use her computer in her room, and I shouldn't be taking any more advantage of her hospitality. I mean, all she did was spend all her time today and last night touring me around, lending me a bike, a bed, and now her computer to use. "Are you almost done? I have to get ready before people come over."

"Yeah! I'm so sorry, I didn't realize how long I had been. I think I'm going to Whistler tomorrow."

"Cool! Whistler's great! You'll love it. So you're almost done with the computer?" There was a dry tone to her voice.

"Yeah, I'm done. Thank you, thank you."

She gave me a cordial smile and waited for me to leave the room before she went in and closed the door.

Devina was an interesting individual. She had the ability to be cordial, helpful, and hospitable, without showing any sign of emotional attachment. She seemed to skillfully avoid any emotional attachment, or reject any attempts at partaking in anything that would lead to such things. It took a lot of convincing for me to treat her to breakfast that morning, and I could see some discomfort and reluctance as I was paying. Or like the way she told me how I would like Whistler. By the tone of her voice, I knew that she could care less whether or not I liked it. If I told her that I was changing my plans and leaving this very instant, I would know exactly what she would say: "Okay, good luck!"

I noticed that the way she acted toward her Mexican friends was different. Her tone of voice would change, showing love and care. Then it would switch toward me and the San Francisco Boys, to something much less personal. I'm not implying that it was a bad thing. In fact it was quite normal for her to express more emotion toward people that she did not meet twenty-four hours prior. We were not her "Hermanos." However I did find it interesting. Maybe it seemed necessary in this big world of Couchsurfing, where the reality of the situation was that you were still letting a stranger into your home, and it was necessary to maintain an air of caution, keeping a certain part of you closed off. As nervous as I was when I walked into Devina's apartment for the first time, she must have been equally nervous to let this disheveled man with a backpack and a wicker hat into her home.

This tough-yet-friendly front of hers must have been even more necessary if she was telling the truth about her volume of visitors. But if there was no emotion, how could she have been enjoying it? What was it about making her home a revolving door of Surfers, that made it worth it for her? I thought that I had answered this question for myself back when she gave me her keys, then again on the Lion's Gate Bridge, but I was doubting both answers. Or maybe I was over-thinking all of this. I recalled what Devina told me about her self-induced hostel: "I hate empty houses—too much unutilized space." Maybe it was as simple as that. The answer was that this website (culture rather) was not black and white. People probably did not host for the same exact reasons. I wondered what Patrice's motives were. I would find out soon enough (I hoped).

I stepped into the kitchen and finished my Kebab with Ian and Doug. It wasn't long before Devina walked out of her room, freshly dressed and on the phone. "Hello? Claude? This is Devina, sorry I missed your call." The three of us gave each other a familiar smile. "You're out front? Cool, I'll let you in." It was déjà vu all over again, as we sat at the little kitchen table, quietly munching on our kebabs. Devina opened the front door and we creeped our heads around the corner to watch seven people with big backpacking packs pile into the living room. There were four girls and three guys. We remained seated and listened to the delightful sounds of French accents.

"...And these are some other Couchsurfers," Devina said as she walked them into the kitchen. "This is Ian, Evan, and Doug. They're from the US." Everyone introduced themselves, but there were too many French sounding names to remember them all. They were young, friendly looking, eager to talk, and more eager to drink when Devina told them of the night's festivities. The Hermanos eventually arrived with a box full of beer and liquor and the night had begun.

The French addition was welcomed into the Vancouver posse with open arms. The drinks flowed as freely as the conversations, and Devina did not hesitate to periodically refill her glass of water. I was able to walk around the party and get some good face time with almost everyone, since we were all so interested in learning about each other's stories and travels. There was never an awkward moment between all of these people who had just met. We were immediate friends, like we were part of some club that allowed anyone from anywhere in the world to connect and feel comfortable with one another. Not to mention that there are so many new things to talk about and learn from someone from another country.

"Where are you from Evan?" asked Carlos.

"Massachusetts."

"Mass-a-tus?" Carlos struggled.

"Near New York—the other side of America." I pointed in a random direction across the room.

"Ahh yes, New York!" he said. Now York is much more internationally known than Massachusetts, not to mention not nearly as much of a mouthful. "I want to go to New York! I hear is nice!" he said.

"Oui-oui, New York is very beautiful," said Francois. "It is similar to Parrii, but not as cool. Haha!" We all laughed, to which Francois added, "Just kissing!"

Carlos and I looked at Francois. "What did you say? Kissing?"

"Oui, kissing, you know, like a joke."

"Ooh!" I said. "Kidding!"

"Yes, kissing!" We all laughed again.

Ben approached me at a later, more inebriated part of the night. "Evan, you say you're from Massatuset, si?"

"Massachusetts. Yes I am," I replied.

"Oh." Ben nodded and looked at me pensively like he was figuring out some deeper meaning in the word Massachusetts."

"Does that make you a junkie?"

I nearly spit up my rum and coke and my eyes grew wide. "What?!"

"You know," said Ben, "a junkie."

Jesus Christ, I know I'm drunk, and I smoke pot here and there, but a junkie?! Who does this guy think he is, calling me a junkie? I wasn't sure if I was more offended than I was confused. "Ben, what do you mean? I don't think you're saying the right thing. Do you know what that means?"

"Si-si," Ben insisted, "like an American. A junkie American." Ben pointed to himself. "We are American too. But you are junkies."

"Ben, now I'm really confused. You're saying that you are American. But you're Mexican. And you're saying that I'm a junkie. But I'm not a drug addict!"

Ben's eyes grew wide. "No! No drugs!" Ben screwed up his face and turned. "Devina! Ven aqui!"

Devina stumbled over with her cup of water. Ben rattled off quick Spanish speech and our translator listened intently. "Okay. Si, entiendo." Devina turned to me. "Ben is trying to say that we are all American, because we are all from America. Like everyone from North and South America can be classified as American."

I nodded. "Okay. That makes sense. But because I'm Amer—I mean from the US, he's calling me something specific, but I think he's mistaken."

Devina turned to Ben and more Spanish ensued. Ben finished his explanation with, "Junkie." Devina looked at him like he was crazy.

Thank God, I was beginning to think that I *was the crazy one.*

"Junkie??" Devina confirmed.

"Si," said Ben.

"I don't know Devina," I said, "last time I checked I wasn't a drug addict."

Devina furrowed her brow in thought. "Junkie? Oh, wait. Oh!" Then she burst out in laughter. "Yankee?" she asked.

"Si! Si!" said Ben. "Junkie!"

I gave an incredulous look. "You meant Yankee?!"

Ben nodded.

"Ooooh my God!" I laughed and gave Ben a big drunk hug. "Yes Ben, I am a Yankee—*not* to be confused with junkie!"

"Latin Americans often say their y's like j's," explained Devina. We all laughed and had a big trans-American hug. I was glad we had gotten that ironed out before I was banished to the street to hang out at the heroin store with my own kind.

The night was filled with French and Spanish pronunciation hiccups. It got worse as the night went on, until eventually we were too drunk to communicate, and resorted to sitting back and watching the Mexicans and French trade off their respective country's soccer victory songs. I was lucky enough to be able to keep my private room, which permitted me to retire from the festivities at my own convenience. I passed out like a true junkie.

DAY 23

I wokc up in an eerily similar state as the day before: same bed, on my sleeping bag, sweatshirt as a pillow, light hitting me through the window, light throb in the head. I was dizzy again as I got up and swirled my way to the bathroom. I took a shower, got dressed, and walked out to the living room to find it empty, with not a trace of remanence from the festivities of the night before. *Did I actually party with a bunch of French, Mexicans, Canadians, and San Franciscans last night?... Maybe it never happened.*

I got the same sense of a Couchsurfer sneaking up behind me. "Ian and Doug left early this morning. The French group left early as well, to do some sightseeing." Devina had this impeccable ability to come in at the exact right time and answer my inner thoughts.

"Ian and Doug must be off to Vancouver Island," I said.

"Yeah," said Devina in her detached abrupt way, and changed the subject. "So my friend Loki should be coming over any minute. We were talking about going to the beach. You're welcome to come, unless you have other plans."

"I'd love to!" I said. "The only thing is, I was going to try to catch a bus up to Whistler in the late afternoon. Will there be enough time to go to the beach?"

Devina nodded. "Yeah, you'll be fine."

I smiled. My event planner once again did her job. I knew I was paying her for something.

So you found a Couchsurfer up in Whistler to stay with?" she asked.

I gave a nervous shrug. "Heh, kind of. It's still a maybe. But I'll figure something out."

"If you don't hear from him or her, I got a tent you could borrow as a last resort. You would just need to come back here to drop it off on your way back—obviously."

I looked at her and shook my head in mock disappointment. "Devina, if you keep doing me all of these favors, I'm going to be in debt to you for the rest of my life! I'll have to become your indentured servant, or something."

"Ha! That would be cool." Devina looked at me. "Evan, listen. You're a Couchsurfer now. This is how we do things. If you stole my tent, it's not a huge loss to me, it's just a tent. It would do more damage to you, because it would be on your conscience."

I nodded. "This is true."

"Plus I'd get your ass kicked off the website."

"Also true—and fair." I liked being told that I was a Couchsurfer. I felt like I had graduated and was being inaugurated into the club. All I had to do was follow the club's code of ethics, which stated that I generally should not be a selfish piece of shit. *I think I could do that.*

"Yo D!" We looked over and a man was standing at Devina's window. He leaned in and smiled.

"Hey Loki," said Devina, "come to the front, I'll let you in."

"That's cool, I got this." Loki was a tall, lanky fellow, and was able to reach his legs over the window frame without much trouble. He looked to be in his late twenties, had African skin, and dressed like a funky hipster, with ankle pants, a cutoff sleeveless shirt, and a small cap.

"Loki, this is Evan, a Couchsurfer."

He swung himself into the living room and extended his hand along with a jovial smile. "Hey, Couchsurfer! How're the waves?"

"Damn good so far. No complaints," I said as I shook his hand. He had a firm, American grip.

"Evan is an American as well," said Devina.

"Oh yeah?" said Loki. "Where from?"

"Massachusetts."

"Cool man, I'm from Detroit."

"Okay, I've never been there but I did pass through Michigan on my way out here."

Loki shook his head. "I haven't been back there in a while. Was it as shitty as I remember it?"

"Um, I don't think so. It was pretty nice actually. I was up in Petoskey."

"Oh, I'm sure that's much nicer than the south. The more north you get, the nicer."

"Yeah? You think so?" I asked.

"Of course! That's why I'm in Canada!" Loki burst out laughing.

"Let's get out of here guys." Devina was back in leader mode. "I say we pick up some sandwiches and bring them with us."

"You're the boss, D." Loki turned to me. "You can always rely on D to lead the pack. When you hang out with her, you just switch to autopilot and let her steer the ship."

I chuckled. "I know exactly what you're talking about." Devina picked up a bag. "I got a blanket, waters, cards, towels—anything else?"

"Shit," I said. "I just realized that I don't have a bathing suit."

"Okay," said Devina with a surefire answer, "we can stop by that thrift store on eighth, no problem. It's on the way."

"Cool!" And we were off. On to another day of following people I had just met, to a place I did not know. *Fuck, I love traveling!*

We walked down a few blocks on the main street, heading toward downtown. This was the first time I had walked anywhere in this city for more than a block, and it gave me a better feel for the neighborhood. Devina didn't live in the nicest part of town, but I could tell that it was going through the oh-so inevitable gentrification transformation process. Take that hip café we went to for brunch the day prior for instance, which was sandwiched between a grimy Chinese launder mat and Indian convenience store.

After a couple blocks we turned onto a street which looked to be fully gentrified. Soon we were in a sea of moustached couples, shaved muts, vegan butcher shops, kosher shellfish markets, and "Canadian Apparel" boutiques: The stench of irony was thickly settled. We walked into an "artist" café that reeked of spiced coffee, and ordered some fancy sandwiches with aioli—or something, and Devina stuffed them in her bag.

A few blocks down, we made it to the aforementioned thrift store. I bought some ugly, blue gym shorts that amused me because they were from the Vancouver Jewish Youth Center. Loki couldn't help himself and he bought a neon tank top. Devina didn't get anything. She stayed content in the corner with her pitcher of water.

We walked a few more blocks and waited at a bus stop which would take us to the beach. Loki and I were deep in conversation. I learned quickly that he could be considered an outspoken guy who got easily riled up. "Man, that's why Bush is a motherfucker. And Americans, they just don't get it! All the facts are laid out in front of them and they're still too stupid to see it."

"Not all Americans, remember. Only half," I corrected.

"I don't know man, if it's that many people against it, then why haven't you taken that motherfucker down? He's been in office for eight years for Christ's sake! Me, I *listened* to the rednecks. They told me to either let Bush bend you over and fuck you, or get the hell out. So I got the hell out!"

"Are you going back?" I asked.

"Not if I can help it. I'll go back if my band goes on tour."

"You're in a band?"

"Loki's amazing at keyboard," said Devina.

"I'm in a few bands," answered Loki.

"Cool, what kind of music do you play?" I asked.

"A lot of stuff. I'll tell you what I *don't* play, is shit!" Loki was still worked up.

The bus ride took thirty minutes through scenery that wasn't too eventful. Just a collection of plain, urban neighborhoods, but I simply watched it all go by with a pleasant grin.

We got off at the end of the line at the University of British Columbia campus, which looked like a mess of unattractive, square buildings. The bus had dropped us off in a parking lot, and we walked across it toward a tall perimeter of dense trees. This was once again where civilization abruptly ended. There was no sign of a beach, but I learned at this point to be prepared for any radical change of scenery at the blink of an eye.

We followed some other beach-prepared groups to an opening in the woods, where there was a railing and stairs that led abruptly downward. A few steps down and the city disappeared and I had entered a bona fide rainforest. Tall trees rose straight up from the cliffside, spreading out up above, to an impenetrable ceiling of lush-green leaves. Thick vines hung down to a forest floor that was covered by prehistorically large, emerald ferns. Down and down we went, covering a good twenty stories until the light broke out from the bottom and I could see glimpses of people, sand, and water.

"By the way Evan," began Devina, "did I explain anything about this beach to you?"

"No, you just told me we were going to a beach. I don't think—ohhhh!" My eyes drew wide as I stepped out of the forest.

"I forgot to mention it's a nude beach." I stopped and Devina walked past me and turned and smiled. "Clothing optional, that is."

She was right. *Some* people had clothing, but they were the minority. We walked out and I took off my shoes, feeling the warm sand envelop my feet and creep in between my toes. The water was dark blue and calm, with tiny waves lapping onto shore. The forest cliffs lined the inner edge of the beach as far as I could see, so there was no development in sight—only forest, beach, and ocean to be enjoyed.

Lots of people were swimming and it looked like they were able to walk a ways out without it getting too deep. Women stood far out from the shore, their exposed breasts only getting wet with the occasional splash. I was surprised at the amount of attractive nudists. Sprightly, perky Twenty Somethings played frisbee, lounged on blankets, drank, and played music. It wasn't often that I went to nude beaches, but I knew enough to know that the common misconception was that they, well, looked like *this*. However, most did not. Most nudists are a bunch of old people with bodies that look as retired as their owners.

Loki ran past me jumping and hollering. All I could see was his big, black, bare-naked butt running away. We watched in amusement as he plunged into the surf.

"Ola! Devina!" We looked over and Juan, Carlos, and Ben were sitting on a blanket close by. The Mexicans were fully clothed, nor did Devina make any hint at taking anything off. In fact Devina didn't even have a bathing suit. She would once again be enjoying the festivities from the sideline, with her trusty glass of water. And me, I couldn't bring myself to join the pasty-ass club. I know, I know what you all are thinking: you are so disappointed in me. But I couldn't shake off my American bashfulness. Besides, I had to show off my brand new (used) pair of shorts.

We walked over to the Hermanos. "Ehh! Junkie!" yelled Ben, and we all laughed.

"Good afternoon to you as well, Ben." I sat down and soaked in the rays as Devina spoke Spanish with her Brothers. It was an identical day to the day before: The sun was ruler over the skies and no spec of cloud dared to invade its domain.

Once my body was brought to roasting temperature, I got up and walked to the surf. I crept up to the edge where the flow reached out before the ebb, and I had the common apprehension, which everyone gets when stepping up to the surf (except for Loki). I wanted to go in so badly but my body was dry and at peace. I looked out to see if I could spot Loki for encouragement, but he was nowhere in my line of sight. There were too many other naked Twenty Somethings splashing around, like beautiful babies in a bath. I let the next wave hit my ankles and braced myself for a freezing shock...but no shock came, only a slight chill: very habitable. This encouraged me and I walked my way in, until I was up to my waist. The water was so calm and refreshing that I thought I was in a spa. I couldn't understand how the water could be so warm. Hundreds of miles south in California, I could barely stick my feet in and would not dare to submerge myself without a wet suit. Water was supposed to get colder as you went north. There must have been some kind of logical, scientific explanation for this (which will once again not be covered in this book). Soon I was submerged, splashing and dunking my head in an explosive fit of giddiness that could only be found in a human under the age of nine. I might have looked crazy because I was doing this by myself, while everyone else had friends to splash around with. But I could care less. I was an expert at amusing myself.

I got my fill and ran back to the blanket, laughing and sopping wet. Devina and the Hermanos were playing a card game, eating aioli sandwiches, and drinking beer or water. They handed me a sandwich and a beer and I reclined on a log that was conveniently situated next to our blanket. "Where's Loki?" I asked. "Did he ever come back to the blanket?"

Devina shook her head. "I haven't seen him since I saw his rear end run into the ocean."

I shrugged and leaned back, then closed my eyes and let the sun hit my face and dry off my body. I was so comfortable that I couldn't imagine moving ever again.

"Do you want to play cards Evan?" I heard Devina's voice from some far off place.

I slowly moved my head left to right. "You should take a swim Devina." I said. The water's amazing.

"Naa, I'm good. Maybe I'll stick my feet in. But it looks like it hit the spot for you."

I calmly nodded.

I would call Devina an organizer and an observer. She had this perpetual desire to bring people together and lead them to fun. Then she took amusement out of watching people react to the world that she created. She did not necessarily have to participate in this world; She was content with simply being there and sipping her water. She did not have to go into the ocean; She could watch the pleasure that Loki or I took out of it. She did not have to drink; She could quietly stand and listen to Juan and I laugh and argue about who are more beautiful, Mexican or American women. And this seemed to be a never-ending, ever evolving adventure for her, as long as she kept hosting Couchsurfers. It was a big part of her life that helped her to keep enjoying it. I opened my eyes and looked at her. She was watching and laughing at Ben and Juan who were yelling at each other in Spanish and pointing to the cards on the blanket. She looked content. As was I.

Once I was dry, I got up and decided to walk around. Maybe I would run into a butt-naked Loki, up to some silly antics. I took a fresh beer and set off. It was a large beach, a couple hockey rinks long at least. This was no family beach. I didn't see any kids. I did see a lot of drunken Twenty Somethings with their damn drug smoking and loud racket.

I caught Loki's naked body lying out spread eagle on a blanket, in the middle of a group of people. One naked guy had a guitar, playing some folk song which sounded in the vain of Neil Young. Next to him was a beautiful, big-breasted girl wearing nothing but trendy sunglasses, lying flat on her back. Two guys with hipster haircuts (long manicured hair with the sides shaved) sat on either side of her and were playing a card game on her stomach. Some of the group watched a man who sat cross-legged. He had long, disheveled hair, a big belly, and a little penis that drooped to the side. A girl sat cross-legged across from him and the man held one of her hands with her palm up, staring at it pensively.

As I approached, Loki noticed me and whispered something to a girl next to him, then pointed at me. The girl got up and skipped over to me, her smallish breasts firmly bouncing with every skip. "Hello Couchsurfer!" and she gave me a big hug. I held the naked stranger's body to mine. She pulled back and had a bright smile. "Welcome to Vancouver! I'm Katrina."

"Nice to meet you. I'm Evan."

"Yo E!" said Loki. "Glad you found us. Come sit."

I sat down and Katrina passed me a joint. "Welcome to Vancouver!" she said again.

It was as if Vancouver's tourism bureau had a "Twenty Something" department, that recruited beautiful, naked women to welcome visitors and hand out drugs. "Thanks," I said, and I took a big puff of the joint and passed it to Loki. It was incredibly smooth. I felt like I could taste how natural it was, like it was freshly picked from some organic patch somewhere in the mountains close by. I was instantly, beautifully high, like an unobtrusive wind had swooped in and lifted me up. This was my introduction to the world renowned, "BC Bud." It was far less intense then the Cali bud, which hit more like an overbearing tornado.

My body relaxed (even more then it was) and I focused my attention on the long haired pot bellied man. "Check this guy out," said Loki, "he's a fortune teller." I listened in and sure enough he was directing his attention to the girl's palm.

He pointed, "This is your love line. It shows that a rocky relationship will expose you to an unexpected encounter, which will turn into a very long and fruitful relationship." The girl nodded with a stoned grin. "And this is—excuse me..." The fortuneteller paused and took a long hit off the joint. The girl giggled as the fortuneteller swayed side to side and exhaled a cloud of smoke. "I'm sorry madamme, I think I need a fortunetelling break."

"That's okay," she said, and pulled her hand away.

Then the fortuneteller perked up and addressed the group. "But I'm ready to tell you all a story!"

"Yay! A story!" said Katrina. Her firm breasts gave a little jiggle of excitement and she nudged closer. We all followed suit and scrunched in around the fortuneteller. He reached out his hand and the man noodling the guitar passed the instrument over. The fortuneteller took it and started finger picking a delicate tune, which lulled the group into a more relaxed state then we already were.

"This is a fairy tale," began the Fortuneteller. "A tale that came out of the great glacial lakes of British Columbia. Lakes that take weeks to get to and some are almost impossible to find—mostly because the wood nymphs are very protective of these sacred places, and they will put out large efforts to alter your course. You may think this unfair, but the forest relies on the wood nymphs to protect that which is most sacred to these ancient woods..."

The Story of Atuk and the Lady of the Deep*

This particular story takes place in one of the most sacred and well-protected lakes in all the forest.

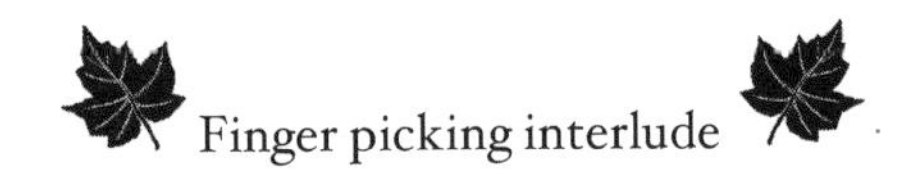

The path to this lake seems simple: Begin at the Grand Pine. Go five thousand five hundred and fifty paces, and turn right. Take the fifth path to the left at the many crossroads. Pass the leaning birch, the elephant rock, and it's right over the ridge. There you will find a glistening lake, bluer than the sky, and sparkling as if the surface hath been covered with sheets of diamonds.

At the bottom of the lake there liveth Her Majesty, the Lady of the Deep, the Queen of the Nymphs, the Mistress of the Mountains. And if you are lucky enough to have found the lake, you are especially lucky to have seen Her Majesty. Only once a day will she arriseth from the deep and bathe her silk body on the Sun Rock. This rock lies in the center of the lake and Her Majesty will only arriseth when the light is absolutely perfectly hitting the rock, which bears the name of Her Majesty up in the Sky. It is exactly

* As told by a nude fortuneteller.

two nymph hours that the sun absolutely perfectly hits the Sun Rock, which is approximately four minutes and thirty-seven seconds in human time. This is the exact amount of time that the Lady of the Deep arriseth from the lake and layeth on the rock, at which point the Lady and Her Majesty up in the Sky, connect and discuss all matters that pertain to the state of earth, and all that liveth and breatheth on, in, under, over, and around it...

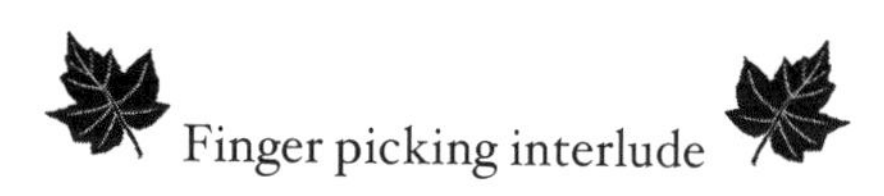

Down in the valley there once was a small town. A peaceful town, one that saw Inuits, Native Canadians, Canadians, and all walks of human life live peacefully for many, many ages. However, it was but a drop in the stream compared to the Forest Dwellers, who saw the forest itself grow from a tiny egg. After all, they were the ones that nurtured this egg, and fed it, and helped it grow to its awesome size that we now know as the great land of British Colombia.

Quietly from the forest the Dwellers watched, as this little town was discovered by some wandering travelers. They were more fascinated than anything else, as they witnessed the little town grow from a tiny shack, to the size that it was when this story takes place. The Forest Dwellers felt a connection to the town, since the town grew just like their egg that they nurtured, which became the forest. They were not particularly happy with this intrusion, but these new people respected the forest, and their surroundings, and never bothered the Forest Dwellers—minus the occasional cutting down of one of their tree friends, or slaying of one of their deer friends. They carefully observed what these people did with their fallen friends. It was agreed that the people used these resources responsibly, making sure that every splinter, every strand of hair, every drop of blood, every pine needle was utilized. They were not a wasteful people, and the Forest Dwellers acknowledged this, and let them go about their ways.

But as the Mistress of the Mountain always reminded them, "You must keep a close watch my children. As respectful as these valley dwellers may appear to be, do not leteth down your guard. I know the potential of these people and they have the ability to wieldeth more power and destruction then you think."

"Yes, your majesty," replied the obedient Forest Dwellers in unison...

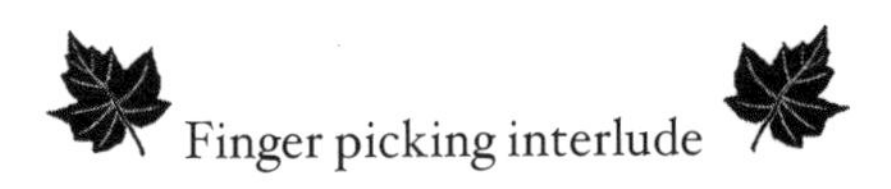

Finger picking interlude

The townspeople did have some knowledge of the Forest Dwellers, but only through gossip and traveling folklore. Naturally there were skeptics. Men would come back from the forest and proclaimeth, "I saw it! I saw a nymph with mine own eyes!" And some would say, "Do tell! Was she as beautiful and fare as we've been told by the stories of yesteryear?" And others would sayeth, "Gobbledigook! You saw no such thing. Yer mind be playing tricks on ye. What did I tell ye about eating the wild Tiger Lilies? They'll make the sky into a pie and a boar into a whore!" And the man would scratcheth his long beard and shaketh his head and say, "I swear on me mummy's bum I saw it! Alas it was only for a second and she was gone but..." And the debates would go on into the night.

These discussions often happened at the Purple Maple, the town pub and center for folklore, gossip, and ugly and pretty rumors of all sorts. People came to listen, boast, toast, and host; laugh, cry, drink, and stay dry; and everything in between. And of all of the rumors spread around, nothing got the jowels moving, the bellies rumbling, and the beer flowing more than the talk of Her Majesty, the Lady of the Deep, the Queen of the Nymphs, the Mistress of the Mountains.

No living man had claimeth to hath seen her, or been to the sacred lake. But they all knew about the Sun Rock and would go to bed dreaming about her unmatched beauty and all the mystery and wonder that she hath beheld. Even the skeptics dreamt about her, secretly in their comfortable beds of goose feather and bear hide, with their maple doors closed so tight so no one could heareth their thoughts...

There were other rumors: Rumors that Her Majesty could bringeth immortality, and great wealth and power to anyone who could manage to cast her out of her fortress in the Deep, and taketh her back to keepeth for their own. This was by far the most dangerous of the rumors and this was what many people thought behind their closed maple doors as they drifted to sleep. They dreamt about power, and wealth, and all of the amazing things they could do. But they all knew not to act on these impulses. They were content with their simple, peaceful lives in their small town, in the valley of the beautiful mountains of British Columbia. This they all knew, except for one man who thought different. His name was Atuk...

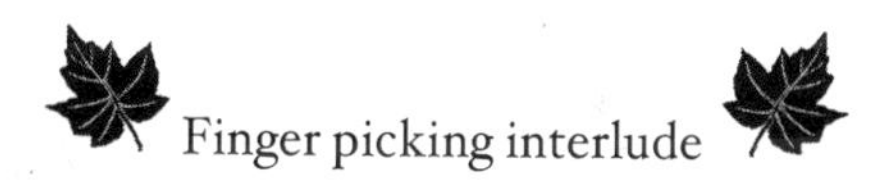

Atuk was a cobbler by trade. He was tall, and well built, and fell into cobbling by sheer convenience. His father was a cobbler, his grandfather was a cobbler, his great grandfather was a cobbler, his great, great, his great, great, great, and his great, great, great, great grandfather, Natar, came down from the Yukon (to escape the inconvenience of the Wooly Mammoths) and settled in to the valley. Everyone in the valley marveled at the shoes Natar had traveled down with from the Yukon. "Natar!" they would say. "You traveled hundreds of steps, up mountains, down through rivers, through snow, and mud, and everything in between. How on Her

Majesty's earth do you keep your shoes looking so new and clean?"

And Natar would take a calm breath and say, "You must respect your shoes to respect yourself. If your shoes crumble, your feet shall followeth, and so will your body follow suit." And all the townspeople would nod and agree and would give Natar their shoes to fix. Before he knew it, he was a full time cobbler.

Atuk knew this story well and respected his great, great, great, great grandfather Natar very much. But he knew deep down in his soul that cobbling was not his ideal path in the tangled mess of moss we call life.

Atuk was still a young lad, but old enough to see all of his adversaries long before taking wives and starting families, with small heirs to whatever business their great, great, great, great grandfathers had foundeth. Atuk had no heir, nor even a companion to produceth one.

As he would wind down the busy day in his quiet, lonely home, he began noticing that his back would ache as he slipped into bed. And he would run his hands along the faint hint of wrinkles that were beginning to form on his face. He attributed this to being so idle every day, cobbling from sun up to sun down. He knew in his heart, that if he did not change something soon, it might be too late.

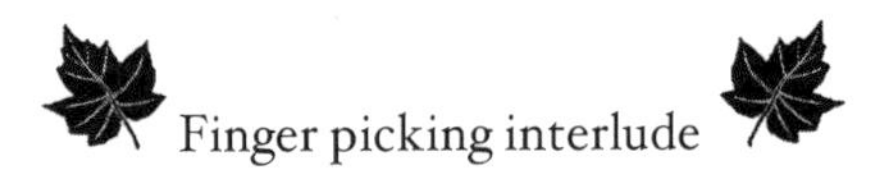
Finger picking interlude

As of late, Atuk would visit the Purple Maple after closing up his cobbleshop. Atuk was not what one would calleth a social creature—which could attribute to why he had not taken a wife yet. But he did find that he had developed a taste for the Malty Maple Bitter Brew, the Purple Maple's popular home brewed concoction. It was just the right thing to calm his senses after a long hard day of cobbling. He would siteth at the same spot at the bar, toward the far end. The spot was strangely never taken, as if everyone knew to save it for him. He liked that spot because it was tucked away in the corner with not much light. He would not be bothered, minus the occasional questions from a town drunkard sitting close by. "Hey Atuk! When is ye going to introduce me to ye special mistress?...What does ye mean ye doesn't have one? Pish-posh! A man as youthful as ye must have a full chest of treasures by now! Barkeep! Another round for good ol' Atuk! A bitter brew for better luck my friend!" And Atuk would bashfully nod and accept his generous gift for good fortune.

But the main reason why Atuk came to the Purple Maple, was for the stories. He loved to hear the incessant banter over the tall tales that travelers told, and he especially kept an ear out for any word on the Lady of the Deep. Her name would be mentioned hither and thither, sometimes as a figure of speech like, "You dived off the cliffs of the Giants?! Not even Her *Majesty* would approve of that!" But Atuk would make sure to listen in when the debates began, and people would hanker and holler, swearing by her existence and how they "knew a friend" who's "great, great grandfather" visited the Sacred Lake and saw the Lady on the Sun Rock and "was blinded by her unsurpassed beauty." Then the skeptics would chime in again with their "nays" and "gobbledigooks."

Atuk would go home at night and feel his back as he crawled into bed, and touch his wrinkles, and stare out his window at the starlit sky with the mountains silhouetted by the moonlight, and say out loud, "I know you're out there your Majesty. One day I will find you. I will seek you out and take you back as my own and we shall liveth our days together till the end of time and thereafter." Then Atuk would drift to sleep, flying, swimming, and wading through thoughts of prosperity and immortality, and the unsurpassable, unimaginable beauty of the Lady of the Deep, the Queen of the Nymphs, the Mistress of the Mountains.

The finger picking stopped. I was lying on my back and I opened my eyes to a clear shade of blue. I turned over and everyone around stirred from their own comfortable positions.

"Is that it??" Katrina said with a scrunched face.

"For now," said the Fortuneteller. "It's a work in progress."

"But I want to know if Atuk finds the Lady of the Deep!" cried someone in the group. We were resorting to our childhood tendencies of whining about what we didn't get.

"I haven't decided if he will or not," said the fortuneteller. "I think I'll have Atuk go on a great adventure to find the lake, but when he gets there, he never finds the Lady and goes home. Any thoughts? I'm open to suggestions."

Everyone sat silently in their own thoughts. "It's a fairy tale!" said a girl. "It *has* to have a happy ending. He can't just go home! He has to get the girl!"

"I don't agrcc," said Loki. "That's just a bullshit Hollywood cnding. I'm sick of those endings. Let him go home empty handed. Like The Rolling Stones said, 'you can't always get what you waaaant!'" Loki sang while a guy took the guitar and began playing the chords to the Stones song.

"If Atuk goes home empty handed, will he feel content, or unfulfilled?" I asked.

Some people nodded in agreement. "Good question," said the Fortuneteller. "This is something I've pondered myself. I think he will have gone on a great adventure to get to the lake. He will discover amazing new things that he had never seen in his entire life as a cobbler, being stuck in the valley. As he returns to his home, he'll be sad that he didn't reach his ultimate goal, but he will not have regretted his journey, one that led him to peril and near death, but was filled with amazing new discoveries and new friends within the Forest Dwellers."

"So the journey was more important then the goal?" someone asked.

The Fortuneteller nodded. "Precisely!"

"But if you try sometimes, you just might find," Loki jumped up and did a dance—his penis doing a mini dance, "you get what you neeeed!"

I looked at my watch and noticed that I had an hour and a half until my bus left for Whistler. I got up and walked with Loki back to Devina's blanket, where Devina and the Hermanos were packing up the stuff. I picked up my phone, which I had tucked in my T-shirt, along with my wallet. These precious items had been kept under the close watch of the Vancouver posse, so I knew they would be safe.

We packed everything up, Loki clothed himself, and we headed back up the cliff, through the rainforest, and back into boring, clothed civilization.

We took the bus back the way we came. Loki got off at the stop before us and we got to fit in a quick goodbye. "Best of luck, Evan," said Loki. "Move to Canada, it's way cooler, and more naked, and all that good stuff."

"Thanks Loki, I'll consider it. You guys have a real good thing going up here."

"Damn right! Okay, until next time! Later D!" And he jumped off the bus.

After I gathered my stuff together at Devina's place and strapped up my bag, Devina came over with a compact rolled up tent in her hands. "Do you still need this?"

I had forgotten about her generous offer. "Um—I mean, no. Well, yes, but you really don't have to—"

She pushed it into my arms. "Here you go."

"I'll be back, I swear," I said.

Devina nodded in her confident way. "I know."

I secured my wicker hat, and it took more effort to sling my bag over my shoulder because the tent was tied to it. I wobbled awkwardly down the street alongside Devina and the Hermanos, but I got used to the new weight by the time we reached the bus that took us downtown. The Vancouver posse led me off the bus and all the way to the front of the bus station. This door-to-door service couldn't be beat.

"Alright dude, have fun in Whistler," said Devina.

"Thank you so much, all of you guys, but I guess this isn't goodbye, I'll see you in a few days," I said.

"Sounds good. Adios!" she said in her usual detached tone.

"Adios amigos!"

"Bye Evan, see-you-soon," said the Hermanos.

"Adios Junkie!" Ben said, laughing hysterically. He was never going to let that go.

I walked into the station and bought my ticket, one way to Whistler. I hesitated on buying a return ticket and decided that I would wait. I wasn't prepared to limit my options, yet.

I had five minutes to spare but made it to my bus no problem. On the front of the bus it said, "Squamish/Whistler." I put my bag in the bottom cargo hold and I stepped onto the bus with my nalgene and my purple notebook with the Grateful Dead sticker on the front and the weed warning sticker on the back. The doors closed behind me, signifying that I was the last person to get on the bus. It wasn't crowded and I got a row to myself, making sure to sit on the left side by a window, in hopes that we would drive along the water. At least this was what I thought would happen, if I had remembered correctly from my map studying back in my room in Amherst.

Stepping on this bus made me feel more at home than when I had stepped *off* the bus for the first time in downtown Vancouver. I was surrounded by people ranging from their twenties to early thirties, who all looked physically fit. They dressed as if they were going to step off the bus and go climb a rock, or hop on a bike. I embraced this outdoor adventure vibe that was thickly settled.

It was mid-late afternoon as the bus mobilized, but the sun was still high in the sky, not yet yielding to its inevitable decent. *Thanks summer solstice.* I needed all of the light I could get if I was going to seek out a campsite and set up.

The bus rolled through the Turquoise City and met up with the road, that twenty-four hours prior had taken me through the forest of Stanley Park. There was no defiant crowd of bicyclists stopping traffic today, and I secretly breathed a hypocritical sigh of relief: I was too anxious to get where I needed to go. We passed over the forest-green beams of the Lion's Gate Bridge and touched ground onto North Vancouver. I got a surge of excitement knowing that my physical being had entered a new step on my journey. Soon enough I would be able to move my little tack on my map up to Whistler as my northernmost point of travel.

This was going to be the beginning of the last great step in this month-long expedition. Part of me felt okay with that. I felt content with what I had done, and seen, and experienced. However the other part of me couldn't stand the fact that I was getting to the end: *This doesn't* have *to be the end, Evan. Keep going, there's nothing stopping you. You can go a few more miles. Just take one more hit of the travel crack pipe. It won't kill you. Trust me Evan, it's worth it.* I wasn't sure what side of myself to go along with. But for the time being, I suppressed it and focused on the present: I was going to Whistler.

The bus veered to the left (west) as it got off the bridge and I was looking across the bay toward Stanley Park. I could see the small bike path under the bridge that I had ridden along. It was filled with other happy bikers on their Saturday afternoon jaunt through the park. From my far up vantage point, they looked like little biking figurines. Then they disappeared as the bus rounded a corner and headed north.

We were driving on Highway 99, also known as the "Sea to Sky Highway." So far it held up to its name and my predictions were right. Shortly after the road ended, a cliff dropped off hundreds of feet down into a channel. On the other side of the channel were mountainous islands. They were the tallest and most magnificent of the mountain islands I had seen thus far. Big, beautiful, tree-lined cliffs dropped down into the channel. It was like looking out at the Yosemite Valley where the mountains dropped down so abruptly, that I could see it in its entirety from its peak to the ocean. Hence, "sea to sky."

It was a two-hour drive from Vancouver to Whistler. We sailed along the channel for a solid hour with my face plastered to the window before we headed inland. That meant only an hour left to Whistler. What a fantastically short drive it was, between one of the world's greatest cities to the world's greatest ski resort. This was a special place. I liked living in special places. *Could I live here?* I was sensing this gravitational pull, which grew stronger along side my expanding knowledge of "Beautiful British Columbia." The idea of heading back to the tired old States wasn't sitting well with me.

We came to a town called, Squamish, at which point we were surrounded by mountains, with no water in sight. I looked around and could see tall cliffs of bare, flat rock rising up close by. I squinted my eyes at the cliffs and I thought that I saw some small human figures attached to the rock, but I wasn't sure. The bus stopped and some of the outdoor adventure people stepped off. We were in the middle of a flat valley and it looked like the town took up most of it (not very large with no tall buildings). At first glance the only interesting aspects to this town were these dramatic cliffs, as well as the fact that the town had such a peculiar name as "Squamish." But mountain towns like these are known to contain more than what meets the eye.

We continued on and once we reached the edge of the valley, we began an ascent up a winding, narrow road. The bus trudged up and up, occasionally squeezing through claustrophobic corridors of rock on either side. Then one side would open up to a quick vista of a valley, followed by mountains, followed by valleys, and mountains, and on, and on, and on. The sun had begun its descent in the sky, and dark shadows were forming on mountainsides where bigger mountains were in the way. These bigger mountains still stood shining and proud. They had extra time to soak up the remaining waning rays.

The road leveled out just short of the two-hour mark. We were in another valley (smaller than Squamish) and up ahead on the right side, a mammoth hill curled upward farther than I could see, and some distinctive cut up trails curved around its slope. As I looked up, I almost missed a large sign on the side of the road that said, "Welcome to Whistler—Bienvenue a Whistler—Home of the 2010 Winter Olympics." I had made it. Not quite how I had planned to make it, but here I was, rolling into Whistler on a bus, alone, with my backpack, and a Couchsurfer's tent.

The bus turned right, past a larger, more extravagant sign with international flags waving that said, "Whistler Blackcomb." Up ahead was a parking lot big enough to fit every car in Vancouver, followed by a group of buildings that were unmistakably hotels and ski resort operations facilities. This was the Whistler Village. Directly behind it was the start of the behemoth ski mountain, which shared the same name of the village, as well as the town. Strings of thick metal crept up the mountain in various directions, starting at the village. These were the chairlifts and from my vantage point, I could tell that most of them patiently sat still, waiting for the cold weather and snow to blanket the then lush-green slopes.

The bus pulled up to a roundabout at the edge of the village and I got up along with the rest of the passengers. As soon as I stepped out I was hit with the fresh, clean, clear, delightful, invigoratingly cool mountain air. The freshness was intensified from the quick transition of coming from a metropolitan area. That was not to say that Vancouver was a stale, suffocating wasteland. I was breathing air in one of the greenest cities in the world. But it still couldn't hold a candle to the quality of the mountain air, no matter how hard it tried.

As I stood at the edge of the Whistler Village and soaked in my surroundings, I couldn't help but feel a sense of doubt. I still needed to figure out where I would be laying my weary carcass that night. Patrice had told me to give him a call when I arrived. Knowing that he was a Couchsurfer, I figured he we basking somewhere up in the mountains, taking advantage of this perfect day—at least that's where I would've been at this moment. *To be a Couchsurfer, one must think like a Couchsurfer.* But I could never be too sure. I took out my phone and the piece of paper that I wrote his number on. I dialed...no ring, straight to voicemail. It wasn't an automated message like Devina's, but I couldn't tell if the message was Patrice's. All I heard was a bunch of fast sentences in what sounded like French, before a robot woman told me to leave a message at the tone...Beeeep! "H—heey, Patrice, this is Evan from Couchsurfing. I just arrived in the Whistler Village and was seeing if you're available to host me tonight. Uh, yeah, please give me a call when you get this. Thanks!"

I decided to take a quick stroll around the village and give Patrice a cushion of time to get back to me. If he didn't, I would need to find someone or something that would steer me in the direction of a campground, or at least a spot where I could set up camp and not be harassed by a Mountie—although the thought of getting harassed by a Mountie had its possibly amusing benefits.

I walked into the village, which was like stepping through a portal and ending up in a chic, downtown shopping center with high-end clothing stores, restaurants, bars, and gift shops. Some tourists walked around, consisting of couples and families, but the village had a generally quiet ambiance. This was to be expected in the off-season. Just like the chairlifts, the stores and boutiques were waiting for winter to arrive, at which point money would follow suit.

The buildings rose high above me and blocked out the sun's rays, leaving me to travel through shadowed corridors. The most light was emanating from up ahead, toward the base of the mountain. I numbly gravitated in that direction, like a moth to the flame. The narrow corridor opened up to a big plaza with a rounded stone fire pit in the middle. This quaint, yet fabricated scene welcomed me with the backdrop of the mountain behind. Past the plaza was a grassy hill, and fifty yards ahead, the chairlifts started. One of the chairlifts was running, and this was the busiest area so far.

People surrounded the chairlift holding mountain bikes, and were decked out in all of the gear necessary to speed down a hill comfortably without mangling their bodies on a fall. Most had helmets with face-masks, gloves, chest pads, shin pads, and elbow pads. I could see why this was necessary when I looked up the hill. These bikers would take the chair lift up (a hook was fastened to the back of the chair for the bike). Then they would proceed to speed back down the hill along an intricate course. This course, which was visible for the plaza to admire, was made up of switchbacks. Every level had its own feature, including big jumps with gaps to clear, or narrow wooden catwalks to maneuver over, or a set of berms to curve around. It looked insanely fun (emphasis on insane which justified all of the protection on these biker's bodies). I later found out that Whistler was the world's premier mountain biking destination. This wasn't hard to believe. It was the world's premier winter destination, why not be the summer's as well?

I was reaching in my pocket to get my camera and instead I felt a vibrating phone. I took it out and saw a number that may have looked French Canadian. I held my breath and answered. "Hello?"

"Yes, hello, is zis Eevin?"

"Yes, this is Evan."

"Hello Eevin! How are you, zis is Patrice!"

"Hey Patrice! I'm good, I'm standing here at the base of Whistler. How are you?"

"I am very good man, I am sorry I missed your call, I was up in ze mountains with no cell phone reception. We were out camping last night and I was not sure if I was coming back tonight, but some friends needed to get back, so we all came back, but we are going to camp somewhere else tonight." He talked fast with an excited tone. "So by ze sound of your message, you are probably looking for a couch to surf on tonight?" He gave a chuckle. "Or maybe ze next few days, yes?" He had a peculiar sounding accent that hinted French but was not quite there.

"Yeah!" I answered. "That is exactly right."

"Okay, well how would you like to go camping with us tonight?"

The question came as a shock but I had an immediate answer that came out of me as naturally as breathing. "Yes! That sounds perfect!"

"Great, so you traveled up by bus from Vancouver, yes?"

"That's correct."

"Okay, no problem, I will come to ze village to pick you up. Probably ten minutes—no longer. Can you be at ze roundabout where ze bus dropped you, in ten minutes?"

"I sure can."

"Good, good, only a few hours left of sunlight so we must act fast, but we should be fine. Okay! See you soon Eevin!"

"See you soon!"

I nearly ran back to the bus stop, as if Patrice was already there and would only wait another minute, before leaving. I got there with nine minutes and thirty seconds to spare, and stood waiting not so patiently.

I looked out across the parking lot to the other side of the valley. More snowcapped peaks rolled into each other under a dark blue, late afternoon sky. Just a few hours prior I was looking out at skyscrapers, and before that the open ocean. How many places on this earth can that be done?

I observed various cars come up to the roundabout, trying to guess which one would be Patrice's. I saw a few luxury SUV's and sedans go by, and didn't have to guess whether or not they belonged to Patrice. Sure enough, wealthy looking people with families stepped out. Then an old beat up two-door approached the roundabout. Loud instrumental rock was blasting out of its confines. I peered in intently to find two younger looking guys taking up the front seats and peering back at me. They pulled up to where I was standing and rolled down the window. They looked like they were in their late twenties, ruffled hair, scruffy beards, with big, genuine smiles. The man in the passenger seat leaned over and yelled over the music. "Eevin?" He asked. I nodded. The passenger got out. He had on a dirty T-shirt, cargo shorts, and sandals (basically me, without a wicker hat). "Hey man! Welcome to Whistler!" I shook the hand of my new guide, Patrice Kirouac. He pointed to my backpack. "Looks like you are ready to go! Zis is good, not much more time to spare. Sorry to rush you, but let's go!"

I got in the back seat and the driver turned around. "Hey, I'm Mattie."

"Evan, nice to meet you."

"Ohhhh, *Evan*!" Mattie turned to Patrice. "Not *Eeeee*vin!"

"Yes!" said Patrice. "Zat is what I said!"

I could already tell that Patrice's accent was going to be a source of amusement. Mattie, on the other hand, did not have an accent. He must have been "normal" Canadian (as opposed to "weird" French Canadian—just kidding Quebec!)

"That's alright, I'll respond to either." I said.

"That's good," said Mattie, "because Patrice won't stop."

Patrice turned to me. "Don't mind Mattie, he's from Ottawa. Very strange people from Ottawa."

"Shut up, you Quebec lunatic. So we have to buy some groceries and beer, get back to my place, load up the van, and we're ready to go. You're coming camping with us, right Evan?" asked Mattie.

"Um, well yeah, I think so, if that's alright." This never got any easier. I couldn't shake the feeling of meeting people and immediately including myself in their plans. Alas I needed to get over it. I was Couchsurfing.

"Of course man, of course," Mattie politely reassured. "Have you been to Whistler before?"

"No, this is my first time, I just got off the bus."

"Cool well I think we finally got some good weather coming, so there should be lots to do."

"Yes, finally!" said Patrice. "Thanks for bringing ze good weather Eevin, we really needed it."

I laughed. "No problem guys I try to help when I can." I was starting to get that familiar feeling again of meeting up with old friends who were connecting after too long a time.

We drove out of the parking lot and turned right up a road, which took us the opposite way of Vancouver. I spotted a lake on the left through some pine trees, and some roads that veered off to condo complexes, and other residential streets. Signs popped up like, "The Pines at Whistler," or "Aspen Grove." I laughed to myself and shook my head. *Resort real estate marketing never changes*. Past that, the condos subsided and we got into neighborhoods with more modest residences. This was the "ski bum" part of town, where the "full timers" lived year-round. No desk job to go back to in the city, no hustle and bustle, just fresh air and fresh pines all year long. I wondered what kinds of jobs these guys had here to sustain their mountain living.

"It sounds like you've been on a great adventure Eevin," said Patrice. He went on to tell me that he had read my profile description, which turned out to be as enticing as I had intended it (at least for a few curious souls). "So your car broke down in California?"

"Yeah, we were having problems with it throughout the drive. It didn't come as a huge surprise when it finally happened. My friend, who was the owner of the car, was a bit on edge for the entire trip because he knew it wasn't running up to par."

"To par?" Patrice curled his eyebrows. Apparently this phrase hadn't made it to Quebec.

"Oh," I corrected myself, "I mean it was not running perfectly like it should have been. Up to standards, rather."

Patrice still looked confused. "Par, like golf par?"

"Yeah, forget it, it's a weird American phrase."

Patrice chuckled. "America has such funny phrases! Like, 'Heavens to Betsy!' What the hell does zat mean?"

I laughed. "I don't think many people have said that since the year nineteen-fifty, but I agree, that's a funny phrase."

"Yes, funny stuff. In Canada, we kind of watch and laugh about things on ze news from America. You guys get caught up in such crazy shit!"

I nodded. "Yeah, I know what you mean."

"I don't mean *you* personally. You are a Couchsurfer so I know you are smarter, eh?"

"Um, I guess so, it's hard for me to say," I said as I shrugged. Then I chuckled to myself. Hearing "eh" made it official. He was French *and* Canadian. He was French Canadian.

We talked, bullshitted, and laughed, with the conversations flowing seamlessly from one topic to the next: from traveling, to life in Canada, to Whistler, to America, to food, to beer.

"Speaking of beer," I said, "I can buy the beer for tonight." This seemed like a good opportunity to chip in and not come off as a camping freeloader. Patrice didn't object. He was far less resistant than Devina.

We pulled in to a parking lot with a little supermarket. I picked out a thirty pack of cheap Canadian beer called, Kokanee. When I brought it to the cash register, I nearly gasped when I saw the price. I learned that Canada's taxation on beer and liquor was higher than America's. This also applied to cigarettes, which was no concern of mine, but there was no question that my inner, disgruntled alcoholic had been awakened.

After the beer and supplies were purchased, we drove off the main road to a residential street. The neighborhood was windy and hilly and we took a succession of turns that I couldn't begin to try to retrace, even if I had paid attention. But I wasn't paying any attention. Instead I was fixated on every individual house that we passed. When I say "individual," I mean exactly that. This was no cookie-cutter suburban neighborhood. Each house had its own unique style. Most were made out of wood (for winter insulation) and metal roofs (for snow resistance). Some were tall A-frames with wide windows lining the flat sides, from top to bottom. Some had flatter roofs but were multiple stories with large wrap around decks that surrounded the perimeter of each floor. Some were set up high on a hill with funky stairs leading up from a little garage. The driveways were packed with boats, bikes, and gear for any outdoor activity imaginable. Porches were crammed with chairs, grills, hammocks, and stringed lights—all items to help with optimal enjoyment of life. And between, around, in front of, and behind each house, stood gloriously large pines.

I marveled at all of these houses, because each one I could realistically see myself happily living in, enjoying life, and sitting on my porch in the summer. Or in the winter, building a grand fire in my fireplace from the wood stacked in my garage. The wood would be stacked next to my kick-ass sport utility vehicle (NOT an SUV, which stands for Stupid Unnecessary Vehicle), which takes me where I want to go in the mountains. My kickass sport utility vehicle would be parked next to my mountain bike, which takes me where I want to go after my car takes me to the trailhead. My mountain bike would be placed next to my skis, which tear up the Whistler Blackcomb slopes when the snow falls deep and powdery. My skis would be placed next to...the list could go on and on.

We turned into a house with a wide wooden deck on the second floor. A stump lay on the front lawn with an axe stuck in it upright, like the sword in the stone. In the driveway was, low and behold, a kickass sport utility vehicle. When we got out I had to admire this monstrosity. It looked like it was driven out of the bush of the Australian Outback, across the ocean floor, and up over the Pacific coastal mountains to Whistler. This was a fucking badass machine that looked like it could conquer anything. Mattie noticed me admiring it. "We'll be taking her to the campsite. It's not a far drive, but there are some tricky bumps that will require her expertise."

"She does look like an expert," I said. I was staring at her jacked up wheels which looked like they were taken from a monster truck.

I followed Patrice and Mattie inside. The bottom floor entrance was a sliding glass door into a kitchen and dining room area. The whole ambiance was cluttered, but homey. There were some posters on the wall of skiers in a graceful position in mid air, snow flying off of a cliff behind them. Cast iron pots and pans hung from the ceiling on hooks that surrounded the kitchen, where a woman was rummaging around, grabbing different camp-worthy objects, and putting them into a large plastic bin. Mattie walked over to her and gave her a lovable kiss on the cheek.

Patrice walked toward the dining room table and greeted a young fellow. His hair was wet, like he had just taken a shower, and he was eating a bowl of pasta. "Luke! Ca va!"

"Hey Patrice, you're back so early!"

"Yes, but we are going back out now to Green Lake. What about you? You are not going to come?"

"Nooo, I'm too tired, I just got back from Squamish. I spent all day climbing the Buttress."

"Ohh, that's awesome! I want to get there so badly! Can we go soon?"

"Of course! You wouldn't believe the view from the top. You can see Whistler and everything." As Luke said this, he had a look of content that I could only be jealous of. This was one of the many perks of living in a mountain town. Maybe he was the little speck that I saw on that rock from the bus.

"Hey, Eevin," Patrice waved me over, "zis is Luke." I walked over and shook his hand. "Eevin is Couchsurfing here from ze US."

"Cool man, nice to meet you. Did you come here to climb?" Luke asked.

I didn't know how to answer that question. *Maybe?* "Um, I don't know. I came to check it *all* out."

"Cool man, Squamish is the place to be if you want to climb. That I can guarantee."

"Thanks, I'll keep that in mind."

"Okay!" announced Mattie. "We're going to load the van and we're good to go." He walked outside with the plastic bin.

The woman walked over to me. She had a similar relaxed smile that Mattie had given when we met. She looked in her thirties, had black hair, and was clearly physically fit. "Hi, I'm Missy."

I shook her hand. "Evan, nice to meet you."

"You're from the States?"

"Yeah, Massachusetts."

"Oh wow! A long way!"

I shook my head in agreement. "Yes indeed."

"Welcome to Whistler, you picked a good time to come. The summer is the best here."

"What about winter?" I asked.

"That's the best too." Missy laughed. "It's all the best—but summer is really special. You're coming camping with us, eh?"

"Yeah."

"You are going to love zis place," said Patrice. "It is ze best, right Missy?"

"No question," she replied.

We turned for the door. "Have fun guys!" Luke said with a mouth full of pasta.

We walked out of the house and over to the Monster Van. It had a sliding door, giving Mattie a big opening to work with. He was grabbing different tubs and chairs, and stacking them neatly and securely inside. A whole bunch of stuff went in, but when I looked inside, there were still two comfortably available seats for two passengers to sit in, like kings on thrones. There was also a great metal rack that spanned the entire roof of the van, with a majestic, wooden, two-person canoe fastened onto it. It even looked like there was more room to put stuff, if the instance arose where our cargo had doubled in size—or tripled—or quadrupled. I had seen this same van in an African safari expedition show on TV once. I think they were carrying an elephant on the roof.

Patrice and I grabbed our bags and threw them in the small aisle between our seats. Mattie closed the sliding door on us, and he and Missy got in the front. "Mattie, your van amazes me," I said.

"Thanks, she's a bad bitch." Mattie turned the ignition, and she roared to life like a lion, then purred like a panther.

"Alright! Making great time guys!" said Patrice.

We cruised back through the neighborhood, and downwards around the beautiful windy bends, past the houses I should have been living in.

"How long have you lived here Patrice?" I asked.

"I used to live here a few years ago. But then I traveled ze world. I got back a few months ago."

"Like the whole world?"

Patrice nodded. "Everywhere: Europe, Africa, Middle East, Asia. And I Couchsurfed everywhere I went. So many great places and wonderful people."

"Wow." I didn't know what to ask someone who said that they traveled everywhere. *I know what I'll ask: Really?? How was it??*

"Okay, of course I do not mean *everywhere*," continued Patrice. "No one can travel everywhere. Just like you cannot read every book. Zat is why it is so great, because you can do it for your entire life without retracing your steps."

That made my crack-traveler body shiver. The thought of devoting one's life to traveling the entire world was dangerously enticing. I tried to put it out of my mind, but it was too late. Patrice had branded me.

We were back on the main road. To our right up ahead, I could see Whistler and Blackcomb peeking up over the tall pine trees.

Missy turned around. "How do you guys know each other?" she asked.

"We actually just met when Mattie and Patrice picked me up." I said this as I glanced at Patrice, and we exchanged a similar look of understanding and laughed. I noticed Missy turn to Mattie and give a strange, not so understanding look. I realized that that may not have sounded as funny to them as it did to Patrice and me. I forgot that these poor, unassuming people were allowing a complete stranger to go camping with them.

"Remember I told you guys about Couchsurfing?" said Patrice. "We met on ze website and Eevin is going to stay with me for a few days."

"Oh, cool, I forgot you mentioned that," said Mattie.

Mattie had already heard, but I repeated the summary of my trip and how I got there. I did this for Missy to hear, as well as for both of them to hear, since they now knew the context. I hoped that my story would aleve any uncomfortable suspicion that may have started to brew. I had faith in them that they would understand. Judging them so far, they seemed like unofficial Couchsurfers, like the Hermanos.

Just as I finished my trip recap (which lasted no more than five minutes time), Mattie made a quick turn off the main road, onto a dirt road. It was a road you wouldn't notice unless purposely looking out for it. It looked laden with rocks, and bumps, and holes, but the Super Van made it feel like a freshly paved street. We were surrounded by thick woods which did not look to let up anywhere ahead. On the contrary, it was getting thicker.

It was a couple minutes of Mattie slowly scanning the side of the road, before he did a double take over his shoulder and stopped abruptly. He backed up the Vanimal about twenty yards (or from blue line to goal line) and sure enough a narrow path into the woods had revealed itself. It looked completely impassable. "I always barely miss it!" said Mattie. He turned toward the entrance. There was an oversized log, followed by a deep ditch. "Hold on!" he said with a grin. He shifted to first gear and slowly rolled the front wheels over the log, which caused the front end to tip up, so for a moment our view was of the tops of the trees and the bluish-purplish sky of the early evening. Then we sunk into the ditch as the back wheels bucked up on the log. Mattie gave her bad bitch some gas and the front wheels rolled over the ditch as the back end dropped down and over, and we were back on flat ground. "Yeah baby!" Mattie patted his baby's dash. "Who's the baddest bitch of them all?"

Missy turned around in time to see me still trying to process what just happened. "That was the tough part. We're almost there."

"Pretty cool, eh Eevin?" said Patrice.

I nodded in unarguable, mouth-gaping approval.

The woods did not stay thick for long and I could see open air up ahead. One and a half more hockey rinks and we were clear out of the woods. The path split in two directions making a small circle around an area with various pull offs for campsites. These were no-thrills sites, consisting of merely a flat grass patch and a stone-round fire pit. There couldn't have been more than four or five sites around the circle, and none were occupied. We were the masters of this domain.

But why go through all the trouble to get to these measly campsites? That was obvious. Directly in front of us where the campsite ended, the lake started. It was wide open and serene, surrounded by cliffs and forest. And above it as a backdrop, towered two great mountains named, Whistler and Blackcomb. They shone far more clear and more exposed then any other view I had seen up till now. If I reached out far enough, I could have grabbed one. This was the kind of place where a professional photographer went, who worked for the Canadian tourism bureau, postcard division. It was where the word "picturesque" came from. Like an orgasm for the eyes. Where the Canadian Prime Minister, or Wayne Gretzky would stand and say into the camera, "Come discover Canada, and enjoy all the untouched beauty we have to offer!" And would be played on Charlotte, North Carolina, or Perth, Australia cable channels—It was fucking gorgeous okay??!!?

We drove around the circle and Mattie took the best site, closest to the lake. The Monster Machine purred to a halt and when Mattie disengaged the ignition, a silence rushed in and enveloped us. Everyone sat and stared, and no one breathed. It was like we made it to heaven and had to take time to fully digest it, starting with our eyes and letting it fill our souls.

"Yep," said Mattie. "I've lived here for almost eleven years, and I just managed to find this amazing place."

This comment planted a grin on me from the tip of one ear, across to the other. *Wow, I've been in Whistler for about eleven minutes...*

If standing on the top of the Lion's Gate Bridge with a thousand bikers had helped me realize the significance of Couchsurfing, this moment was the final blow that pounded the point into the ground for good. It was a piece of my life and soul that I had not realized I was missing, but it made so much sense, now that it was clearly there. I was like a born-again Couchsurfer.

The funny thing was that I had already experienced and acknowledged the essence of Couchsurfing. I had been given advice by a local in Jackson. Becca showed me the true flavor of San Francisco. Linda pampered me like I was in a five-star resort. But now I had found a resource that could help me keep up this untarnished form of traveling. I no longer had to luckily find the right local to ask for advice, or manage to sit next to the right person on a bus, or only be limited to this experience in places where I had friends or family. The entire world had opened itself up to me.

From this point forward, I wanted a local. I wanted to live, breath, feel, taste, and smell what a real person who lived there day to day experienced. And I wanted that person to guide me, not because I was filled with money, but because they were a real person with a genuine interest in showing me all that their home had to offer. This was because they took pleasure in the sheer act of exposing someone new to the beauty that they knew and loved (or in this case, took eleven years to find). And at the end of the experience, I might come out of it with a new friend. My mind had shifted in that simple statement that Mattie had made in his Sport Utility Vehicle as we gazed out at nature's sacred offering, and there was no turning back.

Mattie was the one to break the silence and snap us back to reality. I wasn't sure how long the silence had lasted, it could have been a minute—it could have been centuries. Mattie got out and opened the trunk. He pulled out the large plastic bin and carried it over to the fire pit. Patrice and I got out, and I figured I would help, so I grabbed my case of beer. I opened it and handed each member a can, which was gladly accepted.

"Can I help with anything?" I asked.

"I don't think so," Missy said politely, "Mattie and I have this down like clockwork. You can relax, but thanks for the offer." She didn't have to tell me twice.

Patrice pulled out a fishing rod and walked toward the lake, beckoning me to follow. "Do you fish Eevin?"

"Not often, but yes."

"Me neither. But it is fun to take ze gamble. Who knows what will happen when zat lure drops in. Maybe we will catch a whale!"

We walked to the edge of the lake (twenty feet from the campsite). The surface was a sheet of glass, with no wind to disturb a single molecule. Whistler Blackcomb was getting dark but had a faint halo of golden light that settled on the top of each peak. We had reached dusk and everything about our surrounding was still and quiet, minus the activity of Mattie and Missy who worked diligently but quietly. Patrice fastened a neon rubbery lure on the hook—which could have been mistaken for a gummy worm if you weren't careful—and cast it out. The silence was so heavy around us that I could crisply hear the whip of the rod, the whisp of the line unraveling, the plop of the lure in the water, and the click of the clasp to secure the line. Patrice slowly turned the crank. "Zis is a catch and release lake," he said, "just like ze women in this town!" He let out a bellowing laugh. I laughed and shook my head. *This guy is a riot.*

After he had brought the empty lure back in, he handed it off to me. "Maybe you will have better luck. Zis is a hard lake for fishing."

I repeated the same action, then calmly stood holding the rod, next to the calm lake. Patrice pointed in front of us. "Do you see those houses on ze other side?" I nodded. I could see some docks across the way, and faint wooden stairs leading up to cottages. "My friend Augustin lives in one of those houses. I think it is around ze bend. He will stop by tomorrow on his boat. Maybe we will have better luck if we cast out in ze middle of ze lake. What do you think?"

"Sorry," I said, "but I'm no expert on the subject." I reeled in my empty lure. The fish didn't feel like dining on gummy worms this evening.

Patrice shrugged. "Oh well. Maybe ze fish are already sleeping." Patrice took a swig of his beer, grabbed the rod, and we walked back to the campsite.

Mattie and Missy had made some headway. They had brought firewood with them, which was already lit in the fire pit. Four folding chairs were set up around it. Mattie was sitting in one, staring at the fire and sipping his beer. He grabbed a log and stuck it in, setting the fire ablaze. "Almost ready Miss," he said. Missy nodded. She was sitting at a chair with a small table in front of her, cutting up broccoli.

"Can I offer my help again?" I asked.

"No thanks," said Mattie. "Sit down and relax, it should be ready soon."

I sat down in a chair with my beer, watched the fire, and sipped. Missy set up a small camping stove and put a pot of water over it. The water had come from a large jug. When it boiled, she threw in a few fettucine pasta nests. Then she went back to the cutting board and took out some deliciously multicolored sausages.

I looked over and noticed a jeep rolling into camp. It parked at a site opposite from us around the circle and a young couple got out. The guy looked like a skateboarding stoner. He had long hair, wore board shorts, and a T-shirt. The girl looked like a model. I don't mean to be judgemental, but this pair seemed odd. At first glance this dude looked like he smoked weed, did landscaping, and lived in his parent's basement. The girl looked like she was the daughter of a Turkish emperor. Back in a metropolitan area, you would probably have seen this girl with a rich, Armani-wearing Armenian. But up here in Whistler, the snowboarder reigned king. He was probably the kind of dude that hucked himself out of helicopters and rode down avalanches over cliffs. And she loved him for it.

I directed my attention back to the fire, which at this point was sufficiently stoked. I could feel the heat of the flames, which was nice, but not necessary in this weather. I was still comfortable in my shorts and T-shirt, considering the sun, with its organic heat, was unmistakably gone from this part of the earth. Mattie got up and went over to the Mystery Machine, then walked back with a metal grill that happened to be just the right size to set over the fire. Then the real magic began. Mattie took out a big wok from the plastic bin and set it over the grill. Then came the oil, then the sausage, broccoli, and spices. A sizzle sound erupted with each addition, and aromas crept into our olfactory passages. All eight eyes were fixated on the wok. Then came the chopped garlic. "Mmmmmm," groaned Patrice. I sucked up the saliva that dripped out of my mouth. Then came the fresh pasta and some milky concoction from a mason jar, completing the culinary steps.

"Okay," said executive chef Mattie, "let's grab some bowls." Missy took sets of bowls and forks from the bin. She scooped the delicious substance out of the steaming wok and filled each bowl, passing them around. Once we all possessed a filled bowl of gastronomical goodness, Mattie raised his beer. "Cheers everyone, hope you enjoy pasta alfredo, al Mattie and Missy."

"A-La," corrected Patrice.

We all raised our beers. "Cheers, thank you!" I said.

"Bon appetite," said Missy."

"Bon app-e-*ti*!" said Patrice snobbishly. "Do not pronounce ze T!"

"Shut up Frenchy!" said Mattie.

We drank and ate merrily. The food was as delicious as it looked and smelled—An A-plus as far as pasta alfredo went. There were clear benefits to car camping, which this setup had perfectly summed up. You did not get these luxuries when backpacking. I thought back on the trip in Oregon with Casey. There we sat on hard logs, eating simple salami and cheese quesadillas, around a fire made by what available wood was around. It was a different experience, but neither was necessarily better. Each experience was special in its own way. You get a sense of accomplishment from being able to manage an entire camping situation out of the bag on your back. Then again it is damn good to eat a gourmet meal in comfy camping chairs with a full case of cold beer. It also helped that I was dealing with car camping professionals. I was sure that it had taken Mattie and Missy years of trial and error to build up their camping gear and find exactly what worked and what did not.

The transition from dusk to night had happened during our feast. I looked up and saw a wide array of stars that blanketed the sky, some bright enough to twinkle the surface of the lake. I looked over at our neighbors, who had built a blazing fire as well. The skater-stoner sat in a camping chair, picking away at a guitar. The Turkish princess was walking around arranging things, and completely naked from the waist up. Gravity pulled my loose jaw down, not only because of the reality of the situation, but because I was convinced then that she *had* to be a model, with such a perfectly chiseled chest. I thought I had seen my share of robustly rotund, young female breasts today, but I think I just found the winner. *Oooh Caanadaa. My home and native laaaand...* This place was too much.

When we had our fill of merriment, the topic of sleep was raised. It appeared that nobody in the party had taken pitching a tent into consideration. *Looks like I'm going to be using Devina's tent after all.* But Mattie read my mind. "It's looking like a tent won't be necessary," he said. "I was going to see how the weather panned out and it's what I had hoped for."

"Yeah," said Missy, "I'm fine sleeping outside."

That thought never occurred to me as a possibility, but once I saw the reality of the situation, it made sense. I had not been bitten by any bugs thus far, and the temperature had only dropped a few degrees. If the bug and temperature factors were okay, and the sky was as clear as crystal with no threat of rain, there was nothing stopping us. We all agreed that this was the best option, and when the fire stopped getting stoked and burned down to a glow, we took our sleeping bags, found our own flat patch of soft grass, and bunkered down for the night. I scrunched up my sweatshirt for a pillow (as usual).

Lying on my back, I looked up at the stars. The faint sound of running water on stones was entering my left ear, while light guitar picking from our neighbor, entered the right. It was a perfect mixture to help droop my eyes and lull me to sleep. The day was done and I slept soundly by Green Lake in Whistler, British Columbia. No bugs that bit, no air that chilled, no rain that fell. Maybe British Columbia really *was* the greatest place on earth.

DAY 24

I woke to strange voices, or rather voices of strangers. My eyes shot open in a panic. I was disoriented for a brief time, confused as to why I was buried in a sleeping bag and lying in the grass. I would have thought that by day twenty-four of waking up in a different strange place every morning, my mind would have gotten used to it. But there was still that initial state of panic as I entered into consciousness and thought, *what the fuck am I doing lying outside in the middle of the grass??* Confusion led to relief as I sat up, saw the blue sky above me, the trees and mountains around me, and two friendly folks, Mattie and Missy, working once again around the fire pit. I looked to my other side and Patrice was lying peacefully unconscious in his sleeping bag. A few feet beyond him, the grass sloped down into the water. This was where these strange voices had come from.

I watched a group of people chatting on a raft that was floating by. They wore helmets and lifejackets, and were fashioned with little, useless oars. A man sat in the back of the raft with a big oar, who looked like he knew what he was doing as he lectured something to the others in the raft. I hadn't noticed last night, but the lake fed into a river that stretched back in the direction the raft was heading (away from Whistler Blackcomb). This explained the delightful sound of running water that helped put me to bed. I looked out on the lake and saw a couple more people-filled rafts following in an evenly spaced succession. Whitewater rafting trips. It did not occur to me that Whistler would have sufficient rivers for whitewater rafting. This wasn't hard to believe.

It was a skiing, biking, climbing, and camping destination, why not be rafting as well?

I sat savoring my serene surroundings, and thought about how deeply and soundly I had slept through the night. It was amazing to think that sleeping outside was such a rare phenomenon. Us domesticated humans needed the conditions to be just right: no bugs, not too cold, no precipitation. Whistler was this heavenly place that eliminated those elements. Either that or it was me being a wimpy diva who couldn't handle the "icky outdoors."

I got up and walked over to Mattie and Missy. Mattie sat tending to a freshly blazed fire. Missy was back at her table chopping onions, garlic, and yellow peppers. They looked up smiling and said, "Good Morning," which is Canadian for, "Good Morning."

"Nice night, eh?" said Mattie.

"Amazing!" I said. "I slept straight through."

"Yeah, this weather can't get much better. We had such a long stretch of shitty rain. We're all so relieved it's over and summer is finally here."

"I know what you're talking about..." I proceeded to tell Mattie and Missy about my run-in with the Godzilla rain cloud which had steered away our course in Jackson. It was crazy to think that the weather we were experiencing thousands of miles away, was part of the same cloud that touched here. But I never forgot what my good friend Niko had revealed to us: "A cloud that's stretching from Vancouver to Montreal."

"Jackson Hole, eh?" came a funny French voice from behind me. "You go ski there?" Patrice walked up and took a seat by the fire.

"What? Oh, hey Patrice. No, I was talking about earlier on my road trip, just a few weeks ago. No snow, just a whole lot of rain."

"Oui-oui, fuck ze rain. I like sun and camping."

"Do you like eggs too?" asked Missy.

"Oui-oui, and eggs too."

"Good, because that's what's on the menu. And we're throwing in some veggies. Should I throw in the rest of the sausage from last night?" she asked. The three growing boys nodded their heads up and down with a Pavlovian drool. Missy grabbed the sausage. "That was easy."

Just like dinner, Mattie built up the fire to a blaze and placed the grill over it. Except instead of using the wok, he took out a large cast iron skillet from the seemingly magically bottomless plastic bin. He threw in the veggies and sausage, then cracked ten eggs. They sizzled together in harmonious unison, like an illustrious Mozart symphony.

I looked over to check up on our prom king and queen. The guy was sitting in a camping chair, holding something to his mouth and lighting it. He looked up and blew out a visible puff of smoke. The girl walked around, no longer topless, but her shorts and bikini top made her look like she was about to step onto the set of a summer sportswear catalog photo shoot. My incessant staring was interrupted by a plate, that was set on my lap. The egg/veggie/sausage aroma crept its way up to my nostrils and I dug in. Insatiable lust makes for such a smooth transition into voracious hunger.

As we happily consumed the first meal of the day, I noticed a small boat out on the lake, which was separate from the rafting holding pattern. There was one gentleman inside controlling a motor on the back, and it looked like he was steering in our direction. Patrice noticed me staring, then looked over in the same direction and squinted his eyes. "Is zat Augustin?"

Mattie squinted too. "I think so."

Patrice got up, walked toward shore, and waved his hand. The lone seaman waved back. "Bonjour monsieur Augustin!"

"Patrice! Mattie!" came his far off voice.

The seaman's boat tugged up to shore and Patrice grabbed the front to hold it steady. A man in sandals, board shorts, and a T-shirt stepped out of the boat. He was slightly shorter in stature to Patrice, but a hair taller than Mattie. He had messy blond hair, which stood up from all angles. It must have been the weekend look for this gentleman—although it could have passed as an everyday look, in the bustling, cutthroat metropolis of Whistler. Patrice helped him drag the front of the boat so it securely rested on shore, then they shook hands and walked up to the fire. "Salut mon ami," the man I presumed to be Augustin, said casually.

Another Canadian Frenchy I see.

"Hey Augustin, have a seat," said Missy. Then she passed him over a plate of steaming eggs.

"Ohh! Merci! Zis looks great! A delicious creation from ze kitchen of Missy and Mattie I presume?"

Missy giggled and looked down modestly.

"Augustin!" said Patrice excitedly.

"Yes! Patrice!" mocked Augustin.

"This is Eevin, he arrived yesterday from ze States."

Augustin gave the genuine Whistler smile and extended his hand. "Nice to meet you..." He paused and frowned. "Eevin?"

I shyly nodded and shook his hand.

"Evan! It's Evan!" said Mattie.

"Oh! Eevin. Okay," said Augustin. "Nice to meet you. Welcome to our home. Are these hooligans treating you well?"

"Absolutely, I feel like I'm in a five-star resort."

"Good!" said Patrice. "Only ze best for Couchsurfers."

"Oh, a Couchsurfer," said Augustin, "zat's really cool—and brave. What if we were all axe murderers?"

I thought for a second. "If you all were axe murderers and killed me, I would die happy, because of how much fun I've already had."

"Ahh!" came the amused reaction from my hosts.

"Plus," I continued, "judging by Mattie and Missy's culinary abilities, I would be confident that they would cook me up into some delicious meal."

"Eww!"

"Zat's disgusting, yet strangely appetizing," said Augustin as he plopped a forkful of steaming eggs into his mouth.

We relaxed and conversed a bit longer until Augustin finished his eggs. "So," he said, putting his plate down, "on to ze main event, eh?"

"Yes!" said Patrice as enthusiastically as always. "Bring ze fishing poles, maybe we can catch some real fish!"

We put our plates and forks into the magic bin. I peeked inside and wondered. *Maybe it'll wash everything for us while we're gone.* Then Augustin, Patrice, and I headed toward the boat. Mattie and Missy walked to the Vanetron and began to take down the canoe from the roof. "We'll meet you out there!" said Mattie. The three of us piled into Augustin's boat and the engine sputtered to life.

As we putted away from shore, different elements of my surroundings revealed themselves to me. Like the farther we got into the lake, a snowy peak presented itself, which had been looming over us behind the campsite. To the side of the lake there were large, dramatic cliffs that fell into the water. Tall pines rested on top of the cliffs, but some grabbed onto the sides of the rock. Their roots were spread out, desperately reaching into any rocky crevasse they could find. The water had an emerald-green shine, which was illuminated by the strong sun that was beating straight down onto it.

We stopped in a central spot on the lake. Patrice grabbed his fishing pole and Augustin grabbed one from the floor of the boat. In unison, they cast out on either side, then leaned back to get comfortable, letting out a relaxing sigh. "Ahhhh..." Then there was silence. We all sat in a meditative state. Augustin and Patrice watched their lures, while I slowly turned my head, observing it all. Mattie and Missy gently paddled by on their canoe, looking to be in their own state of serenity.

Patrice broke the silence by reeling in his empty lure. "What do you think, Eevin? Pretty nice, yes?"

"Pretty nice?" I said incredulously. "That's a gross understatement."

"Yes, yes you are right." Patrice shook his head and smiled. "Zis is good, because I want to show you a great time while you are here."

"Thanks Patrice, that's a very gracious gesture. I don't know why I would deserve it, but—"

Patrice held up his hand. "Let me tell you, Eevin. On my travels, no matter where I went—Ghana, Morocco, Italy, Israel, Jordan, Ukraine—wherever—and I went to many more then those. Wherever I was, if I was Couchsurfing, I was treated like a king. My host always made sure zat I was having ze best possible experience they could offer. So I promised myself to make sure zat anyone I hosted would receive ze same hospitality zat was given so graciously to me. It is like, how do you say? Karma."

"Thank you." That was all I could think to say. I was speechless. I couldn't believe this person whom I had known for not even twenty-four hours, was so committed to making sure that my experience was an exceptional one. And he had felt so strongly about it because he was treated so beautifully during his time traveling.

Patrice got me closer to the root of my answer about what was motivating Couchsurfers. He first reinforced my theory of Couchsurfers having different reasons for hosting. Patrice differed from Devina. There was no question his approach was more personal (no doubt due to the fact that he wasn't running a "hostel"). Then he added the element of— "how do you say?"–karma. He was treated so well by so many different kinds of strangers, that he had been trained to love humanity. And now he was trying to share that love and openness with another stranger. He did all of this for zero monetary (or any other type of) gain, save for fostering a new relationship. It was so damn beautiful that I had to stop myself from tearing up.

Each of us took a few turns casting with no luck to be had. Mattie and Missy paddled up to our boat and we put down the rods. "I'm sorry guys," I said. I may have brought the good weather, but I've been known on this trip to scare aware the animals."

"Zat is okay," said Patrice. I have a better activity. A mischievous smile wiped across his face as he pointed up to a cliff on the side of the lake. "Who is feeling lucky?"

"I thought you'd never ask!" Mattie smiled.

"Mattiiiieee," Missy's "concerned significant other" voice came out, "you promised no more of this."

"I promised nothing."

"Full speed ahead!" said Augustin as he started the engine and pointed the boat toward the ominously inviting cliffs.

I knew what plot was afoot, even though it wasn't outwardly spoken. I got the same feeling in the pit of my stomach that I always got when these situations arose. It was the feeling of uncertainty that I was either heading toward wild fun, or impending death. The cliffs grew taller and monstrous as we drew closer. When we were twenty yards from the rock, Augustin turned off the engine.

"Okay!" said Mattie, and he threw off his shirt. The rest of the boys followed.

Missy sat looking concerned and defeated. "Mattie, wait!"

Too late. Mattie dove into the water.

"Missy, I assume you will be manning ze boats?" asked Augustin as lightly as he could. Missy folded her arms and let out a sigh. "Thanks!" and Augustin jumped in.

I looked at Patrice and he gestured his hands toward the water. "After you my friend!" I nodded and jumped in.

Shocking yet refreshing was the feeling I had. I could barely breath, which was, in fact, a good sign. When it got below a certain temperature, I couldn't breath at all and a transformation would start to occur, trying to turn me into a breathless mannequin. At that point I would need to seek land fast, before I fully transformed and sunk like a stone. I followed Augustin's path. Ahead I saw Mattie already climbing out.

I reached the cliff's edge and followed a climbing path, which had clearly been taken before. We were not pioneers of this fruitful yet treacherous land. This idea gave me comfort to know that others had braved this terrain—however there were no signs that confirmed survival. Mattie had scrambled up like an amphetamined adolescent anthropoid, while Augustin was more of a selective sloth, carefully choosing his hand and foot holds. I copied Augustin. A root led to a rock step, which led to a branch, which led to more rock holds. I made sure that every hold was solid and secure before I trusted it to support my weight. "Take your time Eevin!" called Patrice from below. "No reason to rush, I cannot have my Couchsurfer die on me! Haha!"

"Thanks Patrice! You're so reassuring!"

I made it to the top and saw Mattie and Augustin standing proudly on a flat, natural platform carved by the rock. They were deliberating as they looked down and pointed. I walked over and had to stop myself from walking straight over the edge, which abruptly revealed itself only inches from where Mattie stood. I looked over and my organs made a quick dash northward, clawing their way up my torso to get away from this sight of a drop, that looked infinitely higher from here than from down below. "A good forty to forty-five footer," commented Mattie. "Pretty decent size." Augustin laughed trying to keep composure, but I could hear the nervousness in his voice. Patrice walked up and his eyes grew wide. He mumbled some French words to himself that probably translated to, "Jesus Christ almighty, may God have mercy on our souls."

I ignored the drop for a second, and instead looked up at the view. A crown of snowy peaks had revealed themselves around the glistening lake. I wanted to peacefully engross myself in this heavenly view forever, but Mattie took me back to the reality I was reluctantly excited to be in. "It's a clear jump, but it's always good to propel yourself out just to be safe. It gets deep very quickly." A resounding gulp and a nod passed through the crowd.

Missy sat motionless looking up at us: a little body in a little canoe. Behind her were the rafters who were fixated on us as well. I could see one or two people taking pictures, and a few more with video cameras in hand, ready to role tape. "Ladies and gentlemen, welcome to the afternoon event at Green Lake! If you look to your left you can see some Whistler locals getting ready to do what they do best, which is something daring and stupid. Let's hope they don't die folks." I was sure the raft guides were saying something along those lines. At least I hoped that the "Whistler locals" part was added for my benefit. I would die happy *and* as a local.

"Who's first?" asked Mattie.

...Silence.

"Okay, pull my arm why don't you." Mattie took in a relaxing breath and wound up. Before he jumped, I noticed a tattoo on his shoulder. It was a skier, whos skis pointed downward and crossed in an X—or an "iron cross" as it's called. And growing out of the skier's back was a pair of great expanding wings, which implied the skier to be in flight. I watched the tattoo disappear as Mattie took off over the cliff. He slowly formed a gracefully perfect swan dive, heading fingers first into the glimmering water. The tattoo fit Mattie perfectly. He was a true "ski bum:" a lover of the mountains and all the excitement and dangers it had to offer. I envied this love, this lifestyle. It was beautiful, and heroic, and simple. It was pure. So incredibly pure.

Mattie made a small, elegant splash and we all held our breath. Then he popped his head out of the water, shook some beads off his face, and let out a quick, yet jubilant, "Woo!" A resounding applause came from the rafts. Missy sat, arms crossed.

Then there were three...It was apparent that Mattie was the leader and for a brief time we all looked at each other, nervous and dumbfounded. *What the hell do we do? Our leader just jumped off a cliff! But thus was the point of this ridiculous game.* It went back to the age-old question/rebuttal that a mother asked, regarding the mischievous friend. "But if Mattie jumped off of a cliff, would you?" Naturally it is a rhetorical question. But what all you kids don't realize, is that the real answer is, "depends." And in this case it is, "Yes, but there's no way I'm going to do a swan dive."

Patrice was the next victim to step up. "Okay Eevin, if I die, it is your responsibility as a Couchsurfer to notify my mother." I laughed nervously, unsure of how to answer that. Patrice peeked over the edge, then stepped back, breathed a few deep, loud breaths, and launched off. There was no graceful swan dive. He flailed his arms, yelled "Merde!" halfway down, and hit the water with a resounding splash. He surfaced shortly after and let out a triumphant sound. "Yeah!" yelled Mattie, who was treading water to the side.

I looked over at Augustin. He looked a little green. "Go ahead, I'm in no rush," he said. I nodded in acceptance. The time came to meet my maker. I walked to the edge and peaked over. It looked a thousand feet higher than before. But this was no time to clam up, or think too much. The more you thought, the longer you waited, the longer you let the fear build up. I zoned in to see if I could spot any rocks by the water's edge, in case there was a required distance that I needed to make sure to clear. There were no rocks in sight, but I knew to propel myself forward as much as I could, just to be safe. I stepped back and the next (and last) thing to focus on was jumping. A running jump was one of those things that is done a million times, and without any reservations. But when your life depends on it, a second is taken to make sure it will go off in precise fashion. I looked forward and calculated how many steps it was going to take, and which foot I would launch from. *One step left, one step right, then launch at the edge with my left. Okay. That was all of the necessary thinking. Focus. Breath in, breath out, breeeeeeaaaath in, go!*

And I was in the air. Nothing but sparkling water below me, far, far away. When jumping in the air, there is a certain amount of time that your body is used to freefalling for, before it braces for impact. It is about 0.91 seconds. But if there is no impact, the body starts to panic and gets confused as to why it's still freefalling. It was 0.92 seconds when I started screaming and flailing my extremities. I was in the air for another full second before I was under water. The extra second was enough time to put my body in a panicky state, but before it could all be processed in my brain as impending death or excruciating pain, I was resurfacing and gasping for air. A sudden feeling of excitement and pleasure (which is the dictionary definition of "thrill") hit me, and I let out my own triumphant sound. "Yeeeow!" And I swam back to the water's edge.

Patrice was waiting for me, sopping wet and grinning like a giddy child. He held onto a branch and held his other hand out to help me up onto land. "Was zat fucking crazy man or what?!"

"Wow that was high!"

"Hoohoo, woooooo!" Patrice screamed.

We stood there and watched Augustin jump, followed by Mattie who did another olympic-caliber swan dive. Then we scrambled up again and did another. The same nervous feeling came to me when I was about to jump, although this one came with a bit more ease. Two jumps were good enough for me and I swam back to the boat. From there I watched Mattie and Patrice go again.

Missy would tense up when she saw Mattie jump. She had nothing but tender love for her man. "That stupid bastard has really perfected his dive." She admired him too.

I reclined on the boat and let the warm sun dry me as we waited for Patrice and Mattie to swim back. Everyone climbed onto their respective boats, laughing and shaken up by the aftereffects of the thrill.

Augustin was the first to speak. "Okay, I need to drop you guys off and head home to get ready for tonight. Are you guys coming?"

"Ah yes!" said Patrice. "I almost forgot about ze dinner! I will be there. Can Eevin come too?"

"Yes, of course," said Augustin without hesitation. "Everyone is welcome. Mattie? Missy?"

"No, thank you, we have stuff going on," said Mattie.

"I'd love to," said Missy, "but I'm doing a catering event up at the summit lodge tonight."

"No worries," said Augustin, "next time, eh?"

Patrice turned to me. "I had forgot Eevin, Augustin is having a big dinner at his house. I think a lot of my Quebec friends will be there. Is zat okay?"

No, that sounds horrible, why would I want to eat lots of food, drink, and laugh with lots of new people? "Yeah, that sounds fine." My new event manager was executing his job with flying colors.

Augustin dropped us off at the campsite and putted away across the lake. After we packed up the site and strapped ourselves back into the Vanasaurus, Mattie drove us across town. We passed Whistler Village and Mattie took the next left turn which led us up a hill into a neighborhood of condominiums. We were still in resort territory, because above the condos I could see ski trails. These were the condos that people rented in the winter, which were known in the real estate world as, "Ski in, ski out." This was because the condos were touching the ski trail, so in the morning you could quickly finish checking your stocks, then walk out of your backdoor, put your skis on, and get right onto a trail down to a chairlift. Then at the end of the day, you can ski right back to your humble abode, and walk in to enjoy a glass of wine and hors devours, while finding out what the market closed at.

Mattie dropped us off in front of a multi-story condo complex. Before Patrice and I got out of the Man Van, Mattie turned around and extended his hand. "Evan, it was very nice to meet you. Good to have you along. I hope you enjoy the rest of your time here."

I shook his hand. "Thank you Mattie, that was such a fantastic time. You guys are real camping professionals. I can't even express my envy."

"Thanks," said Missy, "we try. Nice to meet you. Bye Patrice."

"Goodbye my friends!" said Patrice. "Another perfect camping trip comes to an end. Until ze next one!"

We got out and Mattie sped off. I followed Patrice into a building and up a flight of stairs. He turned his head as we walked. "Before we get to my flat, I want to let you know zat my roommate Claude, he is a little unsure of Couchsurfing."

I nervously looked at Patrice, bracing myself for what would follow this statement. "Uh huh?"

Patrice shrugged. "It should be fine though. Once he gets to know you, I am sure he will not be so nervous. But he is protective of his stuff, so he has a rule zat you are not aloud in ze house when we are not there."

"Oh, okay, that's totally fine!" I said relieved. "I thought that you were going to say something like, you needed to smuggle me in and if he found out I was staying there, he would kick me out, or kill me, or something."

"Haha! No, not zat bad."

I had not yet been confronted with this element of Couchsurfing. I was a veteran—or part of the "club" as Devina said—at staying in a Couchsurfer's house. But this was a new concept of staying in a Couchsurfer's house, who had non-Couchsurfer roommates. With all of the freedom I was given with Couchsurfing, it did not occur to me that some freedoms could be taken away. I needed to abide by the specific rules of the household, and in this particular case, as it states in section 8.2b on page 55 of the Patrice Couchsurfing Rulebook:

> 8.2b: Any Couchsurfer residing inside said premises, will not be permitted to occupy said premises, while either the Couchsurfing host (Patrice Kirouac) and/or the host's roommate (some dude named Claude) is/are not present in said premises.

This meant that I could not sit alone, relax, and watch TV all day (which one could easily do in their hotel room) unless I was permitted to do so by my host. Although I imagined that it would have been strange in any Couchsurfing situation, if the guest wanted to sit around and watch TV. "Hi! I just traveled halfway across the world to sleep on your couch! Do you have HBO?" Even though this gave me a certain restriction of when I could be in the house, I wasn't worried about it. What I *was* worried about, was meeting this man, Claude. *Who is this guy? Am I going to be staying with someone who's going to be uncomfortable with my presence?*

We walked up a flight of dull, concrete stairs and made it to a hallway with a few doors. Nothing was in the hallway. No doormats, no potted plants, no tacky "welcome to our home" door ornaments. "Most of these places are rented out to vacationers," said Patrice. "It is very quiet in ze off season." *That explains the lack of character. There's no one around.* "But when ze snow is here, zis place gets fun. Especially when you get some crazy college kid neighbors on spring break. Oh man it gets loud and crazy!"

"Do you ever party with them?" I asked.

"Ha! Noo. Well," Patrice paused, then admitted, "maybe a couple of times."

We stopped at a door. "Zis place is okay," Patrice continued. "Not as cool as Mattie's or Augustin's house, but it is convenient because Claude and I work at ze resort."

"What do you guys do?" I had been waiting for an opportunity to ask this question.

"I work on a paint crew. We touch up different buildings during ze warm months. Claude works for ze lifts ops—chairlifts."

"Oh," I nodded. "So you don't paint in the winter?"

"No," he said.

I paused for elaboration but it never came. "Sooo, what do you do instead?"

Patrice shrugged, then said casually, "I do not know, it is still ze summer. I have a lot of time to decide." Patrice opened the door and walked in. I stood for a second, digesting what he just told me. *I need to ponder that for a while.*

I stepped into a good-ol'-fashioned bachelor pad. The living room was untidy, but not dirty. There was a couch, a plant, a half-empty aquarium, and a TV. Adjoining the living room was the dining room with a table. Some papers that resembled bills were strewn across it. The living room and dining room were essentially the same room. Not too large, but enough space for two (plus an occasional guest). Branching from the dining/bill paying area was a small walk-in kitchen.

Sitting at the dining room table was a muscularly large fellow who looked in his mid-thirties. He wore khaki shorts and a tucked in collared shirt. He looked up at us and at first appeared big and mean with the apparent inclination to want to throw me out the window. I held my breath. Then he let go of any strain in his face and gave us an exaggerated smile. He got up and walked over. "Heey! You must be ze Couchsurfer!" he said it almost *too* enthusiastically. I shook his stalky, bone-crushing hand. "I'm Claude! Nice to meet you!" His accent was similar to Patrice's.

"Zis is Eevin," said Patrice.

"Eevin?" confirmed Claude.

I nodded, "Yes, Ee—uhh, Evan. Nice to meet you too. Thank you for letting me stay here."

"Yes, of course!" He looked over at Patrice and said, "My pleasure."

I couldn't tell if this man was genuine, or if his intention was to snap my neck in the middle of the night. He was the first person that I had met in this town who didn't have the unthreatening, disheveled, yet delightfully earnest look, which I had gotten used to at this point. *I wonder if he's judging me as much as I'm judging him.*

Claude spoke to Patrice in French as I stood and blinked. *Great, speaking in code in front of my face.* "Oui, oui," said Patrice.

"Okay Eevin," said Claude as he headed toward the front door, "I need to go out to ze store. I will be back later and we will go to Augustin's. Nice to meet you!" And he left. I listened to his beefy body barrel down the stairs.

Patrice commenced the grand tour. "Okay, so ze kitchen is there, ze bathroom is back there behind ze front door, and zis is your couch!" He pointed to the couch in the living room. It was a fine, faux-leather sofa which looked barely long enough for my feet to prop up on the armrest. "I hope you do not mind," said Patrice, "but I have had a crazy weekend and I think I need to take a nap if I want to be alive at Augustin's tonight. You will not give me a bad reference if I take a nap, will you?"

I laughed. "No Patrice, that is totally fine. I'm not impartial to taking a rest myself. I've had a crazy month."

Patrice laughed and patted my shoulder. "Yes my friend! I know what you mean. Traveling is a whole job in itself!"

Ain't that the truth.

Patrice retired to his room and I stood in the middle of his living room alone. I put my bag down next to the couch in a spot that was out of the way. I took out the Chuck Palahniuk book that I had bought in Seattle and looked around the room. The most attractive part of the condo was a small porch outside the living room, separated by sliding glass doors. I walked out to find a little table with an ashtray and two camping chairs with an empty beer can in the chair's cup holder. The view was a sloping grove of pine trees that rose above the building, shrouding the apartment in shade. These trees must not have permitted much direct sunlight at any time of day. But the air was warm at this mid-day moment and the shade created a nice even temperature. I sat down in a camping chair. The pines relaxed me and I had no desire to move for a while...

"Eevin! Eevin!" I batted my eyes open. Patrice stood above me with a smiling bearded face. I was sitting in the same position in the camping chair, on the porch, with the book resting on my chest. It was still light out but I had no way of knowing how much time had passed, because the shade from the trees made the light look exactly like it did when I dozed off.

"Hey, are we leaving soon?" I asked.

"Oui, oui. Claude is going to drive us. He is taking a quick shower."

Oooh, a shower! I had forgotten about hygienic activities such as these. I hadn't done anything that resembled hygiene since some time in Vancouver. Between that time, I swam in a salt water ocean and a fresh water lake, ate greasy food while getting blissfully shrouded by a smoky fire, and slept on the ground. I hoped that I didn't smell too badly without realizing it. The judgments and rumors could have been running rampant. "Have you met Patrice's visitor yet? He's some *dirty* Couchsurfer. Who knows what nasty hole he's crawled out of."

I managed to get a quick shower in and no more than ten minutes later I had a fresh body, fresh breath, and fresh clothes on. It was a good thing I packed my special occasion eveningwear: shorts, a T-shirt, and Birks. Patrice looked similar. Claude had a button down tucked in shirt and his hair was combed. He had us beat in both strength *and* style.

I stuffed my dirty clothes under my bag. Then I put my toiletries back in the bag's top pocket, which I planned to take out and put back every time I used them. Putting in this effort was not as necessary at Devina's, where I had my own room. But now I was residing in a common space. My goal was to leave as few indications as possible to show that I was staying there. This was the mark of a good guest, but was also a good metaphor for life: Don't leave a fucking mess.

The three of us headed downstairs and out to the street where Mattie had dropped us off. Claude excitedly turned to me. "Hey Eevin, do you like cars?"

No, but I'll humor you. "Yeah! Definitely!"

"Okay then get ready for zis."

We walked across the street and up to a red Alfa Romeo sports car convertible. "Pretty nice, eh?" boasted Claude. "Do you know Alfa Romeo?"

As a matter of fact I did, only because Torino, Italy (where I studied abroad) was where the Fiat headquarters were, and Fiat owned Alfa Romeo. I was able to humor Claude, telling him about how I had toured the factory.

"Oh wow!" he said in that ambiguously genuine, overenthusiastic tone. "I would *LOVE* to go see where those cars are made! Then maybe test-drive some Ferraris or Lamborghinis? You know what I'm saying?" He made a "nudging" gesture with his elbow.

I shook my head. "Yeah! Definitely!"

We drove down the hill and back onto the main road. Claude made some quick gear shifting maneuvers to demonstrate his exceptional automobile prowess, as we cruised top down, past the resort. "Pretty sweet action, eh?"

I shook my head. "Oh yeah!" I wasn't going to break it to Claude, but fast cars didn't exactly get me "wet." Claude had let me sit in front, to get a feel for the "sweet action." I looked back, and Patrice looked as disinterested as I would have looked, had I decided to show it.

"Hey!" shouted Claude. "Do you like golf?"

Oh God, I don't know how much more I can fake. I couldn't find the strength to humor him as much as before. "Um, kind of, I don't play too often."

"Cool! Want to know what I did last summer?"

Is he even listening to me? "Sure, what?"

"I traveled across Canada and played golf in ten golf courses, in ten provinces, in ten days."

I gave my first genuine response. "Really? That's awesome!"

"Yes, and now I'm in ze Guinness Book of ze World Records!"

"Wow! Congratulations!" I really was impressed.

"Claude is a maniac!" said Patrice.

Claude nodded with a proud grin.

I started to reconsider my first impressions of this burly, clean-cut fellow. Maybe he was being genuine. Maybe he was just a *really really* enthusiastic guy. At the very least he had gained some newfound respect from me. I didn't know many people who would travel across a continent in ten days, just to say that they could play golf in every province. I somehow doubted that he had broken any previous records. Maybe he did it for the experience. Or maybe for the sole bragging rights of being in "Ze Guinness Book of ze World Records."

After a quick stop to pick up wine, we eventually made a right turn onto a road that landed us in a quaint neighborhood. We turned onto a street with more beautifully individualistic houses and I could see behind them and through pine branches, some brief glimpses of glimmering water. To fully explain the beauty of this neighborhood, refer to my description of Mattie's neighborhood, and insert a lake in the backyards.

We reached a cul-de-sac and parked by a house with a full driveway of cars that trickled out to the street. Most of the cars I noticed were Suburus, or small trucks. All were vehicles that were prepared for any weather condition that Mother Nature was in the mood to dish out (except for Claude's car but I was sure that he was somehow fully prepared as well).

The house appeared to be one story. It was a modest brick ranch style with a little stone path wrapping around to the back. We took our wine bottles and walked on the path, around to the side of the house, which led to some wooden stairs downward. This revealed another story below. From the back, the house was two levels. The top level, where we walked from, had a large porch. A bar be cue sat with smoke rising from it, and there was a long table set up with mismatched plates and silverware. The whole back wall of the house was made up of windows that looked out onto the lake, which was clear as day from this vantage point. These stairs continued down to a small dock where Augustin's familiar boat sat in the still water, resting from its eventful day.

We turned toward the floor below. A sliding glass door was open and a group of people stood inside with beer or wine glasses in hand. I walked into a wall of French sounds and a bouquet of delicious culinary smells. There was a mix of males and females, all attractive and fit, ranging from mid-twenties to mid-thirties. People were greeting Patrice and Claude and they all got sucked into the French blob. Before I was too overwhelmed, Patrice switched to "Evan-Language" and introduced me like always. "Zis is Eevin, from ze States." Everyone was welcoming and inquisitive. "Where are you from?" "Wow, zat is fantastic! Where did you drive?" "What brings you to Whistler—besides it being ze greatest place on earth, zat is. Haha!" All conversations were pleasant with nothing out of the ordinary as I gave them my schtick.

Nothing out of the ordinary, until I got to chatting with one pleasant fellow named Jean. "So Eevin, you said you were from ze States?"

"Yes. Where are you from?" I asked.

"I have lived here for a few years now, but I came from Quebec."

"Okay, what are you doing here?"

"I am a bartender at ze resort, but zat is not why I moved here. Where are you from in ze States?"

"Massachusetts."

Jean looked curiously intrigued. "Ooh! Boston!"

"Not exactly, but close."

"So are you a Bruins fan?"

I paused in shock. "...What?! A Bruins fan?" *Did I hear him right?* I let out a bellowing laugh and Jean gave me a confused look. "Did you say a Bruins fan?"

"Yes. Is zat strange? You know ze Bruins? Ze hockey team."

"Yes I do. But Jean, I have to be honest with you. Nobody has *ever* asked me if I was a Bruins fan."

"Really? Why not?"

"I've been asked a million times if I was a Red Sox fan, or Patriots, and sometimes Celtics. But never in my life have I been asked about the Bruins. Hockey just isn't as popular down there. But no, I don't think it's strange for you to ask me. In fact it makes a lot of sense. This is Canada and you all love hockey."

Jean nodded. "Zis is true, we love hockey. Do you play hockey?"

"No, I wish I did. Do you?"

"Of course, I am Canadian!" We laughed.

"I did play lacrosse, which is similar," I added.

"Ah yes, lacrosse is very fun. Did you know that it originated in Canada?"

"You don't say! Man, Canada gets cooler by the minute!"

A familiar fellow came over and interrupted. "Hey Evan, how's it going?"

"Hey Augustin! This is a great place you got here."

"Thanks, it's a good little spot. I'm here on my lonesome, so it is nice to have some people over."

"You have this whole place to yourself?"

Augustin chuckled. "No no, my job does not pay nearly zat well. Just zis bottom level is mine. I rent it from ze owners who live above. But zis is their vacation home so I don't see them too often. They give me a low rent and I act as their caretaker. Although zat doesn't involve much, besides refilling the bird feeder and taking their boat out on ze lake to go cliff jumping, haha!"

"Hell yeah!" I said and we slapped five. "That's a great deal!"

The space was small. A living room with a tiny kitchen attached (consisting of a sink, counter, stove, and cupboard), and a hallway in back that led to a bathroom and bedroom. I noticed that hung up on the wall of the living room were three pairs of rugged skis, each one with their own shape and trendy graphics. I pointed over. "Are those yours?"

Augustin nodded. "Yeah, I hang them up in ze summer, figuring it's free wall art. Come over, I'll show you." We walked over and he took each beautiful pair down from the wall, explaining to me which was used for what. "These are my early season skis—you know, before we get a solid base of snow. They're older and I'm not going to cry if I snag a rock or two. I also use them when I work, because I'm a ski instructor." He put them back and took the next pair. They were significantly wider than the previous pair. "These are my powder skis for those deep days. They keep me afloat, but aren't too wide so they stay maneuverable." Next pair: "These are my all around skis..." I stood and watched, eyes bulging and mouth uncontrollably open. I had to catch myself from drooling.

This guy was leading the perfect life that I wanted to lead: live by a beautiful lake, bar be cue with your friends, and ski in fluffy, pillowy powder all winter long at the world's greatest ski resort out your back door. I had entered some insane fantasy dream that I could not wrap my mind around. People weren't supposed to have this much fun with their lives.

Everyone started to move out of the house and up the stairs to the porch. Augustin walked over to the grill with a sizable platter of thickly cut filets of raw, juicy steaks. I put my wine bottle down on the table next to a half-dozen others, then grabbed an open one and poured myself a big glass, with no reason in the world to hold back.

A gorgeous girl with dark hair and eyes bluer than the sky, walked up to me holding a plate full of deviled eggs. *Goddammit I love devilled eggs!!!!!* She gave a big smile showing perfect white teeth, except for one front tooth which was a tad crooked, but it was no deterrent. In fact it was adorable. "Please, you have to try one." Her voice was calm and gentle. She was the devilled egg goddess who hath descended on me from the deliciously tempting land of devils and eggs.

"Oh, you don't have to tell me twice!" I said as I took one. "What is your name?" I asked.

"My name is Angelique. And yours?"

"Evan."

"Ah yes, Eevin. From ze states, yes?"

I nodded dreamily. "How did you know?"

"Patrice, he told everyone. You will have fun with him. He is a wild guy." She gave me a polite smile and walked over to another group, before I was given a chance to tell her that I could be a wild guy too.

I walked to the railing and looked out over the lake, munching on my devilishly good egg. The mustard and paprika were perfectly balanced to the yoke. *Magnifique mon amour, Angelique.* The sun was heading toward the crest of the mountains and a dark amber light was casted over the water, rocks, and pines. The air was perfectly still. It was a mirror image of yesterday's evening, except now we were on the opposite side of the lake, enjoying a glorious bar be cue on the back porch of a lake house. I felt like I was living the life of a millionaire, yet I had yet to find anyone who held a job that gave any indication that they came remotely close to hinting at a status of wealth.

We all sat down at the big table where every seat was accounted for. Someone walked up to the table with a full platter of steaming baked mushroom caps with melted cheese filling. That had to be what I was smelling when I entered the house. There were some "Mmmm's" and "Ahhh's" as the platter was set down at the center of the table. As the mushrooms were passed around, so was a long, fat joint, which as far as I could tell, everyone took a hit off of. That pure British Columbian bud hit me so smoothly and unobtrusively. After the hit, I cleared my palate with a sip of wine, in preparation for a mouthful of baked mushroom, with cheese that I was delighted to find out came from the venerably moldy family of blue cheeses.

"Okay guys!" said Augustin announcing from across the porch at his grill station. "Are we ready for steak?" More "Mmmm's" and "Ahhh's." "Also, is zat joint finished? Can somebody please help the grillmaster with zat?"

A great bowl of mashed potatoes was put down, followed by a long platter of asparagus, freshly plucked from off the grill. Lastly came the platter of steaks. There was enough for everyone to have their own piece. Soon I was looking down at a steaming plate of meat, potatoes, and vegetables. Everyone looked eagerly at their untouched works of art, begging to be devoured.

I'm no expert on French Canadian culture. But if I had to evaluate them by this meal, I would consider them to be a perfectly balanced blend between Europe and North America. We started European, with the plethora of wine and emphasis on the small, individual courses. Then the meal was capstoned by a big American piece of grilled meat.

Augustin sat down at the head of the table and lifted up his glass. "A la votre!"

Everyone picked up their glasses. "Ehh! A la votre!" We all reached in and clinked.

"To summer!" said Patrice. "It is officially here!" People nodded in agreement.

"It doesn't get better then zis," said Jean.

As we ate, most of the conversation around the table was directed toward how good life was for them. Patrice mentioned how fun camping was. Someone else asked who was interested in backpacking the following week. Another talked about a great mountain bike trail they had recently found. There were no complaints about work. In fact there was no mention about work, besides saying in passing, "Yes, I would love to take out ze kayak. My shift ends at three o'clock." Or, "My friend Dave who works at ze restaurant with me, knows a lot about bikes, so he can help you."

Aside from hearing them all talk about their fulfilling, action-packed lives, I was sensing a trend: Missy did catering, Patrice painted, Claude was a "liftie," Jean was a bartender, Augustin was a ski instructor... I had to get to the bottom of this. I leaned over to Patrice, who was sitting next to me. "Hey Patrice," I whispered.

"What's up?"

"Can I ask you something?"

"Sure."

"Do most of you have seasonal jobs?"

Patrice looked around. "Umm, yes I think so. Except Claude, he is a year round lift ops manager. And Dana over there, she works for ze Whistler Tourism Bureau."

"Um," I was embarrassed but I had to ask, "I hope you don't think this is a rude question, but do you all like your jobs?"

Patrice gave me an unaffected look, which I was relieved to see. He shrugged. "No, not especially. But you have to work, you know?"

"And you're okay with that?" I asked.

Patrice gave a confident shake of his head, then dipped a piece of steak in his mashed potatoes and popped it into his mouth. "Absolutely, if it means zat I get to live in a beautiful place such as zis." He swallowed, took a sip of wine, and continued. "I worked in Quebec City for five years at a desk in an office building. All day at ze computer." Patrice made a typing gesture with his hands. "And I made three times as much money as I make here. But I was miserable. So fucking miserable. And I think a lot of people here can give you ze same story. I think zat ze difference between us, and them in ze cities, is zat they live to work, while *we* work to live. Do you know what I am saying?"

I nodded in understanding. It made sense. But on the other hand it seemed like it wasn't supposed to make sense. Why would you spend the first majority of your life in school, then go and paint buildings for a living? There had to be some part of them that was unfulfilled. But if they were, I couldn't tell. Everyone was so happy, smiling, enjoying the company, enjoying the food, enjoying sitting out on a porch with a view of the lake. But how sustainable was this happiness? Augustin didn't have the freedom to use this porch at his free will. The owners of the house were nice enough to let him use it while they were back in the big city, making money to support their vacation home in the mountains. How long could Patrice and Claude live in a cramped bachelor pad together, crashing college parties when tourists came into town? I pondered this, then remembered what Patrice had said earlier. "It is still ze summer, I have a lot of time to decide."

We ate, drank, laughed, and "a la votre'd," as the view of the lake disappeared into the darkness of the night. Claude eventually gave the signal that we had to get going and Patrice agreed. Tomorrow was Monday, which meant back to work for all the painters, lift operators, front desk clerks, and the like. The fun had to stop some time for everyone (even me...eventually).

Under an abundance of unobstructed stars, we cruised back across town. The air was comfortable but just cool enough to give a slight chill with the top down. All the wine I had consumed had amplified my uplifted state, and I grabbed Claude and Patrice's shoulders. "Claude! Patrice! I'm having so much fun, thank you guys for letting me come, that was—oh man—that was so much fun, I love everyone I meet here!"

"No problem man," said Patrice, "our pleasure."

"Hey, would it be alright if I cooked you guys dinner tomorrow night?"

Claude and Patrice looked at each other, and Claude said something in French.

Uh-oh. Did I say something wrong? Something's wrong. I'm too drunk and I ran my mouth.

Patrice nodded. "Yeah sure, zat would be cool."

"Great! Because I owe you guys a lot, you really are treating me so well." I grabbed their shoulders again. "Thank you! This place is awesome!"

"Okay!" laughed Patrice. "You really liked zat wine, eh Eevin?"

"Yeah, it was really good."

We got back and I went to take my sleeping bag out of my pack to set up on the couch.

"Hey Eevin." Patrice walked up to me, looking a little nervous.

"What's up?"

"So remember zat I told you about our rule zat you can not be here when we are not here?"

"Yeah, no problem."

"I forgot to mention zat we get up at six o'clock. We will probably leave ze house at six-thirty. I am sorry but—"

"Okay, no problem," I said. "That will be good, because then I can have a full day to do stuff."

Patrice's worried face flipped around. He appreciated my optimism, which I could guarantee was genuine. I wasn't in Whistler to sleep—that was being saved for my grave. I wanted to take full advantage of the precious time that I had. "Okay man," he continued, "have a good night then. Do you need anything?"

"No, thank you. You've done more than enough my friend."

Patrice smiled and nodded. "Goodnight." He walked into his room and shut the door...

...As soon as I could tell that the house was quiet, I grabbed the laptop that was sitting on the table, grabbed an expensive watch, some DVDs from the TV stand, stuffed it in my bag, and ran out the door. Those suckers never knew what hit 'em.

Just kidding, I rolled out my sleeping bag on the couch and went to sleep.

DAY 25

I woke up in a dark room to doors opening, bodies shuffling, and toilets flushing. I was exhausted and it didn't help that my brain was pounding on the interior of my skull. I looked at my watch and groaned: six o'five. Curse the gods for warping a wakened mind! I wanted to crawl in a hole and die, instead of getting up to tackle a glorious day in Whistler, BC. But the last thing I wanted to happen was to have my hosts waiting for me while I dragged my hungover carcass around to get ready. I mustered up all of my energy, which was needed to peel myself out of my sleeping bag.

I rolled up my sleeping bag and tucked it behind my pack. After I got dressed, I sat back on the couch, waiting for the bathroom to free up. Patrice's door opened and he stumbled out in a groggy daze, dressed in a T-shirt and pants. His pants had various paint marks sloppily swiped across them. "Good morning—" his voice had a low morning tone, "—or good night, I do not know which one it is, it is too dark." He walked into the kitchen and I followed him. He took some items out of the fridge and started making a sandwich. "So Eevin, what are you going to do today? Me, I am going to go paint a wall."

"I was thinking of trying to mountain bike," I said. "Do you know of a place where I can rent one for the day?"

"I know a couple of places I think. But I have a bike you can use. Ze chain is a little screwed up, but it works."

"Really? Are you sure?"

"Yes, no problem. We can get it on ze way out. It is locked up downstairs. Do you need a bag to carry with you? For a water bottle or food?"

This was a good point I hadn't considered. My mobile home was easy to transform into a backpacking pack, but a mountain biking pack was a different story. "Yeah, I guess I do."

"Hold on," said Patrice. He finished up his turkey, cheese, and mayo sandwich, put it in a ziplock bag, walked into his room, and came back with a small daypack. "Here, use zis. Try not to get it too sweaty, eh?"

I took it and said—yep you guessed it—"Thank you." I should have kept a "thank you" tally on my trip. Maybe *I* would have gotten into Ze Guinness Book of ze World Records.

The three of us left the dark building to a brightening sky of navy blue. Some stars still shone, holding on tight before the sun managed to gather enough strength to loosen their grip. There was a chill to the morning mountain air. With that chill came a fresh, clean smell of pine, along with a general clarity that gave my body new life when I breathed in. "Okay, see you all later, have a good day!" said Claude as he turned and hiked up the street toward the resort.

Patrice opened a storage room door outside of the entrance and pulled out a worn-looking mountain bike. "Here you go Eevin, you just need to be careful because sometimes ze chain will back up in ze lowest gear. If zat happens, you need to stop, backpedal a little, and it will reset itself. Any questions?"

"Um, do you know where the trails are?"

Patrice laughed. "Yeah!" Then made a sweeping motion with his hand. "Everywhere!"

I laughed embarrassingly. *Of course.*

"But zat is not a good answer is it. There are some fun trails if you bike past ze village toward Lost Lake. They are easy to get to, I think there are signs for ze lake in ze village."

"Sounds simple enough."

"Do you have a water bottle?"

"Yes, I filled it up and it's in my—I mean *your* bag."

"Good, you are going to need it. I think it will be another beautiful, but hot day. My advice to you is to bike around ze lake, then swim in ze lake and check out all of ze beautiful ladies. I will be swimming there during lunch, around eleven if you want to join."

"Okay, I will plan for that... Wait, how will I find you?"

"Just go where all ze pretty girls are. Zat is where I will be. Okay, have fun, I must go before I am late. Ze world is relying on me to give a good paint job. God only knows what will happen if I do not make it in time!"

"You're right, I won't keep you any longer."

"See you at Lost Lake!"

Patrice was off on foot in the same direction as Claude. I was left with a mountain bike and a bag with my nalgene, my book, and my purple notebook with the Grateful Dead sticker on the front and the weed warning sticker on the back. I stood for a second, wondering if every Couchsurfing host came equipped with a bike to borrow.

I headed in the direction that Patrice and Claude had gone. The village was so large and built up that it was impossible not to find my way there along the roads and small paths. The village was quieter than when I had been through it two days ago, meaning I was practically the only person walking around.

As I searched for some enticing open eatery, I saw a group of adolescents gathered around the big tram building. I thought I was imagining this at first, because they were all dressed in winter gear. They had jackets, goggles, snow pants, hats, boots, and carried around snowboards and skis. I rubbed my eyes and blinked. Nope, I was still looking at a bunch of teens ready to go "hit the slopes." I looked at my watch to make sure that I had not accidentally passed out on Patrice's couch for six months. *Man, that wine was strong!* Then I looked up at the mountain to check that they did not miraculously receive a dumping of snow the night before. No, it was still summer and the slopes were still green.

Across from the tram building I noticed an open café and walked in. I went to the counter where a blond haired, blue-eyed, twenty-year-old goddess stood smiling. "Good morning, can I help you?" Her accent was distinctly Australian.

"Yes, I'll have a small orange juice and a blond Australian—I mean cheese danish."

"Sure thing mate, anything else?"

"No, but I have a question."

"What's up?"

"Do you know what all of those kids are doing out there?"

"Yeah, they're in the ski and snowboard camp, waiting for the tram to staat."

"Ski and snowboard camp? Now? But where—"

"Yeah I know. It seems strange right? But they go up to the glacia' at the top of the mountain where there is snow year round."

My eyes grew wide and I looked up at the mountain. "No way! Really?"

"Yeah, believe it."

"Can the public go up and ski?"

"Naw, it's just for the camp. That would be ripper though, hey?"

I had never heard of anything like that before. Those must have been some serious kid riders (with serious rich parents).

While waiting for my order and thinking about skiing glaciers, I noticed a stack of stickers down on the counter. It said "Winter Olympics, Vancouver, 2010." Under that there was a picture of a skier in some acrobatic form.

"You can take one." I looked up to the smiling Australian goddess holding my orange juice and a danish. "It's free."

"Cool, thanks!" I took the sticker along with my breakfast and sat by the window. I couldn't spare a minute before taking out my purple notebook with the Grateful Dead sticker on the front and the weed warning sticker on the back. I flipped the notebook over and placed the Vancouver Olympics sticker neatly above the weed warning sticker. It fit perfectly.

With that important task out of the way, I enjoyed my breakfast while watching the kids, who were heading into the tram building. A few minutes later I saw a packed tram exit the building, float up a cable, and over a ridge. At that point the tram vanished to some strange snowy land that I couldn't wrap my mind around.

I finished and headed onward out of the village with my bike. Sure enough there were signs pointing to Lost Lake. Onward I went, up a small hill lined with condos, and a left onto a dirt path. The hybrid, all-terrain, mechanical contraption under my body adapted to the dirt and rocks, while the front shocks absorbed all intrusions. It was a short path down a woodsy hill and it cleared out to the lake, which did not seem terribly "lost." I could almost see the roofs of the condos from where I stood. It was a small, round lake, significantly smaller than Green Lake and surrounded by a thick growth of trees. I was both disappointed and relieved to see that there were no cliffs to tempt my impressionable thoughts. I looked across the lake and spotted some faint images of mountain bikers whisping through the trees.

In front of me was a sandy, beachy, lakey place. Out in the water were some floating platforms to swim to. This welcoming, picturesque area was abandoned. No one seemed to have the desire to kick back by the lake with a few beers at seven o'clock in the morning. There was a small building with bathrooms and a snack bar next to me which also showed no sign of life. Whistler wasn't awake yet, except for a bunch of kids skiing on a glacier, and a lonely French Canadian painting a wall. I couldn't ski on a glacier, and I sure as shit wasn't going to paint anything, but I could damn well ride a bike! I saddled up and got ready for physical activity.

Mountain biking was going to be the most physically active event on the trip thus far:

Quick physical activity recap of the trip:
Day 1: Water skiing, Petoskey, Michigan
Day 2: Tennis match, Petoskey, Michigan
Day 7: Hike, Yosemite National Park, California
Day 10: Bike ride, San Francisco/Sausalito, California
Day 11: Kids soccer game, Santa Rosa, California
Day 17: Hike, Eagle Cap Wilderness, Oregon
Day 18: Hike, Eagle Cap Wilderness, Oregon
Day 22: Bike Ride, Vancouver, British Columbia
Day 24: Cliff Jump, Whistler, British Columbia

To my recollection, I did not brake a sweat, nor make myself short of breath while doing any of those activities. This was unfortunate, yet expected. Traveling did not lend itself well to maintaining an exercise routine (let alone any sort of routine). This meant that I was about to enter a world of pain, mixed with ecstasy, mixed with the fact that I had not gone mountain biking since I was twelve. But ready or not, I was going to conquer the world's greatest mountain biking destination...

...And conquer I did. My excitement fueled my adrenaline as I trudged up and down the narrow trails, over rocks, across wooden platform obstacles, and around tight corners. I was a natural born mountain biker. I fucked that shit up. I embraced the pain and exhaustion that came with my body's untrained state. I spit out wads of sticky mucus that my racing lungs were pumping out. I poured sweat and toxins out of my body like a wet, squeezed sponge (which mostly came out of my back and onto Patrice's bag—sorry Patrice). The mountain air helped keep my mind straight and my lungs functional. I traveled through dense forests with occasional breaks to stand at an opening and stare out at hundred-mile mountain views. The sunny heat boiled my already overheated body, but I was given relief by the engulfing shade of the thick pine forest. Before I knew it, I was back onto a path by Lost Lake and it was ten-thirty, which gave me enough time to settle in at the lake and wait for Patrice.

I was on the opposite side of the lake from where I started and I could see that the beach was densely inhabited at this point. I rode along the flat path that circled the lake, where I had seen the people biking earlier from my vantage point on the beach. On my biking adventure, I saw a handful of other bikers. Now that I was by the lake, I was passing by scores of walking couples, families, dogs with their owners, and leisurely bikers (tourists).

I got back to the beach and it became instantly apparent that I had stumbled upon the place where models chose to vacation. It was the Garden of the Gods, where all the sexual deities waited to be picked by the gods, who would come when they were feeling randy. While they waited, they sunned themselves and bathed in Lost Lake. This made me feel out of place, especially when I took my shirt off and blinded the world with my pasty, flabby chest. That is not to say that I am a fat, unattractive person. But I was clearly not fit for the Garden of the Gods. I brushed off that idea and put down my bag and my bike on a grassy area above the beach.

I spared no time before heading toward the glistening water. This was the perfect situation to swim. I had just overworked my body and was drenched with sweat from the physical workout under the sweltering sun. There was only one thing in the world that was going to transcend me into a state of balanced perfection and I was walking straight toward it.

I could hear my body sizzle as I submerged myself in the lake, which was significantly warmer than Green Lake. While submerged, my body temperature was eased down to normal. All of the sweat and accumulated dirt had loosened its grips and was released into the lake, soon to be dissolved by pure mountain water particles. All of this happened before I came up for my first breath.

Close by me, two bikini-clad deities stood waist deep in the water. They carried on casual conversation, most likely complaining about Zeus and Apollo fighting over them. I eavesdropped enough to notice that both had Australian accents, like the girl at the café. This was turning into a trend, but before I could investigate further, my cover was blown by a sneaky French Canadian.

"Eevin! Eevin!" I looked over at the shore where Patrice stood. He looked the same as when we parted in the morning, with a sweaty brow and a few additional paint swipes on his pants. He waved and I waved back as I turned to walk toward shore. But he held up his palm as the universal sign to stop, and he took off his shirt and pants, revealing a pair of swimming shorts ready to go. He marched into the lake with no reservations. Once he hit the water, the look that came across his face had matched the feeling I had gotten when I walked in. "Fuck man, zat feels good!" He walked up to me and dropped down to his knees so only his head poked above the surface. "How was your morning? Did you bike?" he asked.

"Yes, I went on all those trails back there. It was so fun."

"Oh, I am so jealous."

"How was work?" I asked.

"You know, saving ze world one paint stroke at a time. No big deal."

Without further notice, Patrice launched off and swam toward one of the floating docks. I followed, but he pulled ahead in a vigorous front stroke. It looked like he was making up for a lack of intense physical activity in the first half of the day. I wasn't lacking in that department and followed with a slow breaststroke. By the time I reached the dock,

Patrice was lying on his back, eyes closed, and chest heaving. I climbed onto the dock from a small metal ladder and sat down next to him.

I looked out at the lake with the dock lightly lapping up and down atop the windless water. Patrice stayed lying on his back, his eyes closed taking in deep breaths. I could feel the sun going to work at lifting the water from my body. Patrice must have been conscious of this feeling, sprawled out on the hot wooden dock. His body looked to be in complete comfort. Then he lifted his head and an eyelid, and took a glance at his watch before putting his head back down. He scrunched up his face in a look of frustration. "Fuck man, lunch breaks are too short." I chuckled like I knew what he was talking about, but in actuality, I had no idea. I had not experienced the necessity to work a shitty job just to pay the bills and feed myself. I was fresh out of college, where the only thing that I had to work on was how much fun I could have from one minute to the next. I was living in a dream world, which would soon end and reality was going to set in as fast as a hockey stop. The question was, where would that reality set in for me? Patrice decided to turn Whistler into a reality. I was experiencing first hand what it was like to live in it. He got a half hour lunch break from his shitty, meaningless job, but he got to spend it on a dock in the middle of a beautiful lake. I didn't know much about reality. College was not. My trip was not. But I learned enough on this trip to know that it could be a lot worse.

Patrice shot up without notice again and jumped back in, heading full speed to the other platform. I figured that he would lie there for a minute again and jump back in, most likely back to shore to scarf down his sandwich as quick as he swam. I headed back to shore and waited for him. He was in his zone and there was no point in following like some insecure sidekick.

Like I had predicted, he soon swam back and plopped down next to me, taking out his sandwich and scarfing away. He breathed out a large sigh as he chewed. "Did you have lunch?" he asked. I figured that he was talking to me, but he said it as he watched two girls in bikinis walk by.

"No," I said, "I will soon."

"Zat snack bar has really good burgers over there." He pointed to the small building next to the lake. "And a beautiful Australian girl takes your order."

I looked over at the girl he was referring to, then back at Patrice. "Really?"

"Yeah, she is super hot."

"No, I mean really she's Australian? I've noticed a few Australians today. Are there a lot here?"

"Oh yes—Aussies, Brits, Kiwis, they are everywhere—and all beautiful."

"Do you know why so many are here?"

"Because it is very easy for them to live here."

"Why is that?" I asked.

Patrice looked at me surprised, like this was general knowledge. Then he realized, "Ah yes, you would not know zis because you are American. All of ze countries under ze Queen are very easy to travel and live in."

"The Queen? Like of England?"

"Yes, exactly. It is easy to get visas. I do not think it is as easy for you in ze US to live here. I think it used to be easier, but George Bush made it hard for Canadians to live in ze US, so Canada said, 'Okay, we will make it hard too.'"

"How hard is it?"

"They make zis, how do you say? Catch twenty-two?" I nodded and he continued. "If you want to get a work visa, you need to be sponsored by a company here. But you need a work visa to be able to work here."

I thought for a second. "So you can't work without a visa and you can't get a visa without work?"

"Exactly. But not if you are under ze Queen. Then you can come much easier."

"How the hell does that work?"

"I do not know. But I do know zat there are not many Americans here. Zat is probably why." Patrice took the last bite of his sandwich. "I heard zat if you marry a Canadian, it is much easier. So," Patrice swept his hand out to all of the deities around us, "get to work!" We both laughed. "I need to get to work, so I will see you later. I will be back at my house around five."

"Cool! I'd still love to cook you guys dinner if that's okay."

"Yeah, Claude and I would love zat. We can take you to the market after work if you want. But now I have to go save ze world! Good luck finding a wife!" Patrice shot up and was gone.

I got up, went to the snack bar, ordered a cheeseburger from the beautiful Australian girl, considered asking her for her hand in marriage, chickened out, got my burger, and ate reclined on the grass. I felt like my newfound aspirations of moving to Whistler were crushed. I had to enjoy this brief dream while it lasted.

I finished my well-earned burger and laid out, watching the deities, imagining myself going up to each one of them, desperately falling to my knees, asking them to marry me, and envisioning their reactions. I sighed. I didn't have the courage to ask for a stick of gum, let alone marriage. But there must have been some other way. The thought of Patrice talking about Whistler being unattainable made me want it even more.

I got back on my bike with the intention to explore, maybe finding some hidden gems of bike trails, and if I was lucky, another lake full of Australian nymphs. I ventured back to the base area and rode out of the main entrance to the main road. I crossed the road and found a paved path that ran downward through trees and along some condo communities. The path continued past the condos and flattened out, turning into a common flat bike path. The path wasn't densely wooded and about a quarter mile down, opened up. Sure enough I was by another gorgeous lake. This was larger and had a perfect view of Whistler Blackcomb. It was the lake I had noticed when Patrice, Mattie, and I first drove out of Whistler Village. Without fail, more deities lounged and pranced about by a large grassy area in front of the lake. I stopped by a sign that said, "Alta Lake," with a large trail map below it. I found everything I had intended to find without making more than a twenty-minute effort on my bike. I wondered if heaven was anything like this: a casual bike ride to mountain lakes with lounging models.

I figured that I would try some of these trails until I worked up enough heat and energy to want to submerge myself again in a cool body of pristine mountain water. The trails that I picked did not go as smoothly as the Lost Lake trails, nor did I have the stamina that I had that morning. But my short ride was worth it due to a grove of brilliantly green, enormous maple leafs that I biked through. I could have covered my whole midsection with one of these prehistoric plants if I wanted. Canada was giving me some kind of signal to let me know that, "You are here, and you're not going to forget it." Then I made the mistake of touching one, and received a painful prick because the bellies of these leaves were covered in sharp thorns. "And don't think about fucking with us either."

When I sufficiently exhausted my body, I rode back down the hill and out toward the lake. I made my way through the divine garden of Australian accents and walked into the calm water. I stood waste deep for a while, lightly running my hands along the surface. There was so much to look at: the mountains, the water, the trees. At first glance it was those three elements, but I could have kept staring at each element endlessly and continued to find something new and stimulating.

As my sight was getting stimulated, I felt something else stimulating my toes. It felt like things were biting me, but I wasn't actually getting bitten. I looked down and saw a group of small fish the size of minnows. They were hovering around my feet, taking turns attacking them, but attacking was not the right word. Maybe snacking was more accurate. It felt like tiny suction cups were hitting the tops of my feet. They must have thought that they could get nutrients off of my sweaty, smelly foot glands. Once I was fully aware of the situation, I broke out in giddy laughter. I must have looked mentally deranged from the perspective of the three deities who were wading a few yards away. "Just a special grown man laughing at nothing, alone in a lake. Somebody should give him some floaties."

I continued staring at the beautiful scenery as I laughed hysterically from the tickling fish. I never thought that I could live in harmony with something that was trying to eat me, but it seemed to work out for both sides. It was what you would call a "symbiotic relationship." Eventually they seemed to have extracted all of the possible nutrients from my feet and swam on, to find the next sweaty, smelly food source. I got out and relaxed in the garden, taking in the rays from the tirelessly high sun. I took out my book from my sweaty bag of goodies and read (taking some swimming or deity-watching breaks) until it was time to head back to Chateau de Patrice and get ready for an evening feast, prepared by yours truly.

I got back at ten till five and waited for Patrice at the same spot where we had parted in the early morning. At ten after five, I spotted a paint-ridden body come marching up the road. "Eevin! You made it back!" Patrice sounded and looked more lighthearted than he did at lunch. By lighthearted, I meant normal, or the Patrice that I had known for the past couple days who loved to camp, cliff jump, and eat. The Patrice who painted contained more melancholy. "How was your bike ride?"

"Great! I went to Alta Lake."

"Ah yes! Another beautiful lake with beautiful girls."

"You seem to have a lot of those around here," I said.

Patrice smiled. "As life should be, eh?"

I smiled back. *Yes it should.* "Can we still go to the market?" I asked.

"Yes. Claude can take us when he gets back. We just need to wait for zat big ogre. He should be here soon."

We put the bike back and headed up the stairs of his building. "Hey Patrice," I said in my "get ready for another thank you" voice, "I know I've thanked you many times already, but this has been an amazing experience."

Patrice smiled. "Of course man, my pleasure."

"But I hope I'm not occupying too much of your time. Please let me know if there are other things you need to do."

Patrice nodded. "You are right, Eevin. And believe me, I would not do zis if I did not want to. But you are a cool Couchsurfer so I have no problem with it. I would have known not to bring you places after we went camping. And if you were a dickhead during camping, I probably would not have let you stay at my house. As a host, I have no obligation to help anyone who I do not feel comfortable with. But you are cool, and Claude likes you too, so I have no problem showing you all zat Whistler has to offer."

"Have you met any dickhead Couchsurfers?" I asked.

Patrice curled his eyebrows in thought. "Umm, not really. Maybe a couple of weird experiences. Like zis one time in Madrid, I surfed with zis gay man who lived in a one-room studio. And zat night he had sex with some random guy, while I tried to sleep on ze floor next to them."

"What did you do?"

"I pretended to sleep, and found another person's couch ze next night, instead of staying with him again." Patrice shrugged. "It was not zat big of a deal. Just a little too close for my liking. What is ze worst zat happens? God forbid you book a room at a hotel, right?"

I laughed. "Hotel rooms: for emergencies only."

Patrice laughed too. "You got it!"

We were up in Patrice's apartment at that point, and Claude arrived soon after. We spent little time in transition, and were out the door and back into Claude's sweet ride, with the top down.

We coasted out to the main road and turned right toward Green Lake. When we got to the Whistler Village entrance, Patrice, who was in the front passenger seat, spotted a guy on the side of the road with his thumb sticking out. He pointed at him. "Eh, Claude, l'auto-stoppeur." Without any discussion or pause for thought, Claude slowed and stopped next to the young man. He was in his twenties with stylish sunglasses and a neon tank top with a bright logo of a snowboard company on it.

"Where are you heading?" asked Claude.

"Just to Rainbow Station." His demeanor said anything but psycho killer.

"Hop in," said Claude, "we're headed past zat way."

The man got in the back and sat next to me. I was a tad nervous, but the whole Couchsurfing/road trip experience had done a good job of desensitizing me toward meeting any and all strangers at any given time, in any given circumstance.

"Thanks for the lift guys. Nice day, eh?" He sounded like a laid back surfer with a deep Canadian accent.

"Yeah man, are you coming from work?" asked Claude.

"Yeah, I work over at Dubh Linn Gate. I've been doing afternoons lately."

"Oh, cool," said Patrice, "do you know Joseph? He is a server."

"Yeah! Joseph's the best. What's your name?"

"Patrice, zis is Claude and Eevin."

"What's up guys? I'm Sabastian. People call me Sab. Did you guys get out and enjoy this sick day we had?"

"Yeah," I said proudly, "I got some good mountain biking in around Lost Lake."

"Sick! I love those trails—oh, right up here is good."

Claude pulled over.

"Cool, thanks a lot guys, Patrice, um, Claude and..."

"Evan," I said and extended my hand.

"Evan! That's right, nice to meet you all." Before shaking my hand, he reached into his pocket, then took his hand out and shook it. "Thanks a lot guys, I'll see you around, eh?"

And he got out. I looked down and a small nugget of marijuana sat in my hand. I laughed. "He gave us some weed!"

"Cool," said Patrice.

"Here," I said and handed him the nug.

"Thanks! I am sure I can find some use for zis." And we continued on as if nothing happened.

I had not been in many hitchhiking situations in my life, and I have never expected it to go as smoothly and nonchalantly as that. "I take it you guys pick up hitchhikers a lot?" I asked.

"Yes, all ze time," said Claude.

"I hitchhike everywhere," said Patrice. "In Whistler zat is. Maybe not so much in ze cities."

"You think Whistler is a lot safer?" I asked.

"Yes, of course. Zis is a small ski town. Ze only people hitchhiking are ze ski bums. And practically everyone who lives here are ski bums. If you are not, then you are probably a tourist—or a big rich guy. And I do not see rich guys hitchhiking too often. Unless their six SUV's broke down."

I never thought that such trustworthy places like these existed. I also noticed people didn't go crazy about locking their bikes, or houses, or cars. Theft didn't seem to be at the forefront of everybody's mind here. This was for good reason: It did not need to be. I was in a place of beautiful people, beautiful scenery, with endless outdoor activities, and no crime. What else do you need? I had never felt so in love with a place. I had to find a way to live here.

A five-minute drive in total, and we arrived at the small supermarket. It was time to switch energy to dinner for Patrice and Claude. I wasn't sure what I was going to make. I didn't know why, but I walked out of the store with baby scallops, pasta, squash, garlic, lemon, a bottle of wine, and a big loaf of bread. I wasn't sure how I was going to cook this, but I was caught up in wanting to give back to my host, who had generously showed me so much, which included a new way to live.

We got back to the condo and I went straight to work in their kitchen. I boiled the pasta, fried the scallops with some oil, put the squash in a baking pan with butter, stuck that in the oven, chopped garlic (enough for the sauce and bread), put the garlic in a saucepan with lemon and butter, mixed this sauce with the scallops, threw in the cooked pasta, cut the bread in half, scattered on the remaining garlic with more oil and butter, stuck it in the oven, popped open the wine bottle, then woke up and dinner was served.

Patrice and Claude had been sitting at the table on laptops, probably dealing with real life things. "Wow Eevin, this looks great!" "Yes, thank you Eevin."

We sat down and poured the wine. I raised my glass. "A la votre!"

"Ehhhh!" said my impressed French Canadian hosts. "He's learning!"

I kept my glass raised. "Thank you guys again. I know I've said it ten million times already, but this really was a special experience for me. This place is like nowhere else I've been and meeting all of you has been just as unique as Whistler itself."

"Thank you Eevin," said Claude. "I was not sure about ze whole Couchsurfing thing when Patrice brought it up, but I think zat it worked out very well. I mean, I can't complain about a free dinner! I probably would have eaten cereal!"

"Well I certainly I hope that this will taste better."

We started eating and I must give credit where credit's due. I hadn't considered myself a good cook, but my motivation to want to give back to my hosts had boosted some untapped culinary skill. It was like, how do you say? Karma?

Delicious food and wine led to delightful conversation. "Where do you go after zis?" asked Patrice.

"This is actually the end." I couldn't believe the words were coming out of my mouth. "I go back to Vancouver, then down to Seattle where I'll get a flight back to the East Coast." <By the way, I booked a flight back to Massachusetts at some point, but I spared the details. For all interested parties, here is a summary: I borrowed a computer, I went to a website, I compared prices, I booked a ticket, I felt sad. It was as exciting as it sounds.> "Speaking of that, do you have a bus schedule?" I asked.

"Bus schedule, what for?" asked Patrice.

"Um, to get back to Vancouver." I wasn't sure what he was asking. The question seemed obvious.

"Ze bus is a waste of time and money," said Claude. "Just hitchhike."

"Really? All the way to Vancouver?"

"Yeah, no problem. You go to zat place where we picked up zat guy Sab today, down at ze end of ze resort entrance. Go to ze other side of ze street in ze direction of Vancouver."

"You're absolutely sure?" I said.

"Absolutely man, people do it every day. It's the easiest thing to do around here."

"Okay, if you say so." I had learned today that local rides around this town merited sticking your thumb out to get to your five-minute-or-less destination—but we were talking about a two-hour journey to a city. Like everything else, I put my trust in it. *Hitchhike to Vancouver? Sure! I'm sold!*

Patrice's plate was clean. He looked like he was deep in thought as he grabbed the wine bottle and refilled his glass and mine. "How long have you been on ze road?" he asked.

"It will have been just shy of a month. But I felt like I've been going nonstop for years."

Patrice nodded. "A month is a good amount of time to be away from home. Long enough to feel like you are living, as opposed to vacationing, but short enough to be able to return to your normal life without much interruption."

"How long did you say you were traveling?" I asked.

"Two years."

"Wow."

"I stayed ze longest in certain spots for one month, but a week on average."

"Did you miss your home?"

Patrice weighed the question in his head. "Yes...and no. No because I was living a different amazing dream every day. Yes because sometimes I was tired of it. I wanted to stop moving and stay put, but stay put in a familiar place." Patrice furrowed his brow, like he thought of something that concerned him. "At one point I traveled to Morocco, where I got very sick. I was stuck in a bed for two weeks, only getting up to vomit or release diarrhea. I thought to myself, 'what a horrible choice I had made by traveling for so long.' I was so far away from any friends and family. Nor did I tell my parents about being sick, because I did not want them to worry. Then I started thinking about how foolish it was to be traveling and not working at my old, steady desk job in Quebec City. I could have been nice and healthy, sitting at my desk, with my family and friends close by. But instead I was sick, alone, poor, and vulnerable in a foreign country. I got a lot of anxiety."

Patrice took a sip and continued. "But I got better and marched on. And when I look back at ze whole thing, I do not regret it, except maybe zat it was too long. But when you travel, you are taking a risk and putting yourself out there to gain experience. And whether I was vomiting in a Moroccan toilet hole, too weak to bat ze flies off of my head, or swimming in a Mediterranean lagoon, I was involved in an unforgettable experience which will make me a stronger, more well-rounded person to inhabit ze earth."

Patrice looked back from me to his glass and took another sip. Everything he said was said seriously, like he was tapping into a hard memory. Then he smiled. "Morocco is amazing though, you have to go if you get a chance."

"I would love to," I said. "Maybe I will change my flight to Morocco instead of Massachusetts."

"Good idea! Let me tell you about zat time I arrived when..." Patrice went into a story about Morocco, which segued into other traveling stories that I was able to tell from my Europe trip, as well as this one.

Before we knew it, the wine was finished and it was past the painter's bedtime. Claude had said goodnight an hour prior. We said a brief goodbye and thanks, so I could get back to telling Patrice about how Wallace, Gill, and I had found the hot springs in Nevada. Eventually we had to cut ourselves off and head to bed.

"Unfortunately another early wake up for us, my friend," said Patrice.

I shook my head. "Not a problem." We said goodnight and I settled in for my last night in this enchanting world, before beginning my process of backtracking.

A long avoided deadline had been reached with my trip. I had a scheduled flight from Seattle to Hartford, Connecticut, leaving two days from now. I laid on their faux-leather couch in my sleeping bag, thinking about this new feeling. It was a feeling that had not entered my realm of thought in a long time: I was going home. Did I want to? Just like Patrice had said, "yes and no." I felt the need to never stop, to continue searching and exploring, to keep attacking my five senses with the foreign excitement of the unknown. But I did feel content. I had reached my goal to make it to Beautiful British Columbia, along with a multitude of other detailed goals in between. And like Patrice had said, I had these unforgettable experiences which I could keep as part of who I was. If I lived under a rock for the rest of my life, I still had this month to cherish in my mind. Although living under a rock was not a goal I had in life. I went to sleep thinking about the realistic possibility of building a cool house under a rock. *I could live there,* I thought, *but I'd rather live here.*

DAY 26

I woke up to nothing. I looked at my watch: five-sixteen. I closed my eyes again, knowing that I could get at least forty-five more minutes before life started to move in the house. But I knew that I could not fall back asleep. It was that feeling of waking up and the mind springs to life leaving you involuntarily awake and alert. No grogginess, no unavoidable desire to drift back into dreams. The floodgates of my mind had opened and were filling with the realities to come. Soon. Soon I would get up. Soon I would leave Whistler. Soon I would be on a plane back to where I started. Soon this would all be a fond memory. My sleeping bag was too hot so I wiggled out and laid on top. I kept my eyes closed and waited, and thought.

Eventually a muffled sound of beeping could be heard from another room. Then it stopped. A few more minutes of silence passed before the beeping started again. A body mass moved around, creaking the floors.

I got up and gathered my stuff. I put on my pair of shorts, which were noticeably smelling like I had mountain biked into a campfire. I rummaged through my bag for any clean clothing. All that I could find was a T-shirt. *So it goes.*

Patrice walked out the same as the previous morning, crossing the room like a lifeless zombie toward the kitchen. He finished his bag lunch and went back to his room as Claude came out ready to go. He looked like he was in a rush. "Have a good day, Eevin. See you later." He turned toward the front door, then caught himself and turned around. "Oh, you are leaving, eh?"

I nodded. "Yeah, pretty soon."

"You were just becoming a normal part of ze house!"

I appreciated that he expressed comfort with my presence, but I kept to a modest response. "Hopefully I can leave before that happens."

He extended his hand. "Great to meet you man, thanks for ze dinner last night. Please come back anytime!"

"Thank you Claude."

"I'm sorry, but I'm late. Good luck hitchhiking, don't get stabbed!" He laughed and I gave him an uneasy look. "Kidding! You'll be fine. Safe travels!" And like that, the Canadian golf legend was gone.

Patrice came out shortly after, prepared to paint the world. "Are you ready to go Eevin?"

"Yes, one second!" I zipped my pack and grabbed Devina's tent which sat idly by the corner of the couch. I slung my big red pack over my shoulder, and fastened my wicker cowboy hat on my head, for one last time.

We walked out and I followed Patrice up the hill toward the village. The sky was an ominously overcast grey. As we walked, Patrice grumbled to me about the pain in the ass paint job he was supposed to do today. I didn't think he had the specific intention of telling me. He was going to complain to anyone in his presence and I happened to be there. I guess it wasn't always sunshine and happiness in heaven either.

We got to a path that split. One way headed downward, the other way headed up. Patrice stopped. "Okay Eevin," he pointed down the path, "zat way will take you through ze village and out to ze intersection. I have to go zis way to get to work." Then he shook his head. "I am sorry you won't be around zis afternoon. A group of us play a round of disc golf every Tuesday."

I bit my tongue and thought I was going to have a nervous breakdown. *How could I leave Whistler without playing disc golf??* I spent a fraction of a second trying to figure out how I could spend another day here and still make it down to Seattle for my flight. *If I skip Vancouver, I can go straight to Seattle and—damnit I have Devina's tent! It's no use... Put down the crack pipe Evan.* "I'd love to," I said. "In fact I'd love to stay here forever. But for now I'll take a rain check. We'll play when I come back."

"Fair enough." He extended his hand with a smile. "Zis is where our paths diverge—until next time."

I shook the hand of my gracious Couchsurfing host, as well as a new friend.

"Patrice, I have one more thing that I've been meaning to ask you."

"What's up?"

"Your last name is Kirouac, right?"

Patrice smiled. "Yes it is. And no I am not related to Jack Kerouac. I get zat a lot."

"Okay, just making sure."

Patrice shrugged. "But I heard zat his parents were French Canadian, so you never know."

"Is that so..."

"Any other important questions? Unfortunately I cannot talk for too much longer."

I shook my head. "No, that's it. I won't keep you from saving the world. I think I've already said thank you enough."

"Like I said Eevin, karma. Just make sure to pass it on and do it for someone else."

"I will."

Patrice took the high road and I took the low road into the village. I was cut loose again from another safe haven and I was back to a lonesome traveler. However, if I was able to make it back to Vancouver alive without getting slashed up from hitchhiking, I would get another complimentary night with an old Couchsurfing compadre.

First I needed to fill my belly and break my heart again at the café in the village. Across from the café, the little rich kids were out, lounging with their snowboards, ready to go up the mountain and do what no other kid got to do in the whole northern hemisphere.

After getting my heart broken and finishing my meal, I walked out of the café and watched again as the tram station rumbled and the tram left the building packed with the kids. They headed up the mountain for their magical, unimaginable day on a glacier. I turned and walked the opposite direction, away from the mountain, away from the village, on my way to impending doom, or just a free ride to Vancouver.

When I made it out of the village by the bus drop off, I paused and took my bag off. I opened the top zipper and took out my knife that I had bought for five dollars in Nevada, and put it in my pocket. I may have been on a roll with trusting in my fellow man, but that didn't mean I could let my guard down.

At the end of the road was a traffic light, which was the spot where Claude had told me to go. Standing by a traffic light made sense because when people were stopped at the light, they had time to see the lonely, car-less individual, and have time to decide whether or not to pick them up. It was harder on a straight road, where they would have already been flying by and could not make a quick enough decision to slow down.

I looked across the road that I had to cross, to be in the right direction toward Vancouver. Low and behold, a man was standing there with his thumb out. *You have to be kidding me. There's a hitchhiking line?? So be it.* As I crossed the street, I pretended not to notice him, but I could tell that he was eyeing me. I was sure that he was thinking, *You have to be kidding me. I got competition?* When I got to the other side of the street, I turned to face the traffic. He stood thirty feet behind me. I put my bag down and stuck my thumb out, assuming that I was doing it right.

"Hey!"

Shit, is he yelling at me?

"Hey you!" I reluctantly turned. He looked at me sternly and pointed behind him. "Back of the line!"

Without thinking too much, I did what I was told. I grabbed my stuff and walked past him.

"Come on, dude," he said as I walked by, "first-come, first-serve."

"Right, sorry." That was stupid of me. It made sense. If someone stopped, they would have seen me first. He was there first, so he was supposed to get picked up first. Even hitchhiking had its rules.

We stood there and watched as car after car passed us by. I would get my hopes up when a car would stop at the traffic light. I would be too afraid to look them in the eye, but I tried to make my face soft and non-threatening, with a slight smile. Nobody stopped. Ten minutes passed. Twenty. Twenty-five. This was turning out to be useless. Either the high volume of two hitchhikers was overwhelming for these drivers, or this whole hitchhiking culture wasn't living up to its reputation. I thought back on when I had bought my bus ticket for Whistler. *Why did I only buy one way? I could have had an easy ticket in my hand and been on the road by now. What I need to do is drag myself back to the Village and find somewhere to buy a bus—*

Then something happened. The other hitchhiker gave a defeated huff. He turned his head and sneered at me, then stormed across the street. My spot in line was bumped up! This had to be a good sign. But my patience was still running low. I could have only waited for another five minutes before—*Wait, what's that truck doing?* It had its blinker on and was slowing down. When it passed me, it pulled up on the side. I was as nervous as I was excited. I looked over across the street where the defeated hitchhiker was standing and staring. *Sorry dude, you lost your place in line!* I ran up with my bag to the passenger window.

A friendly-looking middle-aged man in construction clothes rolled the window down. "Where you headed?" he asked.

"Vancouver."

He nodded. "Okay, I can take you about eight kilometers down to Function Junction."

I had no idea where he was talking about or how far that was, but it sounded good. I glanced back at the other hitchhiker who had already turned and was walking toward the village. "Okay!" I hopped in and we were off.

My driver looked big and muscular enough to have his way with me if he wanted, but I tried to put that thought aside. "Do you live in Vancouver?" He sounded a lot nicer than he looked.

"No, I'm from the states, just traveling around."

"Oooh the States, eh?"

"Yeah." I didn't feel like giving my shtick, but I did feel the necessity as the hitchhiker to strike up some kind of conversation. "Are you heading to work?"

"Yep. I'm a construction contractor. We're building a facility for the Olympics."

"Oh, that's cool. But they aren't for another two years, right?"

"Yeah, two thousand ten, but we've been building and planning for a while now."

"Really? It takes that long?"

"Oh yaah, it takes quite a few years to get ready to host..."

We talked about the Olympics for the rest of our ride, which lasted ten more minutes, before he dropped me off at another intersection. "Sorry I couldn't take you farther but you shouldn't have a problem getting another ride."

"Great, thanks a lot and good luck with the construction!"

"Thanks, best of luck to you, eh!"

It was a nice ride but he didn't bring me far. Neither was there an option, where he dropped me off, to get a bus ticket instead. But there was no reason to feel defeated yet. I stuck out my thumb with a little more confidence this time. And waddayaknow, as soon as my thumb went out, a beat-up sedan pulled over. This dude was about my age, and by the looks of him, snowboarded for a living. He rolled down the window. "Hey bro, I'm headed to Squamish. What about you?"

"Vancouver."

"Right on bro, hop in!"

I assumed that I was in luck again. This guy looked too harmlessly stoned to want to take advantage of me.

The conversation started out the same as before. Where was I headed, what was I doing there, visa versa. He lived in Whistler but worked at an outdoor outfitters store in Squamish.

"Sick dude, you're from the States, eh?"

"Yes."

"Are you from Colorado?"

"No, I've visited it though, it's very nice."

"You know what's my favorite part of Colorado?"

Hmm, let me guess. Snowboarding? "What's that?"

"South Park. You know that show?" he asked.

I laughed. That was like asking a Canadian if he knew what language they spoke in Quebec. "Yes I do! I love that show."

"Oh man, South Park cracks me up!" Then he started to sing the words to "Blame Canada." That got me laughing more, because he decided to quote the most insulting song toward his own country that South Park (or any American show) has created. "I love when they make fun of Canada."

"Really? You're not insulted?"

"Pfff!" He scoffed at my ridiculous question. "Hell no! It makes no sense! Does my head disconnect from my jaw?"

I nodded. "You have a good point there."

We ended up talking for the entirety of our forty-minute ride about how much South Park hated on Canada and how much this guy not only felt no insult from it, but was (better yet) wildly entertained. The way he talked made it seem like he represented the general sentiment of Canadians. It was accurate with the overall attitude that I had noticed in these people: laid back, lighthearted, genuine, and in this case, they had the humble gift of not taking themselves seriously. "If South Park wants to make fun of us, fine. We don't care." I found these to be admirable qualities. Canada was doing something right. They knew better than to get caught up in the "crazy shit" as Patrice had so eloquently put it.

I left the guy's car laughing, as he dropped me off at another intersection in Squamish. We each exchanged a friendly, "Later dude!" and parted ways to live out our own lives, never to cross paths again on this great earth, in this lifetime. If I was lucky, the next time we would run into each other would be as butterflies, and we would laugh again about our favorite South Park episodes while fluttering about in the forest.

I was close to where the bus had stopped on my way up. This guy (whose name I had never gotten) left me with high spirits. I knew that I would need one more easy ride to take me the rest of the way to the city, since there weren't many more opportunities to stop between Squamish and the Lion's Gate Bridge. Out my thumb went again and this time with a proud air of confidence.

Car after car passed with no more than a bat of an eye in my direction. My confidence stayed for a brief time before it turned to dismay. After twenty minutes, my thumb began to droop. The overcast clouds covered the sun and dropped the temperature to a level that I wasn't used to. The cool mountain air blew up my shorts and through my thin cotton T-shirt. I shivered in chilly fear, forgetting that mountain weather wasn't perfect all the time. In fact when it got bad, it got *really* bad. I looked up at the cliff where I had seen the climbers. It looked cold and barren. The only thing that clung to the sides were dark patches of fog. *It could be worse. It could be raining... But what if it starts?* The clouds looked like they could change their mind at any moment. I pictured myself soaking wet with my thumb out. The occasional car would drive by, close enough to spray me with dirty road water. Just like the weather in the mountains, hitchhiking wasn't all fun and games.

At minute thirty-two, with my thumb drooping by my side and my eyes fixated up at the menacingly dark clouds, I heard the sound of a piercing, muffler-less engine approaching me. I looked down to see a small two-door VW hatchback come speeding up, and nearly run me over, before turning sharply in front of me, and screeching to a halt. I cautiously walked up to the side. The passenger window rolled down and a mean-looking high school age kid with a shaved head, stuck his head out and eyed me from wicker hat to Birks. He looked mean but had an air of fear about him as well. A disheveled, meaner-looking man in his thirties leaned over from the driver's seat. He had music playing at a blaring volume, but turned it down to plain loud. "Where you going?" yelled the man. It sounded more like a command than a question.

I had a bad feeling about this outfit. *Don't take this ride Evan. Do NOT take this ride!* "Vancouver," I said. *What are you thinking??... I don't know! What was I supposed to say? Nowhere?*

The man and kid looked at each other like, "What did he just say??" The guy looked back at me. "I can drop you off downtown. Okay?"

No! Not okay! "Uhh, okay."

The kid was staring at me and the man shoved him. "Hey, get out!" The kid got out of the car and pulled back his seat so I could crawl in the back. The car reeked of old cigarettes and a hint of marijuana. Garbage, empty beer cans, and power tools littered the back seat and floor. I squeezed in with my bag resting across my lap. The kid rolled back his seat which cramped up my legs, and he got in. I was trapped. The man cranked the music back up and put his full weight on the pedal.

The music was top-forty American pop, which at its blaring volume could not drown out the screaming engine. *Who are these people?* The man wasn't old enough to be the kid's father. The kid sat motionless while the man bobbed his head up and down at a violent pace. Whether he was doing it to the music or for some other reason (pill related), I was far from knowing.

They sped along as if I didn't exist. The kid seemed to be too scared to speak. The man was in his own world. The more I watched his movements, the more apparent it appeared that he was on some sort of drug of the amphetamine variety. We sped down the windy two-lane highway and any chance the guy got, he would shift gear and swerve into the oncoming lane to pass a car.

We had made it back to the part of the road where it dropped down from the guardrail to the water channels hundreds of feet below. I could see why the kid sat nervously silent. This man had some death wish that I had been so lucky enough to cross paths with. One slip on a turn and we would be launching off the side. When I had traveled the opposite way on the bus, this was my favorite part of the trip. Now I had nothing but fear for these treacherous cliffs that could lead to the end of my life.

After what seemed like an eternity of nerve-wracking, ear-splittingly loud silence, we approached a construction zone. There is a first time in one's life for everything. I had done a lot of things for the first time on this trip. But of all my firsts, I had never anticipated hitchhiking in a car, that deliberately drove straight into a construction zone. It was a coned off dirt pile with various heavy equipment strewn about. The man found an opening and swerved in, then skidded to a stop in the middle of the site. I plunged my hand into my pocket and felt for my knife. It was still there and I made sure to have a solid grip on it. Once we were stopped, the guy reached into the center console and as quickly and aggressively as he did everything else, he pulled out a large bag of weed and a book of rolling papers. Then he proceeded with an addict's expert precision, to break up some weed and roll it into a joint. The kid sat there motionless. I did the same, clutching my knife, while occasionally and as calmly as I could, looking back to see when a cop was going to pull in and assess this absurd situation.

When he finished (it took no more than a minute) he took out a lighter, lit the joint, and as he held it firmly in his lips, my driver wrenched the car in gear and sped back onto the highway. I doubted that smoking a joint was any significant offense in British Columbia. But combined with trespassing in a construction zone, with God-knows what other drugs were in the car, and a hitchhiker to boot (maybe even a kidnapped boy), the offense may have been more serious.

The weed seemed to calm the guy's nerves and his movements were less erratic. I looked in the rearview mirror and noticed that his blood-shot eyes were on me. Finally he spoke. "So what's going on in Squamish?"

I gulped and answered. "I actually came from Vancouver."

The guy frowned and looked over at the kid like *I* was the crazy one. "What? Buddy, that's where we're taking you."

"I mean, sorry, I meant Whistler. I came from Whistler," I said nervously.

He looked over at the boy, then nodded. "You on vacation or something?"

"Yeah."

"Where from?"

I wasn't sure how much information to divulge to these people. Would they try to take advantage of me if they knew I was from the states? I couldn't think fast enough. All I could think of was Vancouver, and I didn't know that city well enough to make up a fake story. "I'm from the States."

"Did you have some friends up here or something?"

"No, I'm on my own."

"Where did you stay? A hotel?"

"No, I Couchsurfed." *What the hell Evan? Why are you blurting this shit out? Just keep your mouth shut!*

The man and kid gave each other a confused look. "Couchsurfed? Like sleeping on couches?"

"Yeah, it's a website where you can request to sleep on people's couches, or whatever other amenity they have to offer."

"Like just random people?"

"Yeah." I said this with the utmost confidence.

"But what if they're like a psychopath or some shit?"

You're one to talk. "I haven't met one yet."

The man shook his head. "That's sounds fuckin' weird."

Our conversation didn't last much longer and it was back to extremely loud pop silence for the remainder of the trip. I had solace in the fact that they were so turned off by the idea of Couchsurfing. I didn't consider it to be an exclusive thing, but it wasn't for everybody. It took a certain kind of person to be a Couchsurfer. That kind of person was a traveler. And one of the many traits—if not the most important trait of being a traveler, was being open-minded. This trait did not include labeling something off-the-bat as "fuckin' weird."

I tuned out the music and looked at the coastal British Columbian mountains. I thought about all the beauty I had confronted on my trip, which was a byproduct of keeping an open mind. I thought about its unexpected turns, its people, and its time alone. I thought about its mountains, oceans, fields, cities, snow, rain, sun, stars, cars, buses, boats, monster vans, friends, new friends, old friends, family, quesadillas, camp stoves, microbrews, tents, pirate ships, Christians, and Couchsurfers. Its Michigan lakes, Idaho wind, Oregon trees, and Dakota prairie that went on and on and on...

My chauffeurs dropped me off in downtown Vancouver like they had promised. I gave a quick thank you, but I didn't think they heard it over the music, and they sped off.

This time I was not lost. I knew which bus that I needed to take to get to Devina's. When I arrived, she was having a party with the Hermanos, five Swedes, and a Japanese couple. I handed Devina back her unharmed tent. She gave me a warm smile, which felt like it had a tinge more warmth than usual. "I knew you'd bring it back."

DAY 27

What better a day to head back into my home country, then on July Fourth?

I took a bus from Vancouver to Seattle, and Seattle to Tacoma, and learned from the uneventful ride, that taking the route through the San Juan Islands was—without question—the right choice.

Mr. Evan was greeted by Jessie, Asher, Zebadiah, Adam, Linda, and Toby. We sat on a blanket in a park by the water and watched the evening fireworks. Zebadiah sat on my lap.

My trip was coming to an end. It was my final cry of "freedom" (no Independence Day pun intended) before I was to hit the real world. A heavy weight was about to fall on me. It was a weight I had held suspended for a month. Certain times during the trip I would look up and see it hanging there, but I would never fixate on it for too long, and bring my attention back to the window of whatever vehicle I had found myself in, looking out to whatever newfound beauty was being presented to me. But the weight could hold no longer. As I watched the explosions light up the sky, I also watched the weight fall on me with all the questions I already knew it had. "Now what? You've avoided the real world for long enough. What are you going to do with your life?" These were all questions I was expected to answer when I sat there with Casey at graduation. But I chose to stall them for a month.

However, this trip had managed to give me more answers than I thought. I got to see many lives that people led. What was so important to all of them? Why did Jenny love to live by a lake in northern Michigan? Why did Becca love the San Francisco city life? Why did Casey choose to work in a small town in Eastern Oregon? Why did Adam and Linda pick up and move across the country to live in a Seattle suburb? Why did Devina want to leave Vancouver and move to Mexico? Why did Patrice love Whistler so much? It seemed so clear. They had put location before everything else. Any kind of job or career was an afterthought. This was what I needed to do. I needed to pick a place to live, where I knew that I would be happy. I thought about all the places that I had visited on my trip and what seemed like the best fit for me. As Zebadiah and I admired the fireworks that exploded above us, I smiled. I didn't have to think twice about the answer...

People often say that lightening never strikes twice. I thought that it would have never happened in a million years, but I managed to spend another night in the pirate ship.

DAY 28

Linda, Asher, and Zebediah drove me to the airport. I was given another divine medley of Christian rock sing-alongs, this time with a three-part harmony.

The cross-country flight took about as long as it took Wallace, Gill, and me to drive from Santa Rosa to Mendocino. Ian and Doug were right. Sitting on a plane was not as exciting—especially not as much as driving along Highway 1. I looked out of the plane's window, thirty thousand feet down, to see the path that I had spent a month crossing over, as well as the endless amount that I did not get the chance to see. "No one can travel everywhere," said Patrice. "Just like you cannot read every book. Zat is why it is so great, because you can do it for your entire life without retracing your steps."

The Hartford-Bradley airport is a small airport outside of Hartford, Connecticut. It caters to the Northern Connecticut/Western Massachusetts region, which is not so densely populated. However that is a subjective statement, depending on where you're from. It would have seemed like an overcrowded metropolis in the eyes of a small town feller from a place like Manhatten, Nevada. "You got that right. That's how we like it out here," said the Bartender. "Hell with them!" said the old man at the slot machine. Needless to say, it wasn't hard for Wallace to find me, or I to find him, even if he was driving up in an unrecognizable sedan. I had a moment of confusion seeing him in this foreign car. *What the hell is he driving in? Where's the Suburu? Oooohhhh right.* There wasn't much to say about his new car, besides that it lacked all character that our shitass pile of rust possessed (may she rest in peace).

My heart was filled with joy when I saw that scruffy, blue-eyed brute. "Wallace!" I ran up and gave him a big hug.

"Heey buddy." It never ceased to be refreshingly amusing to hear how low his bassy voice was.

We rode north along Route 91, which brought us up to Northampton. On the way we passed the exit for Route 90, the exit we took twenty-eight days prior, bound for Rochester, New York. *Was it twenty-eight days, or years?* We took the Northampton exit to get to Amherst.

When we got off the exit and slowed down, I took in all the recognizable elements of my home: the humid air, the smell of the fresh grass, the green deciduous leaves. It felt good to recognize. I thought I had forgotten what recognition felt like. It felt like comfort.

Then we were back in my old house. It was no longer mine, but Wallace and a few friends took over the rent, so it stayed in admirable hands. I walked through the house, observing all the unfamiliar new furniture, and walked out to the back porch. That skinny friend of mine sat sipping a beer, relaxing in a chair.

"Gill!"

"Heeeey! Kenward!" He got up and gave me a big, boney hug.

After a jovial reunion, I was handed my favorite local beer, from Berkshire Brewing Company. That familiar taste of malt on my mouth was able to merge body, mind, and soul. It wasn't until that moment that I could truly say I was back home. We sat down on the porch chairs, engulfed inside a typical warm summer night in the Northeast. When we had left, spring was packing its bags and on its way out. Now summer was in full bloom. Out in the dark field, the fireflies roamed their secret metropolis, with brief blinks of light steering their way.

Then I looked up to the dark shadow of the mountain that tormented me for so long before my trip. It looked bigger than I remembered. At this point the leaves must have turned a full summer green. An urge came over me and I decided that tomorrow I would go out and take a long hike. I couldn't wait. I couldn't wait to do all the things I loved, that came with summer in the Northeast. This feeling had felt so forgotten and unappreciated. I thought about how Patrice must have felt after coming home from abroad. This had to be similar.

The three of us sat back in the deck chairs. They looked at me like they were eager to hear me speak, so I did. "How was the drive back?" We all laughed. I knew what the answer was and they knew that I knew.

"Aweful," said Gill. We drove straight through. It took us forty-eight hours. All we did was alternate driving and sleeping."

"Forty-eight hours!? That's crazy! Why did you do that? What was the rush?"

"We," Wallace began then paused. He was unsure of his words. "We just had to get back." It wasn't a sufficient answer but he made it sound like he didn't want to be prodded for the real one, and I simply nodded.

"Tell us about your trip," said Gill.

"Oh man, where do I begin?"

"How about where we last saw you, outside of a hotel in Eureka, getting into your friend's car."

I tried to hit every important point without getting bogged down in details. Portland, Casey, Pirate ships, Swiss women, Vancouver, Couchsurfing—but when I made it to Whistler, I got more in depth and animated. "...you guys really got to see it to believe it. This place was heaven."

"Heaven? Like perfection?"

"If not, it's damn close. The mountains, the lakes, the people—everyone was geared for the outdoors. No one gave a shit about jobs, or money, or big houses, status—none of that bullshit. They were perfectly happy to live their lives in this amazing place where you could camp, swim, bike—literally do any outdoor activity that your heart desires—"

Wallace cut me off. "What do the people do for work?"

I shrugged. "Like I said, who cares? They paint, or bartend, or do whatever to pay the bills. Just stuff to get by. But none of that matters! They get out of work and live amazing lives and are, well, in heaven."

"It sounds like *you* were in heaven," said Gill.

"I was. I was. And guys, I think I'm sold." I took a deep breath and smiled. "I'm going to try to move out there."

"When?" asked Gill.

I shrugged. "I don't know, tomorrow? Next week? It will take some planning. I know I need to figure out some bureaucracy bullshit with getting into Canada as a US citizen but—"

"Did anybody have families?" Wallace cut me off and I looked at him.

"What do you mean?"

"All of these people living these," he held his hands up in quotations, "'perfect' lives. Did they happen to have any other responsibilities besides taking care of themselves?" Wallace gave me a serious look, his blue eyes nearly blinding mine.

"Um, well, no, I don't think so," I said.

"Then of course it was easy to live like that. But it's not like they can sustain it—unless they want to be 'ski bums' forever." Wallace crossed his arms and looked at me for an answer.

I didn't have one.

That night I was able to fish out my old bed which had been put in storage above the garage. I also found my sheets and a lamp that I could set up temporarily. I nestled into bed and propped up my pillow. Then I took out my purple notebook with the Grateful Dead sticker on the front, and the weed warning sticker on the back, with the Vancouver Olympics sticker above it. I opened it up and flipped past some pages. One page had random scratches of phone numbers, directions to Becca's house, and Patrice's name at the bottom. Kirouac was underlined with a question mark. The next page had my poem I had written by the San Francisco Bay. The next page was the list that I had made of all of the things to transfer from the broken down Suburu, to my backpack.

I flipped to the next page which was blank. I thought for a second, then grabbed a pen and wrote, "It wasn't looking good."

ORIGINAL ROUTE ——

REVISED ROUTE - - - -

FOR THE HISTORY BOOKS ➤—➤

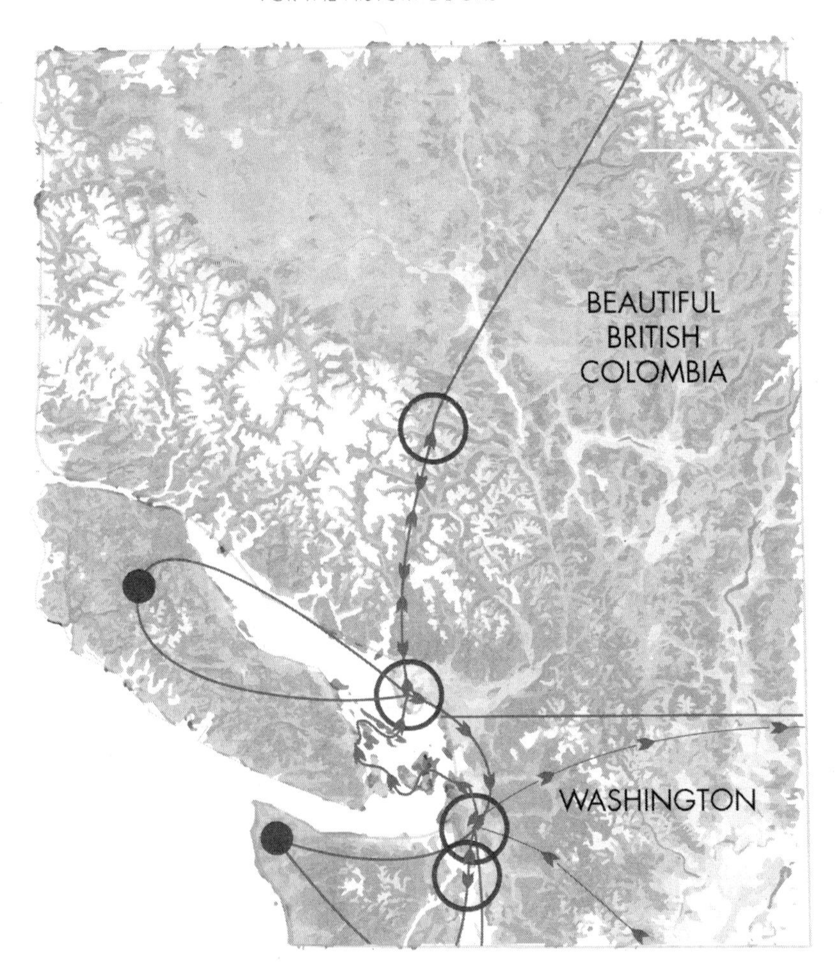

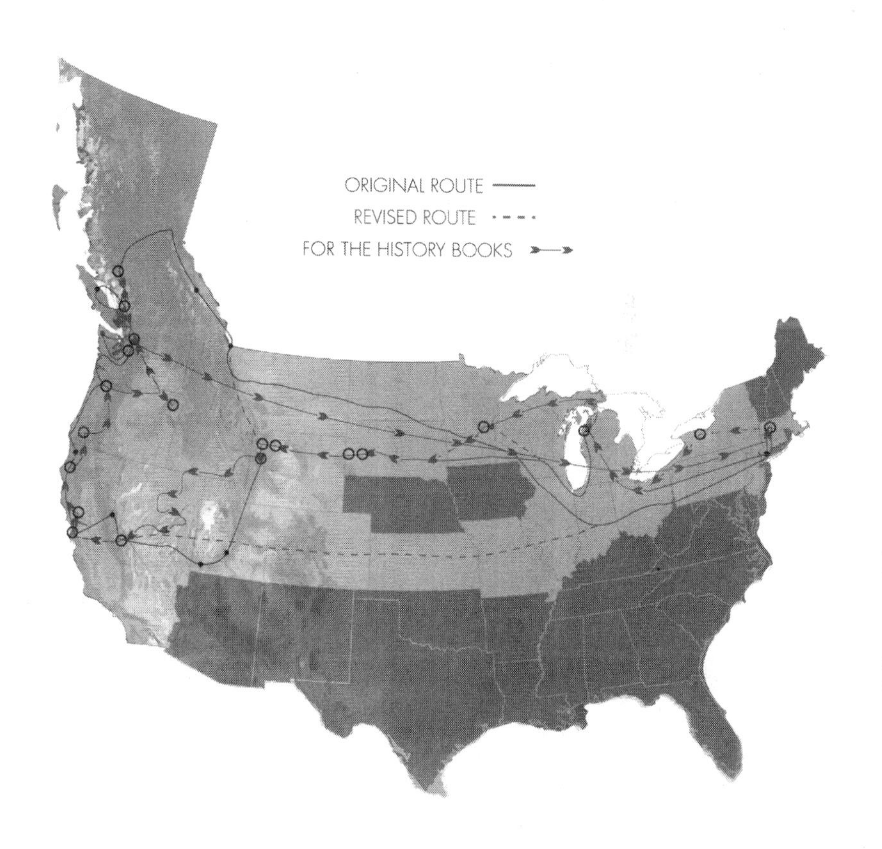
ORIGINAL ROUTE
REVISED ROUTE
FOR THE HISTORY BOOKS

EPILOGUE

I met up for lunch with my friend Kyle in midtown Manhattan (the East coast Manhattan). He was an old college friend whom I had not seen for a while after we graduated, because he had spent a year teaching English in Japan. After his return, he landed a job working for a PR firm near Times Square.

I was making my rounds to catch up with various friends in the city, because I was on my way out of the Northeast, moving to San Francisco. I had my new car (manual transmission of course) packed with as much as I could fit. Everything that I couldn't fit I sold. This was going to mark my fourth cross-country road trip since the first one with Wallace, Gill, Me, Myself, and I. <Sorry, these other trips do not have corresponding books.>

I was able to grab Kyle during his lunch break. We got falafel sandwiches to go, from a bustling counter-service café, a block away from his office. The café was packed with corporate lunch-breakers like him. He talked to me at the same speed of the sandwich makers, along with the cars going by outside, and the exchange of money all around. "Do you know what you want?-Good.-Order fast.-I think we have time to go to my favorite lunch spot around the corner.-Got it?-Good.-Let's go." Kyle spoke fast back in college as well, so I figured that he felt right at home in the Big Apple... But this didn't turn out to be the case.

His "favorite lunch spot" was a row of concrete benches between two skyscrapers, with some scrawny trees planted in between each bench. Once we were sitting and eating, his usual erratic fast-talking had changed to a calm level-headedness. "Work is alright, I guess," he confessed. "Sometimes this city really gets to me. It gets so crazy."

"Even for you?" I asked in jest.

He chuckled, knowing what I was referring to. "Yeah, I know I was Mr. A.D.D. in college. But I don't think I'm like that anymore. Japan helped a lot with calming me down. I still don't feel content though."

I nodded, sensing his melancholy. He looked defeated, like he went to Japan to find himself, and came back, only to get the same PR job that he would have gotten regardless of where he traveled and what he experienced.

"I don't know," he looked down at his half-eaten sandwich, "I don't think PR is for me." He shrugged. "But it could be worse. The benefits are good. And Suzy and I are getting more serious, so a job like this is good to have for that kind of stuff."

"What kind of stuff?" I asked.

"You know, families, and dogs, and shit." He sounded as excited as his soggy sandwich.

The sun, which had been shining on our little concrete slab, moved on past the skyscraper and we were cast under the shadow of the impenetrable fifty-story block. The temperature dropped noticeably and became as comfortable as the concrete that our cramped behinds were sitting on. Kyle looked up at where the sun had last been seen, then looked down at his watch. "Fuck man," he said, "lunch breaks are too short." He wrapped up the rest of his sandwich and stood up. I stood up with him and he gave me a brotherly hug. "Good luck in San Francisco. I heard they have good Chinese food."

I nodded. "Yeah they do. Come visit sometime."

"Sure," he said unconvincingly, "sounds fun."